WAGNER: VOLUME I

CURT VON WESTERNHAGEN

WAGNER

A BIOGRAPHY

VOLUME I

TRANSLATED BY MARY WHITTALL

CAMBRIDGE UNIVERSITY PRESS

CAMBRIDGE

LONDON · NEW YORK · MELBOURNE

Published by the Syndics of the Cambridge University Press
The Pitt Building, Trumpington Street, Cambridge CB2 1RP
Bentley House, 200 Euston Road, London NW1 2DB
32 East 57th Street, New York, NY 10022, USA
296 Beaconsfield Parade, Middle Park, Melbourne 3206, Australia

First published in English translation 1978

Phototypeset by Western Printing Services Ltd, Bristol

Printed in Great Britain at the University Press, Cambridge

Library of Congress Cataloguing in Publication Data

Westernhagen, Curt von.
Wagner: a biography.

Bibliography: v. 2, p.
Includes index.
1. Wagner, Richard, 1813–1883. 2. Composers –
Germany – Biography.
ML410.W1W55   782.1′092′4   [B]   78–2397

ISBN 0 521 21930 2 Volume I
ISBN 0 521 21932 9 Volume II

CONTENTS

Volume I

Contents

ILLUSTRATIONS

between pages 8 and 9

Sources

Archiv für Kunst und Geschichte, Berlin: plates 1, 5b, 6, 9a, 9b, 11, 13, 16a
Bibliothèque Nationale, Paris: plate 12a
Historisches Museum der Stadt Wien, Vienna: plate 14b
Metropolitan Museum of Art (Gift of Frederick Loeser, 1889): plate 16b
Radio Times Hulton Picture Library: plates 4a, 7a, 7b
Richard Wagner Gedenkstätte, Bayreuth: plates 2a, 2b, 3a, 3b, 4b, 5a, 8a, 8b, 10a, 10b, 12b, 14a, 15a, 15b

PREFACE TO THE ENGLISH EDITION

When Ernest Newman published the first volume of his *Life of Richard Wagner* in 1933 he justified the undertaking on the grounds that during the previous twenty years 'so much new and vital first-hand matter has come to light that one's old conception of the story has had to be modified at a hundred points' (p. vii). Since his final volume appeared in 1946 another thirty years have passed, during which a new perspective has opened on the Wagner phenomenon, and a wealth of new material has become available.

I must say at once that the importance of Newman's *Life* as the standard work has in no way been diminished. There are many delicate issues which can be presented with sufficient detail and thoroughness only in a work of so large a compass. Outstanding in this respect is his treatment of the 'Nietzsche affair': no one should forgo the pleasure and instruction of reading his chapters on that subject. I am equally sure that Newman himself would have welcomed my additions to the tale.

The bibliography of the present work gives some idea of the variety of publications that have appeared since 1946. I will confine myself here to mentioning those that contain documentary material of biographical importance. Foremost among them are the Burrell Collection, consisting almost entirely of letters, previously known only through the inadequate and misleading *Catalogue of the Burrell Collection* (London, 1929), and the second volume of Max Fehr's *Richard Wagners Schweizer Zeit*. Then there are Cosima's intimate letters to Judith Gautier, and two other collections which, though published before 1946, escaped Newman's net: her letters to Gobineau, published in the *Revue Hebdomaire* in 1938, and the second volume of her letters to Nietzsche (1871–7), which appeared in 1940. The edition of Wagner's complete correspondence in chronological order is planned to be in fifteen volumes in all; the three volumes published to date go up to 1851 and contain some new documents, but for the most part they republish, as far as possible in their original form, letters that have appeared in print before. As well as these collections, a number of isolated letters have been published which have helped to correct misconceptions (or worse) that had been current for decades: for instance the three letters from Nietzsche to Cosima discovered in 1964 by Joachim Bergfeld, and the letter from the philosopher's sister Elisabeth Förster-Nietzsche to Frau Overbeck, published by Erich F. Podach, in which Elisabeth admits that she did not dare call on Wagner when she was in Bayreuth for *Parsifal* in 1882, thereby giving the lie to her touching story of her 'farewell visit' and Wagner's heart-rending message for Nietzsche. (EFWN, p. 279) This more than confirms Newman's suspicions about 'Elisabeth's false witness', yet innocents still rely on her testimony even today.

Podach was the first Nietzsche scholar to take account of the findings of Wagnerian scholarship as well, among other things the documents from the Wagner Archives that I published in the appendix of my book *Richard Wagner. Sein Werk, sein Wesen, seine Welt* (1956), which included Wagner's correspondence with Nietzsche's doctor, Dr Otto Eiser of Frankfurt am Main, and the three short letters Nietzsche sent to Cosima–Ariadne at the onset of his madness (the one commonly circulated before that date was apocryphal and was based, according to Podach, on an oral communication of Elisabeth's). Podach's own publications have been of the greatest importance to the reassessment of the popular Nietzsche–Wagner legend, notably his *Friedrich Nietzsches Werke des Zusammenbruchs*, containing authentic texts of *Nietzsche contra Wagner* and *Ecce Homo* based on the original manuscripts in the Nietzsche Archives, and his *Ein Blick in Notizbücher Nietzsches*, which includes an analysis of Nietzsche's 'Ariadne' fantasies.

International interest was aroused in 1976 by the publication of a letter Wagner wrote to his American dentist Dr Jenkins, on 8 February 1880, discussing his idea of emigrating to the United States. It gave rise to my article 'Wagner's Emigration Utopia', in the Bayreuth Festival programme for *Götterdämmerung* in 1976.

Newman lamented in the mid–1930s: 'It is a thousand pities that his brother-in-law Brockhaus [actually Heinrich, the brother of his brothers-in-law] confiscated his library on his flight from Dresden: the mere titles of some of the books might have told us a good deal we should like to know about Wagner's reading and thinking.' (NLRW, II, p. 51) In 1966, through the kind cooperation of the publishing firm of F. A. Brockhaus of Wiesbaden, I not only had access to that library (which they have now presented to the Richard Wagner Foundation in Bayreuth) for my own use, but also published a catalogue of it, with commentary, for the use of others. I have also had the opportunity to consult the unpublished manuscript catalogue of the Wahnfried library, and so familiarize myself with the books Wagner read in his later years, from the Upanishads to the works of his 'great eccentric' contemporary, Thomas Carlyle.[1] As a result I have been able to incorporate in my biographical account of the events of Wagner's life a parallel history of his intellectual life.

Other interesting documents have been published in G. Leprince's *Présence de Wagner* and Martin Vogel's *Apollinisch und Dionysisch*, while the iconography has been enriched by Willi Schuh's *Renoir und Wagner* and Martin Geck's *Die Bildnisse Richard Wagners*, an anthology of portraits including the one painted for King Ludwig by Friedrich Pecht, which is now in the Metropolitan Museum of Art in New York.

New material in the field of Wagner's compositions ranges from exercises dating from his teens, done for his teacher Theodor Weinlig – including a four-part vocal fugue 'Dein ist das Reich' and a sonata in A major with a fugato in place of a scherzo (published by Otto Daube) – to the 1850 'Washington Sketch' for *Siegfrieds Tod* (published by Robert W. Bailey), the composition sketch of thirty bars that did not, in the end, go into *Tristan*, and my own study, with numerous musical examples, of the composition sketches for the *Ring*.

In the last year or two considerable attention has been focused for various reasons on Cosima's diaries. Carl Friedrich Glasenapp, the friend of my own youth in Riga, had the complete manuscript in front of him in 1907–9, when he was writing the sixth volume (838 pp., published 1911) of his *Das Leben Richard Wagners* and was preparing the fifth edition of Volume V (416 pp., published 1912), though he did not actually identify the diaries as his source. A copy he made of them at the time is no longer in existence. He wove his extracts from the diaries into his text in indirect speech, only very occasionally giving verbatim quotations between quotation marks, and confined his selection to the realm of ideas and art, but Richard Graf du Moulin Eckart also cited more personal events in the first volume of his life of Cosima (1929), such as her last interview with Hans von Bülow. In his preface Du Moulin writes: 'I cannot forget how she even made her diaries available to me for my work . . . Naturally I made the fullest use of them [pp. 422–999 of his book], although it will never be possible to exhaust their riches. But they afforded the basis of the depiction of her unique relationship to Richard Wagner and of the light in which his wife regarded his genius.' Du Moulin here pinpoints the value of his extracts: they are the 'basis', the primary source of any biography, and they already reflect the 'riches' that a complete edition of the diaries can only enhance.

Eva Chamberlain, Richard and Cosima's younger daughter, made a selection of 'entries from Mama's diaries for Maestro Toscanini' (15 April 1874 to 30 January 1883), amounting to 130 quarto pages of Wagner's observations about his own work and about literature, music and life in general. The same selection was published, with some unimportant differences, by Hans von Wolzogen in *Bayreuther Blätter* between 1936 and 1938.

My own quotations from the diaries are taken from these three sources. (In the case of the *Bayreuther Blätter* extracts I compared the printed text with Eva Chamberlain's original manuscript.) At the time of writing, the first volume of the complete edition of the diaries has appeared (CT, I, covering the years 1869–77 – and see the Postscript to the Preface, below), and in general it confirms the reliability of the earlier selections; they may contain occasional minor errors in interpretation or the decipherment of Cosima's handwriting, but CT itself is not faultless in that respect. Some of Wagner's remarks on his compositional procedures at the time when he was writing *Parsifal*, which are given in exactly the same form in BBL and CT, were obviously misunderstood and wrongly taken down by Cosima herself; where quoted here they have been corrected, without comment, after comparison with the score.

CT can make a valuable contribution to the dating of letters which have previously been uncertainly or mistakenly dated: one instance is the correspondence between Wagner and Catulle Mendès, immediately before and after the Siege of Paris, where the precise dating is of some importance.

It should be emphasized that Glasenapp and Du Moulin did not

overlook or deliberately suppress anything of biographical importance in their use of the diaries. Since Cosima wrote them expressly
and intentionally for her children there was never any question of
their containing any 'sensations'. On the other hand, if one com-
pares the accounts of certain episodes where the details are of the
essence (such as the Munich productions of *Rheingold* and *Walküre*)
in the diaries and in the biographies, the latter are unquestionably
superior in being able to draw on a wider range of documentation.

The diaries are fascinating precisely because of their subjective
limitations: the reader feels as though he or she were actually
present, from the night and its dreams, through the morning and its
work to the evenings spent reading and making music. There is,
however, no overlooking the fact that the underlying mood of the
diaries stems from Cosima and not Richard. Even actual facts are
given a surprising colouring for being seen through her eyes. For
instance, though she records a large number of the nonentities who
called at Wahnfried she does not even mention Anton Bruckner's
visit in September 1873; he is referred to only once, apropos of
Wagner's running through his Third Symphony on 8 February
1875, when she calls him the 'poor organist Bruckner from Vienna'.

If the diaries were our only source we should never have heard
about Wagner's extraordinary love affair with Judith Gautier and all
its fantasies. The only reference is in the entry for 24 December
1877, when Cosima notes that the purchase of Christmas presents
in Paris for herself had given rise to a lengthy correspondence
between Richard and Judith. The true character of the correspondence cannot have remained a secret from her, but she had the
good sense to say nothing whatever about it, in the certainty that it
was a passing fancy that would die down of its own accord.

On the other hand it is disappointing to find so little about
Nietzsche's visits to Tribschen and Bayreuth. By contrast, her
numerous letters to him are a mine of information. Nietzsche's
French biographer, Charles Andler, has a shrewd comment on
this: 'Cosima Wagner, entre les deux hommes, supérieurement
coquette, attisait à son insu leur rivalité.'

The earlier published extracts failed me in only one instance: they
do not refer to Wagner's acquaintance with Gustav Nottebohm's
edition of Beethoven's sketches for the Choral Symphony, and his
recognition of the parallels with his own way of working. 'Richard
says it's similar for him, it's almost never possible for him to use

something in the form in which he first wrote it down, it's like a mark to indicate that one has got something in one's head, but quite different, and so one finds it eventually.'(CT, I, p. 917) The comment confirms the thesis I advanced in *The Forging of the 'Ring'*.

The case of Wagner's Brown Book, published entire for the first time in 1975, is rather different. This diary–cum–notebook kept by Wagner from 1865 to 1882 was intended for Cosima's eyes only, and it was started at a moment when their relationship had reached its crisis. Its private nature is emphasized by the fact that Eva Chamberlain thought fit to paste over five sides (which have now been uncovered again) and to cut out and destroy seven further pages (fourteen sides). Since it was published by my own publishers, Atlantis Verlag of Zürich, I have been able to add some valuable material from it to the English and the second German editions of this biography, thanks to the cooperation of Atlantis Verlag and the editor, Joachim Bergfeld.

I would like at this point to avert one possible misunderstanding: if I have spoken hitherto exclusively of the biographical value of documentation, it does not mean that I am a champion of the current fashion for so-called 'documentary biographies' or 'studies'. Their alleged greater 'objectivity' is deceptive: the subjective answerability of the compilers begins with the selection of material, indeed with the selection of the sources, for the general reader is not in the position to judge the reliability or credibility of the witnesses.

In addition, there is something I like to call the 'counterpoint' of facts, which is particularly pertinent to an account of the life and work of Wagner. One need do no more than contemplate the events of a two–year period such as 1856–7: the completion of *Die Walküre*, the prose scenario of *Die Sieger*, the conception of a new ending for *Götterdämmerung*, the start of the composition of *Siegfried*, the first musical ideas for *Tristan*, the prose scenario of *Parsifal*, the text of *Tristan* and the composition sketch of the first act, the first Wesendonk songs – surely no one can believe that a reversion to a primitive chronicle method could begin to give an adequate idea of the strains and tensions, both personal and artistic, that are concealed behind those dates and facts!

Finally I must refer to an element in this book which Giulio Cogni, in his review of the Italian edition, called (perhaps a little grandiloquently) the 'valore artistico del volume'.[2] I would like to

think that the 'valore artistico' consists above all in the mastery of
the immense quantities of material. I have spotlighted elements in
the first half of Wagner's life, of which he left a perceptive and
reliable account in *Mein Leben*, in a series of essay-like chapters, and
then adopted a narrative sequence of epic scenes as the means of
giving an impression of the second half in its entirety, so far as the
limitations of space permitted.

The reader may be puzzled by the absence of one thing: the raised
eyebrows of the moralist. As Furtwängler once observed, a com-
plaint about 'Wagner's bad character' is a normal part of the ritual.[3]
Nor was Wagner the first: 'They would all like to be shot of me,'
Goethe said to Eckermann two years before his death, 'and as
there's nothing they can touch in my talent, they have a go at my
character instead.' Schopenhauer's comment on that particular
school of Goethean biography was that because a great mind and
spirit had made the human race an incomparable gift they thought
they were justified in 'dragging his moral personality before their
judgement seat'.[4]

My own intention, by contrast, is to display the personality
complete with its inner contradictions, its *creative polarity*, and to
leave judgement to the reader. This is perhaps not unconnected
with the fact that, of the four academic disciplines Goethe's Faust
lists with such disgust (philosophy, medicine, law 'and, alas', theology), my own life has been spent in medicine, the one least likely to
predispose its practitioners to moralizing.

Curt von Westernhagen

Preetz/Holstein. May 1977

POSTSCRIPT TO THE PREFACE

The second volume of Cosima Wagner's diaries was published in July 1977, shortly after the second German edition and the English edition of this biography had both gone to press. As the editors point out in their preface, it differs from the first volume in two important respects: in its greater depth and detail – the period from 1 January 1878 to 12 February 1883 occupies no fewer than 1081 pages (whereas the first volume covers nearly ten years) – and in the stronger light this greater length throws on the personality and attitudes of Cosima herself. From a detailed record of the activities of Richard Wagner, the diaries become the intimate chronicle of their married life; the change is reflected even in the style, especially of such epic passages as the months in Palermo. On the other hand, the account of the vicissitudes attending the rehearsals and the performances of *Parsifal* suffers from the lack of the broader, general lines a more detached narrator might have given.

Although these daily notes were inevitably written in haste, they are stamped with Cosima's own personal style, as we know it from her letters to Chamberlain and Nietzsche, even if they never aspire to the elegance of her correspondence in French with Gobineau and Judith Gautier. Her own sympathies and antipathies are more strongly in evidence than in her earlier volume, not only in the expression of her anti-Semitic and anti-French feelings – in the latter one recognizes the renegade – but also in her attitude towards individuals in Wagner's life. Even in the Munich period his friends had the sense that she was cutting him off from direct contact with others, which was perhaps the outcome not so much of a real dislike on her part as of a conscious lack of gregariousness.

This is particularly obvious in her treatment of the women

Wagner knew, especially Minna and Mathilde Wesendonk. The fact that Wagner had made Mathilde Maier a formal proposal of marriage (conditional on Minna's death) on 25 June 1864 inspired Cosima to commemorate religiously each anniversary of that 28 November 1863 in Berlin when she and Wagner had 'vowed to belong only to each other', in order to assert her own prior claim on him.

As for Wagner's last romance, with Judith Gautier, Cosima certainly knew of it by 27 January 1878, at the very latest. Writing to Judith on that day, after joking about the 'fâcheries' they were both experiencing in their attempts to translate *Parsifal*, she went on a little more seriously: 'Cependant vous savez bien, méchante, que toutes les questions ne sont pas vidées, mais motus, je compte sur vous pour prendre un bel élan de confiance, digne de vous et de notre amitié!'

I do not believe that the apostrophes to 'suffering – O my old companion' in her entries in the diary in 12 and 14 February 1878 have anything to do with that, however, but rather express the effect on her of three letters from Bülow (29 December 1877, 14 and 17 January 1878) which, after two years of silence, reopened her old wound, the trauma of her guilt towards him. (The letters are referred to in DMCW, I, pp. 816f., but for the full texts one must go to NBB, pp. 516–20.)

She had nothing to fear from Judith: 'Vous avez trouvé un ami digne de vous [Benedictus], "ce que l'on rêve et ne trouve pas", me disiez-vous ici.' (26 February 1878) The correspondence between the two women continued until 1893, conducted for the most part on terms of cordial friendship. Nevertheless, Cosima found it advisable to shield Richard from seeing too much of Judith during her visits to Bayreuth in 1881 and again, for *Parsifal*, in 1882 – and to say as little about them as possible in her diary. She mentions the presence of Mathilde Maier, and the delight with which Wagner greeted her, at the dinner for the artists and other friends on the day after the dress rehearsal (CT, II, p. 984), but it is left to an impeccable witness, Friedrich Eckstein, who made the pilgrimage from Vienna to Bayreuth on foot, to tell us in all innocence that Wagner's neighbour at table was a young woman in a linen sailor's blouse with a bright red neckerchief, who laughed a great deal and chattered to the Meister in melodious French.

Quite apart from such retouching, one must always bear in mind, when reading memoirs, that everyone involved in a conversation hears – and records – something different. The classic case is the different records of conversations with Goethe made by Eckermann and by Chancellor von Müller, on the frequent occasions when both were present at the same time. There is a striking example in Wagner's case, too. Ludwig Schemann's account of a conversation on the afternoon of 31 May 1882, when Hans von Wolzogen was also present, is cited in Chapter 31 of this book. It made an indelible impression on Schemann, because he sensed that what Wagner said was a testament. He ended his account: 'Wagner had become increasingly sad, he prolonged our leavetaking, bade us farewell over and over again and accompanied us right to the front door. I may have seen him grander and more overpowering on other occasions, but never nobler.' The reader should set that, and the rest of the account on pp. 579–80, against what stuck in Cosima's memory:

> 31 May 1882. A visit from Dr Schemann and Wolzogen rather upset Richard, he came back to Cherubini and said people ought to exercise much more criticism. 'You bury your noses in books, and all the time there's so much that needs doing. Military band music, for instance: am I to endure it that my son, or someone like Stein, will have to march to that music? Conservatories, concert organizations, they all need taking in hand, but instead of that we just nibble at I don't know what.'

There is material evidence, in the form of some of Cosima's notebooks preserved in the Richard Wagner Museum in Bayreuth, which makes it all the more appropriate to compare her practice with that of Eckermann, who wrote up his records of Goethe's conversations from notes taken on the spot. In April 1972 *Fränkischer Heimatbote*, the monthly supplement of Bayreuth's daily newspaper *Nordbayerischer Kurier*, published an article about one of these notebooks, describing it as the 'original manuscript of Cosima Wagner's last diary'. Now that the texts of the diaries are available in full, we can see that this document was not one of the actual diaries but the 'second notebook' which Wagner gave Cosima on 26 October 1882 in the Piazza San Marco, after he had been on an independent shopping expedition. (CT, II, p. 1033; the 'first' notebook was presumably the one 'with a swallow on it' that he gave her the day before.) He wrote an inscription on the first page:

Gemeines Karnickel
für Tages-Artikel!
Mach mich nur schlecht,
dann geschieht mir recht!
   Adieu! – Oh!
   26. Oct. 1882.
R. W. Ges. Schr. T. II.

('A common "carnicle" for the daily article! Make me out to be bad, it'll only serve me right! Adieu! Oh! 26 October 1882. R. W. Collected Writings, Vol. II.')

The sense of this curious 'dedication' is that Wagner, possessing little Italian, had spoken French in order to make his purchase, referring to the notebook as 'un carnet'; perhaps by way of an Italian word of his own imagining ('carnuccio'?) he ended up with the German word 'Karnickel' (which means a 'rabbit' in the zoological sense but also a 'donkey' of the human variety). 'Article' has the same range of meaning in German as in English, so a 'daily article' is not only an article for daily use but suggests here that he knew perfectly well that Cosima would use the notebook for her daily 'piece' about him in her diary – which is probably also the point of the reference to his 'collected writings'. It's a typical piece of Wagner's punning light verse.

The next entry on the same page is in pencil and in Cosima's handwriting: '27ten Freitag. Gute Nacht trotz Kaffee, Gespräch kath. Kirche, Professoren über lieben.' ('27th, Friday. Good night in spite of coffee. Conversation Catholic church, professors on dear' [i.e. 'on the dear Lord'].) These are the topics that provide the substance of the entry in her diary for that date. (CT, II, p. 1033)

A second facsimile accompanying the *Fränkischer Heimatbote* article gives her notes for what became the entries for Wednesday and Thursday, 27 and 28 December 1882. A line has been drawn across the page from bottom left to top right, as if to signify that it is finished with. The article also includes facsimiles of the two drawings Paul Zhukovsky made of Wagner in the same notebook on 10 and 12 February 1883 (cf. Martin Geck, *Die Bildnisse Richard Wagners*, p. 157).

There can be no doubt that this notebook contains the original notes from which Cosima wrote up her diary from 27 October 1882 to 12 February 1883. That it was not the first such notebook is

demonstrated by Cosima's reference to her 'little notebook' on 14
October 1882 (CT, II, p. 1024); the editors' note at this juncture is
somewhat perfunctory (p. 1278). It would be interesting to compare the text of the notebooks with that of the diaries. It might well
reveal a subjective bias on Cosima's part. As a 'well-informed
Frenchwoman' remarked, 'elle n'est pas pour rien la fille de
Madame d'Agoult'. (Ludwig Schemann, *Lebensfahrten eines Deut-
schen*, pp. 135f.)

That is not to deny the positive value of Cosima's use of preliminary notes in writing up her diaries; it is the guarantee of the
accuracy of her dating of events, which, as we shall see, is of crucial
importance on some occasions.

The editorial annotation and comment in this second volume of
Cosima's diaries are lavish and, in the main, exemplary. It includes
an appendix of errata from the first volume.

C.v.W.

January 1978

ACKNOWLEDGEMENTS

The author wishes to thank all those whose assistance and coopera-
tion have helped him in his work: Frau Winifred Wagner for
permission to publish material from the Wagner Archives in
Bayreuth, and for the run of the library in Wahnfried; Frau Gertrud
Strobel for looking out the archival material; Verlag F. A. Brock-
haus of Wiesbaden for access to Wagner's Dresden library and Frau
Susanne Brockhaus for her catalogue of it; Dr Joachim Bergfeld and
Dr Manfred Eger, Bayreuth, for the use of documents from the
Richard-Wagner-Gedenkstätte; Dr Dietrich Mack, Bayreuth, for
information about Cosima's diaries; Herr Erich Neumann, East
Berlin, for the emendation of some points arising in the first edition;
Dr Arnold Whittall, London, for making English-language additions to the bibliography; and last but not least Mrs Mary Whittall
for the skill and care she has again shown in translating one of my
books.

C.v.W.

The translator wishes to acknowledge the kind permission of
Thames & Hudson Ltd to re-use her versions of a number of
documents that appeared previously in *Wagner: A Documentary
Study*, compiled and edited by Herbert Barth et al. (London, 1975).

M.W.

SUMMARY BIBLIOGRAPHY

With a key to the abbreviations employed in the text

A comprehensive bibliography appears at the end of Vol. II.

BB   Bülow, Hans von, *Briefe*. 7 vols. Leipzig, 1899–1908

BBL   *Bayreuther Blätter*. Monthly, later quarterly periodical, ed. by Hans von Wolzogen. Chemnitz, later Bayreuth, 1878–1938

CT   Wagner, Cosima, *Die Tagebücher*, ed. by M. Gregor-Dellin and D. Mack. 2 vols. Munich, 1976–7. (An English translation is in preparation. See the Preface and its Postscript, above)

CWFN   *Die Briefe Cosima Wagners an Friedrich Nietzsche*, ed. by E. Thierbach. 2 vols. Weimar, 1938–40

DMCW   Du Moulin Eckart, Richard Graf, *Cosima Wagner. Ein Lebens- und Charakterbild*. 2 vols. Munich, 1929–31

EFWN   Förster-Nietzsche, Elisabeth, *Wagner und Nietzsche zur Zeit ihrer Freundschaft*. Munich, 1915

FHKF   Herzfeld, Friedrich, *Königsfreundschaft. Ludwig II. und Richard Wagner*. Leipzig, 1939

FWSZ   Fehr, Max, *Richard Wagners Schweizer Zeit*. 2 vols. Aarau, 1934–53

GLRW   Glasenapp, Carl Friedrich, *Das Leben Richard Wagners*. Definitive edn, 6 vols. Leipzig, 1905–12. (Modern reprint, Wiesbaden and Liechtenstein) (First edn, 2 vols, 1876–7)

JKWF   Kapp, Julius, *Wagner und die Frauen*. Final edn, Berlin–Wunsiedel, 1951. (First edn, 1912; numerous subsequent edns)

KLRW   König Ludwig II. und Richard Wagner, *Briefwechsel*, ed. by Otto Strobel. 5 vols. Karlsruhe, 1936–9

LJG   Wagner, Richard and Cosima, *Lettres à Judith Gautier*, ed. by Léon Guichard. Paris, 1964

LWVR   Lippert, Woldemar, *Richard Wagners Verbannung und Rückkehr 1849–62*. Dresden, 1927

ML   Wagner, Richard, *Mein Leben*. 1st authentic edn. Munich, 1963. (First edn, 1911)

MMCW   Millenkovich-Morold, Max, *Cosima Wagner. Ein Lebensbild*. Leipzig, 1937

MWKS Morold, Max, *Wagners Kampf und Sieg, dargestellt in seinen Beziehungen zu Wien*. 2 vols. Zürich, Leipzig, Vienna, 1950 (First edn, 1930)

NBB   Bülow, Hans von, *Neue Briefe*, ed. by R. du Moulin Eckart. Munich, 1927

NLRW Newman, Ernest, *The life of Richard Wagner*. 4 vols. New York, 1933–46. (There are some discrepancies between the pagination of the New York printing and the London edn of 1933–47. The author's references are to the New York edn, which is also that reprinted, London and Cambridge, 1976)

RWAP *The letters of Richard Wagner to Anton Pusinelli*, ed. by E. Lenrow. New York, 1932

RWBC Wagner, Richard, *Briefe. Die Sammlung Burrell*, ed. by J. N. Burk. Frankfurt am Main, 1953. (*Letters of Richard Wagner: The Burrell Collection*, ed. with notes by John N. Burk, was first publ. in New York, 1950, with the documents in translation. The German edn has the documents in the original and the editorial matter in translation. Page references in the present work are to the German edn, and quotations from the documents are newly translated for the sake of stylistic consistency)

RWGB *Richard Wagners Gesammelte Briefe*, ed. by J. Kapp and E. Kastner. 2 vols. Leipzig, 1914

RWGS Wagner, Richard, *Gesammelte Schriften und Dichtungen*, vols 1–10. 4th edn. Leipzig, 1907 (Reprint, Hildesheim, 1976)
      – *Sämtliche Schriften und Dichtungen*. Vols 11–16. 6th edn. Leipzig, n. d.

RWSB Wagner, Richard, *Sämtliche Briefe*, ed. by G. Strobel and W. Wolf. Leipzig, 1967– (See below, Vol. II, p. 617)

SERD Richard Wagner, *Skizzen und Entwürfe zur 'Ring'-Dichtung*, ed. by Otto Strobel. Munich, 1930

SRLW Röckl, Sebastian, *Ludwig II. und Richard Wagner*, 2 vols. Munich, 1913–19

TWLF Tiersot, Julien, ed. *Lettres françaises de Richard Wagner*. Paris, 1935

Part I: The Early Years (1813–1840)

1

The Wagner Family[1]

Germany was only beginning to recover from the horrors of the Thirty Years' War in 1651 when Martin Wagner, a schoolmaster and son of a silver-miner, Moritz Wagner, left Freiberg in Saxony, where he had been born in 1603. His destination was the village of Hohburg, seventeen miles east of Leipzig, and his journey took him past Wurzen, which the Swedes had razed to the ground in spite of its defences. Hohburg, too, had been devastated, the inhabitants had fled and the benefice had been vacant for years. Now, as the villagers gradually returned, their first move was to appoint a schoolmaster to make good their children's neglected education, to work diligently and in the fear of God at instructing them in the true Christian religion and in all Christian doctrines and virtues. It was another four years before a pastor arrived, and then Martin had additionally to assume the duties of sexton, hearing catechisms, singing in the church and playing the organ.

The Wagners remained in the district of the Hohburg hills for the next hundred years, working as village schoolmasters and cantors. In 1666 Martin's son Samuel 'satisfied the examiners' in Thammenhain. In those years there was little enough cause for satisfaction in life or work in those poverty-stricken villages. The plague stalked the land; warning placards were erected on the roads. An appeal was made to the monastery of Meissen to help the 'poor schoolmaster' of Thammenhain. In 1703 his son Emanuel was appointed schoolmaster and organist in Kühren, after having been 'heard by several in singing and in reading and well liked'. 'May God prosper and bless his appointment,' the scribe continues, 'because he has played the clavier for several years too.'

Emanuel's eldest son, Samuel, Richard Wagner's great-grandfather, was the last of the composer's ancestors to follow this career. After contact with a loftier educational sphere as servant–pupil to the Evangelical Superintendent in Borna, he went to Müglenz, at first as deputy to the old teacher there – who had to pay him from his own meagre salary – and eventually, after qualifying, as schoolmaster, cantor and organist 'with singing, reading and organ-playing, likewise bellringing and winding the church clock'.

When Samuel died in 1750, the same year as Bach, his eldest son Gottlob Friedrich was fourteen. He is next heard of in Leipzig in 1755 as a Thomaner, a pupil at the Thomasschule. 'The *subjectum* is not bad *in litteris*,' a friendly cleric wrote in a letter of recommendation to the pastor of Müglenz, 'and since he is young you ought to be able to mould him yet. I think the best thing he could do would be to leave Leipzig, because otherwise the all too great licence of the other Thomaner may lead his as yet innocent nature astray!' This advice was not followed, however, and in 1759 Gottlob Friedrich enrolled at Leipzig University to read theology.

Saxony was doing badly in the war with Prussia at that time and Frederick the Great made his winter quarters in what was then known as the Königshaus (later the Thomäsches Haus) in the market square in Leipzig. Napoleon stayed in the same house before the Battle of the Nations in 1813 and later, as a child, Richard Wagner spent the night there when he visited his father's sister, his aunt Friederike. The portraits of fine ladies in hooped skirts, with youthful faces and powdered hair, that still hung on the walls of its abandoned state apartments, filled his imagination with terrifying visions of ghosts.

His friend's fears about the harm that might be done to Gottlob Friedrich's innocent nature were not unfounded: in the thirteenth semester of his university studies he appears in the register of the Thomaskirche, on 23 March 1765, as the father of a child born to Johanna Sophie Eichelin, spinster, the daughter of the respected schoolmaster Gottlob Friedrich Eichel. That was the end of his career as a theologian, and he was lucky to get the job of excise officer at the Ranstadt gate of the city. When young Goethe arrived from Frankfurt to study in Leipzig that October, he must have paid his gate dues to Richard Wagner's grandfather. Unlike Goethe, who assiduously suppressed the information that his grandfather was a tailor, Wagner was not the least ashamed of his forebear. When a caller at Wahnfried mentioned that his father had been musical director (a municipal appointment) in his home town, Wagner interrupted him with '*Stadtmusikus*, you say? You do us an honour then. My grandfather was a tollgate-keeper in Leipzig.'

It was four years before Gottlob Friedrich was able to marry Johanna Sophie. He wanted their two sons (the first child had died) to succeed where he had failed. The elder, Karl Friedrich (born 18 June 1770) – Richard's father – studied law, the younger theology. Friedrich Wagner became registrar at the police headquarters in Leipzig. In 1798 he married Johanna Rosine Pätz, the twenty-three-year-old daughter of a master baker from Weissenfels. They had nine children in fourteen years of marriage, the youngest, Richard, born only six months before his father's death, so that he had no memory of him at all; and as though Friedrich Wagner was destined to remain completely unknown to posterity, no portrait of him survives.

Among what is known of him, the outstanding characteristic was a passion for the theatre, not unmixed with a gallant enthusiasm for some of the actresses, as Richard gathered from his mother's recollections. As well as other lawyers and tradesmen and their families, the regular visitors to their home included the members of the Seconda troupe. The plays of Lessing and Schiller were in the company's repertory and the first performance ever of *Die Jungfrau von Orleans* was a red-letter day for the Wagner family; as the crowd pressed around the theatre exit, all heads were bared as Schiller's tall figure appeared, and mothers lifted their children up to see: 'Look, here he comes, that's him!'

Friedrich Wagner himself acted, in Goethe's *Die Mitschuldigen* for instance, in amateur performances in a room in the Thomäsches Haus. When E. T. A. Hoffmann came to Leipzig in 1813, as musical director of the Seconda company, the first thing he did was visit the inn the actors always patronized. 'Evening in the Grüne Linde', he wrote in his diary. 'Registrar Wagner, an exotic character who imitates Opitz, Iffland etc., really rather well – he seems to be an adherent of the better school, *un poco exaltato* after imbibing a lot of rum.'

They were stirring times when Richard Wagner first glimpsed the light of day on 22 May 1813, between the allied defeat at Bautzen and the Battle of the Nations outside Leipzig. He was born in the house of the Red and White Lion in a street called Der Brühl, and the majestic lion crouching over the porch of the house sends one's thoughts forward over seven decades to that other house, on the Grand Canal, adorned with a frieze of eagles, where his life ended. The birth of a genius is enveloped in a kind of mystery. And in Wagner's case there are in addition two genealogical mysteries.

The truce agreed on 4 June gave his parents the chance to take a holiday with their new baby in the pretty village of Stötteritz just outside the city, where Friedrich celebrated his forty-third birthday. He was recalled to Leipzig in July, when Napoleon arrived to review his troops, and he was appointed interpreter and acting chief of police by Marshal Davoust. Then at last, on 16 August, the child's christening, delayed by the events of the war, was able to take place in the Thomaskirche, where he received the names Wilhelm Richard.

The truce expired and on 16 October the thunder of cannon announced the start of the battle of Leipzig. The fighting reached the suburbs of the city by 19 October. The tocsin was rung in Der Brühl and when Johanna Wagner leant out of the window she saw the emperor galloping past bareheaded, having lost his hat in his haste. The following days and weeks demanded every ounce of strength Friedrich Wagner possessed, as he worked to restore order. The bodies of men and horses littered the streets in the suburbs, the dead and wounded lay together in the great hall of the Gewandhaus, and an epidemic of typhus broke out, eventually claiming Friedrich himself as one of its victims. His wife published an announcement in the local newspaper:

> A victim of his duties, my husband Carl Friedrich
> Wilhelm Wagner, chief registrar at the Royal Police
> Headquarters, died on 23 November, in his
> fourty-fourth year, far too early for me and my eight
> growing children. His worth as man and as friend has
> been proved to me especially by the exceptionally
> delicate concern his friends have shown for the
> well-being of me and my children at this time, but
> this has also made me all the more sensible of the
> magnitude of my loss.

There was one friend in particular who at once took the family into his care: Ludwig Geyer. Ludwig Heinrich Christian Geyer was born on 21 January 1779 in Eisleben, in the district of Halle, the son of the clerk to the justices, Christian Gottlieb Geyer. He enrolled at

Leipzig University in 1798 to study law, but had to give up his studies when his father died. Portrait-painting had been a hobby of his, and he now started to attend classes at Oeser's (later Tischbein's) 'Academy of Drawing, Painting and Architecture', where he painted 'old men and young girls'. He became friendly with Friedrich Wagner in 1800, and it was Friedrich who discovered his acting talent, invited him to take part in amateur performances and so set him on the professional career that led Geyer eventually to the Saxon court theatre.

In the summer of 1813 he was playing in Teplitz (now Teplice) in Bohemia with the Seconda company. 'I would have loved to come to Leipzig,' he wrote to Friedrich in Stötteritz on 6 June; 'Teplitz arouses my indifference, not to say dislike.' He invited his friends to visit him in Teplitz, and as her husband was recalled to Leipzig in July Johanna went without him, and was inscribed in the register of visitors on 21 July 1813. Ernest Newman's argument (NLRW, II, pp. 608ff.) that the only explanation for this journey of Johanna's in wartime was that she was anxious to show her two-month-old son to his alleged natural father – so indirectly supporting the hypothesis of Geyer's paternity – does not stand up to close scrutiny. Johanna used to take the warm baths at Teplitz every year, and the spa was more secure against war and war's alarums at that particular time than Leipzig, the centre of military activity. Goethe was in Teplitz at the same time, and his diary confirms that the town was quiet, with its descriptions of the comings and goings of other visitors, of his own mineralogical expeditions, of parties and visits to the theatre. A performance of Schiller's *Don Carlos* that he mentions will have given him the opportunity to see Geyer as King Philip, one of his best parts. There is only one reference to the war, a 'gloomy military–political conversation' on 25 July. The idyllic calm ended with the expiry of the truce on 10 August. All visitors had to leave Teplitz, and Johanna too returned to Leipzig.

Geyer hurried to Leipzig to offer help and comfort immediately after Friedrich's death, but had to return to Dresden, where the Seconda company was playing. When his daughter Cäcilie, in 1870, sent her half-brother Richard the letters Geyer had written to their mother at that period, he told her that he had been not just touched, but profoundly moved by them. 'It is seldom in civil life that we see so plain an example of complete self-sacrifice for a noble purpose as we find in this case . . . I think I now understand this relationship completely, although I find it extremely difficult to express my view of it. It seems to me as if our father Geyer believed he was expiating some guilt in sacrificing himself for the whole family.' (14 January 1870)

And yet the whole tone and content of the letters contradict the suspicion Wagner was voicing. 'Over the bier of 1813 you allow the ties of friendship to be fastened yet more tightly,' Geyer wrote to Johanna at the end of the year; 'the invitation to do so is great and noble.' It is only very gradually that the note of love and longing enters what he writes. 'Heaven is very well disposed towards us, it has given me the gratifying vocation of being your friend,' he wrote on 28 January 1814. 'I have a great deal to talk to you about, and I can barely wait until the time when I shall be able to have a heart-to-heart talk with you on the dear old sofa.' Johanna was of one mind with him, and they were married on 28 August 1814.

If Wagner's suspicion was well founded, why should Geyer have expressed himself with such restraint in these letters? (He even uses the formal 'Sie' in addressing her.) Indeed, Wagner himself later changed his mind. The entry in Cosima's diary for 26 November 1878 includes the following: 'I ask Richard: "I suppose Father Geyer was your father?" Richard replies: "I don't think so – my mother loved him – 'elective affinities'." '

But in 1870, still under the impression Geyer's letters had first made on him, he must have said something to Friedrich Nietzsche about his initial suspicion, for in 1888 the latter inserted a footnote in *The Wagner Case*: 'Was Wagner German at all? There is some reason to ask . . . His father was an actor called Geyer. A vulture [Geyer] is almost the same as an eagle [Adler].' Readers at once seized upon what he was hinting – that Wagner was a Jew. They assumed that his one-time friend, who had read the first proofs of Wagner's autobiography, which was still not generally available, must have more, and more reliable, information about the matter. But the inference was Nietzsche's own invention. Geyer is an old German surname, the most famous bearer of it being Florian Geyer, a nobleman who sided with the peasants in the Peasants' War in the early sixteenth century, and there is no onomastic justification for linking it with Adler, which is almost exclusively Jewish. Otto Bournot's research into the family background of Wagner's step-father, published in 1913, revealed that Geyer's ancestors had been organists and cantors at the Evangelical church in Eisleben (where

1. View of Leipzig from the east, around 1820

2b. Johanna Rosine Wagner, née Pätz

2a. Ludwig Geyer

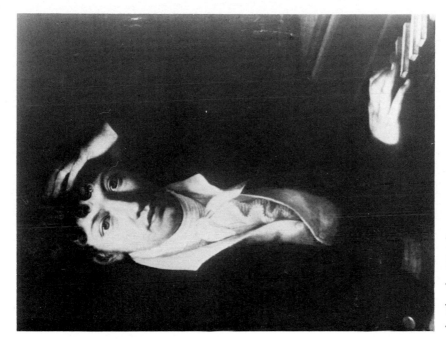

3b. Theodor Weinlig

3a. Adolf Wagner

4b. Giacomo Meyerbeer

4a. Vincenzo Bellini

5b. Wagner's house in Riga

5a. Wagner around 1850: drawing by
Ernest Benedikt Kietz

Extra-Beilage zu Eberhardt's Allgem. Polizei-Anzeiger.
Band XXXVI N° 47.

Richard Wagner

ehemal. Capellmeister und politischer
Flüchtling aus Dresden.

am 30. v. M. aus derselben aber entlassen und an das Landgericht zu Lauenburg behufs Einleitung einer neuen Untersuchung, abgeliefert worden. 11/6. 53.

651) **Kahlert,** Georg Bernhard, Webergeselle aus Rudolstadt bei Gotha. Alter: 27 Jahr; Größe: 5' 8''; Haare: dunkelblond; Augen: braun. Besond. Kennz.: eine Narbe über dem linken Auge und eine dergl. am rechten Handknöchel. Er kam kürzlich nach Altenburg, trat dort als Hochstapler auf und erregte zunächst dadurch die Aufmerksamkeit der Polizei, daß er zwei Erinnerungszeichen an den schleswig-holsteinischen Krieg in Kreuzesform auf der Brust trug, weshalb er zur Haft kam. Bei der der über ihn eingeleiteten Untersuchung hat sich etwas Weiteres nicht ergeben, als daß Kahlert, wie auch seine Heimathsbehörde ihn bezeichnet, ein Vagabond und Schwindler ist; er zeigte sich aber in Altenburg während seiner Untersuchung auch als frecher Lügner, weshalb er körperlich gezüchtigt wurde. Am 30. Mai d. J. ist er unter Anrechnung des Arrests als Strafe, in seine Heimath abgeschoben worden. 11/6. 53.

Politisch gefährliche Individuen.

652) **Wagner,** Richard, ehemaliger Capellmeister aus Dresden, einer der hervorragendsten Anhänger der Umsturzpartei, welcher wegen Theilnahme an der Revolution in Dresden im Mai 1849 (Bd. XXVIII, S. 220 und Bd. XXVII, S. 306) steckbrieflich verfolgt wird, soll dem Vernehmen nach beabsichtigen, sich von Zürich aus, woselbst er sich gegenwärtig aufhält, nach Deutschland zu begeben. Behufs seiner Habhaftwerdung wird ein Porträt Wagner's, der im Betretungsfalle zu verhaften und an das königl. Stadtgericht zu Dresden abzuliefern sein dürfte, hier beigefügt. 11/6. 53.

653) **v. Wittenburg,** Max, aus Neiße (Jul. Bd. XXXIII, S. 230), ist am 18. April d. J. aus Breslau, wohin er am 17. April zurückgeführt war, ausgewiesen worden. Der Aufenthalt im Reichenbacher Kreise ist ihm verboten worden. 11/6. 53.

Erledigungen

a) **Heinecke,** Eduard, aus Eisenberg (Bd. XXXVI, S. 217), ist ergriffen.
b) **Töpfer,** Amalie Antoinette, aus Ohrdruf (Bd. XXXVI, S. 231).
c) **Gut,** Carl Friedrich, aus Zembichen (Bd. XXXVI, S. 265), ist zu Marburg verhaftet worden.

Redacteur: H. Müller. — Druck der Teubner'schen Officin in Dresden.
Hierzu eine Extra-Beilage.

6. The warrant for Wagner's arrest after the revolution of 1849, from Eberhardt's *Allgemeiner Polizei-Anzeiger* 1853

7b. Arthur Schopenhauer

7a. Minna Planer

8b. Anton Pusinelli

8a. Eduard Devrient

9a. Dresden Opera House, designed by Gottfried Semper

9b. Villa Wesendonk, near Zürich

11. The end of the Prelude to *Tristan und Isolde*: an autograph sketch dated 15 December 1859

12b. Hans von Bülow

12a. Charles Baudelaire

13. Letter from Wagner to King Ludwig dated 3 May 1864: 'Theurer huldvoller König!'

14b. Eduard Hanslick

14a. King Ludwig II

15b. Jessie Laussot-Taylor

15a. Eliza Wille

16b. Wagner around 1864: painting by Friedrich Pecht, with a bust of King Ludwig in the background

16a. Cosima von Bülow around 1860: drawing by Claire Charnacé

Luther was born and died) since the seventeenth century. The earliest known, Benjamin Geyer (died 1720), was the municipal director of music; the fact that he lived in the so-called 'church house' in Watzdorf from 1686 to 1693 shows that he held a post at the Andreaskirche there.

The other genealogical 'mystery' concerns Johanna Wagner. In *Mein Leben* Wagner says that she never gave any of her children a full account, or many details, of her own origins. 'She came from Weissenfels and acknowledged that her parents had been bakers there . . . A remarkable circumstance was that she was sent to a select educational establishment in Leipzig and enjoyed there the care of one she called a "high-ranking fatherly friend", whom she later identified as a prince of Weimar, to whom her family in Weissenfels was greatly obliged. Her education at the establishment seems to have ended abruptly on the sudden death of that fatherly friend.'

It was to this that Houston Stewart Chamberlain, Wagner's son-in-law, was alluding when he wrote to a teacher, one Hellmundt, on 12 December 1913: 'There is not a single missing link in his mother's descent, and the little secret it contains is no secret to initiates, and allows her family tree to be traced back to the twelfth century.'[2] In other words, it was assumed that Wagner's mother was the natural daughter of Prince Friedrich Ferdinand Constantin of Weimar (1758–93), the younger brother of Goethe's patron, Grand Duke Karl August. Prince Constantin is known to have been musical and a libertine. His military tutor, Karl von Knebel, wrote: 'The prince passed his time in reading, writing and, above all, music. This was his favourite occupation, and he possessed no small talent in it. He found nearly every instrument easy; indeed, he cured himself of an indisposition by prolonged music-making.' His youthful amours did not always lack consequences: he once returned to Weimar from Paris with a Madame Darsaincourt, who bore him a son who was raised in a forester's family.[3]

The Prince Constantin hypothesis was accepted not only in the inner circle at Wahnfried but – more important – even by so dispassionate an enquirer as Newman. Why, he argued, would a prince of Weimar have sent the daughter of a Weissenfels baker to receive an education above the average for her class in Leipzig, 'unless for very good reasons of his own'? He met the objection that Constantin was only sixteen when Johanna was born by referring to his, and his brother's, known precocity. (NLRW, II, pp. 613ff.)

The one curious thing is that Mrs Burrell, the founder of the famous collection of Wagner documents now in the Curtis Institute of Music in Philadelphia, never heard of the hypothesis. She began her researches in the 1890s, when there must still have been memories in a small town like Weissenfels of the mother of so famous a person as Wagner. And what did she learn there? She heard 'from more than one source', 'with variations', that Johanna Rosine Pätz was selected by Karl August and Goethe for the theatre in Weimar, and that Friedrich Wagner had made her acquaintance through Goethe. (NLRW, II, pp. 617ff.)

After the accretions of legend have been removed, the most likely facts are these: after the death of her mother in 1789 and her father's remarriage, Johanna was selected for a career as an actress, not by Karl August but by Constantin; her education for the stage was then ended four years later when the prince died.

But it is almost symptomatic of the extraordinary impression Wagner made, especially on his contemporaries, that even his parentage was a matter to be surrounded by mystery and legend.

No less remarkable is the prophecy made over his cradle. Jean Paul wrote in his preface to E. T. A. Hoffmann's *Fantasiestücke*: 'Until now Apollo has always cast the gift of poetry with his right hand and the gift of music with his left to two people so far apart from each other that to this day we still await the man who will write both the text and the music of a true opera.' That preface, dated 24 November 1813, was written in Jean Paul's home town, Bayreuth.

2

Wagner's Mother

In the autumn of 1814 the family moved to Dresden, where Geyer was well known as a portrait-painter, actor at the court theatre and playwright. His play *Der Bethlehemitische Kindermord* – in spite of its title, 'The Massacre of the Innocents', it is a comedy about the ups and downs of an artist's life – even earned him a certain posthumous reputation when it was published many years later in the cheap and comprehensive series of popular classics, Reclams Universalbibliothek.

Johanna reigned in the hospitable house in the Moritzstrasse, amidst her flock of children, which was increased in the following year by a black-haired daughter, Cäcilie. Geyer's portrait of his wife shows her as still youthful, apparently on the point of going out in her bonnet and shawl, then suddenly turning back, perhaps in response to a call from the artist, and catching at her shawl, as it slides from her shoulder, with her left hand; her full oval face is turned towards the spectator, smiling and with some surprise in her large eyes.

Wagner described her as 'a woman remarkable in the eyes of all who knew her'. Certainly in his own case the memory of her is a thread running through his whole life and work. Only a few days before his death he dreamed of her, 'young and graceful, a radiant vision'.

Her chief attributes were a good temper and a sense of humour, according to *Mein Leben*, but the strain of caring for her large family stifled the expression of maternal tenderness. Wagner could hardly remember ever having been caressed by her, and so was the more strongly affected by one occasion when, as he was being borne sleepily off to bed and raised tearful eyes to her,

she smiled warmly and made an affectionate remark about him to
a visitor.

'What made the strongest impression upon me was the unusual,
almost histrionic fervour with which she spoke of the great and
beautiful in art. But she always told me that she did not include
theatrical art in her enthusiasm, but only poetry, music and painting; indeed she frequently came close to threatening to curse me, if
I, too, should ever want to go into the theatre.' (ML, pp. 18f.)

She had good reason to fear that he might, for four of her other
children did. Her eldest son, Albert, who was very like Richard in
appearance, gave up his medical studies, to Geyer's displeasure, and
became an opera singer; Rosalie and Luise were trained as actresses,
at the wish of their father, and made their debuts at an early age in
little plays Geyer wrote specially for them – Rosalie with such
success that she was engaged for the court theatre; and a younger
sister, Klara, possessing a pretty voice, could not resist the lure of
opera.

In spite of Johanna's pleas and threats, Richard, too, embarked on
a theatrical career at the age of nineteen. Two letters she wrote him,
the only ones by her to survive, assail the wretchedness of the life he
had chosen, which she feared would estrange him from her and
from his own better self.

The first was written apropos of his falling out with the husband
of his sister Luise, the wealthy publisher and bookseller Friedrich
Brockhaus, who had remonstrated with the young director of
music at the Magdeburg theatre when he arrived home in 1835 with
nothing to his name but debts and 'a very intelligent poodle'. 'This
humiliation in front of Fritz is buried in the very depths of my
heart,' Richard had complained to her, 'and I am tormented by the
bitterest self-reproach for having handed him the right to humiliate
me.' (25 July 1835) He must have expressed his feelings even more
strongly in a later letter announcing the forthcoming première of
Das Liebesverbot, to which she replied on 9 March 1836. (Her
attitude to German orthographic conventions was even more wilful
than that of Goethe's mother; her spelling, notably, was coloured
by the Saxon tendency, in speech, to lengthen vowels and voice all
consonants.)

My dear boy, pray tell me how this false, ever bitterer
trait got into your once guileless heart? it will be 3, 4

years before you realize that you were certainly wrong;
the letter got into Rosalie's hands . . .: your heartlessness
upset her the whole day . . .

I am greatly relieved that you have now decided to
present your opera in Magdeburg and conduct it
yourself, but good Richard what did you want to let
that great advantage slip out of your hands for? . . .
Now may God bless you and your plan; oh only believe
that I really yearn for you! I am always afraid time, and
things, will snatch your heart from me! God preserve
this one reward for me on earth! . . .

And another thing dear Richard, you have made me
very worried about your circumstances in Magdeburg, I
can . . . very well imagine that you often have great
money trouble now, but my dear good son! if you are
victorious it will gain you a lot of respect and so you
will show what the resolution of a noble youth can do,
what a comfort! what a hope for your mother! my good
heart's boy!

Yes yes I rejoice over you greatly in private! for I know
your purpose is good and noble.

The second letter was written in the following year, after he had
moved to Riga. It had been a painful year for her: Richard had
married the actress Minna Planer against his family's wishes, only
to have her run off with another man soon afterwards, and Rosalie,
who was married to Dr Oswald Marbach, had died in childbirth on
12 October 1837.

My heart's dear son! That's what you were before you
tore yourself out of my heart; but a mother's heart
remains the same, only the circumstances are changed!
Yes! dear Dear God!! It was you three, you, my sainted
angel Rosalie, poor Cecilie, who I had at my side
longest. The final loss of your heart and filial love cost
me many sleep less nights . . .

I heard the description of your Domestic
Circumstances in Königsberg with true distress, I cannot
understand how *a Female Creature can Hurt and Use so
young a man in this way*! . . . A well-brought-up
gentlewoman is certainly incapable of behaving so after

the worst treatment if she ever loved a man, and he so
young!

My angel Rosalie was too pure to go into a better
world unreconciled with you; before I left she had a
long talk with me about you on a walk, she said that
Louise Brockhaus had too little faith in you, and your
talent! but, she had great hopes for the future, if only!
you are surrounded by people with enough
understanding intelligence and a measure of nobility! for
only that, and it can still all go well with him! that's
what she said! and I said Amen![1]

The apparent estrangement was only an expression of youthful
defiance. 'I hope you did not believe that I had ever for a moment
forgotten you,' Wagner wrote from Meudon on 12 September
1841, after hearing of the reception of *Rienzi* in Dresden,

even when you heard nothing from me! Oh, I'm sure
I've already told you that there were times when I really
went out of my way not to stir up your sympathy for
my affairs again. But I was praying to God to preserve
your life and health, for I hoped that in time my own
efforts would win me a prize which would add to the
pleasure of showing my face at home once more . . .
Everyone who wants to attain true inward and outward
independence must uncompromisingly . . . follow the
path that his earnest inclination and a certain inner,
irresistible prompting tell him to follow . . .

I would look foolish if I put into words what I think
of – what I hope for – for what are thoughts and
hopes! But things *must* turn out right eventually, and the
person who most deserves his good fortune is one who
has come through the tempest safely and has known bad
fortune!

Even later, the memory of the years during which, for the sake of
his career in the theatre, he had kept himself aloof from his mother,
who was 'good but ignorant in this respect', was painful to him.
Nevertheless he encouraged the young Hans von Bülow, whose
wish to be a professional musician was opposed by his parents, to
muster the same energy as he had himself when he had not allowed

even the most noble of natural ties to hinder him in his right to self-determination. (To Franziska von Bülow, 19 September 1850)

Johanna lived to witness the beginning of her son's success. She tried to be reconciled with Minna, whose behaviour in Königsberg she was unable to forgive; even so they seem to have quarrelled again over the old grievance, when they were both taking the waters in Teplitz in July 1842. Wagner passionately took his wife's part in a letter headed 'for you alone', in which he commiserated with her over his mother's 'nagging', which he felt to be beneath his own notice. 'But it is quite different for you. Everybody ought to treat you, my dear wife, with special consideration, firstly because you deserve it in every way, and secondly because rough treatment hurts you more deeply than anybody else, for reasons that are very easily understood.' (Undated, RWBC, pp. 612f.)

In the end Minna's domestic virtues prevailed on her mother-in-law to forgive and forget. In a letter that can probably be dated just before the first performance of *Tannhäuser* in 1845, she thanked Minna most warmly for the love and attention she had been shown while she was staying with the couple. 'A mother's greeting and a kiss to my good old Richard! It makes me happy to see him prosper in everything he undertakes.' (RWBC, p. 621)

After spending her last years in a state of near childishness, she died in February 1848, shortly before the revolution broke out, and so was spared Richard's exile. It was a bitterly cold morning, Wagner wrote, when they laid her coffin in the grave. Instead of scattering earth in the grave in light handfuls, they had to drop it in frozen clods, which startled him by their rumble. 'On my short journey back to Dresden, the clear sense of my complete isolation came over me for the first time.'

His mother meant security to him, and this is the role assigned to motherhood in his works. It is not particularly overt in his auto-biographical and anecdotal writing or dicta, but operates at a deeper level of his subconscious. Once, in later life, recalling how he had taken a risky climb on to the school roof as a boy, he added that he had had a fit of vertigo and thought he was done for. In his terror he had thought of his mother, and that thought, like invoking the protection of a higher power, had given him the courage to reach the safety of the skylight again. In just the same way Siegfried calls on his mother in the moment when he learns fear.

There is even a letter Wagner wrote to his mother, dated 19

September 1846, which anticipates Siegfried's state of mind in the scene under the linden tree: 'My good little mother, however many strange things have come between us, how quickly they all vanish! When I leave the smoke of the town for a beautiful leafy valley, lie down on the moss, look at the slender trees, listen to a bird singing, until in my sense of ease a tear forms that I am happy to leave undried – it's as though I were stretching out my hand to you from the whole chaos of strange events.' And later he once, in conversation, referred to the Woodbird in *Siegfried* as the voice of 'Sieglinde's maternal soul'.

Cosima noted in her diary on 4 January 1878 that Wagner told her that 'when he had argued with his mother as a child he had shown a compulsion to confess'. This is like Parsifal, who has run away from his mother and is stricken with a passionate metaphysical sense of guilt in the second act, as the reality of her death comes home to him.

Such elements rose out of Wagner's subconscious and appeared in his work involuntarily. The connection is even more mysterious when the theme of Parsifal's self-reproach in the second act – 'Die Mutter, die Mutter konnt' ich vergessen!' – is recalled in a majestic fortissimo by the woodwind and horns in the third–act transformation music, as if, on the point of assuming his royal office, Parsifal remembers the security his mother gave him.

It is characteristic of Wagner and his work that a few pages about his mother should open perspectives of this breadth and depth. His life and his work are a fabric closely woven together from threads that run continuously from the earliest experiences of his childhood to the work that was his 'farewell to the world'.

3

Boyhood

It was a small thin boy that grew up in the charge of his sisters, pale, with a high forehead and bright blue eyes – 'blue as the sea', Judith Gautier wrote when she first met Wagner at Tribschen. His health was poor and caused his mother great and constant anxiety; once, when he was particularly ill with a childhood disease, she almost gave him up altogether. He suffered from a very early age from an allergic sensitivity of the skin, which continued to trouble him throughout his life and was the reason for the famous silk underwear. But just as the grown man, forever suffering and complaining about it, had an incredible capacity for hard work, so the child, for all his delicacy, possessed a prodigious fund of vitality and was always ready for mischief and hair-raising adventures – Geyer called him 'the cossack'. On a visit to Geyer's brother, a goldsmith, in Eisleben, he never stopped fighting the local boys, and when a troupe of rope-walkers set up their act in the marketplace, he at once tried to imitate them; to the end of his days he used to horrify Cosima by climbing every tree in the garden.

He himself denied that he was an infant prodigy. It would have been hard, indeed, to discover one particular outstanding talent in the abundance of his gifts. But there were signs that he was different from other children: he was observant far beyond his years, and he possessed an imagination which brought even inanimate objects so vividly to life that he was sometimes terrified by them. Mime's vision of Fafner in Act I of *Siegfried* is an objectification of his own earliest fears put to comic use.

His stepfather had plans for him, though they did not include the theatre. It would have pleased him best if Richard had shown a talent for painting, but after a number of fruitless attempts to capture the boy's interest, he had to admit defeat on that particular front.

In his autobiography Wagner describes how he was summoned home from Possendorf, where he had started school with the pastor, because his stepfather was dying. He was taken to the bedside and experienced the sensation that it was all happening in a dream. 'In the next room my mother invited me to play what I had learned on the piano, her intention being to distract father with the sound: I played "Üb' immer Treu und Redlichkeit"; then father asked my mother, "Do you think he might have a talent for music?"

'At first light the next morning mother entered the large room where we children slept, came to each bed in turn and told us, sobbing, that our father was dead, saying something to each of us like a blessing; to me she said, "He hoped to make something out of you." '

'I recollect', Wagner confessed, 'that for a long time I imagined that I would come to something.'

Geyer died too soon (on 30 September 1821) to have been able to influence the boy's development. His most lasting effect on him was perhaps through his friendship with Carl Maria von Weber. '*He* inspired me with enthusiasm for music. I wish somebody could have seen me at the performance of *Der Freischütz*, in the little old theatre, conducted by Weber. It is a blessing to experience the impact of an elect being in childhood.' When Weber passed the house after rehearsals, Richard called his little sister Cäcilie to the window: 'Look, there's the greatest man alive! You can't have any idea how great he is!' 'Not to be emperor, not to be king, but to stand there like that and conduct like that': that was his sole desire when he saw and heard Weber conducting *Freischütz* once again. And the composer of *Parsifal* could still remember the 'tonic–harmonic thrill', the sense of the 'daemonic' that came over him on hearing the first bars of the overture, 'something peculiar to me, too'. 'Formal beauty, on its own, was a matter of indifference to me . . . Nobody else had much of a chance after I had heard that adagio introduction.'

His stepfather and his brothers and sisters introduced the child to the world of the theatre. Artists were frequent visitors in the Geyer household; they made trips into the country together, picnicking in the open air, and once Weber acted as cook. While Dresden, the capital of Saxony, was described at that date as a 'colony of court officials', with an appropriate decorum prevailing in social behaviour, manners in this charming, lively-minded circle were friendly and relaxed.

What attracted him to the theatre was, by Wagner's own account, not so much the search for entertainment as the pleasurable excitement of a purely imaginary world, a fascination often close to horror, 'something mysteriously ghostly about the beards, wigs and costumes, which the addition of music only intensified'. Through his sisters he was able to go behind the scenes and explore backstage and the wardrobe rooms, and a single piece of scenery or a costume was enough to transport him at a stroke to 'that fascinating daemonium'. He used to watch his sisters sewing the more delicate costumes at home, and just touching them was enough to set his heart racing.

The discovery of a puppet theatre that had belonged to his stepfather, with lovely sets Geyer had painted himself, at once inspired the boy to write a play of derring-do, which made his sisters laugh uncontrollably when they found it and must have been his first essay in dramatic form. Seeing a puppet theatre half a century later, after he had written *Götterdämmerung*, moved him, as we shall see, to comment on the essence of mimic art, present even in this primordial form of theatre.

The whole of the boy's small world was filled with marvellous happenings; it is characteristic that E. T. A. Hoffmann's fairy tale *Der Goldene Topf*, which was set in Dresden (and which was written in the year of Richard's birth), remained a favourite of his all his life, with its mixture of the realistic and the fantastic, reminding him of his first childhood.

Wagner's first experience of the wider world took the shape of a journey to Prague, on foot, and his account of it – including his falling passionately in love with two pretty sisters and even encountering a blind harpist – reads like a chapter out of *Wilhelm Meister*. The volcanic soil of Bohemia was to stir his imagination mysteriously again on a later occasion.

The five years he spent as a pupil at the Kreuzschule in Dresden (1822–7) provided an important classical counterbalance to the romanticism on which his imagination fed. It is rare for an artist of genius to praise his school as highly as Wagner did in his autobiography. Greek history and mythology aroused so great an enthusiasm in him that, while his neglect of Latin incurred punishment, he plunged into the study of Greek, so as to be able to hear his heroes speaking in their own language. His teacher, Magister Sillig, confidently predicted a career as a classical scholar for him. Newman's doubts as to the accuracy of these claims are refuted by the record of extra work done by the third-form pupils on their own initiative in the Michaelmas term of 1826: the thirteen-year-old Wagner was the only one in the class to submit a translation of the first three books of the *Odyssey*. (GLRW, I, p. 103)

His early classical studies ranged widely. Professor Friedrich Creuzer of Heidelberg published a book entitled *Symbolism and Mythology of Ancient Peoples, with Special Reference to the Greeks*, which stirred up quite a controversy. Johann Heinrich Voss, whose translation of Homer is still the standard German version, wrote an *Antisymbolism* in reply. It is astonishing to read Wagner reminding an old school friend, in a letter from Riga in November 1838, of how they had sworn 'death to Creuzer's *Symbolism*' – when still in the third form! He later formed a less harsh opinion of Creuzer's thesis and had the book in his library in Wahnfried.

When the family moved back to Leipzig in 1827 his interest in classics was encouraged by his father's younger brother, Adolf Wagner. 'God, when I remember Uncle Adolf!' he said to Cosima. 'I would have been proud to introduce you to him, and to tell you I was descended from the same stock. His conversation was refined and mild, his mind was cultivated, noble and free. He was a true disciple of Goethe.'

Adolf Wagner had just published his magnum opus, *Parnasso italiano*, an anthology including texts by Dante, Petrarch, Ariosto and Tasso. He dedicated it 'al principe de' poeti, Goethe', who sent him a silver goblet in thanks. 'I have used it for many years in joy and sorrow, and it has witnessed manifold events. Use it yourself as often and refresh your memory of me in the enjoyment of wine, which belongs, like poetry, to those products of spirit and intelligence with which humanity has come close to rivalling nature itself.' (29 October 1827)

Richard used to accompany his uncle on afternoon walks outside the city gates and the sight of them deep in talk may well have raised a smile in passers-by. He liked to spend his evenings in his uncle's house, too: when Adolf read a Sophoclean tragedy aloud, it revealed a new, previously unknown side of the Greek spirit to him, one which was to be of decisive importance for his own work.

He had in the meantime discovered Shakespeare by his own initiative, and his enthusiasm grew to an obsession. 'I can remember dreaming in my early adolescence that Shakespeare was *alive*, and I saw him and spoke to him, face to face.'

For all his passion for music, the bent for poetry seemed to be winning the upper hand. While still at the Kreuzschule he had won the prize for a poem on the death of a fellow-pupil. It had even been printed and his mother folded her hands in prayerful gratitude at this first proof of her youngest son's gifts.

'It was now beyond doubt that I was going to be a poet.' The outcome of this conviction was a five-act tragedy, *Leubald*, at which he worked in secret for two years (1826–8). (RWGS, XVI, pp. 179ff.) The only person in the secret was his sister Ottilie. Once when he was reading her one of the most blood-curdling scenes, a violent thunderstorm broke out. 'As the lightning flashed and the thunder rolled right overhead, my sister tried to persuade me to abandon the reading, but she soon realized it was impossible to stop me, and sat it out with a touching devotion.'

He laughed at it later in life: it was compounded of *Hamlet* and *Lear*, forty-two people died in it and most of them had to reappear as ghosts in the last act, since he had run out of characters. But he took it very seriously at the time, and the monstrous progeny of his imagination sprang up from his bedroom floor with such vitality that they frightened even their creator.

At fourteen he believed he had found his vocation, chosen his future path.

4

Beethoven

'Then came Beethoven.' The look and tone of voice with which Wagner once spoke these words, in the course of a conversation tracing the development of German music, amounted to an experience in themselves, according to Hans von Wolzogen: as if the name of Beethoven heralded the dawn of a new world.

Beethoven did open a new world to Wagner himself. The start of the overture to *Fidelio*, with its use of horns and woodwind, had an effect on him similar to that of the *Freischütz* overture. He asked his sisters about Beethoven and was told that he had just died. His deafness, his lonely life, a lithographed portrait and now his untimely death conjured up the impression of the 'most sublime, transcendental originality'. And when he heard the incidental music to *Egmont* he knew he had to write music like that for his own tragedy.

Beethoven, too, was admitted to the world of his imagination, and in his dreams Beethoven's image was mingled now with Shakespeare's. This conjunction of the poet and the composer was a first, confused intimation of his own future creative activity. It was while he was in this state of mind that he had two great Beethovenian experiences: he saw Schröder-Devrient in the part of Fidelio and he immersed himself in the score of the Ninth Symphony.

The Leipzig theatre reopened in August 1829, after a closure of over a year, now under the supervision of the intendant of the court theatre in Dresden. Its priorities included not only high production standards but also a varied and worthwhile repertory. Since his sister Rosalie was a member of the company, Wagner had no difficulty in getting into performances whenever he wanted to. If it had been the mysterious and fantastic elements in the theatre that had attracted him as a child, now, at sixteen, under the spell of Shakespeare, Schiller and Goethe, he was seized for the first time by a more 'aware' passion for the stage.

It was then that a kind of miracle occurred, turning his artistic sensibility in a new direction, determining the course of his whole life: Wilhelmine Schröder-Devrient, then twenty-four and at the height of her fame, came from Dresden for a short season as guest artist, and sang the title role in *Fidelio*.

In the opera's second act, as the music transfigures the drama, and as Leonora frees her husband from the darkness of his cell, it was to the boy, listening with bated breath, as if she was leading him, too, into the broad daylight of his hitherto dimly perceived artistic ideal. He scribbled a hasty note, handed it in at the singer's hotel and ran off into the night like a madman. From that day forward, he wrote, his life would have a new meaning, and if she should ever hear his name acclaimed in the world of art, then she might care to remember that it was she who had made him that evening what he thereupon swore to become. 'When I look back at the whole of my life,' he affirmed years later, 'I can discover no other experience that I could compare with this for the effect it had on me.'

He would have written a work worthy of that great woman there and then, if he had been able. The fact that he could not filled him with despair over his literary and musical experiments and cast him for a while into a frenzy of youthful excesses. He dedicated his essay *On Actors and Singers* (1872) to her memory, and the figure of Tragedy in the sgraffito over the front door of Wahnfried bears the face of Schröder-Devrient, a mysterious yet overt memorial to that seminal experience of his teens.

No such ideal interpreter guided him in his other Beethovenian experience. He had to find the meaning and the soul in the dumb notation of the score for himself. Some of the earliest of his childhood impressions were revived. As a small boy he had never been able to go past the palace of Prince Anton in Dresden without trembling at the mysterious sound of fifths that seemed to come from the violin held by one of the stone figures decorating the baroque façade. The haunting impression was the stronger because of a picture he knew well in which Death played the violin to a dying man. Later, when he attended afternoon concerts in the Grosser Garten park, on the outskirts of Dresden, the sound of the orchestra tuning struck him like the summoning of a spirit world in which he first set foot with the opening bars of the *Freischütz* overture.

Music was a 'daemonium' to him, a 'mystically sublime immensity', and tonic, third and fifth appeared to him in half-waking dreams as tangible, physical entities. Reading his favourite author, E. T. A. Hoffmann, fed his susceptibilities, and he even believed he had found the original of one of Hoffmann's characters, Kapellmeister Kreisler, in a half-crazy musical fanatic in Leipzig. This mysticism was only a youthful manifestation of the completely individual sensitivity to music that gives his works their special character: the sounds perceptible to sense are only the surface layer of the impulses contracting and relaxing in the depth of the soul: the music is more than music.

Opening the score to the Choral Symphony, he was struck by the fifths, the ghostly echo from his childhood, the 'Fundamental' of his own life. This symphony must contain the secret of all secrets! He set to, to copy the score laboriously by hand, until late into the night. Once the first light of day surprised him at his task and with a shriek he buried his face in the pillows as if he had seen a ghost. Since there was no piano reduction for two hands at that time, this seventeen-year-old undertook the task. The specimens of it published by Otto Daube show that his mysticism was allied to a genuine musical understanding: not only does it offer a clear, playable piano version, but there are places in the Adagio where its rendering of the melodic line is superior to Otto Singer's later version.[1]

After he had finished the first movement he wrote to Franz Schott, the publisher, in Mainz, on 6 October 1830 – the letter is the earliest by him that survives:

> Beethoven's last glorious symphony has long been the
> subject of my study, and the closer my acquaintance
> with its high quality, the more saddened I have been
> that it is still so much misunderstood, so much
> disregarded by the majority of the musical public . . .
> My enthusiasm was great enough to embolden me to
> undertake a two-hand piano version of it myself, and so
> it is that I have so far arranged the first, and perhaps the
> most difficult, movement as clearly and as fully as
> possible. I am now therefore approaching your respected

publishing house, to enquire whether you would be
interested in taking an arrangement of this kind (for
naturally I am unwilling to proceed further with such a
laborious task without that assurance) . . . I therefore ask
you most respectfully for a speedy reply.

Schott's reply was noncommittal, but he met Wagner at the next
Easter Fair in Leipzig and took the complete piano score away with
him to study it. He was obviously amazed to find his would-be
collaborator so young. After waiting several months for Schott's
decision, Wagner wrote to him again on 6 August 1831:

Since I have been waiting vainly for an offer from you
for over three months, I have come to the conclusion
that you have been expecting me to state my terms,
which I herewith hasten to do. I am sure, Sir, that you
will not think it exorbitant if I ask for 1 louisdor per
fascicle for this protracted, difficult and important task,
which no one else has as yet attempted in view of its
unusual demands, that is a total of 8 louisdor, which will
certainly be recouped tenfold by the sales of this
important work.

Even this tempting commercial prospect could not persuade
Schott to undertake publication. After he had returned the manuscript at the end of 1831, Wagner sent it back to him in June 1832:

I do not ask for any honorarium for it, but if you would
care to make me a gift in return you would make me
your grateful debtor. Might I perhaps request you to
send me, through Herr Härtel: Beethoven 1) Missa
Solemnis (D major), full score and piano reduction; 2)
Beethoven Symphony no, 9, full score; 3) idem 2
quartets, score, and 4) Hummel's arrangements of
Beethoven's symphonies? The sooner, the more
gratifying.

Schott complied with this request but did not publish the
arrangement of the Choral Symphony. Forty years later Wagner
asked him for it again, as a present for Cosima: 'My dear wife is in a
perpetual state of excitement, as much at the thought of the gift you
are sending her . . . as at the continuing delay in its arrival. You

would have to be as truly obsessed with my poor manuscript as this dear woman is, to be able to understand her state.' (3 January 1872) In return he dedicated a piano piece, *Albumblatt* in E♭ major, to Frau Betty Schott.

This earliest publishing venture not only gives a glimpse of his study of Beethoven, but it also reveals Wagner in toto, his enthusiasm, his persistence and not least his not unjustified self-confidence.

In the short story he wrote in Paris in 1840, *A Pilgrimage to Beethoven*, Wagner recounts the impact of Beethoven on him in fictional terms, when he has a German musician say, 'I don't really know what career had been planned for me, I only remember that one evening I heard a Beethoven symphony for the first time, that I thereupon fell ill with a fever, and when I recovered, I had become a musician.' (*Eine Pilgerfahrt zu Beethoven*, RWGS, I, pp. 90ff.) The extraordinary and unique thing about his further development was that he had been separately inspired by two Beethovens, first the dramatist and then the symphonist. Each of the experiences addressed itself to a different side of his own talent – hence the initial 'fever'. The ambition to combine these two strands in a single work of art sprang from his own genius. The whole story of his artistic endeavours, as theorist and practitioner, is the struggle to synthesize music as drama with music as symphony, in symphonic drama. That is what distinguishes him not only from other musicians, but also from his master Beethoven.

5

Studiosus Musicae

The address Wagner gave on his early letters to Schott was 'Leipzig, in the Pichhof by the Halle Gate'. His mother and three of his sisters lived in a comfortable apartment on the first floor, with a fine view of the Promenade, a broad leafy avenue following the line of the old city walls, and the scene of Richard's secret poetic and musical experiments was a 'wonderfully small bedroom'.

Outside that room he ran wild. His self-esteem suffered a blow when he was put into a class in the Nikolaischule in Leipzig lower than the one he had been in in Dresden, and his enjoyment of his lessons was completely spoiled. He abandoned everything else and studied only music. By the time his family found out about it, he had not attended school for six months.

The family in conclave decided that there was no further way of preventing him from devoting himself to music, and his brother-in-law Friedrich Brockhaus proposed sending him to Weimar to study the piano with Hummel.

How was he to explain that music to him did not mean playing an instrument, but composing? He felt that the only course open to him was to make a complete break with his surroundings. It was the first of many times in his life when he was to feel the same. Whenever external circumstances threatened to overwhelm him, he was always able to find an escape route. On this occasion he gained admission to the Thomasschule in order to continue studying, but, as he said, he left that, too, without having made the least effort to reap any advantage from it. On 23 February 1831 he matriculated at the university in Leipzig as a music student.

Not the least of the university's attractions was the glamour attached to the status of student, which had impressed him even as a

27

schoolboy. He joined the 'Saxonia' fraternity and even before the session began he already had fights pending with several experienced duellists. That he escaped with a whole skin from these challenges was due to a series of remarkable accidents of the kind that continued to help him in tight corners throughout his life. His account of this wild, dissipated period is written with such disarming frankness that Mrs Burrell, his admirer and biographer, who secretly got hold of a copy of the private printing of *Mein Leben*, could not bring herself to believe it but took it to be a fabrication of Cosima, whom she detested.

His inner life can be gauged from the fact that he still found the time for music and the self-possession to compose a number of pieces which, as he later remarked, bore much the same relationship to Beethoven as *Leubald* to Shakespeare. All the same, at the age of seventeen and still a schoolboy, he had an Overture in B♭ major performed in the theatre in Leipzig, on 24 December 1830. With gleeful self-mockery he tells in *Mein Leben* of how the drumbeat that recurred in every fifth bar put the audience into fits of laughter. The conductor, Heinrich Dorn, found the work unusual but recognized something in it that commanded attention.

Ever since Eduard Hanslick called Wagner a 'dilettante' and Nietzsche repeated it with rhetorical insistence, it has been bandied about, not only by laymen but by musical scholars who ought to have known that his 'miraculous scores', in Richard Strauss's phrase,[1] could not possibly have been written by an amateur.

The more detailed account found in *Mein Leben* already demonstrated that Wagner's remark in the *Autobiographical Sketch* of 1842 – that his study with Weinlig came to a halt within less than six months – cannot be taken literally. But the full extent of his formal studies has only been known since Otto Daube published his survey of Wagner's 'apprenticeship'.

At fifteen he borrowed Johann Bernhard Logier's newly published *Methode des Generalbasses* from the lending library run by Friedrich Wieck, Clara Schumann's father, so as to be able to paint the apparitions in his great tragedy in the proper musical colours. He found it tougher going than he had expected, and the accumulating library dues were, he asserted, the first and root cause of the financial difficulties that troubled him throughout the rest of his life.

Seeing that he would make no progress on his own, without

telling his family he began lessons in harmony with Christian Gottlieb Müller, a violinist in the theatre orchestra. He soon found the rules Müller expounded and the work he set too arid, and he went back to the 'artistic hauntings' of Hoffmann's *Fantasiestücke*, which were far more to his taste as a source of instruction. Even when he resumed lessons with Müller, after he had had to confess to his family the amounts he owed him in fees, harmonic theory could not hold his interest for long, and by summer he was neglecting his studies entirely. His move to the university brought no improvement – on the contrary, that was when his career in taverns and gaming houses really got under way.

At this point his mother plucked up her courage and went to ask Christian Theodor Weinlig, the cantor of the Thomaskirche, to give her son lessons. Weinlig, born in 1780, had studied in Bologna and was an adherent of Padre Martini's conservative Italian school. He had a formidable reputation as a contrapuntalist and had been appointed to J. S. Bach's old post in 1823. His health was poor and at first he would not yield to Johanna's fervent pleas to teach her son, but a fugue Richard had brought with him and shyly proffered changed his mind: he saw at once that the prospective pupil had talent and only lacked instruction. He agreed to teach him but made one condition: for six months he was to compose nothing at all but only to follow his master's precepts.

At first it seemed that the course was doomed to end like all the others; things reached the point at which Weinlig told him he wanted nothing more to do with him. But this coincided with another harrowing event: Richard had collected his mother's pension and in the course of a single evening's card playing had lost it and won it back again in one desperate play; thereupon he had sworn never to touch a card again. It was, he later confessed, the turning point of his life. But it also signified the turning point of his career as a musician. He begged his teacher's forgiveness and Weinlig agreed to persist with him. From then on the lessons were a joy to Wagner; the most difficult technical problems seemed to solve themselves like a game, so that he sometimes wondered if he was really learning anything.

When his English friend Edward Dannreuther asked him in 1877 for the secret of Weinlig's method, which had effected such results, Wagner replied:

Weinlig had no special method, but he was clear headed
and practical. Indeed, you cannot teach composition . . .
All you can do is, to point to some working example,
some particular piece, set a task in that direction, and
correct the pupil's work. This is what Weinlig did with
me. He chose a piece, generally something of Mozart's,
drew attention to its construction, relative length and
balance of sections, principal modulations, number and
quality of themes, and general character of the
movement. Then he set the task: you shall write about
so many bars, divide into so many sections with
modulations to correspond so and so, the themes shall
be so many, and of such and such a character. Similarly
he would set contrapuntal exercises, canons, fugues – he
analysed an example minutely and then gave simple
directions how I was to go to work . . . With infinite
kindness he would put his finger on some defective bit and
explain the why and wherefore of the alterations he thought
desirable. I readily saw what he was aiming at and soon
managed to please him . . . Music should be taught all
round on such a simple plan.[2]

This understanding between teacher and pupil, as Daube observes,
lives on in Hans Sachs's workshop, as he explains the rules of
mastersong to Walther.

Wagner regretted, in later life, the loss of an exercise book containing the fugues of the Leipzig period. But some of the counterpoint exercises, with Weinlig's corrections, are preserved in the
Wagner Archives and very attractively illustrate Wagner's account
of his lessons, above all a four–part vocal fugue on the text 'Dein ist
das Reich von Ewigkeit zu Ewigkeit, Amen' (published by Daube).

Wagner's mother had the shock of her life one day when Weinlig
paid her a formal call. Accustomed to hearing nothing but complaints from Richard's teachers, she was prepared for the worst, but
instead the cantor explained that he had considered it his duty to call
on her to render account of his pupil's progress. It was quite
remarkable, but the young man already knew for himself everything he could have taught him. And when she enquired about the
fees due after six months of lessons Weinlig replied that it would be
wrong of him to expect payment in addition to the pleasure it had

been to teach her son. His pupil's diligence and the hopes he himself nurtured for him were payment enough.

To give his student the chance to show that he had got rid of all his bombast, Weinlig set him the task of writing a sonata after the pattern of one of a childlike simplicity by Pleyel. Although Wagner constructed his Bb major Sonata from the simplest harmonic and thematic relationships, it breathes the spirit, not of Pleyel, but of Mozart, whom he was then just coming fully to know and love. In recognition of his self-restraint Weinlig got Breitkopf & Härtel to publish it, and his acceptance of the dedication on the title page shows he saw no reason to be ashamed of this piece qualifying the apprentice as journeyman.

As a reward Wagner was then allowed to compose his Fantasia in F♯ minor for piano in as free a form as he liked. Its interest lies in the fact that for the first time we encounter here anticipations of the kind of uniquely Wagnerian thematic shapes that were later to characterize *Die Walküre* and *Tristan*.

Finally, one day when he presented his teacher with a particularly elaborate double fugue, Weinlig told him he might as well frame it and hang it on the wall, he had nothing more to teach him. 'You will probably never write canons or fugues; but what you have acquired is independence. You can stand on your own feet now, and you know that you are capable of the utmost expertise, if you ever need it.' Although this marked the end of a good six months of strict apprenticeship, Weinlig remained his 'friendly adviser'.

Wagner now proceeded to study on his own. What he still had to learn could only be learned from the masters, Mozart, Beethoven and Bach, whose *Well-tempered Clavier* he tried to unlock on his own. Newman devotes several pages of inimitable irony to Wagner's 'academic enemies', who could not conceive how anybody could even dare to compose without having been through their school; what conservatory of any age could ever have taught him what he found out for himself? The truth is that he went on learning all his life, but he could do it only in his own way, aiming straight at a target that his contemporaries could not even see.

That his study of Beethoven had profited from Weinlig's instruction is illustrated by the A major Piano Sonata and the C major Symphony, both of 1832. The sonata, which Daube publishes, is decidedly the most important of Wagner's juvenilia. The main theme of the first movement, stated at the outset, is a true symphonic theme in the Beethovenian sense, driven forward by an inner dynamic and providing the material for a lively development section. Its pulsating rhythm persists in the quieter final bars, as if preparing for the impassioned, sombre Adagio molto e assai espressivo (F♯ minor). It was a bold stroke to follow this with a free three-part fugue instead of a scherzo, finishing with a cadence which already prefigures the succeeding theme and leads without a break into the finale (A major), which is also in first-movement form.

Wagner's next composition, in the early summer of 1832, was the C major Symphony. He had been completely cut off from external life, he wrote to his friend Theodor Apel, and his interior life was all the stronger for it. 'I was forsaken by God and the world. So my godlike music had to come, and you must believe me when I say that in this state I worked on my most powerful work to date, my symphony, and finished it within six weeks.' (16 December 1832)

This early work still gave him pleasure at the end of his life; he thought it a not uninteresting example of the effect Beethoven's works, then still not well known, had on a young man like him. 'I also enjoyed putting my study of counterpoint to the test: there are some stretto passages in it I can only call devilish.' When the symphony was performed again in 1882 he wrote of it, in Fritzsch's *Musikalisches Wochenblatt*, that if it contained any recognizable trait of Richard Wagner it was probably the boundless confidence that he already possessed, caring for nothing even then, and remaining immune to the hypocrisy that since then had infected the Germans totally. (RWGS, X, pp. 309ff.) He then goes on to say that 'the theme – no! let's call it the melody of the second movement (Andante)' shows the capacity he already had for writing in an elegiac vein, 'although it would probably never have seen the light of day without the Andante of [Beethoven's] C minor Symphony and the Allegretto of the A major', but, as Paul Bekker very rightly comments, his dependence on Beethoven is no greater than that of Brahms in his most mature works.

After finishing his symphony Wagner went to Bohemia again, on the track of his early love, in particular of the elder of the two young sisters. 'Picture Jenny as an Ideal of beauty, and add my ardent fantasy, and you have it in a nutshell,' he told Apel. But a bitter disappointment was in store for him. He found the young ladies surrounded by a gang of witless, horsy admirers, whom they permitted to pay clumsy court to them in the most unfeeling fashion. 'Oh, and – you can imagine all the things that can wound an ardent love; – but what is capable of killing it is more dreadful by far! – learn it from me and send me your sympathy: – she was not worthy of my love!' He had some consolation in an artistic triumph, however, when Dionys Weber, the director of the Prague Conservatory, conducted his students in the first performance of the C major Symphony. The occasion induced a friend to write what was probably the first of those satiric verse apostrophes, not always so good-natured, that rained on Wagner throughout his later career, likening his approach to Weber to the assault on Dionysius the tyrant in Schiller's *Die Bürgschaft*.

The symphony was played before the Euterpe Society in Leipzig in the December, followed by a performance in the Gewandhaus on 10 January 1833. Demoiselle Clara Wieck played a concerto by Pixis in the same concert. 'Now, listen to this,' she had already written to Robert Schumann after the Euterpe concert; 'Herr Wagner has soared above you. They performed a symphony by him that is said to be as like Beethoven's A major Symphony as two peas.'

Wagner managed to get three other orchestral works performed during the course of 1832: a Concert Overture in D minor in the Gewandhaus, an overture to Raupach's play *König Enzio* in the theatre, and a Concert Overture in C major, again in the Gewandhaus. His teacher Weinlig had used all his influence to help him, Wagner explained, in the belief that public performance was an experience of cardinal importance, 'and I am happy to say that it never did me any harm, but on the contrary, I had two great advantages from it: in addition to finding out increasingly clearly, by listening to the things myself, what was needed to achieve my ends, I also had the pleasure of having the eyes of the public directed towards me with interest.'

Half a century later he spoke of what had motivated him in his early works. The conversation had turned to the spread of his fame. 'Oh, yes,' he said, 'one has in abundance in age what one wished for in youth, but I can't say I ever wished for fame – no, for something that was distinctly mine, a real melody that was my own, something that wasn't Beethoven or Weber. That was all I aimed at when

I started to compose; I never went in for sophisticated ponderings like Schumann.' (2 March 1882)

In the meantime, during his visit to Bohemia, his manner of working had taken a new turn that was to prove of decisive importance.

6

The First Three Operas

Wagner brought home with him from Prague his first text for an opera, *Die Hochzeit* ('The Wedding'). The letter in which he poured out his heartache to Apel ended, 'Enough, enough, all too much already. For in spite of the endless void in my bosom I still discover in myself a longing for love; – and what makes me really angry is that I look thoroughly well and in the best of health!' It was hardly surprising, for he had applied the time-honoured remedy of all unhappy lovers and worked off his anguish in writing: 'Such were the circumstances in which I drew up the text of my opera, and it was finished by the time I got back to Leipzig about a fortnight ago.' (16 December 1832)

He later called it a night-piece of the blackest hue, devoid of any gleam of light, any of the usual operatic adornments. *Werther* was much on his mind at the time: not only did he give his characters Ossianic names but a passage in another letter to Apel, describing Jenny at the piano, was stolen from Goethe's novel, as he confessed in the margin. (14 March 1833)

The subject was one he had found years before in J. G. Büsching's history of medieval chivalry, *Ritterzeit und Ritterwesen*. Two kings wish to set the seal on a peace made after years of enmity, so the son of one is invited to attend the wedding of the other's daughter. The young man falls passionately in love with the bride. As she comes out of the church their eyes meet. She tries to collect herself: 'Mein Gatte, sprich, wer ist der fremde Mann?' ('Husband, tell me, who is that stranger?'; cf. Senta's 'Mein Vater, sprich, wer ist der Fremde?'). That night the disturbing guest climbs up to the window of the room where she is waiting for her bridegroom. After a moment of hesitation she struggles with the intruder and succeeds in hurling him down to the courtyard below. The cause of his death remains a mystery, but as the court observes the proper ceremonies the princess collapses lifeless on his bier.

It is an early variant on the *Tristan* theme: 'Er sah mir in die Augen'. Wagner wrote the music for the first scene, and a septet won Weinlig's approval for its clarity and singability. There is even an authentic Wagnerian motive repeated several times in the accompaniment to a recitative. But his sister Rosalie, whose opinion meant more to him than anyone else's, felt nothing but revulsion for the grisly story, so he 'annulled and tore up' his text. The score of the first scene is all that survives, and it was performed in Rostock in February 1933, exactly one hundred years after its composition.

It was not offended vanity that made him abandon it. Rosalie, 'little sprite' as her stepfather called her, was his 'maternal' sister. There is a picture of her at the piano: while her fingers seem to be gliding over the keys, she looks out at us, clear-eyed. She believed in Richard from the first and suffered immeasurably at his teenage dissipation. Now that her faith in him was restored he wanted to prove by this summary act how much he valued her judgement. It was she who, by her playing of Gretchen in 1830, had inspired him to write his Seven Compositions for Goethe's *Faust*; he revised the sketches in 1832 and proudly inscribed them 'opus 5'. The melodrama 'Ach neige, du Schmerzensreiche' already foreshadows the future composer of music dramas.

There is reason to regret that he did not complete his first opera: it would have been much more personal, much less 'operatic', in short much more Wagnerian than the next three. But he may have been guided by a sure instinct that he was not yet musically ready for this tragedy of love and death.

He now made another important discovery. Heinrich Laube, the young editor of the *Zeitung für die Elegante Welt*, who had recognized the promise in the C major Symphony when he reviewed it, offered him a libretto which he had originally thought of sending to Meyerbeer. It gave Wagner a shock. He had renounced his boyish ambitions to be a poet and his only aim now was to be a composer, but only he could know what sort of text would serve for an opera of his own composing.

He had already started another text of his own. He took the plot of *Die Feen* ('The Fairies') from Gozzi's fairy tale *La donna serpente*, but made some characteristic changes to it. The fairy Ada is cursed by her human husband Arindal, who fails the tests he has to undergo; she turns to stone until he releases her through the power of music and both enter the realm of fairyland together as immortals. This simple tale, which again is set in an Ossianic ambience, bears some typical Wagnerian trademarks: the forbidden question, the hunter's pity for the animal he has wounded, the idea of redemption. But these features are planted in an operatic hothouse of transformation scenes, choruses and ballets, and the ideal couple are flanked by a more down-to-earth pair as well as a burlesque pair.

In order to devote himself to the composition of his opera Richard turned down the offer of a post in Zürich, though with a bad conscience as he was being supported by Rosalie. At the end of January 1833 he accepted an offer from his brother Albert, who was working in the theatre in Würzburg, directing opera. By chance there was a vacancy there for a lowly post as chorus master, constituting Wagner's first practical engagement in a theatre.

'Yes, Theodor, now my future is bearing down hard on me,' he wrote to Apel, 'life is beginning to take a serious shape externally as well. I shall have to find myself a sanctuary for the summer, so that I can finish my opera by the winter.' (14 March 1833) His months in Würzburg were not so oppressive and serious that he failed to find inclination and opportunity for amatory escapades, but he nevertheless pursued his work with characteristic obsession. He had finished the finale of the last act the day before yesterday, he wrote to Rosalie on 11 December. 'It was exactly twelve noon, and the bells were ringing from all the towers as I wrote Finis at the bottom.' All that remained for him to do was orchestrate the last act, and here another characteristic reveals itself: his 'somewhat pedantic manner' of writing out even the first draft of the score as cleanly and tidily as possible would probably hold him up for another three weeks. It was dreadful, he complained nearly half a century later when he made a mistake in scoring *Parsifal*, to have been given 'pedantry and genius' in one bag – veritable torture! But the compensation for posterity is that his own fair copies of his scores are masterpieces of calligraphy.

He was unshakably convinced that his opera would be a success. 'It all flowed from my inmost soul – and they say that's how to reach into the souls of others.' His sisters had already put in a word for him at the Leipzig theatre. He was allowed to submit his score, and his only concern was that the forces there might not be adequate to its demands. 'It's a pity about the female principals in your company – I really need a first-rate voice and compelling acting ability – someone like Devrient would be no bad thing,' he wrote to Rosalie. (11 December 1833)

However, the bass singer and producer Franz Hauser, on whose sole judgement acceptance of *Die Feen* depended, was the last person in the world to like it. He was a knowledgeable and competent musician, but he thought Mozart over-elaborate, approved only of Gluck and regretted that Bach had written no operas. The twenty-year-old composer wrote him not so much a letter as a dissertation, which began with an expression of appreciation of Hauser's profound discernment and warm-hearted frankness, but then erupted in total youthful self-confidence: 'You dislike my opera; even more, you dislike the whole direction that I follow.' (March 1834)

Die Feen was not refused but postponed until Wagner had lost interest in it: 'If they don't stop fouling things up soon, I'll take the score back from under their noses.' It was eventually performed for the first time in Munich in 1888, but by then its only interest was historical. It is in fact very informative about the stage in Wagner's development at which it was written. The overture, for a start, is not just a medley of the opera's tunes, but a dramatically motivated symphonic movement after the models of Beethoven and Weber. The two themes of the Allegro are well shaped, only the energetic cantilena which ends the whole is no more than perfunctory: it was not until the coda to Elisabeth's greeting of the Hall of Song that he managed to write one with his own authentic stamp. All the operatic accessories are conventional, but the dramatic high spots – Arindal's 'echo' aria, Ada's scene and aria 'Weh mir, so nah der fürchterlichen Stunde', Arindal's mad scene – are uncannily competent for so young and inexperienced a composer. One particularly impressive feature is the use, probably quite unthinking, of a kind of leitmotiv: the opening bars of the romance of the wicked witch Dilnovaz are quoted several times, in various rhythmic and harmonic transformations, as a 'witchery' motive.[1]

Even while a production of *Die Feen* was still being discussed, Wagner had an artistic experience that seemed to cast doubt on all his ideals. Once again Schröder-Devrient came to Leipzig, but this time to sing Romeo in Bellini's *Montecchi e Capuletti*, a work with a ridiculously facile libretto and music of a vapidness that left Wagner under no illusions. How was it possible, he wondered, that it nevertheless made an impression far stronger than all those contemporary German operas that were so much better made? The search for the answer to this unsettling question drew his first piece of critical writing from him, on German opera (*Die deutsche Oper*, RWGS, XII, pp. 1ff.), which was published in the *Zeitung für die Elegante Welt* in June 1834. In it he renounced the 'academic' music of Spohr and Marschner, not sparing even his idol Weber's *Euryanthe*, and paid homage to the vocal beauty of Italian opera, in which the singing is as natural as speech and fills the characters with warm life. With youthful extremism he wrote off all the achievements of German opera: he would never forget, he wrote, the impression that the recent performance of Bellini's opera had made on him, blessing his ears – heartily weary of eternal allegorizing orchestral tumult – with simple, noble song again. When he wrote about Bellini again, five years later, he still voiced the wish that German composers would think of a way of treating singing in such a fashion: 'Song, song, and again I say, song, you Germans!' (*Bellini*, 1839; RWGS, XII, pp. 19ff.)

The time had not yet come when he would realize that the sure way to produce an incomparable work of art would be to combine this elemental song with texts and music of a high quality. From this point of view his enthusiasm for Bellini was not wasted and he always retained a sense of gratitude to the Italian. Once, when he was playing over melodies from *Romeo*, *La Straniera* and *Norma* at Wahnfried, he said: 'For all its *pauvreté*, there's true passion and emotion there, it only needs the right soprano to stand up and sing it and it can sweep you off your feet. I learned something from this that Messrs Brahms and Co. never learned, and put it into my melody.'

Intoxicated with Bellini, Heinse's *Ardinghello* and Heinrich Laube's *Das Junge Europa*, he and Theodor Apel set off for Bohemia, the land of his youthful romances, in June 1834. He tells in his autobiography of the easy life they led in Teplitz and how, driving back to their inn in the dusk of a summer night, stretched out comfortably in their elegant carriage, they felt they had passed the day like young gods.

On some fine mornings he stole away from Apel to climb the hill to the Schlackenburg castle. Here, with a rolling view of sunny hills and valleys spread before him, he wrote the first outline of a new opera, *Das Liebesverbot* ('The Ban on Love'), which was to be the artistic expression of his new 'young European' outlook on life. This time his source was *Measure for Measure*, treated rather freely. He transposed the scene from Shakespeare's never-never Vienna to sixteenth-century Palermo – perhaps in homage to the Sicilian Bellini – and transformed the basically serious theme of the operation of justice into a condemnation of hypocrisy and moral bigotry and a glorification of free love.

But he was overcome with forebodings in the midst of this heady mood. 'Will the happy days I am enjoying at the moment perhaps soon take revenge on me?' he wondered in a letter to Rosalie. 'I am often overcome . . . by a distressing sense of unrest which urges me to return home the sooner the better, I feel as though something is waiting for me there, which I will need all my resources to encounter.' (3 July 1834) His instinct was correct. When he did return to Leipzig he found a letter waiting, offering him the post of musical director to the Magdeburg theatre company, which was spending the summer playing in Bad Lauchstädt, between Leipzig and Halle. It marked the end of his youth, he declared in *Mein Leben*. While he had not remained altogether a stranger to excitements and errors, it was not until this moment that care entered his life.

Wagner's account of what he found in Lauchstädt is a classic description of a provincial theatrical company: the schnapps-drinking manager Bethmann, whom a subvention from the king of Prussia could not keep from chronic bankruptcy; Frau Bethmann reclining on a couch, whiling away the hours with an ageing bass; the producer Schmale discussing with the stage manager, a toothless bag of bones, just how they were to put on *Don Giovanni* the following Sunday now that the Merseburg municipal band were unable to come to rehearsals.

Wagner saw at once that it was no place for him. Intent solely on escaping as politely as possible, he asked for assistance in finding somewhere to stay. A young actor promised to find him lodgings in the same house as the prettiest and most adorable girl in Lauchstädt, the company's leading lady, Minna Planer.

Chance brought him face to face with her at the door of the house. The sight of her was in striking contrast to the bad impressions he had hitherto received on that fateful morning. 'Very graceful and fresh as a daisy in appearance, the young actress was decorous and gravely assured in her movement and demeanour, which lent an agreeably enchanting dignity to the kind expression on her face . . . After I had been presented to her in the front entrance hall as the new musical director, and she, surprised to see one so young bearing this title, had formed a first impression of me, she kindly introduced me to the landlady, asking her to be sure and make me comfortable, and then went off down the street, with a calm, self-confident gait, to attend the rehearsal.'

He took the room on the spot and agreed to conduct *Don Giovanni* on the Sunday.

The description of Minna and his wooing of her that he dictated to Cosima in 1866 has every appearance of being scrupulously fair. When the love letters he wrote to her at that time were published in 1950 along with the rest of the Burrell Collection, the editor, John N. Burk, expressed the view that comparing them with the account in *Mein Leben* revealed the astonishing accuracy of Wagner's later recollection, and agreement in every essential between the letters and the autobiography.

Minna had embarked on a theatrical career not out of inclination but in order to support herself and her parents. At fifteen she had been seduced by an army officer, Ernst Rudolf von Einsiedel, and had a daughter, Natalie, who passed as her younger sister all her life. Natalie often spent long periods in the Wagner home and achieved fame later, as Minna's heir, as the owner of important Wagner papers which she sold to Mrs Burrell in the 1890s.

Without any particular gift for the expression of deeper emotions, Minna's success on the stage was due to the beauty and distinction of her appearance. She was much in demand as an actress and much courted as a woman. While she maintained a polite reserve in the face of the often all too blunt offers she received, she believed it was in the interests of her career not to refuse small favours to theatre directors and well-to-do patrons. When Wagner remonstrated with her she replied that people like that were less importunate than certain young conductors. She fended off his passionate advances for a long time, and even when they were acknowledged lovers she tried time and again to withdraw from the relationship.

One evening she told him that she wanted to leave Magdeburg and take up an engagement at the Königstadt theatre in Berlin. She left early the next morning, to cut short all his objections. 'The morning mist in which I saw you rolling away shivered in my tears. Minna, Minna, I suddenly became horribly certain that the coach was tearing you away from me for ever and ever.' A year earlier he had outlined his plans for his artistic future to Apel: after seeing *Das Liebesverbot* performed, he was going to go to Italy to write an Italian opera: in short, lead the itinerant life of a freelance composer. By his attachment to Minna he had condemned himself to abandon that plan and stay in the small-theatre milieu he detested; now he reminded her of it: 'I have sacrificed every condition of my life to you and you cannot sacrifice two good parts for me!' (4 November 1835)

'What a state I'm in now,' he wrote to Apel the next day. 'My God! My God! – If I wanted to be up-to-date, now would surely be the right moment for separation – but it's no good. My heart is broken – broken like any bourgeois.'

What it was that attracted Wagner so irresistibly to Minna is a perennial question. She lacked the intelligence to understand him and the heart to have faith in him. Did she ever love him? She was incapable of a great passion. His mother and sisters all tried to dissuade him from the liaison, he could see the truth of all this for himself – and walked on to his fate and hers with his eyes wide open.

The first meeting in Lauchstädt, which left so indelible an impression on him, gives the answer: it was the maternal quality in her that drew and held him. Eros and the dependence on a mother-figure conjoined, deep down in his nature, to exercise a power stronger than all reason.

The passion of his love letters overflowed into the music of *Das Liebesverbot*. 'At seven o'clock in the morning I sit down and write to you,' he told his 'ferne Geliebte' in a letter of 8 November. 'Then I work steadily until one at my opera, which has grown back to its full strength in me again and has become one within me with the possession of you.'

When he once played the *Liebesverbot* overture to Cosima, she said she preferred that of *Die Feen*, to which he replied that the later one had more genius in it. The element of personal experience gave his third opera, for all its weaknesses, a spark of real life, which time has not extinguished. The British première at University College, London in 1965 surprised the critics with its melodiousness: its Italianisms look back to Rossini and forward to the young Verdi.

One composer rarely encountered in it is the mature Wagner.

The adagio ensemble 'Sie schweiget in stummem Schmerz' already
has something in its structure, though not in its melodic writing, of
the great ensemble in the second act of *Tannhäuser*, 'Seht mich, die
Jungfrau . . . ', just as Isabella is in general terms a precursor of
Elisabeth. The relentless theme of the decree forbidding love,
which runs through the whole opera, has the function of a genuine
leitmotiv, while the melody and harmonization of the 'Salve regina
coeli' already contains, note for note, the Grace theme from *Tannhäuser*.

In *A Communication to my Friends*, the review of his artistic
development to date that Wagner made in 1851, as much (or more)
for his own benefit as for his friends, he wrote that a comparison of
Das Liebesverbot with *Die Feen* would show that he had it in him to
develop in either of two totally contrary directions: the earlier work
showed the sacred earnest with which his instincts had originally
responded to stimulus, but his experiences had nurtured an
unabashed inclination to unbridled sensuality, which ran directly
counter. Then he makes an admission that allows a glimpse of his
struggle to improve and refine his work: 'Striking the right balance
between the two was the task of my subsequent artistic development.'

His later opinion of his 'wild' early work was not very high; with
a few exceptions everything about it was 'horrifying, atrocious,
revolting'; only the orchestration was good, it was something he
had been able to do from his mother's womb. He dedicated the
score to King Ludwig in 1866 with a quatrain at once penitential and
rueful:

> Ich irrte einst und möcht' es nun verbüßen,
> wie mach' ich mich der Jugendsünde frei?
> Ihr Werk leg' ich demütig Dir zu Füßen,
> daß Deine Gnade ihm Erlösung sei.

(Once I erred and now I would do penance; how can I be rid of my
youthful sin? I humbly lay its work at your feet, so that your grace may
redeem it.)

The first performance of *Das Liebesverbot* took place in Magdeburg on 29 March 1836, conducted by the composer. As the
police objected to the title it was changed to 'The Novice of
Palermo'. The company was on the point of breaking up altogether,
and none of the singers had troubled to learn their parts properly, so

that what happened on the stage was more like a 'musical shadow-play'. Wagner had placed great hopes on the second performance, as it was to be his benefit, but the auditorium was almost empty. The stage stayed empty, too. Certain of the principals chose that evening to allow their amorous wrangles to come to a head, a knife was pulled and blood was shed behind the scenes. The producer had to step before the curtain and inform the tiny audience that unforeseen circumstances prevented the performance from taking place.

That was the end of Wagner's career in Magdeburg. He arrived in Berlin on 18 May to enter into fruitless negotiations to get his opera staged at the Königstadt theatre and on 7 July he went to Königsberg in pursuit of Minna, who had been engaged at the theatre there.

They were married in the church at Tragheim near Königsberg on 24 November. As the pastor held out the closed prayerbook for the couple to place on it the rings they were to exchange, the bridegroom seemed not to be paying attention. It had struck him at that moment, with the clarity of a vision, that his whole being was caught in two separate currents at different depths: 'The upper, open to the sunlight, swept me away as if in a dream, while the lower held me fast in the grip of a profound, incomprehensible terror.'

7

Rienzi

Wagner's premonition that his ill-considered marriage would prove doubly culpable was confirmed all too soon. The debts he had already amassed before the wedding, and Minna's belief that she owed it to herself to improve her financial position by 'making the most of her personal popularity' gave rise to violent scenes. He was at last appointed musical director of the Königsberg theatre on 1 April 1837. He returned home from rehearsals one evening to make the dreadful discovery that Minna had run off with a rich merchant called Dietrich, whose familiarity with her had aroused his resentment from the first. 'Death in his heart', he hurried after her and at last caught up with her in Dresden, at her parents' house, where she had taken refuge after Dietrich had left her. Her reproachful avowals that she had only wanted to escape from a hopeless situation that was all his fault turned his indignation into pity and self-recrimination. After he had succeeded in obtaining the musical directorship in Riga she was ready to go with him to Blasewitz, just outside Dresden, to spend the time before he was due in Riga. Her mood really seemed much improved. But when she failed to return from a short trip she had told him she was making with a family of friends, he learned that she had stayed in a hotel in Dresden with Dietrich for several days and that both had since disappeared.[1]

'With that I knew enough to ask my fate why, when I was still so young, I was doomed to undergo so frightful an experience, one, it seemed, that would poison the whole of my life.' As he relates in *Mein Leben*, he poured out his anguish to his sister Ottilie, who had now been married for several years to the Indianologist Hermann Brockhaus, and lived in a lovely villa in the Grosser Garten in

Dresden. Walking there from Blasewitz every day, he felt as though he was leaving a desert for a paradise. Brother and sister understood each other without the need for explanations, and he found in his brother-in-law a man of scholarship and intelligence, who re-awoke his dormant desire for a better education and was the first to introduce him to the literature of India.

At this time of great emotional suffering, his peculiar strength asserted itself, instinctively countering the pain with increased artis-tic activity. He had read Bulwer Lytton's novel *Rienzi, the Last of the Roman Tribunes*, and conceived an admiration for the hero, while Minna was still with him at Blasewitz. Now he sat down and drafted the scenario of a five-act opera based on it, deliberately making it on such a scale that getting it performed must of necessity take him out of the sphere of small theatres.

He was due to sail from Lübeck to Riga early in August, but the sailing was delayed by contrary winds, so he was forced to spend a week in a squalid sailors' tavern in Travemünde. He spent the time reading *Till Eulenspiegel*, which first gave him the idea of writing an 'authentically German comic opera'. When he drafted the text of *Der Junge Siegfried* fourteen years later, the memory of it came back to him, he claimed. It was another of the secrets of his creative processes that a seed, once planted in his mind, never died but germinated sooner or later. The maturing was a process of con-tinual enrichment.

Karl von Holtei, the director of the Riga theatre, had been under the impression that he was engaging an advocate of the light Italian and French repertory expected by his audiences. He had no suspi-cion that Wagner's recent experiences, culminating in the shock of the death of his sister Rosalie, had set in train an inner transforma-tion, leading him back to the 'sacred earnest' of his original artistic ideas. From this initial misunderstanding relations between the two men grew steadily worse, till Wagner reached the point of regard-ing Holtei as his worst enemy. Despite that, Holtei never had any reason to complain of a lack of zeal on the part of his young musical director, whose rehearsals, he averred, would be the death of his singers.

A new prima donna expected at the theatre failed to arrive, so Holtei welcomed Wagner's suggestion that Minna's younger sister Amalie be engaged in her place. Amalie wrote to accept and reported that Minna was ill and unhappy and living with her parents. Wagner, aware that his wife had been staying in a hotel in Hamburg with Dietrich for a substantial period, asked Amalie to spare him any news of her and instructed a friend in Königsberg to start divorce proceedings.

'Hereupon, Minna herself appealed to me with a truly affecting letter, in which she frankly admitted her infidelity . . . I had never heard such words from Minna, and I was never to hear their like from her again, except on one moving occasion many years later, when the same mode of expression had an equally upsetting effect on me and completely won me over.'

He replied that he himself had been most to blame in what had occurred and that they should never mention the matter again. 'Come to me, my wife,' he pleaded in a second letter, 'let me heal your wounds, it shall be the office of my love.' (Riga, undated; RWBC, pp. 115ff.) The two sisters arrived in Riga on 19 October.

It has been objected that the only evidence of Minna's infidelity is Wagner's own account of the episode in his autobiography. Newman shrewdly pointed out that the *absence* from the Burrell Collection of the first letter asking him to forgive her is the conclusive proof of her guilt. She forgot that Wagner had referred to it at some length in a letter of 18 May 1859,[2] thus irrefutably proving its existence. 'Poor Minna little foresaw', Newman concludes, 'that by thus covering her tracks, as she imagined, she was delivering herself up to the hunters!' (NLRW, I, p. 234)

Wagner's Riga repertory included operas by Mozart, Weber, Cherubini, Bellini, Rossini, Boieldieu, Auber and Meyerbeer. Forty years later he recalled the elevated, ennobled sentiments Méhul's magnificent *Joseph* had inspired in him. However, his theatrical activities were not enough to satisfy him, and he planned a series of six symphony concerts for the winter season of 1838–9. To win the support of the twenty-four members of his little orchestra he composed the first of his proposals for orchestral and theatrical reform, distinguished, like all its successors, by its blend of idealism and grasp of the practical.

> I think I am safe in saying that I am doing no more than meeting the wishes of my respected colleagues in the orchestra when I hereby propose to them a cycle of orchestral concerts, to take place during this coming

winter, which shall be regarded expressly as an
enterprise of the orchestra and undertaken for its own
benefit.

He goes on to suggest subscription and admission prices, the basis
on which profits should be calculated and shared, the fees for
soloists and so on.

> Our audiences as a whole will probably never have been
> accustomed to the more serious musical pleasures of the
> kind we shall offer them in due course, and it will
> therefore be necessary to attract them with more
> obvious enjoyments as well; in this respect I have in
> mind the Leipzig subscription concerts . . . Following
> that precedent, not only must the knowledgeable be
> offered the prospect of elevating musical pleasures, but
> the other sectors of the audience must also be given the
> opportunity to see and converse with one another,
> which could take place easily in the long interval.

He does not omit to advocate a buffet, in the charge of a Swiss
baker. The pecuniary gains might be but small in the first season, he
warned, but it was to be hoped that the success of the undertaking
would grow from one year to the next. Apart from that, every artist
was bound to value the idea behind the concerts. For his part, he
declared in advance, he renounced all financial gain and refused a
fee. (11 September 1838; RWBC, pp. 455ff.)

His popularity with the orchestra may be judged from the fact
that all twenty-four signed the document. Contrary to the note
made by the editor of the Burrell Collection, the first series of
concerts did in fact take place. For the first time since his teens
Wagner again had first-hand contact with Beethoven, conducting
six of the symphonies (nos. 3–8) and the Leonora Overture no. 3
(RWSB, I, p. 350). He also encountered the other great inspirational
genius of his youth, Shakespeare, when a production of *King Lear*
gave him the chance to attend rehearsals as well as the performance.

In a mood of enthusiasm that could not but strike him as a
mockery of his actual situation, he also completed the text of *Rienzi*
and composed the first two acts during the autumn of 1838. Hans
von Bülow's *bon mot*, that *Rienzi* was Meyerbeer's best opera, has
more than a grain of truth in it, but it is even more Spontini than

Meyerbeer. During his short stay in Berlin in June 1836 Wagner had heard *Fernand Cortez*, conducted by the composer. Although the soloists left him cold, he had been surprised by the precision and vigour of the chorus and corps de ballet: his eyes were opened to the 'peculiar impressiveness of theatrical presentation on the large scale'. The impression remained with him while he was thinking out *Rienzi*.

Compared with the character in the novel, Wagner's hero is nobler, a tragic spirit in the mould of Lohengrin. Although he was aiming at strong dramatic effects Wagner avoided everything in his source that would have seemed merely theatrical on the stage. He played through each scene to his friends in the evenings, as he finished them. Heinrich Dorn, who had conducted the first performance of the 'drumbeat' overture and had now also been washed ashore in Riga, described the occasions: Amalie sang the female roles, the men sang whatever they could make out from the sketches, and Minna wiped the sweat from Wagner's brow as he accompanied them on the elderly borrowed grand piano, while the clatter of the broken strings mingled with the rousing strains of Freedom.

Two of the occasional compositions of the Riga period should be mentioned. One is the setting of a poem, *Der Tannenbaum*, by Georg Scheurlin, in E♭ minor, a key Wagner called 'Livonian'. It is interesting to see how he develops an eloquent accompaniment out of a flowing, animated motive, rather in the style of the string figurations accompanying Brünnhilde's defence of her actions in the third act of *Die Walküre*: 'Weil für dich im Auge das Eine ich hielt . . .' The other is the orchestration of a duet from Rossini's *I Marinari*: adding low horn notes to the low strings and using the bassoon to link string phrases in order to depict the gentle stir of the sea at dusk are truly Wagnerian effects, in the view of Alfred Einstein. When it comes to the storm he uses all the available registers of the orchestra, from the piccolo to the drumroll, but the most inspired feature is the sparing, and therefore all the more effective, use of trombones. In that respect it looks beyond *Rienzi* and might be a study for the *Holländer*.

Ever since Wagner had begun to set his sights on Paris, he had been trying to establish connections there. In the autumn of 1836 he sent the scenario of an opera, *Die Hohe Braut* ('The High-Born Bride'), to Eugène Scribe, suggesting to the librettist that he might make a French libretto from it and then get the Opéra Comique to commission Wagner to compose it. Receiving no reply he wrote again in the spring of 1837 and included the score of *Das Liebesverbot* as his credentials. At the same time he wrote to 'Monsieur Meyerbeer, compositeur et chevalier de légion d'honneur à Paris', telling him that he had sent *Das Liebesverbot* to Scribe with the request that he would show it to Meyerbeer. 'It would be . . . quite out of order for me to give vent to clumsy praises of your genius, but I will this much: I see in you the complete fulfilment of the German composer who has mastered the superior elements of the Italian and French school, in order to make the creations of his genius *universal*.' He made so bold, he went on, as to cherish the hope that it would be from Meyerbeer himself that he would learn his fate, 'which I place herewith wholly in your hands, appealing to your heart'.[3] It was also in this period that he wrote an essay, not published at the time, on Meyerbeer's *Les Huguenots*, which also praises the cosmopolitan, universal qualities of his style. This was once given the date of 1840 but Richard Sternfeld, the editor of the later volumes of RWGS, pointed out that Wagner's attitude towards Meyerbeer had already cooled considerably by then. (XII, pp. 22ff., 422) Newman, too, demonstrates that his admiration of Meyerbeer's 'successful eclecticism' yielded, after he had left Riga, to a consciousness of his own German mission. (NLRW, I, p. 224)

This time Scribe replied, politely but noncommittally, in June 1837 and Wagner consoled himself with the thought that he had at least established a Parisian connection. 'There is no quashing me now, with my hopes and plans.' (To August Lewald, November 1838) In fact his Paris sortie became a matter of urgency rather sooner than he wished. Holtei, who had to leave Riga suddenly in January 1839 to escape embarrassing disclosures, had already secretly engaged Wagner's friend Dorn as conductor for the coming season. Since the new director was bound by his contract, Wagner asked him at least to pay him an advance that had been agreed on: in return he declared himself available for any work the management might wish to offload on to him, unless it were polishing boots or drawing water, which would be the last straw. Though he and Minna made every effort to supplement their income with concerts and benefit performances, he could not scrape enough to pay off all his debts, so they were forced to leave secretly and without passports.

The story of their flight over the Russian frontier and their rough sea passage from Pillau (now Baltiysk) to London is one of the most exciting episodes of *Mein Leben*. We will return to it when we reach the composition of *Der Fliegende Holländer*, which owed its 'individual poetico-musical colouring' to the voyage. It was characteristic of Wagner's later works, too, that while he was still working on one piece the characters and melodies of another, often diametrically different, work were already taking shape and maturing in a half-conscious region of his mind.

They landed in Boulogne on 20 August and stayed four weeks there, during which time Wagner completed the orchestration of the second act of *Rienzi* and seized the opportunity to call on Meyerbeer, who was also staying in the town and whose proverbial amiability made the most favourable impression on Wagner. He patiently listened as Wagner read him the text of the first three acts and agreed to read the score of the first two, which Wagner left with him. On a subsequent visit he assured Wagner of his interest in the work and promised to recommend him to the manager and chef d'orchestre of the Opéra, so that Wagner was ready to thank his stars for having brought him to Boulogne just at that time.

Only a very short time elapsed after his arrival in Paris on 17 September before he found that all the recommendations from others and all his own efforts were of no consequence. The manager of the Grand Opéra took impassive note of Meyerbeer's letter of recommendation but Wagner heard no more from him: evidently he had read large numbers of such letters in his time. At an orchestral rehearsal Habeneck, the chef d'orchestre, played through an overture that Wagner had written in Magdeburg for Theodor Apel's play *Columbus* and decided that he had no further obligation for the time being. In order to make himself known Wagner composed French romances for famous singers, who were kind enough to sing them to him but confessed for the rest that they did not know what else they should do about them.

Of these vocal pieces, *Dors mon enfant* is a charming trial run for the Spinning chorus in the *Holländer*. *Les deux grenadiers* was a setting of a French translation of Heine's poem. 'I hear that you have composed Heine's "Grenadiers",' Wagner wrote to Schumann on 29 December 1840, 'and that the *Marseillaise* turns up in it at the end. I set it, too, last winter, and I used the *Marseillaise* at the end, too. Highly significant!' It is typical that the lyric composer gave the tune to the voice, while the dramatist put it in the accompaniment.

At last a possibility of success seemed to beckon. Meyerbeer had referred Wagner and *Das Liebesverbot* to Anténor Joly, the director of the Théâtre de la Renaissance. Since Joly demurred, Wagner turned to his 'dear master' with another cry for help: if he still remembered him, perhaps he would care to compel the wicked Anténor to produce the opera by issuing a kind of ukase or bull. 'Terrorization is the only way and you, revered Autocrat of all the Notes, are the only one who can apply it. I have no other hope of salvation in this world but through you.' (18 January 1840)

It worked. Joly agreed to put the opera on, subject only to an audition of some of its numbers by the committee. With typical optimism Wagner believed he was home and dry. He at once signed the lease for a comfortable apartment in the Rue du Helder, instead of the *hôtel garni* where they had been living. On 15 April 1840, the day they moved in with their few worldly goods, he heard that the Théâtre de la Renaissance was bankrupt and had closed. This bolt from the blue revealed the vanity of the prospects that had opened before him. Cynics, Newman remarks, hinted to him later that Meyerbeer must have known of the impending bankruptcy and had his own reasons for detaching Wagner from the Opéra and directing him towards this moribund institution. This is another case, he goes on resignedly, in which there does not seem the least likelihood of our ever knowing the whole truth. (NLRW, I, p. 280)

Wagner's only friends in Paris were a few Germans as poor and lacking in influence as himself: a musical historian, who kept his real name a secret and called himself Anders (a German surname, but the word also means 'other' or 'otherwise'), and who in spite of his extensive learning had risen no higher than a post in the music department of the Bibliothèque Royale; Samuel Lehrs, a classical scholar from Königsberg, whose abilities were ruthlessly exploited by the publisher Ambroise-Firmin Didot in his famous editions of the Greek classics; Ernst Benedikt Kietz, a portrait-painter who, according to Wagner, worked so slowly that his models died of old age before he finished. They were all drawn to Wagner by his enthusiasm, some of which he imparted to them.

The painter Friedrich Pecht became another friend. He was an acquaintance of Heinrich Laube, who was newly arrived from Germany, and was taking him on a tour of the Louvre galleries one day when Laube announced that he was about to meet another fellow-countryman. A few minutes later they were greeted by a handsome young couple and the notably elegant, even distinguished-looking young man was introduced to him as Richard Wagner. 'Evidently distrait and with his mind on other things than Rubens and Paul Veronese,' Pecht recalled, 'Wagner seemed to me very agreeable, but he did not strike me as a particularly impressive personality: I found him decidedly too good-looking and too dainty. There was a certain delicate sheen to him, but there was certainly something unapproachable about him too, which might have roused the attention of a more careful observer.'

On one occasion, when Laube introduced them to Heinrich Heine, the reserve Wagner had hitherto maintained thawed and he demonstrated his peculiar resilience, his rare ability to preserve his freedom, his loftiest aspirations, intact in the midst of the greatest need and distress. He was a superb raconteur and possessed the most discerning eye for the comic, the sharpest ear for the sound of nature and the surest taste for all kinds of beauty, including the visual arts. He held listeners spellbound with the story of his recent adventures at sea, one event following another like a 'flurry of snow'. Heine, whom normally nothing could move, raised his hands in supplication at such confidence in a German.

Pecht remarks in his memoirs that Wagner's friends had noticed how this one year in Paris had matured him, made him another person altogether. It made another artist of him, too. On a murky evening in November 1839, at a rehearsal by Habeneck and the Conservatoire orchestra of the first three movements of the Choral Symphony, the return to the ideals of his boyhood, which had already started in Riga, was shatteringly and immediately accomplished. His adolescent enthusiasm for the symphony had known no bounds, as long as he had known it only from the score, but a performance he heard in the Gewandhaus at seventeen had shaken his faith in Beethoven and himself. Now, in his own words, the scales fell from his eyes: he realized the crucial importance of a good performance. Habeneck had rehearsed the Ninth for years, bar by bar, until he and the orchestra had gradually come to a clear view of its musical substance. The French instrumentalists, trained in the lyric Italian school, understood that the melody, the song, was the essence of all music – that was their secret. 'That magnificent orchestra simply *sang* the symphony.'

This powerful experience, and the reaction against the misery of his circumstances, inspired him with the wish to write something that would give him inward satisfaction. 'So I wrote an overture to *Faust*.' Finished on 12 January 1840, it was intended to be the first movement of a *Faust* symphony, the second movement of which, 'Gretchen', he already had in his head. The overture is his first wholly underivative work of substantial size. The key, D minor, looks both backward to the Ninth and forward to the *Holländer*.

The experience also had a literary outcome in the short story *A Pilgrimage to Beethoven*, which appeared in the *Gazette Musicale*, 19 November–3 December 1840. He put into Beethoven's mouth his own interpretation of the final chorus of the Choral Symphony: 'Think of the wild, primitive feelings, soaring out and away into the infinite, presented by the orchestra, as being brought up against the clear, defined emotion of the human heart, presented by the chorus.' The encounter would have a beneficial, soothing effect on the turmoil of the primitive feelings, while the human heart, opening to admit those feelings, would be infinitely strengthened and enlarged. This was the first time Wagner put into words what he conceived to be his own life's work, the synthesis of symphony and song.

He was even drawn to the idea of a monumental biography of Beethoven in the following year. His friend Anders, who owned a comprehensive collection of data and documents, but possessed no literary talent, offered him the use of his material. Looking first for a publisher, Wagner wrote that the book would be no mere pedantic parade of learning and undigested quotations. It would be more like a novel about an artist's life than a chronological enumeration of dates and anecdotes. For all that, however, it would contain nothing that would not stand up to the most rigorous critical scrutiny. Woven into the historical narrative would be a comprehensive account of the musical epoch which, created by Beethoven's genius, cast its mantle over all music written since. (To Heinrich Laube, 13 March 1841)

For all his winning words, he failed to interest a single German publisher in the project. It would undoubtedly have been a very idiosyncratic but also a very stimulating book.

In the meantime Wagner had resumed the composition of *Rienzi*, starting the orchestral sketch of the third act on 15 February 1840, but with the composition of the *Faust* Overture a few weeks before he had already advanced far beyond the opera.

He undoubtedly cast the material of *Rienzi* in a dramatic mould but, as he later said himself, viewed through the glass of an operatic composer, as a 'grand opera' with brilliant finales to each of the five acts, hymns, processions and the musical clash of arms. It possesses some wonderful things which are already completely and authentically Wagner: the swelling A on the trumpets which, like the A major chord of the *Lohengrin* prelude or the E♭ major of the *Rheingold* introduction, raised the curtain on the magic realm of the soul where the drama is to be enacted; or the way a melodic line is filled with an inner dynamic by harmonic impulses, as for example in isolated bars of the Prayer; but above all the audacious, exhilarating development of the melody of 'Santo Spirito, cavaliere' at the end of the overture and of the whole opera, which already attains the height of similar motivic intensification in the later works. But in the midst of these, without warning, it plummets down to banal melodies à la Spontini and Meyerbeer.

There is no way to disguise this dichotomy, which is rooted in the basic conception of the work. The most unfortunate kind of retouching, however well meant, is when directors try to turn the opera into a music drama, which only succeeds in underlining its musical inadequacies. If *Rienzi* is produced in the style of grand opera, which is what it is, then the hearer accepts its weaknesses as those of the genre and is all the more delighted by the elements of inspiration which go beyond the limitations. The most important thing is to preserve the youthful exuberance, for better or for worse, as the one thing that lends a particular charm to the ineptitude of any artist's early works.

Even so, Wagner's own liking for his 'bawler *Rienzi*' soon cooled. 'I am very sorry to learn that you have made the acquaintance of my *Rienzi*,' he wrote to his Berlin admirer Alwine Frommann on 27 October 1845; 'I do not like the monster.' If the composer of *Tristan* defended the work in a letter, virtually a dissertation, that he wrote to the tenor Albert Niemann, long after he had lost all interest or sympathy with it, it was only because he desperately needed the money that a revival would bring. (25 January 1859) But he politely declined the invitation to its Paris première in 1869: he had always regarded it as one of the many ironies of his career that *Rienzi*, specifically written with Paris in mind, had never been performed there 'when this work of my young manhood still retained the whole of its youthful freshness for me'. (To Judith Gautier, early March 1869)

Part II: The First Creative Period (1841–1848)

8

Der Fliegende Holländer

The notes Wagner made in his Red Book during the voyage from Pillau to London include the following:

> 27 [July 1839] in storm on the Skager-Rack [sic].
> 28 Storm.
> 29 Stormy west wind forced us to run into a Norwegian small harbour in the region of Arendal. Ashore with Minna in the evening. Marvellous blocks of rock in the sea. Place Sand-Wigke.

It was one of the most wonderful impressions of his life, he later confirmed in his autobiography, when the ship slipped into the gigantic rocky chasm of a Norwegian fjord. 'An inexpressible happiness seized hold of me when the echo of the immense granite walls threw back the shout of the crew as they dropped anchor and hoisted sail [sic: a landlubber, Wagner evidently thought this expression meant its opposite]. The short rhythmic cries settled in me like a mightily comforting portent and soon formed into the theme of the sailors' song in my *Fliegender Holländer*, the idea of which I already carried within me.' He learned that the fishing village where they were was called Sandwike and was a few miles from Arendal. On the hundredth anniversary of the landfall, in 1939, the Norwegian Wagnerian singer Gunnar Graarud proved that, of the six places with the same name in the vicinity of Arendal, it must have been Sandviken on Boröya. It was with some excitement that he himself set the echo flying which had once resounded to the 'Hallojos' of the crew of the *Thetis*.[1]

This account of the genesis of the *Holländer* is complemented by a tale, recalled by Pecht, that Wagner told his friends in Paris when the experience was still fresh in his mind: the whistling of the wind in the rigging had seemed such an extraordinarily demonic sound that when another ship suddenly came into sight and as suddenly disappeared again in the darkness he had thought it must be the Flying Dutchman, and ever since then he had been composing music to the legend in his head.

The legend was well known and there were versions in several different languages. Wagner had come across it in Riga, and his creative imagination had at once been stirred by the version in Heine's *Memoiren des Herrn von Schnabelewopski*, according to which the damned sea-captain could be redeemed only by the love of a woman. This is apparently Heine's own invention, and it is obvious that he introduced it for a purely satirical purpose: 'The moral of the tale for women is that they take care not to marry a Flying Dutchman; and we men can learn from it how women are our destruction at the best of times.'

Wagner ignored Heine's moral but took up the idea of redemption with passionate sincerity and stored it away in his memory, where the dramatic and musical seeds ripened for another two years while he went on working on *Rienzi*.

To gain a conception of Paris in the 1830s and 1840s, the reader needs only to turn to Flaubert's *Education sentimentale*. There is a very close link between the milieu of the novel and that in which Wagner found himself. Flaubert's heroine, the sensitive, noble wife of the art-dealer, is based on the wife of the music publisher Maurice Schlesinger, Wagner's strange patron and employer. Perhaps we may even go so far as to glimpse in the poor devil of a painter, who scrapes a living with badly paid occasional work for the owner of the art gallery, the shadowy outline of the unknown German musician who was grateful when Schlesinger commissioned him to make arrangements for piano and cornet of operatic numbers by Donizetti and Halévy.

'Dearest Monsieur Schlesinger,' Wagner wrote in December 1840, 'I have been sitting here over the proofs of the score [of Donizetti's *La favorita*] since eight o'clock on Saturday morning until this moment, with a few hours' sleep. There were times, I can assure you, when I was on the verge of going out of my mind, and closer to tears than laughter . . . I am a poor devil and must be satisfied with whatever I can earn; but I am often driven to the despairing question: What is Monsieur Schlesinger paying me for this work!. . . A most cordial greeting from your obedient servant, R. Wagner. Tuesday morning, nine o'clock.'

A few pages of a diary from this period have survived. 'Tears came unbidden to my eyes again just now; is it cowardly or a sign of unhappiness to surrender gladly to tears? – a sick German apprentice was here – I told him to come to breakfast again; Minna reminded me that she would have to spend the last of our money just to buy bread. You poor, poor creature! I suppose you're right – things are bad with us.' And a week later: 'Explained to my wife, on our walk, what our financial position is; I am sorry for the poor woman from the bottom of my soul! It's a sad business! I want to work!' (RWGS, XVI, pp. 4ff.)

His work was not enough to save him from the debtors' prison. He does not mention it in *Mein Leben*, but a letter Minna wrote to Theodor Apel on 28 October 1840 gives him away. 'Richard had to leave me this morning and go into the debtors' prison,' she wrote. The Burrell Collection includes four tiny numbered scraps of paper in Richard's hand – evidently all he could get hold of in prison – which are a draft of that letter. The first of the scraps, with the admission of being in prison, is missing, presumably suppressed by Minna or Natalie, which demonstrates once again that the destruction of a document can conclusively prove its content.[2]

Many years later, a reference by Malwida von Meysenbug to his Paris days was still enough to bring the tears to Wagner's eyes: it had been a pit of baseness, he said, and added, turning to Cosima, she could not begin to imagine the atmosphere in which he had lived.

He admits in his autobiography that his short story *An End in Paris* was written in revenge for all the shame he had endured. It was published in the *Gazette Musicale*, 31 January – 11 February 1841, under the title *Un musicien étranger à Paris*. 'Hoffmann could never have written anything like this!' Heine exclaimed in admiration. The underlying note of authentic experience is what makes it so much more impressive than any mere 'tales of the imagination'. Wagner never wrote simpler prose than this. 'We buried him. It was a cold, grey day and there were but a few of us . . . The first chill air of winter made us breathless; none of us could speak and there was no funeral oration. Nevertheless, let it be known to you that he whom we buried was a good man and a fine German musician.' The whole story ends with the famous credo: 'I believe in God, Mozart and Beethoven.' (*Ein Ende in Paris*, RWGS, I, pp. 114ff.) It was Wagner's way of telling the small group of friends who used to meet at his lodgings of an evening that the young man who had come to Paris with such high hopes two years earlier really was dead now.

His intellectual horizons had changed, too. After the recall to his own destiny that hearing the Ninth Symphony again had meant, a new world had been opened for him by the music of Berlioz. 'The bad taste in the externals' of the *Romeo and Juliet* Symphony, Wagner wrote to Ferdinand Heine, a producer at the Dresden theatre, had made him recoil violently from a composer whom he nonetheless regarded as a musician of genius. Berlioz was so isolated among the French that the proper development of his immense powers was made exceptionally hard for him. 'His is a highly poetic nature, and this is all the more amazing since he is a thorough Frenchman in every other respect and can express himself only in extremes. It is not long since I made up my mind about Berlioz, really only since I heard his *Symphonie fantastique* about three months ago.' (27 March 1841)

'Anybody here in Paris who hears this symphony', Wagner wrote in one of his articles for the *Dresdner Abendzeitung* (5 May 1841),

> must truly believe that he is listening to a wonder, the like of which he has never heard before. An immense inner wealth, a heroic imagination, force out a flood of passions as if from a crater; what we behold are clouds of smoke of colossal proportions, broken and shaped into fleeting forms only by flashes of lightning and jets of flame. It is all immense, bold but infinitely agonizing. Nowhere is there any formal beauty, nowhere the majestically serene flow to whose assured motion we might entrust ourselves in hope. After the *Symphonie fantastique*, the first movement of Beethoven's C minor Symphony would have been a welcome relief. (RWGS, XII, pp. 87ff.)

His third musical experience was another to recall him to himself: a performance of *Der Freischütz*. In spite of the vow he had once made to his friend Apel – 'Now and for all time, I shall never again pay homage to our Germanity, and all the glories of your Leipzig classicism are not enough to lead me back to that course' – it was precisely the German qualities in the music of the opera that fell on his ear like the far-off but never forgotten voice of home and childhood. Berlioz had forced the simple words of the huntsmen and peasants into the straitjacket of recitative, the director of the Opéra saw fit to cast it with singers of the second rank, and the performers were unaware of the difference between *Romantik* and *romantisme*. But as the lads of the village clasped their girls by the hand and led them into the inn, as night started to fall in the shadow of the tall pine trees and the sound of the dance music died away in the evening stillness, it was like a stab in the heart to the unhappy German musician: 'I felt a burning hot wound . . . O dreaming, dear to every German heart! O romance of forest, of evening, of stars, of the village clock striking seven! How happy is *he* who can believe, feel, dream with you! How glad am *I* to be German!' (RWGS, I, pp. 220ff.)

But at the same time something was set in train in him that was to have revolutionary consequences: a reaction against the ideal of 'modern civilization'. Paris was the 'point of culmination' of the direction in which the world was now running, he wrote to King Ludwig on 18 July 1867. All other cities were only 'stations' on the same road. Paris

> is the heart of modern civilization, whither its blood flows and whence it circulates to the members again. Once when it was my ambition to be a famous opera composer my good genius took me straight to that heart; there I was at the fountainhead, and there I was able to recognize in full and at once what I might have spent half a lifetime learning in any of the 'stations'. For this sure recognition of the true and proper face of things, it is Paris that I must thank.

The personal and artistic experiences outlined here combined to rid Wagner of the chimera of being a 'famous opera composer'. He had first had to lose himself in order to find himself again with the conception of *Der Fliegende Holländer*. The letter of 3 May 1840 in which he told Meyerbeer about the first prose sketch of the work reveals not only the desperation of his position but also a far more disquieting sense that his whole personality was in dissolution.

> I have reached a point where I have no choice but to sell
> myself to somebody in return for help in the most
> material sense. But my head and my heart are already no
> longer mine – they belong to you, my master; – all I
> have left are at most my hands – do you want to make
> use of them? – I can see that I must become your slave
> in mind and body in order to obtain the food and the
> strength to carry out the work which will express my
> gratitude to you one day. (RWSB, I, pp. 384ff.)

But he had hardly taken the letter to the post before he regretted
it. 'You will understand', he wrote on 4 June,

> the shame and bitter self-reproach that I now feel for
> having permitted myself, in an hour when all the painful
> and worrying experiences of the most recent period of
> my life were thronging through my head, to reach a
> degree of exaltation where I failed to see that I totally
> overstepped the boundary of modesty and delicate
> feeling.

He enclosed the prose sketch of the *Holländer* with this letter, asking
Meyerbeer to bring it to the attention of the new director of the
Opéra, Léon Pillet. (RWSB, I, pp. 392ff.)

Hearing nothing, he wrote to Meyerbeer again on 26 July. 'I
venture only this one request: if, with your superior insight and the
degree of interest which you perhaps still have in me, you think it
proper and it is convenient for you, then I beseech you in all
humility to put in a good word for me and my "winged Dutchman" (one act), of which I have a few numbers ready for audition.'
(RWSB, I, pp. 400ff.) He heard at last that Pillet liked the subject and
wanted to buy it so that he could have it set by one of the composers
he had under contract. Pleas and representations were of no avail:
Wagner was told it would be at least seven years before it could be
his turn to be offered even the smallest commission. He had the wit
to accept the 500 francs he was offered and use the money to finance
his own composition of *Der Fliegende Holländer*, abandoning *Le
Vaisseau Fantôme* to its fate. (2 July 1841)

Pillet commissioned a libretto from two writers who 'botched'
the tale, to Heine's distress, and the music was written by the
director of the Opéra chorus, Pierre-Louis Dietsch. The opera was
first performed in 1842 and was given ten further performances.

When the prose sketch for the *Holländer* was published in 1933 it was revealed that the action still took place on the coast of Scotland, as in Heine. Daland was called 'the father', Mary 'the nurse', Erik 'Georg'. The daughter was called 'Anna', which apparently contradicted Julius Kapp's claim that her name was originally 'Minna'. But in Dietsch's opera the girl actually is called Minna, a name that can only have originated in Wagner's very first draft, in homage to his wife, who may well have appeared to him on occasion like a comforter 'im nächtigen Gewühl'.[3] He obviously changed the names later to put a distance between his own text and the sketch he had sold. The name 'Senta' presents something of a mystery: there is no trace whatever of its existence before he used it, even in Scandinavia. Hans von Wolzogen thought that the girl who waited on Wagner in the house of a Norwegian captain in Sandviken may have been introduced to him as 'tjenta' ('servant'), which he took to be her name and later remembered inexactly as Senta.

The fact that Wagner had written the texts and music of three numbers – the Norwegian sailors' chorus, the song of the Dutchman's ghostly crew and Senta's Ballad – for an audition that never took place, proved in the end to be the most significant outcome of his struggle for recognition in Paris, affecting not only the composition of the *Holländer* itself but the whole development of his creative technique. In writing the Ballad he unknowingly planted the 'thematic seed' of the whole work. When he moved from Paris to Meudon in the summer of 1841 and wrote the composition sketch, he found that the existing thematic idea involuntarily permeated the entire work, showing him how to shape the legend in which the surge of the sea is ever present. He later said that the *Holländer* marked the beginning of his career as a poet – as opposed to a mere manufacturer of librettos – but it would be even more true to say that it was also the start of his career as a musician, for this was the first demonstration of his peculiar ability to develop the themes of a whole work from the motivic germs of a single original melody. The only thing lacking at this stage was the technique for pursuing this principle to its fullest extent: the *Holländer* still contains operatic passages which do not cohere organically with the thematic fabric.

He tried later to alleviate the discrepancy between his artistic intention and his musical ability at the time of composition. In 1852 he purged the writing for the brass of some crudities. The reasons he gave for altering the chord accompanying Senta's scream in the second act were typical of the process as a whole: the original instrumentation was too coarse, too literal; the sudden appearance of the Dutchman is what should startle the audience, not the sound of the brass and kettledrum. On 19 January 1860, after writing *Tristan*, he added the final theme of redemption to the end of the overture. He wrote to Mathilde Wesendonk that he had not been able to find the right ending before. 'We shall become omnipotent, if we just go on playing with the world.' (10 April 1860) A letter Cosima wrote to King Ludwig reveals that in 1865, between the completion of *Meistersinger* and the resumption of the *Ring*, Wagner considered revising the *Holländer* to make it worthy to stand beside *Tannhäuser* and *Lohengrin*. (DMCW, I, pp. 319f.) One might suppose that he meant only the eradication of the more conventional elements, but his intentions went much further. 'He is thinking of revising *Der Fliegende Holländer*,' Cosima wrote in 1878. 'Senta's Ballad is in a folk style, he thinks, but it is not truly characteristic of the *Holländer*.' (DMCW, I, p. 846) And in 1881 he told her about the new version he had written of the Ballad but had unfortunately lost. (BBL 1938, p. 3)

However, the new, Wagnerian characteristics of this early work are so overwhelming that they made him forget his reservations on each occasion. 'On the whole I found the work very interesting, going back to it,' he confessed to Theodor Uhlig in 1852; 'it has an uncommonly penetrating colouring, of the utmost sureness.' (Letter of 25 March) Later he once said that it was without precedent in operatic history: what distinguished the *Holländer* from similar romantic operas by Marschner or Weber was that the supernatural, the miraculous or demonic elements, were not external forces but proceeded directly out of the characters of the protagonists and were therefore artistically credible.

When Wagner heard the opera again in Munich in 1880, despite the deficiencies of the performance he was moved to tears. What he went through while writing the work is revealed by three annotations to the orchestral sketch. At the end of the second act: '13 August. Money troubles start again tomorrow!!' At the end of the third: 'Finis. Richard Wagner. Meudon, 22 August 1841, in need and tribulation.' But at the end of the overture, written last, we find: 'Paris, 5 November 1841. Per asp[e]ra ad astra. God grant it! Richard Wagner.'

For his fortunes had taken a turn for the better in the interval, encouraging him to have faith in his star. After all his efforts to get *Rienzi* performed in Paris had proved vain, he set his hopes on Dresden: not only would the ideal tenor, Tichatschek, be available for the name part, but he would also be able to make something of his personal connections. He had finished the score on 19 November 1840. On 1 December he addressed a petition to the King of Saxony, Friedrich August, not forgetting to remind him of his stepfather's years at the Saxon court theatre, and expressing the wish that his first large-scale work might see the light on the soil of his homeland, with the favour of the patronage of his all-gracious lord and king. On 4 December he sent the score to the intendant, Freiherr von Lüttichau, and in the covering letter pointed out how the visual splendours the work demanded for its production would demonstrate the magnificent appurtenances of the new opera house.

At the same time he wrote to a whole string of the leading figures in the theatre in Dresden: Schröder-Devrient, who still remembered the favourable impression he had made on her in Magdeburg; Hofrat Winkler, the theatre secretary and an old friend of his family, who had published Wagner's articles from Paris in his newspaper, the *Abendzeitung*; the musical director, Kapellmeister Reissiger, with whom Wagner remembered enjoying a drinking spree and who had to be approached with particular tact as an opera composer himself. The most valuable friends and helpers proved to be the producer Ferdinand Heine, who had been one of Geyer's colleagues, and the chorus master Wilhelm Fischer.

In the end Meyerbeer too lent his support with a letter to Lüttichau, dated 18 March 1841: 'Herr Richard Wagner of Leipzig is a young composer who possesses not only a thorough musical grounding but also a great deal of imagination, and whose situation as a whole seems to deserve active sympathy in his homeland in every respect.'

An impatient second letter from Wagner crossed with Lüttichau's reply, dated 29 June 1841: after giving the libretto and the score his careful consideration, he was happy to assure him that his opera had been accepted 'and will be presented at the Court Theatre as soon as possible, I hope during the course of next winter'.

Hoping to steal a march on the Parisian *Vaisseau Fantôme*, Wagner sent the text of the *Holländer*, which had been rejected by the intendant of the Munich opera, Küstner, as 'unsuitable for Germany', to the intendant of the Berlin Court Opera, Count von Redern, with a covering letter dated 27 June 1841 asking for the honour of a first performance: 'This. . . is quite a short opera, at least not intended to fill an evening, but rather to share a programme with a short ballet or play.'

Although he had received no answer he sent Redern the score as well on 20 November, venturing to hope that the opera might be performed before the current season was out. At the same time he appealed to Meyerbeer again: having a stupid libretto and a sizeable chunk of score on his hands he had been able to think of nothing better to do with them than to pack them both up and send them off to Berlin, where he knew they would be left to rot. 'Then the gospel was revealed to me, for it is written by your own venerated hand: "I will try to find favour in the eyes of Count von Redern!" . . . God grant that every day of your blessed life be a joy to you and may He never darken your vision with sorrow: that is the sincere prayer of your most sincere pupil and servant Richard Wagner.' (Early December 1841)

Meyerbeer's diary has the following entry for 7 December 1841: 'Call on Redern, to recommend the score of *Der Fliegende Holländer* by Richard Wagner to him.' He took the score away with him to read and sent it back to Redern on 9 December. 'I have already had the privilege, the day before yesterday, of talking to Your Honour about this promising composer who doubly deserves, both for his talent and for his extremely straitened circumstances, that the major court theatres, as the official guardians of German art, should not bar their stages to him.' A few days later, on 14 December, Wagner at last received the news that the text and the score had been approved and had been particularly warmly recommended by Meyerbeer.

'Think of me and accept in advance my warmest thanks for the inestimable services your friendship has rendered me', Wagner hastened to write to his champion. 'If I thought that you could be much happier than you are I would wish you the attainment of the highest happiness; as it is I must be merely an egoist and ask you to let me share a small part of your good fortune and your fame.' (Mid–December 1841)

It very soon transpired, however, that Redern's approval, gratifying though it was, was not at all the same thing as a binding commitment to stage the work.

9

Tannhäuser

Yet another experience of Wagner's time in Paris that set his thinking along a new path was reading Friedrich Raumer's history of the
Hohenstaufens, of which Goethe said that it brought the 'faded
ghosts' of the past back to life. The one thing that most fascinated
Wagner in the book was Raumer's depiction of the character of
Frederick II, a masterpiece of historico-psychological reconstruction. He struggled in vain to find the proper artistic channel for
portraying Frederick until it occurred to him that his son Manfred
offered a more tractable related subject. During the winter of
1841–2 he wrote the text of a five-act historical opera, *Die Sarazenin*
('The Saracen Woman'). It is prophesied that the heroine Fatima,
the love-child of Frederick and a Saracen princess, will perform
miracles in advancing Manfred's renown, as long as she does not
surrender to him in love. She appears to him with inspired
prophecies at decisive moments in battle and leads him on from one
victory to another. When Manfred falls passionately in love with
her, she is stabbed to death by the young Saracen who has loved her
since childhood, and Manfred realizes that he will never know
happiness again. (RWGS, XI, pp. 230ff.)

Though it seemed reasonably effective to him, Wagner was
unable to feel any great enthusiasm for the text. He later showed it
to Schröder-Devrient, when she complained that she was 'pining'
for his music, if only he would write the right part for her, but she
rejected it: she had known too many lovers herself to have any
sympathy for the idea that a prophetess, like Schiller's Joan of Arc,
might not with impunity be a woman too.

Steeping himself in the atmosphere of the German Middle
Ages to which Raumer had introduced him, Wagner had also

encountered the old folk ballad of Tannhäuser and Venus. He had already known the story from Ludwig Tieck's *Phantasus*, but that modern retelling, with its 'mystical titillation, its Catholic frivolity', had not inspired him to put it in dramatic form. The tale of the Singers' War at the Wartburg, which has no connection with Tannhäuser at all, had also been known to him since boyhood from E. T. A. Hoffmann's version.

But then one day one of the companions of his Parisian misfortune, Samuel Lehrs, lent him a volume of the historical and literary proceedings of the Royal German Society of Königsberg, with a paper on the Wartburg 'war' by C. T. L. Lucas, which acquainted Wagner with the legend's original form. The most important thing he culled from it was the hypothesis, advanced by Lucas with some caution, that the Heinrich von Ofterdingen of the poem may have been identical with the minnesinger Tannhäuser. This was the spark that led to the fusion of the two subjects in Wagner's imagination: all at once he had a drama that threw the *Sarazenin* into the shade.

Now that *Rienzi* and the *Holländer* had been accepted for performance, he was impatient to get back to Germany. He and Minna took a tearful leave from Lehrs, Kietz and Anders on 7 April 1842. They sensed that they would not see Lehrs again, for he suffered from a severe pulmonary disease. The *diligence* carried them along the boulevards on a smiling spring morning. On the far side of the Rhine the weather was cold and grey, and Wagner took it as a good omen that the first rays of sunshine they saw again were falling on the Wartburg. As they drove through the valley towards it he sketched the scenery which he later described to the Parisian stage designer who painted the sets for the first production of *Tannhäuser* in Dresden.

He spent his first days in Leipzig and Dresden in a dream, meeting his mother and sisters again. He had to pull himself together sharply to attend to his affairs. In Berlin he learned that Redern had resigned and his successor was to be Küstner – the same Küstner who had turned down the *Holländer* for Munich as 'unsuitable for Germany'. Although not now able to refuse a work which met 'every requirement of the critical standards of the Royal Prussian Court Opera', he delayed production long enough for the première finally to take place in Dresden on 2 January 1843, while the first performance in Berlin was not until 7 January 1844.

This setback in Berlin was not the only disappointment of the high hopes Wagner had had of Germany. The Dresden opera, too, failed to conceal from him that it found him all too tempestuous. Only Ferdinand Heine and Wilhelm Fischer greeted his arrival with sincere pleasure. In every other respect the Dresden he had known had vanished: the hundred friends he had once had no longer existed. The city itself no longer meant anything to him, and if he was going to be a failure he felt he would rather be one in Paris than in Dresden. 'I have no geographical preferences and my homeland, apart from its beautiful ranges of hills, its valleys and its woodlands, is actually repellent to me. These Saxons are an accursed race – mean, dozy, cloddish, idle and coarse – what have I to do with them?' (To Lehrs, 12 June 1842)

Above all he was still the same 'penniless Johnny', as he complained to his half-sister Cäcilie, 'with glorious prospects and a meaningless present'. His sisters and their husbands had joined forces to ensure him a modest monthly income until the profits he hoped for from *Rienzi* materialized. He would have been well off if it had not been for his old creditors . . . and for his Parisian debts! He was obliged to make some operatic arrangements to pay off an advance from Maurice Schlesinger. He sent him one such piece of forced labour from Teplitz, where he had gone for a cure, on 25 June 1842: '*La Reine de Chypre* – Airs arrangés en quatuor pour 2 violons, alto et basse en 3 suites par Richard Wagner. Musique de F. Halévy.' 'My damned Parisian obligations still weigh abominably upon me, just when I would be gloriously ready to get on with a new work, I have got to force it all back inside myself – in order to write arrangements.' (To Ernst Benedikt Kietz, 1 July 1842)

He managed to get away, though, for a walking holiday as in the old days, going to the Schreckenstein in the Erzgebirge near Aussig (now Ústí) on the Elbe to think out the plot of the 'Venusberg', as the new work was still called. He slept on straw in the small guest room, and the solitude so fired his imagination that in a recrudescence of his teenage japes he spent an entire night clambering about among the castle ruins wearing nothing but a sheet, a living apparition. One day he climbed the Wostrai, the highest mountain in the district, and suddenly came upon a shepherd, lying on a slope and playing a lively dance tune. 'At once I was in the chorus of pilgrims, passing the shepherd as they wend their way through the valley.' He saw Carlo Dolci's *Madonna* in the parish church in Aussig, and told Kietz that he had found the painting extraordinarily delightful, and that if Tannhäuser had seen it, it would have explained fully how he came to transfer his devotion from Venus to the Virgin without any great access of piety. 'Anyway, now I have a clear idea of the saintly Elisabeth.' (6 September; RWBC, p. 188)

Saint Elisabeth of Hungary was the daughter-in-law of Landgrave Hermann of Thuringia and does not appear in Wagner's sources. In the medieval version of the Singers' War it is the landgrave's wife, Sophia, who spreads out her cloak to shield Ofterdingen as the knights advance upon him. Hoffmann turns this figure into a beautiful widow, Mathilde von Falkenstein, who is wooed by Wolfram and Ofterdingen. It was a stroke of genius on Wagner's part to substitute Saint Elisabeth, and make her the landgrave's virginal niece, so gaining a worthy counterpart to Venus.

Some of the pages of the notebook in which Wagner wrote the prose sketch have survived in the Burrell Collection: '2–8 June 1842. Schreckenstein bei Aussig. Spacious grotto with side galleries hidden from view . . . Luxuriant circle of the half-naked forms of beautiful virgins, scattered amorous groups. Singing. *Celebration of love.*'

Glasenapp also published a page of music sketches of the same date, comprising the first version of the principal themes: 'Venusberg', 'Pilgrims', 'Act II finale', 'Act III opening' and so on. The shepherd boy's shawm solo is sketched on another page, in a form totally different from the eventual version. (GLRW, I, pp. 445f.)

The prospect of seeing *Rienzi* take the stage in full panoply in the very near future brought Wagner hurrying back from Teplitz on 18 July, to keep an eye on the 'idlers in Dresden'. He had sent a list of enquiries while he was still in Paris: 'How have the parts been cast? Are my suggestions useful and good, and are they being adopted? . . . The management must spare no expense or trouble – because with operas like mine there's no middle way – you know what I mean! – Just listen to me! An emperor is nothing to me: "Do this! Do that!" as if I had only to command!' (To Ferdinand Heine, undated; RWBC, p. 145)

He had no reason to complain of any lack of zeal on the part of the performers. The work and his own presence at rehearsals increased their enthusiasm daily. The first time they rehearsed the scene with the messengers of peace at the beginning of Act II, Schröder-Devrient was unable to restrain her tears, while Tichatschek, who was singing Rienzi, declared that the B minor ensemble in the Act III finale was so fine that they ought to pay for the privilege of singing it, whereupon he produced a silver groschen and the others followed his example. This charade was repeated at every rehearsal – 'Here comes the new groschen passage' – until Schröder-Devrient wailed that it would make a pauper of her. 'And none of them suspected', Wagner confessed, 'that this honorarium they paid as a joke was only too welcome to my wife and me, to pay for our dinner.'

He wooed the easygoing musical director Reissiger, who attributed his own failures as a composer to bad librettos, with a verse text of *Die Hohe Braut*, the scenario of which he had sent to Scribe in 1836. Reissiger's initial interest was cooled by his wife's suspicion that it was some kind of trap, so he turned it down and had an actor write him another libretto on the wreck of the *Medusa*. Wagner later adopted the title as an appropriate expression for the failure of operatic hopes: if Liszt had not championed him, he said, he too might have sunk without trace like Reissiger's *Medusa*.

Lüttichau was the only person of whom he complained, in a letter to Kietz: the countless misunderstandings that arose daily from the intendant's 'uncommon obtuseness and stupidity' placed continual obstacles in his way, and removing them was like forever mucking out a stable. (To E. B. Kietz, 6 September 1842, RWBC, p. 146)

Nothing in his previous or ensuing experience resembled the state of mind in which he looked forward to the first performance on 20 October. The success went far beyond his wildest expectations. People recognized that, *Euryanthe* and *Les Huguenots* notwithstanding, here was something audacious and new. Financially, too, it was unusually successful: the management could put it on again and again and always fill the house, initially at increased prices. The composer was not so lucky: except for Berlin, no German opera house paid royalties, but only made a single payment, which varied with the size of the house. Lüttichau believed he was being extremely generous when he offered Wagner 300 talers.

At the same time he was preparing the first performance of *Der Fliegende Holländer*. Schröder-Devrient, who had had to be content with a supporting role in *Rienzi*, was singing Senta. She did not find it easy to learn a new part and her moods sometimes made Wagner despair. His patience gave out: Devrient was a sow and a bitch, he wrote to Minna, no one knew the trouble she was giving him. But he was soon reconciled with her again: 'I dare say it will be a long time before our Creator produces anyone like her again,' he wrote to Kietz; 'the wealth, the power of her passion, the turbulence and force of the inner daemon, combined with such genuine femininity, lovableness and kindness of heart . . . our artistic collaboration was quite remarkable: a whole book could be written about us working on the part of Senta!' (8 April 1843; RWBC, pp. 246f.) When he came to create his Brünnhilde, he wrote later, it was her example that showed him how: 'the example that she, the mime, set the dramatist and that I alone, of all those to whom she gave it, have followed'. It was certainly her inspired performance as Senta, seemingly completely isolated on the stage, that made the first performance of the *Holländer* a success. Wagner could not disguise from himself the fact that his stark, sombre dramatic ballad was not greatly to the public taste: for the first time he had cause to consider that his inner promptings might be at odds with outward success.

While he was still pondering this new problem he received an offer from Lüttichau of an assistant conductor's post, which had become vacant through a death. 'I hasten to inform Your Excellency', he replied on 5 January 1843, 'that after mature reflection on my part I believe it necessary to explain, with regard to the proposals kindly made to me by Your Excellency this morning, why I find it impossible, in the given circumstances, to accept a probationary appointment as a conductor to the royal orchestra.' The example of the leading Parisian orchestras had shown him the extent of the organizational measures that would be necessary to raise the standards of artistic discipline in Dresden. 'To have any success in this latter, highly important matter, I would need authority in the full sense of the word.'

Instinct warned him against accepting a post which would certainly conflict with his vocation, and he thought his stipulations would avert the impending disaster. 'I am still in a very great dilemma,' he wrote to his brother Albert; 'of course I would like to keep my freedom for the next few years. I am in my prime now, when my productive powers are at their most vigorous.' (3 December 1842)

But everything seemed to conspire against him: Lüttichau offered him the post on a permanent basis at an annual salary of 1500 talers and without a probationary year; it was Minna's dearest wish to relinquish the 'vagabond life' for middle-class security and respectability; Weber's widow implored him not to abandon her husband's life work.

'More than anything else,' he confessed, 'I was moved by my own enthusiastic faith, never completely extinguished at any time in my life, that the place to which fate had led me – Dresden, as it then chanced – was where the first step might be taken in transforming the familiar, where the unknown might be born.' (ML, p. 293)

The appointment of Richard Wagner as kapellmeister to the court of the King of Saxony was announced on 2 February 1843. 'I often have stupid expenses,' he wrote to Lehrs; 'now I've got to have a court uniform made, which is going to cost me about 100 talers! Isn't it nonsense?' Eliza Wille tells of an evening ten years later in Zürich, when he disappeared for a moment during dinner, to return wearing his court dress. Stooping slightly, rubbing his hands, and with a sarcastic smile on his lips, he turned to his wife: 'Oh yes, Minna, I dare say it was very nice, and you were pleased with me in those days. My poor wife, what a shame the uniform got too tight for me!'

At last he found time, after this eventful winter, to devote himself to *Tannhäuser* again. He finished the text early in April. He meant to start composing during a summer holiday in Teplitz, but a feverish excitement prevented him from getting anywhere with it. The beginning of the composition sketch, which is in the Burrell Collection, is dated as late as November 1843. Like all the composition sketches of the later works, this first continuous draft on two or three staves was written down in sequence and with hardly any alterations. Here and there details of characteristic instrumentation are given. Even a chord as completely without precedent as the sustained dissonance at 'Naht euch dem *Stran*–de' in the chorus of Sirens is found there, exactly as if such an effect was common currency.

He spent six happy weeks in the autumn of 1844 at Fischer's vineyard outside Loschwitz, where he completed the sketch of the second act on 15 October. He sketched the third act after his return to Dresden, keeping himself in form with frequent, solitary walks. He finished the full score on 13 April 1845. 'My whole being had been so consumed in the work that the closer I got to the end, the more convinced I grew that sudden death would prevent me from reaching it, so that as I wrote the last note I rejoiced as if I had just escaped some mortal danger.'

The reason for this degree of involvement lies in the fact that this work expresses the essence of his own nature as no other does. The two opposing tendencies in himself which he described, apropos of *Die Feen* and *Das Liebesverbot*, as the 'sacred earnest' of his instinctive responses and the 'inclination to unbridled sensuality' are also the two dominating characteristics of his protagonist. Wagner went on to say, in that context, that the object of his further development as an artist would be to achieve a balance between the two: the conflict between them is the actual subject of *Tannhäuser* and it is triumphantly resolved. As Wagner pointed out in his note on the overture, the distinguishing feature of *Tannhäuser* is that it ends with the reconciliation of the two elements: 'Spirit and senses, God and Nature embrace in the holy, uniting kiss of love.' (RWGS, V, pp. 177ff.)

It is one of the ironies of Wagner's career that this very conciliatory resolution dragged him into an interconfessional wrangle, with the charge of having been got at by the Catholics. Then and later nothing was further from him than any kind of sectarian commitment. When the Berlin music critic Karl Gaillard took exception to the wording of the concluding couplet:

> Hoch über aller Welt ist Gott,
> und sein Erbarmen ist kein Spott!

he replied that he had left the lines like that 'because in my view "Spott" ['mockery'] is not a forced rhyme, but the most apt poetic word to express the perversion of divine mercy by a hard-hearted priesthood. God be my help!' (5 June 1845)

Gaillard had in fact criticized several passages in the text, and it shows how seriously Wagner now took the words, that he reconsidered and changed the lines in Wolfram's song to the Evening Star:

> Wie Todesahnung, Dämm'rung sinkt hernieder,
> umhüllt das Tal mit schwärzlichem Gefieder

to:

> Wie Todesahnung, Dämm'rung deckt die Lande,
> umhüllt das Tal mit schwärzlichem Gewande

substituting the image of dusk covering the valley with a dark cloak instead of the rather precious plumage of the first version. After finishing the prose scenario, he had written to Kietz that he would try to make the verse text 'as good as possible'.

But Wagner's poetry consists not only in his words but also in his visual imagery. Wilhelm Furtwängler cites the transformation of the Venusberg into the valley below the Wartburg as a particularly remarkable example:

> We think that we have never experienced a May morning quite like it, God's world has never seemed so beautiful as now. The reason is psychological: we are seeing the scene with Tannhäuser's eyes, and his cry 'Allmächtiger, dir sei Dank! [sic] Groß sind die Wunder deiner Gnade!' is thus one of the most sublime moments in world literature. And what else can you call the person who was capable of creating such a moment but a poet?[1]

It is very hard for us today to realize how daring and strange the music first sounded to Wagner's contemporaries. 'Wagner has finished another opera,' Schumann wrote to Mendelssohn, 'the fellow is certainly inventive and bold beyond belief. . . but truly he isn't capable of thinking out and writing four bars in succession of beautiful, or hardly even competent, music.' After hearing a performance, however, he admitted: 'I must take back some of what I said . . . it's all quite different on the stage. I was quite carried away.' Later still, it is true, this enthusiasm abated somewhat. He wrote to a friend that when he heard the operas in the theatre, he could not help but be deeply moved at many passages; though it was not bright sunlight that Wagner's genius radiated, it was often a mysterious magic that mastered the senses. But he found the music slight divorced from the stage, often downright dilettante, insubstantial and distasteful. 'The future will be its judge.' (To Karl Debrois von Bruyck, 8 May 1853)

Mendelssohn conducted the overture in the Gewandhaus in 1846, but adopted so fast a tempo that no sense could be made of it. The young Hans von Bülow described it as an 'execution' in every sense of the word. Hans Pfitzner tells how his father, who was an orchestral violinist, caught a supercilious smile on Mendelssohn's face as the last note died away, as much as to say 'we classicists know what to think of music like this'. Newman comments on the harm the performance did Wagner.

But he had been prepared for hostility. He had written to Kietz that he expected this opera to be a 'great revolution; I feel that I have made giant strides towards my ideal in it. Strictly between ourselves!' (18 December 1844; RWBC, pp. 188f.)

When the curtain fell on the première in Dresden in 19 October 1845, in spite of the friendly reception from the audience Wagner had the distinct impression that the dramatic climaxes had misfired. Tichatschek, vocally overwhelming as Rienzi, had been unable to project the contrition of 'Zum Heil den Sündigen zu führen' in the Act II finale, or to lend conviction to the dramatic motivation of the Rome narration. Wagner's niece Johanna, too, whose youth gave general delight in the second act, was not up to the demands of the Prayer in the third – a passage Wagner always valued particularly highly for its simplicity – which had to be partly cut in the following performances.

There was, additionally, a weakness in the work which Wagner attributed to his lack of dramaturgical experience. In its original version the opera ended without the appearance of Venus or of the cortège with Elisabeth's body, but only with a glow from the mountain and the distant sound of a bell tolling, so that it was not at all clear to the audience what was happening. Wagner rewrote the close twice before arriving at the eventual version.

Wagner was conscious even then of another weakness, the 'sketchy and awkward' writing of the part of Venus, but he was unable to do anything about it until he revised the work for Paris in 1861.

In the last years of his life he used to say he wanted to produce *Tannhäuser* at Bayreuth: as a drama it was now perfected – and yet not quite, after all, because there were things in the music that had not been sufficiently worked out. On 22 January 1883, only a few days before his death, Cosima noted in her diary: 'Conversation this evening, which Richard brought to a close with the Shepherd's Song and Pilgrims' Chorus. He said he still owed the world a *Tannhäuser*.' Whether he meant another version of the work or just a production is not altogether clear. Another remark of a few weeks earlier, whose meaning is quite clear, has hitherto been overlooked. Speaking of his dispute with the Berlin publisher Fürstner, who had withheld his opera from him, he added: 'If I want to revise *Tannhäuser* now, I haven't got a score.' (GLRW, VI, p. 716)

The work was a turning point in his career in one more, very particular sense: in it he attained at last to full awareness of his creative processes. Immediately after finishing the composition sketch of the first act he wrote to Gaillard on 30 January 1844:

> Before I begin to write a single line of verse, or even to outline a scene, I am already intoxicated by the musical aroma of my creation, I have all the notes, all the characteristic motives in my head, so that when the verses have been written and the scenes satisfactorily constructed, then so far as I am concerned the opera itself is already finished.

Some eighteen months later a court official, Hofrat Gustav Klemm, sent him a libretto by a lady, asking him to set it. Wagner replied that, with the greatest respect for the librettist, he hoped, in the name of Heaven, that she would not be offended by his refusal. It was not that he had a low opinion of her work, but he had arrived at the conclusion that if anything more of significance was to be accomplished in opera, it could only come about by the union of poet and composer in one person. He went on with an admission that tells much about his creative psychology: the whole of his productive power, and especially his musical power, was founded on the fact that he shaped and developed his material in such a way that even he himself could not distinguish between 'what is done by the poet and what by the musician'. (20 June 1845)

10

Hofkapellmeister in Dresden

'I have been told quite frankly that I am expected to reorganize musical affairs here on genuinely artistic lines', Wagner wrote to Lehrs on 7 April 1843, a few weeks after his appointment to the musical directorship in Dresden. The expectations seemed justified by the success of the first opera entrusted to his direction, Gluck's *Armide* – a sign of especial confidence in him, as it had never been performed in Dresden before. He had taken pains to render the score less stiff by careful modification of the incessant crotchet movement of the instrumental accompaniment. 'Everyone was beside themselves with the nuances that I got the orchestra and the singers to observe: the king . . . sent me a message of thanks and the most extravagant praise while the performance was still going on.'

One aspect of the performance that everybody commented on was the accompaniment, restrained, soft, yet always perfectly clear; and later in life Wagner himself liked to recall the expressive style of the singing. He used to sing the second-act chorus, 'Beklagt sei er, der nie genossen, wo ihm Nektarströme flossen' ('Ah, quelle erreur, quelle folie, de ne pas jouir de la vie!') as an example, first in the style he had once heard in Berlin and then as he had performed it in Dresden. His parody of the stiff, dry delivery of the Berlin singers was extremely funny; the serious, wonderfully subtle nuances of the second version seemed to demonstrate the abundance of his dramatic skill almost as fully as if it were a live stage performance.

It is not surprising that at the time this success earned him the reputation of a particular love for Gluck. When he conducted *Don Giovanni* three weeks later he had to take over a production originally conducted by someone else and by then hallowed by tradition. He had only one rehearsal in which to loosen the stranglehold of familiarity, and he wrestled in vain with the resistance of the orchestra and its ambitious leader Lipinski, whom Wagner indeed respected as an artist. The press complained of Wagner's 'Parisian tempos'. At the next meeting of the general board of management, Lipinski launched a violent attack to which Wagner replied, aroused, as he confessed, 'to a state where I forgot the propriety due to the occasion'.

He attempted to justify himself the following day in a letter to the intendant. He repeated his promise not to try to alter the accepted tempos of familiar operas without consultation, but pointed out that 'traditions' of that kind were not always so sacrosanct as they appeared. Before he conducted a rehearsal of *Euryanthe*, Weber's widow had implored him to do away at last with the errors of tempo that had taken root. 'Your Excellency will see from this how performance of an opera originally rehearsed and conducted by the composer, with the same performers and in the same theatre, can diverge from the original and authentic conception in the course of twenty years; and my question now is, who will vouch for the authenticity of the tradition in the case of an opera that was first given here fifty or more years ago and was never performed here under the direction of the composer?' (2 May 1843)

It is significant that the anti-Wagner faction took his attitude to Mozart as the grounds for an attack on him. There was nothing that could so discredit a musician in public opinion as the assertion that he despised Mozart. Wagner retorted: 'A stupid remark that I feel almost ashamed even to protest about.' (RWGS, XII, p. 210)

It had been no empty rhetoric when the German musician in his Parisian tale died professing his faith in Beethoven and Mozart. A biography of Mozart, read to him when he was only six, had made an undying impression on him. The only musical biography he bought during this period in Dresden was the German translation of Alexander Ulibishev's life of Mozart (1847); and in spite of the persistent hostility shown toward himself by Otto Jahn (hostility that did not always leave him untouched, as Jahn had the ear of his publisher Härtel), he had a copy of Jahn's *Mozart* in the library at Wahnfried.

He was possessed by a sense of the tragedy of Mozart's life, spent 'as if under the vivisector's knife'. His finest works had been written between present exultancy and anxiety about what the next hour might bring. When Wagner saw an *Adoration of the Kings* in a church in Siena he exclaimed: 'All these signs of honour in childhood, the shepherds and the kings and the angels – where were they later? Mozart suffered the same fate!'

The overture to *Die Zauberflöte* was his earliest musical love: it captured so exactly the note of a fairy tale. He conducted it in Mannheim in 1871 at the concert celebrating the founding of the German Richard Wagner Society. He often reminisced about his childhood impressions when Mozart was played at Wahnfried. He had discovered the C minor Fantasy at his Uncle Adolf's house and had dreamt about it for ages afterwards. The Requiem had aroused wild enthusiasm in him: it was beautiful, he said at Wahnfried, the work of a pious spirit, one who went to church and was moved by religion, and yet totally unecclesiastical. Going through the maskers' quartet from *Don Giovanni*, he said that it was what he had always hoped to emulate when he was young. One evening they sang the trio from Act II of *Zauberflöte*, 'Die Stunde schlägt, nun müßt ihr scheiden'; as a boy he had thought it the most sublime of all music, melancholy and consoling at the same time.

During his studies with Weinlig he had tried to discover the secret of Mozart's fluency and lightness in solving difficult technical problems. In particular he tried to emulate the fugal finale of the great C major Symphony, 'magnificent, never surpassed', as he called it years later, and at eighteen he wrote a fugato as the finale of his C major Concert Overture, 'the very best that I could do, as I thought at the time, in honour of my new exemplar'. In the last years of his life he liked to call himself the 'last Mozartian'. He played Brünnhilde's E major passage from the last act of *Die Walküre*, 'Der diese Liebe mir ins Herz gelegt', and lamented the general failure to appreciate his sense of beauty which, he believed, made him 'Mozart's successor'.

He worked hard to introduce Mozart to his friends. Wolzogen records that, reared as he had been in unquestioning veneration of Mozart, it was through Wagner that he had first been made fully aware of the genius of *Figaro*. Humperdinck says that the most interesting evenings at Wahnfried were those when Wagner performed scenes from Mozart's operas, *Die Entführung* for example, giving them a freshness that was wholly delightful.

He believed the key to Mozartian performance lay in singing. He explained to Luise Dustmann how to take breath in Donna Anna's great aria so as to be able to sing the bar leading into the return of the

main theme and the theme itself in one breath. He wrote in the
album of a young soprano, who had just sung Susanna's aria for
him, 'Long breath – beautiful soul'. Mozart, he said, had breathed
the same expressive beauty into his orchestral writing: 'The whole
of the Andante of the C major Symphony is a vocal aria; I would
like to write words to it and then hear it sung by a Catalani.' He gave
Hans von Bülow advice on how the famous 'Swan' Andante of the
Eb major Symphony should be played: the difficulty here, he wrote,
lay in finding an overall tempo that did not drag, and yet still
allowing the main theme its due. If it was played without any
nuance in the tempo the whole magic of it was lost. (18 March 1868)

What aroused the Dresden public in the 1840s to protest at what
they called 'Parisian tempos' was Wagner's effort to breathe the life
back into Mozart's cantilenas, which they were accustomed to hear
played 'smoothly and neatly', very much as a matter of course.

When the Dresden critic Carl Banck accused him, after a performance of *Figaro* in 1846, three years after that first *Don Giovanni*, of
the wrong tempos and of ignorance of Mozart, Wagner was provoked to reply:

> C. B. is wrong in supposing he needs to tell me to
> enquire among older musicians about the authentic
> tradition of tempos in Mozart's operas. In the case of
> *Figaro*, in particular, I have assembled a large number of
> very reliable testimonies, notably from the late director
> of the Prague Conservatory, Dionys Weber; as an
> eye-and-ear-witness of the first performance of *Figaro*
> and of the rehearsals that preceded it, under Mozart's
> own direction, he told me that, for instance, the master
> could never get the tempo of the overture fast enough
> and, in order to maintain the momentum, continually
> whipped up the pace wherever the nature of the theme
> allowed it.

Wagner gave a number of other examples and finally, in full consciousness of his own quality, took a stand above the level of
theoretical discussion: when the development of creative powers of
his own had given a conductor a finer instinct for the performance
of the work of another genius, he communicated that instinct to the
musicians, too, and the resulting performance could justly be
regarded as perfect in itself, even though there might be differences

of opinion over details; 'above all we may assume that the creator of the work would prefer this kind of performance to every other, because every creative artist knows from experience that, for his own work as for every other, the letter kills and the spirit gives life'. (RWGS, XII, pp. 208ff.)

Wagner's court appointment and his conductorship of the Dresden Liedertafel choral society meant that he sometimes had to write music for special occasions. At the unveiling of a memorial to King Friedrich August I in the Zwinger in Dresden, he conducted a performance of a 'simple song for men's voices of a restrained character', and when Friedrich August II returned from a journey to England on 12 August 1844, Wagner greeted him at the royal country palace at Pillnitz with a choral and orchestral work, 'His loyal subjects' greeting to Friedrich August the beloved', in which the march from *Tannhäuser* was already to be heard.

He broke new ground when asked to write a large-scale work for a festival. Instead of an oratorio, in order to alleviate the monotony of male-voice choral singing, he wrote a 'biblical scene', *Das Liebesmahl der Apostel* ('The Love-Feast of the Apostles'), dedicated to the widow of his teacher, Theodor Weinlig.

A choir of twelve hundred singers, on a platform that almost entirely filled the nave of the Frauenkirche, was divided into separate choruses of disciples and apostles, greeting and answering each other, lamenting and comforting and finally uniting in a mighty crescendo: 'Send' uns deinen heiligen Geist' ('Send us Thy Holy Spirit'). In reply a choir of forty of the best voices was heard from high up in the dome: 'Seid getrost, ich bin euch nah' ('Take comfort, I am near you'). Then the one-hundred-strong orchestra, placed out of sight of the audience, began to play. The disciples asked each other, wonderingly, 'Welch Brausen erfüllt die Luft?' ('What rushing fills the air?') The work ended with the affirmation: 'Wir sind bereit, in alle Welt zu ziehen, kräftig zu trotzen jeder Schmach und Not!' ('We are ready to go out into all lands, doughtily defying every disgrace and hardship') – words that almost anticipate the chorus of the Grail knights: 'Treu bis zum Tod, fest jedem Müh'n, zu wirken des Heilands Werke.' The ethereal quality of the voices high in the roof, the powerful sound of the 'rushing mighty wind' as the orchestra entered at the outpouring of the Holy Spirit, made an unforgettable impression, the critic Richard Pohl recalled. Wagner himself was not altogether satisfied with this occasional piece: it was over thirty years before he was able to realize the scenic and musical potential of his vision, when he came to write the Grail scenes in *Parsifal*.

There was another ceremony very close to his heart. For years efforts had been made to get the mortal remains of Carl Maria von Weber brought to Dresden from London, but they had always met with obstacles. Now Wagner was elected to the committee, in the hope that his energy would overcome the difficulties. The most stubborn opposition came from the intendant, and a strong light is thrown on Lüttichau's capacities by his asking why so much fuss should be made about Weber. What if the widows of all the hofkapellmeisters who happened to die abroad claimed the right to have their husbands' bodies brought home with pomp and circumstance?

But at last all the obstacles were overcome. On 14 December 1844, on an icy winter evening, thousands of people lined the streets as the procession with the coffin, followed by a sea of blazing torches, made its way from the bank of the Elbe to the chapel of the Catholic cemetery. Wagner had written a funeral march, using motives from *Euryanthe*, for eighty wind instruments, carefully employing them in their softer registers and replacing viola tremolos with muffled drums. He gave a moving address at the graveside the following day: 'Rest here, then. Let this unadorned spot watch over the remains that are so dear to us . . . (RWGS, II, pp. 46ff.) Hearing his own voice, he seemed to see himself as a separate person, standing in front of him and speaking. He stopped for a moment, till he remembered that he was there to speak, not to listen. It was one of those moments of self-forgetting that he experienced sometimes when he was inwardly tense. The ceremony ended with a chorus he had composed for the occasion, 'Hebt an den Sang, ihr Zeugen dieser Stunde'. (RWGS, II, p. 49)

The generous imagination Wagner brought to his post at the opera is illustrated by an episode that immediately preceded Weber's burial. A new production of *La Vestale* was scheduled and he had pressed for Spontini to be invited to conduct his opera. Spontini, by now an old man, accepted, but his orchestral requirements – 'six ou sept excellentes contrebasses' were a minimum (RWBC, pp. 295f.) – appalled all concerned. Wagner's description of this episode, a mixture of respect and amusement, is one of the funniest passages in *Mein Leben*. 'He has character,' he said later.

'You see before you a proud devil who doesn't understand a joke, who wears all his orders. But what a difference belief in oneself makes, how decidedly drastic it is, when compared with Brahms, for instance.' He acknowledged a large debt to Spontini: the first-act finale of *Lohengrin*, 'this continuity of singing', really derived from him more than Weber. One evening he played from *La Vestale* to Cosima, Julia's plea to the High Priestess and her monologue, and then said, 'a man who wrote something like that is sacred to me'.

The greatest moment of Wagner's career in Dresden was the performance of the Choral Symphony on 5 April 1846. For the third time the 'Fundamental of his own life' was sounded at a critical moment in his development. The first time had been in his teens, he wrote, as a mystical sign of his vocation; the second in Paris, recalling him to his true path and lighting his way. Much that he had experienced since then had driven him to despair and doubt, as yet unexpressed. But the despair he had tried to hide from his friends was now transformed into enthusiastic optimism by the Ninth Symphony. Anyone who had come upon him unawares with the score open in front of him would have asked if this was the behaviour to be expected of a conductor by appointment to His Majesty the King of Saxony. Fortunately, he concluded, he was spared visits from the respectable musicians, well versed in the classical masters, who were his colleagues.

Reissiger had conducted the symphony in Dresden eight years earlier, on which occasion it had been a dismal failure – a judgement which the conductor fully endorsed. Now when Wagner proposed it for the annual Palm Sunday concert in aid of the orchestral pension fund he roused general dismay. The orchestral management wanted to take the matter to the king himself, and a newspaper asked if this 'carnival music' could be considered appropriate to the solemnity of the day.

By a masterpiece of diplomacy, in spite of all the opposition, Wagner had his way. The performance was to be given in what was known as the Old Opera House, where, in the days when the Electors of Saxony were also Kings of Poland, spectacular operatic productions had been mounted with processions of horsemen and wild animals, and which was now used for court balls and concerts. On those occasions the orchestra was seated in a wide semicircle only two desks deep, an arrangement which, Wagner remarked, broke every rule and was probably without parallel anywhere in the world. His diplomacy scored a further success in that he won from Lüttichau not only the permission to have the platform rebuilt but also the 200 talers to do it. In his request he wrote that he and the theatre machinist had calculated the design for the fairly complicated structure with mathematical accuracy. 'May it please Your Excellency to observe, in studying the plan, that the areas coloured red designate the position of the choir, rising in amphitheatrical tiers at the sides to above the level of the orchestra, and presenting an imposing spectacle, while it will face the conductor from every side and, not being buried in itself, will be heard very strongly and clearly from every seat in the audience.' (4 March 1846)

When Wagner stepped on to the podium at the first rehearsal he slammed shut the score that had been placed there for him and began to conduct the gigantic work by heart, something that was unheard of in those days. He met the full force of the players' resistance in these rehearsals. Time and again, as he rapped his baton to stop them, they shouted, 'But we haven't got D♭, we've got D!' Whereupon Wagner replied, calmly but firmly, 'Well, alter it, it must be D♭.' He paid particular attention to the woodwind. The famous oboist Kummer later confessed that at every emendation he had whispered furiously to his neighbour, 'if only the beggar knew what he was up to!'

Wagner's method of conducting rehearsals was quite different from that of Habeneck, the director of the Paris Conservatoire orchestra, who, according to Berlioz, conducted Beethoven's symphonies from the first violin part. While Habeneck gradually picked his way from the part to the whole, from technical accuracy to interpretative understanding, Wagner already had an overall conception of the work when he arrived at the first rehearsal. Within this framework he then sought to bring out the 'melos' – for him the quintessence of all music – from the broad, sweeping melodic lines down to the tiniest fragments to which the composer had reduced his themes. He made fun of German conductors who could not sing a melody rightly or even wrongly and for whom music was 'a curiously abstract thing floating somewhere between grammar, arithmetic and gymnastics'. At his rehearsals of the Ninth Symphony in London, many years later, he did not hesitate, for his part, to sing the recitative of the cellos and basses, which the players at first took as a joke until the meaning of the unusual phrase suddenly dawned on them.

In Dresden, too, he devoted twelve special rehearsals to the string recitative passages, until they really sounded like human voices singing. Niels Gade, who had come over from Leipzig, said he would gladly have paid twice as much for his ticket if he could only have heard that recitative again. It was only in the rendering of some of the more delicate passages that Wagner found he could not match, then or later, the quality of the Paris orchestra: neither in Dresden nor in London could he prevent the strings, at the rising semiquaver figurations in bars 116–23 of the first movement, from falling straight into the usual crescendo instead of observing the even pianissimo expressly required, which he had heard from the French players who had been trained in the lyrical Italian school. It was true that the passage expressed dissatisfaction, unrest, yearning, whatever the dynamics; but the precise nature of those feelings could only be expressed when it was performed as Beethoven directed: when the delicately 'sung' G♭ was answered by an equally delicately 'sung' G, then the hearer was initiated, as if by magic, into the mysteries of the spirit that was speaking there. (RWGS, VIII, pp. 271ff.)

As well as technical problems of that kind, Wagner believed that a further cause of lack of clarity in the projection of Beethoven's melodies lay in certain weaknesses in the scoring. The instrumental grouping was always superb, but the composer was sometimes mistaken about the relative strengths of individual instruments, and anyone who could help to remedy that was doing him a service. On this occasion in Dresden he went no further himself than doubling the woodwind in the second theme of the Scherzo, so that they could be heard against the string accompaniment in octaves. As a result, he felt, the theme was heard properly for the first time in the symphony's existence.

It was of the highest significance, Wagner said, that Beethoven had marked the tempestuous, anguished first movement 'Maestoso'. Wagner always regarded 'Allegro maestoso', in any music, as possessing a wider range of meaning than any other tempo; no other had such a need of modification when maintained over a long period and particularly when the treatment of the thematic material was markedly episodic. By selecting not too fast a main tempo and keeping to it, with modifications, throughout the movement, Wagner imbued it with an inner tension, so that even in the brief moments of wistful happiness the listener did not forget that he was

on the edge of the abyss. 'That's the demonic cauldron,' he once
commented, 'which has always been there, bubbling, but nobody
heard it.'

He was convinced from the first that the success of the performance would stand or fall by the effectiveness of the singing. He
made Mitterwurzer – who, as Wolfram, had been the only member
of the cast to understand the stylistic requirements of *Tannhäuser* –
sing 'O Freunde, nicht diese Töne' over and over again and then
exclaimed impatiently, 'That won't do, if you can't sing it better
than that, you'd better not sing it at all.' Mitterwurzer said nothing
but looked at him intently; then he started again and sang the line
thrillingly.

Recognizing that only a massive array of enthusiastic singers
would be able to meet the demands of the choral writing, Wagner
enrolled a choir of three hundred, whom he roused to a pitch of
genuine ecstasy in rehearsals. He showed them that 'Seid
umschlungen, Millionen!' and above all the line 'Brüder, überm
Sternenzelt' cannot be sung in an ordinary manner but must be
proclaimed exaltedly. Untiringly he sang these lines with them
with the enthusiasm he knew how to impart, and did not stop until
his own voice, which penetrated the sound of the chorus in every
bar to begin with, could no longer be heard. The result, according
to someone who attended the rehearsals, was something no one
who heard it would ever forget.[1]

In performance Wagner stood very still: his head raised, the
upper part of his body hardly moving, his left hand at his side, his
right hand holding the baton, conducting with the wrist, not the
whole arm. His passion was now outwardly restrained, expressing
itself in his face, above all in his eyes, which he called the most
important means of communicating his wishes. As he conducted
without a score – which the Dresden press decried as an affectation –
he looked at his players all the time and each felt that his eye was on
him. Now and again he stopped beating time in order to let a
melodic line, such as the low strings' recitative, 'speak'. At other
times he showed the power he wielded over the players with his
baton, coaxing from them the most delicate pianissimo, outbursts
of despair, ecstasies of enthusiasm. He said once that the spell he
seemed to cast on an orchestra was admired, but no one realized
what his magic cost him.

His programme note for the Dresden Ninth consisted of quota-

tions from Goethe's *Faust*; it was taken by some as proof of a purely
literary and imagistic approach to Beethoven's music, though the
performance itself should have proved otherwise. As he said himself later: what was expressed in that first movement could not be
put into words, though he had tried. Instead, he had sought to
induce in the audience, by reference to one of the greatest works of
poetry, that 'elevation of sensibility' without which Beethoven
could neither be performed nor appreciated.

About a month before the performance, Wagner sent the intendant a memorandum on the court orchestra. It was published for
the first time by Julius Kapp in 1910, and Richard Sternfeld included
it in the twelfth volume of the complete writings in 1912. It runs to
more than fifty pages of print and is one of the most important
documents of Wagner's life.

> I have spent the last three months, taking the greatest
> pains, in subjecting everything I thought necessary to
> the strictest and most exact scrutiny, carefully weighing
> every point, leading to the revision and rewriting of
> some paragraphs two, three and even four times, and
> have now at last completed the enclosed work, in
> respect of which I beg to assure Your Excellency that I
> have not been motivated by any ulterior consideration.
> I trust that Your Excellency will accept the outcome of
> my labours with your accustomed kindness and above
> all will remain favourably inclined towards me, who
> have so much reason to be obliged to you.

The document is a detailed plan for improving the court
orchestra and bringing it up to strength. Nothing is overlooked :
the manning of the individual sections with 'Kammermusiker' and
'Akzessisten' (full-timers and part-timers), in which section we
learn that at that time one of the double basses also had to play the
bass tuba, prompting Wagner to urge a rise of at least 50 talers a year
for the overworked man, 'because he has to play two instruments
and needs the best nourishment possible to give him the strength';
the purchase of new instruments such as a double-pedal harp; a
roster for the string-players, dividing their duties fairly between
operas with their widely varying requirements, farces, ballets and
divertissements, and summer performances; above all, a concen-
trated seating plan for the orchestra: for good ensemble, the width

should never be more than twice the depth. The paper culminates in two proposals: the institution of orchestral concerts, and the erection of a new concert-hall complex facing the Zwinger, with elegant apartments at the front of the building that could be let at very advantageous rents, and two concert halls, a large and a small, at the back. Finally there are tables with exact reckonings of the current expenditure on the orchestra and of the additional sums needed if the plan were put into operation: the difference would be no more than 1750 talers a year.

There is not a sentence in the memorandum, Newman remarks, that does not carry its own justification. It is the work of an idealist, but not a fantasist. Above all, it is the work of a man who places the interests of art above his own personal interest. Why else should Wagner care about the future of the King of Saxony's orchestra? His sacrifice of three months of his scanty leisure to this work is an example of selflessness almost without parallel in the history of musical institutions. The people who accused him of egoism simply did not know him. He may well have shown egoism in daily life, like most of us. 'But as an artist he was from first to last beyond fear and above reproach.' (NLRW, I, pp. 463ff.)

He had to wait a year for an answer and when it came, early in 1847, his plan was rejected. The experience played a decisive part in driving him into the arms of political discontent and revolution. Another factor was the appointment of a new dramaturg to the court theatre in the person of Karl Gutzkow, who did not restrict the exercise of his dictatorial power to plays but extended it to operas. 'My pain at being condemned, under these conditions, to suffer ever greater dissatisfaction and consequent lack of activity . . . is so great and sincere that, were external circumstances more favourable, I would undoubtedly already have sought to leave His Majesty's service altogether,' Wagner wrote to Lüttichau on 9 July 1847. 'Notwithstanding, however, I cannot remain in thrall to these circumstances, and should Your Excellency not see your way, officially, at the very least to removing Dr Gutzkow from any involvement in operatic matters . . . I am fully determined to leave it to the wisdom of His Majesty the King to decide to what extent and in what manner my proven abilities as dramatic composer and conductor of good music in His Majesty's service could be employed so that an honorarium could be paid me, sufficient at the least to insure the obligations I have already incurred towards the pension fund, but without laying on me any official connections or duties in relation to operatic matters.'

He could not regard it as other than a curse that the whole of his creative prompting was towards dramatic form, he wrote to Ferdinand Heine on 6 August, because he was forced to see the complete mockery of all his aspirations in the miserable constitution of the Dresden theatre. 'Perhaps you've already heard something of my break with Lüttichau about three weeks ago; it was so completely decisive that there can be no thought of reconciliation, especially from my side: the occasion of it was Gutzkow. But in fact the particular circumstances are quite unimportant: it's the old fight of knowledge and conviction against the brute despotism of ignorance.'

11

Germanic Myth and Greek Tragedy

Two intellectual experiences while Wagner was in Dresden, though apparently remote from his musical activities, proved to be of decisive importance in his further development: his encounters with Germanic myth and with Greek tragedy.

Ever since Lehrs, whose interests embraced German antiquities as well as the classics, had introduced him in Paris to the legends of the Wartburg War, Tannhäuser and Lohengrin, he had not rested in his efforts to learn more. Now in Dresden a major book on the subject had fallen into his hands, and when he went to Teplitz on holiday in July 1843 people noticed that on his solitary walks he always took with him a bottle of mineral water and the one book. It was Jacob Grimm's *German Mythology*.[1]

The first impression was extraordinarily exciting. He could discern only a 'rough, fissured terrain, overgrown with tangled scrub', and looked in vain for any structural outlines or defined forms. And yet the book exerted a magical fascination over him. This was the feverish excitement that prevented him from composing *Tannhäuser* during that summer.

Slowly the tangle of gods and heroes, heaven and earth, time and eternity, fate and salvation – assembled by Grimm with a true 'devotion to the insignificant' – began to clear, and he began to make out a world of living figures, 'three-dimensional and primevally akin': he saw them before him, understood their speech and could not fathom how it was that he already knew their ways so well. 'I can describe the effect of this on my spirit in no other way but by calling it a complete rebirth,' he wrote a quarter of a century later in *Mein Leben*, 'and just as we are moved and amazed at the intoxicating joy of children when they experience their first, new, instantaneous perceptions, so too my own looks radiated delight at a similar miraculous perception of a world in which, until then, I had been like a child in the womb, apprehending but blind.'

Wagner improved on this initial experience, which bears all the signs of an intuition of genius, with further study. In October 1843 he moved into a pleasant, spacious flat on the Ostra-Allee, with a view of the Zwinger. There were three things that made it particularly dear to him: a concert grand by Breitkopf & Härtel; Cornelius's title-page to the *Nibelungenlied* (it still exists, in its original frame, in the Wagner Archives in Bayreuth); but above all the library that he built up in accordance with the programme of reading he set himself, in the classics, medieval German and history. After his flight the library was retained by Heinrich Brockhaus, the brother of his brothers-in-law Friedrich and Hermann, as security for 500 talers he had lent Wagner in 1846. To begin with Wagner hoped he would soon be able to redeem his books. 'One other request, my dear Hermann,' he wrote on 2 February 1851, 'please ask Heinrich from me to keep the library together, as he acquired it. He will probably be relieved of it before long, when he has had his money back, so I would be obliged to him if he would look on the books only as security, not as payment.' But Wagner's constantly fluctuating fortunes and his perennial financial troubles meant that he had to give up the hope of redeeming the library. In the end he lost interest in it altogether, when he began to form a new collection in Tribschen and Bayreuth.[2]

What he could not buy he borrowed from the State Library, with the help and advice of the librarian, Hofrat Dr Grässe, himself an authority on Germanic myth and legend and a literary historian – and, incidentally, the founding father of 'Wagnerology'. Stimulated by the Grimm brothers, he went back to the Nordic sources: the Eddas, the Vilkina and Niflunga sagas, the Heimskringla and the Volsunga saga. Paul Hermann, whose German translation of Icelandic sagas was published in 1923, came to the conclusion that Wagner must have acquired a good enough command of Old Norse to be able to understand the original texts, using F. H. von der Hagen's translation as a crib: that, at least, is the inference to be drawn from his characteristic use of certain words, such as 'fahren', 'fällen' and 'taugen', in their archaic senses. In *Mein Leben* Wagner claimed to have made himself as familiar with Old Norse literature as was possible without a 'fluent' knowledge of the language –

which does not exclude the possibility of his having a rudimentary knowledge of it. This hypothesis was confirmed by the discovery of a copy of Ludwig Ettmüller's edition of the Vaulu-Spá (Völuspa, 'Sayings of the Prophetess'), comprising the original Old Norse text, a German translation, a commentary and a vocabulary, in Wagner's Dresden library. This is an important key to the language of his texts, especially the *Ring*.

Goethe confessed that though he had known the tales from the Eddas from an early age and enjoyed retelling them, he had never been able to draw them into the orbit of his poetry because, unlike the figures of Greek mythology, they completely eluded his power of visualization.[3] What was it then that gave Wagner the power to breathe life into the nebulous Nordic figures of Germanic myth so effectively that they gained a validity that held good beyond the frontiers of the German nations? It was that perception of them as 'primevally akin', 'primevally indigenous'. He was helped to this by the example of Jacob Grimm, who had made a thorough exploration of the Norse myths in order to rediscover the lost German myths. It was supremely fascinating, Grimm wrote to F. C. Dahlmann, to learn to distinguish between what was typical and what was individual. He took from the Nordic sources whatever the German folk tradition confirmed as being common Germanic material, and added some traits from German legend, folk tales, popular superstition and custom, which – though often handed down in a pallid and distorted form – nevertheless betrayed mythic origins. In this way he succeeded against all odds in restoring to view the *German* mythology, the outlines of which had been obliterated and obscured by the accretions of a thousand years.

Wagner was to adapt Grimm's methods to the composition of his poetic text: he 'translated' the Germanic myths from Scandinavian into German, or rather, so far as the heroic sagas are concerned, he translated them back into German, for long before Icelandic skalds had told of the exploits of Sigurd, German singers at the courts of Frankish kings in the sixth century had sung of Siegfried. The difference between the old German and the old Scandinavian poems should not be under-estimated. Andreas Heusler, one of the great authorities on ancient Germanic literature, said that the difference between the character and the environment of the two societies meant that a gentler spirit pervaded the German epics, while the

Germanic heroic ideal was pushed to its extreme in the Nordic cycles.

The long and half-unconscious process of assimilation and Germanization of the Germanic myths was spread out over the years from the seminal experience in Teplitz in the summer of 1843 to the first version he wrote down in 1848, *The Nibelung Myth as the Scenario for a Drama* (*Der Nibelungenmythos als Entwurf zu einem Drama*, RWGS, II, pp. 156ff.).[4] One obvious outward sign of it is the use of German forms of the names, and Oswald Spengler's use of the Norse form 'Fafnir' in his critique of the *Ring* in *The Decline of the West* indicates that at the time of writing he knew it only at second-hand.[5] The scene of the action is transferred from chill, foggy cliffs and coastlines to an Alpine landscape, to German forests and the autumnal Rhine valley. The Nordic savagery of the characters is tempered by generosity and warmth of heart, gruesomeness is transformed into grandeur. Characteristics from German folk tales are introduced as well, in the spirit of Jacob Grimm: Wagner even discerns the prototype of Till Eulenspiegel in Siegfried, the boy who sets out to learn fear, just as Grimm, too, sees something of 'Eulenspiegel's temper' in Siegfried in the smithy. Mime's exclamation

> Nun ward ich so alt
> wie Höhl und Wald
> und hab' nicht sowas gesehn!

comes almost word for word out of the Grimm brothers' version of the Hessian tale of the goblin changeling (who, when tricked into revealing himself, cries out: 'Nun bin ich so alt wie der Westerwald und hab' nicht gesehn, daß man in Schalen kocht').

Finally, Wagner's setting of the tales to music can be regarded as another act of Germanization, for whereas the Norwegian and Icelandic poets recited their lays, the Germans – at least as represented by the Goths, Franks, Friesians and Angles – sang them to the accompaniment of the harp.[6]

In his later phase Nietzsche borrowed a term from Paul Bourget's writing on French *romantisme*, and spoke of a kind of *'exotisme'* in Wagner's 'Edda personages', comparable to that in Victor Hugo's *Les Orientales*, a yearning of the modern soul for the piquant attractions of what was remote and foreign: but it is abundantly plain that the comparison is completely without foundation. Even if Wagner had wanted to, he would have been incapable of creating a work of art out of nothing more than an impulsive yearning for the exotic.

On the other hand, the champions of a Nordic ideal have accused him of precisely the opposite: that he failed to preserve the spirit of the Old Norse poems. They are quite right, though not in the sense they meant: Wagner simply never intended to preserve that spirit. His aim was more specifically German: he was confident that even the text on its own was something the nation would treasure, in years to come as well as in the present. His purpose was simultaneously more than merely German. He made fun of his imitators, who stuffed their works with unpronounceable gods and heroes and for whom the exotic, the curious, was precisely the attraction. For him the transposition of the Germanic myths to a more local, German setting was the means whereby he could develop the universally human elements of the myths: 'My heart, my spirit were inhabited by an ultimate, supreme world glory; the old German World-Ash, the Norns' tree, through me was to spread its mighty crown of foliage over every feeling human heart.' (KLRW, II, p. 215)

But before he was ready for that, another, seemingly unrelated precondition had to be fulfilled. His boyhood reading of Greek literature under the tutelage of his Uncle Adolf and his schoolmaster Sillig had ended prematurely when he stopped going to school. But the desire for the 'eternals of humanist culture' stayed with him even during the distractions of his wanderjahre, and in the midst of his Parisian misery he used to say to Lehrs that he wished he could read the Greek Classical authors in the original. With the wisdom of experience Lehrs advised him against the attempt: Greek could be read with true enjoyment only if it were studied seriously. He added, as a well-meaning consolation, that with the music he had in him Wagner would probably manage to learn as much as he pleased without the help of lexicons or grammars. In saying so he expressed an awareness of an inner association, though he could hardly have realized its full significance at the time.

As Wagner took up the Greeks again now in Dresden, he did it 'in order to approach the studies I had undertaken in Old and Middle High German in the proper frame of mind'. He made it easier for himself this time by reading them in translation.

In April 1847 his debts had driven him to move into a less expensive flat in the Marcolini Palais some distance from the city centre. The mansion had a quiet, spacious garden at the rear, laid out in the French style. After spending his mornings working on the orchestral sketch of *Lohengrin*, he used to take refuge from the summer heat in the shade of the old trees and there steep himself in the world of Greek civilization.

The 'intoxicating picture of a day in the Attic theatre' arose before him out of the pages of Droysen's translation of Aeschylus and the accompanying description of performances of the tragedies. He imagined the sight of twenty thousand Greeks filling the wide semicircle of the theatre of Dionysus at the foot of the Acropolis, and himself sitting among them as the action unfolded, watching the chorus of Argive elders, decked in wreaths, enter the *orchestra* and, to the accompaniment of the Apollonian cithara and the Dionysian aulos, begin to intone the mighty *parodos* of the *Oresteia*, in which, as Walter Kranz says, we first hear the soft, deep, heavy notes which form the mysterious primeval source of the trilogy, 'just as the prelude of Wagner's Nibelung trilogy is a sea of sound out of which the giant work rises up'.[7]

Ancient destiny is fulfilled on the *skene* in front of the palace of the Atrides. Between the exchanges of dialogue the action is ever present in the songs of the chorus, dipping down into the primeval origins of music. Narratives and commentaries give the background to the tragic action in words, music and dance. 'One can only marvel . . . at the weave of the primeval tapestry,' Goethe wrote to Wilhelm von Humboldt after reading the *Agamemnon*. 'The intermingling of past, present and future is so felicitous that one becomes oneself a seer, that is, like a god.'

After the crushing weight of the first play comes *The Libation-Bearers* with its persistent, ever renewed wail of lamentation. Many years later, after reading the *commos* of the *Choephore* aloud, Wagner said it reminded him of his own *Tristan*.

The third play, *The Eumenides*, strikes yet another note. The elders tell of the horror that seized all the onlookers at the Furies' sudden appearance. Beginning with the earliest sounds of childish babbling, they sing the invocation, accompanied only by the deepest notes of the aulos, and, wearing the black, snake-haired masks of the Furies themselves, they tread the measured dance 'to chain and ensnare the guilty one's mind'.

Athena appears at the door of her temple, lifts the curse and grants redemption through mercy and kindness where the stricter evaluations of justice have failed. Night has fallen on the festival crowd. Women and girls in white robes, with flowers in their hair and torches in their hands, come out of the stage temple to accompany the chorus, transformed from Furies to Kindly Ones, to their new shrine.

Wagner experienced as vividly as if he were there how the tragedy was transformed, as it ran its course, into a celebration in which the goddess, the Eumenides, and the whole audience all had a part to play. He confessed that as he read he was in a transport, from which he never recovered to the extent of being fully reconciled to modern literature again. 'My ideas about the significance of drama, and of the theatre in particular, took their definitive shape under the impact of those impressions.'(ML, pp. 402f.)

Greek drama had for far too long been regarded as a purely literary creation, in which music played at most an ancillary, decorative role. 'It was different in Athens,' Herder has a Greek say; 'our pronunciation, our declamation, our gestures and music are all lost to you, yet your room feels too small, your house is filled with ringing spirits of the air, when you but read our Greek dramas. Imagine this determinedly advancing, ever-changing melos; hear it in your mind and fall silent over your silent theatre.'

Wagner's reliving of the Greek experience through the spirit of music was not just a consequence of antiquarian studies, but was a response of his creative disposition and practice. With the music he had in him, as Lehrs had prophesied, he was able to experience the work of Aeschylus across more than two millennia, with an immediacy that had been granted to no other person in modern times. Nietzsche writes: 'There are such affinities between Aeschylus and Wagner as to be an almost tangible reminder of the relative nature of all concepts of time; it is very nearly as though some things belong next to each other and time is only a mist that makes it hard for our eyes to see that they do.'

That this was more than a rhetorical conceit has been confirmed by more recent research showing that the example of Aeschylus was the essential factor that enabled Wagner to create his drama out of the ruins of Germanic myth. It is a successor to Greek art of a very different order from the classicism of the Renaissance or the eighteenth century, lying not in the adoption of material or the imitation of forms but in an inner affinity.

In the course of this Greek summer of 1847 he pressed on through the other tragedians to Aristophanes, whose *Birds* exhilarated and delighted him, and to Plato, whose *Symposium* afforded him such a view of the beauty of life in Athens that he felt more at home there than in the modern world. The musicians, artists and writers among whom he moved were puzzled to hear him talking about Greek literature and history and not about music. A young Austrian poet, Johannes Nordmann, who was introduced to him by Wilhelmine Schröder-Devrient, was impressed above all by the profundity of Wagner's general culture. 'He talked about the Greek dramatists with a sympathy and understanding that one would seek in vain among some university professors; but even at that date I noticed that his favourite topic was German myth. The hour that I spent under the spell of his conversation became, in recollection, like attendance at a sacrament of the mind.' (GLRW, II, p. 203)

In the midst of his financial worries, professional frustrations and efforts to gain public recognition for his operas, it was his Greek studies that enabled Wagner to escape time and the world and filled him with a happiness more durable than he ever experienced before.

12

Lohengrin

At the same time as he had read the poem of the Singers' War in Paris, Wagner had read a long-winded Middle High German version of the legend of Lohengrin, the son of Parsifal the Grail King, placed by its author in the mouth of Wolfram von Eschenbach, who in fact wrote a very brief outline of the tale at the end of his *Parzival*. Far from stimulating his creative imagination, if anything this version put Wagner off: he found it bathed the figure of Lohengrin in a mystic gloom that inspired the same distaste that he felt for crudely carved and painted images of saints. 'The old German poem which records this most poetic of legends is the paltriest and most pedestrian thing of its kind that has come down to us.' (To Albert Wagner, 4 August 1845)

But as the first impression faded, the essence of the legend grew clearer in his mind. Significantly he came to recognize a prototype in Greek mythology, in the story of the fateful love of the god Zeus for a human woman, Semele. For the time being, however, he was unable to discover the right form in which to cast the legend, which was left to mature, half-forgotten, at the back of his mind until it was ready for realization.

In June 1845, immediately after finishing *Tannhäuser*, Wagner vowed solemnly to do nothing for a year but 'live off the fat' of his library, for if a dramatic work was to have any significance and originality he felt that it must be the product of a distinct period in the creator's life that was a recognizable advance on previous stages. 'An advance, a period of that importance is not going to be made every six months; only several years will suffice to produce the stage of full maturity.' (To Karl Gaillard, 5 June 1845) He did not realize that he had already made the advance and embarked on the next period.

A few weeks later he went to Marienbad to take the cure. On the way he made a brief stop in Leipzig; Heinrich Brockhaus, who took him on the town, noted in his diary that he was in a state of extreme nervous debility, and that music was a torment to him for the present. But Marienbad was enjoying magnificent weather and this soon restored his spirits. Every morning he went walking in the woods on the outskirts of the town, carrying a fat volume that contained Wolfram's *Titurel* and *Parzival* and the epic poem of Lohengrin. Lying beside a stream in the shade of the trees, he communed with the strange and yet familiar figures of the cycle of Grail legends. Once again, as with *Das Liebesverbot* and *Tannhäuser*, the volcanic soil of Bohemia stimulated his imagination: suddenly the Grail knight stood before him fully armed in a finished dramatic form. Mindful of his doctor's warning to avoid any work of an agitating or exciting character, he sought diversion in drafting a comedy on the mastersingers' guild of Nuremberg, to be an appendage, like a satyr play, to the more serious minstrels' conflict of *Tannhäuser*.

But in vain. One day, while sitting in a bath of medicinal waters, the longing to get on with *Lohengrin* overcame him with such force that he cut short the prescribed time for soaking, pulled on his clothes, rushed home like a madman and began to write the prose scenario. He even sketched one of the principal musical themes of the third act, 'Fühl' ich zu dir so süß mein Herz entbrennen', in the margin.[1]

He had spent nearly all the time in the woods and on the hills, he wrote to his brother Albert, but his thoughts had been unable to rest, 'and consequently yesterday I finished writing out a very detailed plan for *Lohengrin*, which I am greatly pleased with, indeed I freely confess that it fills me with joy and pride . . . My inventive and creative powers are fully engaged in this work.' (4 August 1845)

Once back in Dresden he took only a few weeks to write the verse text. The structure of the text of *Tannhäuser* had demonstrated Wagner's skill in its blending of the two legends of the Wartburg and the Venusberg; now he united countless threads from legendary and historical sources in a simple, easily comprehensible action. The sources are a particularly rewarding field of research in the case of *Lohengrin* but, without going into detail, suffice it to mention here the works by C. T. Lucas, Joseph Görres, the Grimms, Karl Lachmann, San Marte and Karl Simrock that Wagner owned in Dresden. One work, which he himself acknowledged as a source, was missing from his library, but that may have been due to its size: Jacob Grimm's *Weistümer*, about early German legal precedents, three of the seven volumes of which had been published by 1842. Several elements in the plot show that he must also have known Grimm's *Deutsche Rechtsaltertümer* ('Antiquities of German Law') of 1828: the conduct of the trial in the first act, Telramund's defiance of sentence (the offence of 'Urteilsschelte') in the second, and Lohengrin's bringing of a 'charge against the dead' in the third.[2] After the failure of *Konradin*, Ferdinand Hiller's opera about the last of the Hohenstaufens, Wagner admitted that perhaps he was partly to blame, for not having advised Hiller to read the *Weistümer*.

Many years later he told Cosima he was about to say something that would sound very like self-praise: he thought that in *Lohengrin* he had painted a 'perfect picture of the Middle Ages'.

Specifically, *Lohengrin* portrays the early, Romanesque Middle Ages, as opposed to the High Gothic era of *Tannhäuser*. 'There is much too much ceremonial for the noble, naïve simplicity of that time,' he wrote to Ferdinand Heine in 1853, apropos of the Weimar production:

> What gives my *Lohengrin* its individual colouring is
> precisely the fact that what we see is an old *German*
> kingdom in its loveliest, most ideal form. Nobody here
> does anything for reasons merely of the custom or
> etiquette of the court, but on the contrary everyone
> present takes a personal interest in every move; there is
> no despotic splendour here, with 'bodyguards' (oh! oh!)
> pressing back the crowd to 'make way' for the lords and
> ladies, but small boys in attendance on a young woman,
> for whom everyone gladly moves aside voluntarily . . .
> Look at my herald, how he sings as if everything
> affected him personally! (RWBC, p. 444)

This historical setting is necessary if the arrival of Lohengrin is to have the effect of a supernatural world invading the real world, and there is nothing worse than enveloping the work in a generalized fairy-tale atmosphere and so blurring the contrast between the two worlds which are destined from the outset to conflict tragically. The accurate representation of the historical setting fulfils another important dramaturgical function: the relationship of Lohengrin and Elsa is not another tragedy of the passions, like *Tannhäuser*. Their tragedy is grounded in a very sensitive area of male and female psychology and the sphere of action is a purely mental one. This inner action needs the powerful contrast and counterweight on the stage of an external action, provided here by the historical conflicts of immediate national interests and the larger concepts of empire, and of paganism and Christianity.

One consequence of the interiority of the conflict between Lohengrin and Elsa was that Wagner himself hesitated for a time over the necessity of a tragic outcome. One of the people in Dresden to whom he read the text was a literary amateur, Dr Hermann Franck, by whose opinion, delivered with cool discrimination and restraint, he set particular store. Franck considered that the punishment of Elsa by the departure of Lohengrin was repugnant. He recognized that it was in accord with the elevated poetic ambience of the legend, but doubted whether it would satisfy an audience's tragic sense in the theatre. Infected by this doubt, Wagner considered alternative endings, with Lohengrin forgoing his higher nature in order to remain with Elsa, or with both undertaking a penance and withdrawing from the world together. But when he discussed the question with Frau von Lüttichau, the intendant's wife, a woman of discernment, she retorted that Franck must be completely devoid of poetry if he could not see that *Lohengrin* could only end tragically.

Four years after he had finished it Wagner was again stricken with doubts about the ending, when the writer Adolf Stahr raised the same objections as Franck. The identical nature of his criticism made Wagner – who by then had moved some way away from the frame of mind in which he had written the work – hesitate again, and he wrote a hasty letter to Stahr conceding that he was right. This upset Liszt, who had defended Lohengrin's behaviour against Stahr, but Wagner soon changed his mind again. At the time he was writing the autobiographical essay *A Communication to my Friends*, which recalled to him the spirit in which he had written *Lohengrin*, and he now recognized the work as the tragedy of the artist, who puts his faith in the power of love to understand, when the world about him has lost the ability to love or understand – an archetype, even, of the tragedy of life in the modern world. (*Eine Mitteilung an meine Freunde*, RWGS, IV, p. 297)

On the day that he took the manuscript of the *Communication* to the post in Zürich he wrote to Liszt: 'Just two words – *you* were *right* about *Lohengrin* – not Stahr. I retract my endorsement of his opinion – it was too hasty!' (23 August 1851)

That was not the last occasion on which Wagner was to consider the implications of the tragedy of *Lohengrin*. When he was writing a preface for a French prose translation of the texts of his operas, in 1860, he was obliged to subject them all to close scrutiny. In doing so he was greatly moved by *Lohengrin*, he told Mathilde Wesendonk, and he could not help regarding it as the most tragic, because reconcilement was to be found only if a fearfully wide view of the world was taken. But he no longer dreamt of denying the necessity of the tragedy: he had read Schopenhauer and the Indian philosophers and now he sought reconcilement, at least notionally, beyond the bounds of time and space, in the idea of the myth of rebirth. (Early August 1860)

In spite of his complete absorption by his subject Wagner did not immediately throw himself into the composition of the music after completing the text in November 1845. The work lay fallow throughout the winter while he immersed himself ever deeper in its underlying mood: the sense of his isolation as a creative artist had overpowered him, he said. It is reflected in the short notices he published in the press around that time, in anticipation of his performance of the Choral Symphony: the world with which Beethoven had grown familiar was, alas, the world of loneliness. He had been seized by an immense longing to turn to the real world and to share its joys and happiness. 'Receive him, take him to your hearts, listen in amazement to the wonders of his language, in whose new-found wealth you will soon experience wonders and sublimities such as you have never heard before.' (RWGS, XII, pp. 205ff.)

In May 1846 Wagner and Minna, with a dog called Peps and a parrot called Papo, retired for three months to the peace of the village of Gross-Graupa, near the royal summer palace of Pillnitz. 'God be praised, I am in the country!... I am living in a completely unspoiled village – I am the first townie who has ever rented rooms here.' (To Gaillard, 21 May) The sculptor Gustav Adolf Kietz, the younger brother of Ernst Benedikt, who visited them there,

recorded how Wagner, returning home from a walk, greeted him in
the highest of spirits. After dining Kietz had seen over the accommodation, which consisted of two whitewashed rooms with the
most primitive furnishings. And in a place like that, he added,
Richard Wagner, whose love of luxury was already a byword, felt
completely happy![3]

But before he started composing he had, as always, to get his
theories clear in his head, which he did this time in a letter to Franck:
'Of course I've argued with you a great deal: we are still not of one
mind over *Lohengrin*; but I've settled down to it again feeling
completely fresh, and I'm now quite clear about it in *my own* mind.'
The music would leave nobody in any doubt as to how Lohengrin
himself felt: the one great advantage of uniting a text with music
seemed to him to be that it enabled characters to be presented
in a certain 'three-dimensional concentration and entirety', which
would only be weakened by too much 'subsidiary motivation'. 'If
your conscience lets you, do give me your blessing for my work,
for I am buckling down to it now with inexpressible pleasure and
great hopes: – you will like my music this time – I think that I have
again learned a great deal.' (30 May 1846) He finished the composition sketch of the whole opera on 30 July, just two and a half
months after starting it.[4]

On 29 July he received a visit from the sixteen-year-old Hans von
Bülow, already an ardent admirer of his works. Wagner wrote in
his album: 'If there glows in you a true, pure warmth for art, then
the fair flame will surely kindle one day; but knowledge is what will
feed and fan the glow until it becomes a strong flame.'

He began the orchestral sketch in September, after returning to
Dresden, and for the first and only time he started with the third act
of the work. Clearly he wanted to establish the controversial tragic
ending as soon as possible.

He interrupted the composition in December, in order to prepare
Gluck's *Iphigenia in Aulis* for performance. Discovering the customary Spontinian retouchings in the Berlin score, he sent for the
Paris edition, the text and music of which he then revised as spar-
ingly as possible, so that his own hand should be imperceptible. The
only part he had to alter completely was the customary happy
ending, which Goethe's *Iphigenie* had rendered quite unacceptable;
in place of the marriage of Iphigenia, he had Artemis appear *ex
machina* and wrote for her an arioso recitative in which she claims

Iphigenia as her priestess, to serve her on a distant shore, and exhorts the quarrelling Greeks to make up their differences:

> Nicht dürste ich nach Iphigenias Blut,
> es ist ihr hoher Geist, den ich erkor!
> Mein Opfer führ ich in ein fernes Land,
> als Priesterin dort meine Huld zu lehren . . .
> Nun seid versöhnt, versöhnet bin auch ich!
> Die Winde wehn, ruhmvoll sei eure Fahrt!

A marginal note in his own copy refers to his reading of Euripides.

Most important of all, he corrected a long-standing error about Gluck's intentions as to the tempos of the overture. When in 1854 Wagner wrote a concert ending for the overture to replace Mozart's, he defended his views in an article published in the *Neue Zeitschrift für Musik*. (RWGS, V, pp. 111ff.) Newman commented that no one today would think of disputing Wagner's reading of the overture.

This revival of *Iphigenia in Aulis*, which was decried at that time as Gluck's most dated work, was an act of the same order as the performance of the Choral Symphony. It is interesting to note that Wagner's edition of the opera still met with Hanslick's approval at the time of his feud with Wagner: he said that it combined a conservative sense of the characteristic features of the past with a clear-eyed recognition of the needs of the present day. The additions in the last act increased the dramatic effect without forcing themselves into the foreground of the attention.[5]

We can perceive an inner association between Wagner's interest in Greek society and literature, his editing of *Iphigenia* in the spirit of Euripidean tragedy and the composition of *Lohengrin*: just as Artemis's recitative recalls the style of *Lohengrin*, so *Lohengrin* breathes something of the Apollonian spirit of Greek drama. The good spirits nurtured by his Greek studies enabled Wagner to finish the orchestral sketch of the first and second acts and the prelude by 28 August 1847, and he wrote the full score in an incredibly short time, between 1 January and 28 April 1848.

'I took pains this time to place the music in so sure and plastic a relationship to the text and action that I can feel completely confident in the result. Trust me, and don't just put it down to infatuation with my own work,' he wrote to Liszt. (2 July 1850)

The plasticity to which he refers is well prepared by the text itself, in its avoidance of any secondary elements to distract from the central plot. The first act is a model of exposition. The events prior to the stage action are recounted in the charges made by Telramund and in Elsa's narration of her dream in such a form that they become active elements, anticipating the intervention of a higher power. The fact that Lohengrin's arrival with the swan has become the butt of endless facetious comment is due to the shortcomings of naturalistic representation when it comes to miraculous events, not to the poetry of the event itself: Pfitzner calls it 'one of the most marvellous moments, for both the eye and the heart, in all Wagner's work, and thus in all drama'.[6] After the trial by combat has revealed the 'judgement of Heaven', the feelings of everyone present, which have been poised tensely between hope and fear, find release in the joyful outpouring of the final chorus. As a result the musical line is at liberty to develop without restraint. Richard Strauss wrote to his librettist Hugo von Hofmannsthal that when he was asked to name a model operatic first act he always came back to the first act of *Lohengrin*.[7]

The spirit of the music governs even details of the text. While they were working on *Der Rosenkavalier* Strauss wrote to Hofmannsthal that he would like to have a 'contemplative ensemble' in the second act: after the bursting of some dramatic bombshell the action ought to stand suspended while everyone was lost in thought. As an example he cited the ensemble 'In wildem Brüten darf ich sie gewahren' from the second act of *Lohengrin*,[8] and in fact Wagner already anticipated this ensemble in his prose sketch, to play precisely the role of a general reflective pause after a dramatic explosion, the sudden appearance of Telramund. In the margin he noted 'Adagio', the only tempo marking in the whole of the scenario (in the score the passage is marked 'moderately slow' after a 'fast', which amounts to the same, relatively speaking). Strauss and Wagner both recognized the same deep-seated musical need.

There is one instance, too, where the process of melodic invention can be observed in action. One day in 1850, when Wagner was leafing through the vocal score, he noticed how, at Elsa's appearance at her window before dawn in the second act, the clarinet plays a motive in B♭ major which is then heard again, 'fully developed, broad and resounding', as she goes to the church in her bridal array in broad daylight. This brought it home to him, he told Uhlig, just how his themes came into existence 'always in the context and in accord with the character of a plastic phenomenon'. 'Might it not interest you to speak your mind about how the thematic formal structure is bound to lead on to ever new formations along the lines I have started to explore?' He was by then alive to the principle of motivic development that he had used unconsciously in the *Holländer* and would bring to the peak of perfection in the *Ring*.

It is even possible to discern in *Lohengrin* the outlines of those extended musical forms which Alfred Lorenz traced in the later works. The first act, for instance, falls into three main sections: the first, concluding with Elsa's narration of her dream, ends with Lohengrin's motive in A♭ major; the second, of equal length, reaches to Lohengrin's entrance and ends with the same motive in A major; the third, twice as long and more excited in mood, culminates in the motive in B♭ major. Each time, therefore, the motive is raised a semitone: an indication that Wagner was conscious of these three large-scale periods as such. The resulting schema could be called a Bar-form on a very large scale, with the first Stollen of 270 bars, the second of 297 bars and the Abgesang of 562 bars.[9]

The musical framework of the entire opera is equally well constructed: the A major prelude to the first act is paralleled by its reprise in the third act in Lohengrin's Grail narration in the same key. Wagner cut the second part of this narration just before the first performance, from 'Nun höret noch, wie ich zu euch gekommen' to 'wo ihr in Gott mich alle landen saht'.[10] 'I have sung it to myself over and over again and am convinced that this second section would only lower the temperature,' he wrote to Liszt. (2 July 1850) Though he only referred here to the dramatic effect of the cut, it can also be justified in terms of the musical form: it meant that the narration as revised corresponds to the Act I prelude in length, too.

The harmonic technique is more sophisticated than in *Tannhäuser*. Wagner cited as an example the three polyphonic woodwind phrases accompanying Elsa's entrance in Act I, 'Sie naht, die hart Beklagte'. Uhlig, who was going to do the vocal score, was amazed when he saw how far the music modulated in so few bars, and even more amazed when he played them through and discovered how natural the modulation sounded. (RWGS, X, pp. 191f.) Heinrich Porges wrote an introduction to *Lohengrin* for King Ludwig,[11] and when he read it to Wagner the latter drew his attention to the significance of modulations of that kind: when Elsa's theme is played after her line 'Dir geb' ich alles, was ich bin!', the modulation to A♭ major represents the expression in her eyes, which strikes to Lohengrin's innermost soul and kindles love in his heart. Whereas up to that moment his words have sounded rather studied, he now speaks from the bottom of his heart. 'He got out the vocal score', Porges goes on, 'and sang the passage with truly thrilling expression. He is inimitable in his ability to strike home to the unique point of a psychological motive.'

The use of the chorus, going far beyond its conventional operatic role, illustrates the influence of Wagner's reading of Aeschylus. Porges draws attention to some of the particular felicities. At Lohengrin's entrance the male half of the chorus is divided into two four-part ensembles, who toss brief exclamations to and fro between small groups, until they all come together in a resounding fortissimo cry of 'Ein Wunder! Ein Wunder!', and only then do the women, falling on their knees, join in with 'Dank, du Herr und Gott . . .'. Then, while Lohengrin gazes sadly after the swan, in the sempre pianissimo 'Wie faßt uns selig süßes Grauen', Wagner uses the new technique of having the altos and tenors (the first tenors falsetto) sing in unison, which results in a unique veiled timbre.

Lohengrin marks the end of Wagner's first creative period, but it already belongs to the second in one respect: the instrumentation. Before the pupil advances to the polyphonic writing of *Tristan* and *Meistersinger*, Richard Strauss advises in his edition of Berlioz's treatise on instrumentation, he ought to study the 'model compendium' of the score of *Lohengrin*: the treatment of the wind instruments, in particular, is on an unprecedented level of perfection. Wagner assigns specific timbres to individual characters and situations, which had never previously been done with complete consistency. In order to enrich his palette for this purpose he extended the romantic principle of 'tonal blending', devising new instrumental combinations, and he also adapted the preclassical principle of employing the various timbral groups like the different stops of an organ. Supplementing the woodwind with the so-called 'third group' – cor anglais and bass clarinet – meant that he could now paint any triad in any homogeneous primary colour he chose.

Wagner used his new orchestral sound most perfectly in two utterly different passages: in the prelude to the opera and in the scene between Ortrud and Telramund at the beginning of the second act. In the latter he succeeded in expressing the threatening and seductive power of evil in pure sound, above all by the use of the bass clarinet and of the flute in its very lowest register. The 'blue–silver beauty' of the prelude, as Thomas Mann called it, is achieved by the following means: the four strophic variations on the Grail theme, played in changing registers in a slow crescendo by the violins, woodwind, horns and other brass in turn, are framed by the violins in eight parts – four solo instruments and the rest divided – during which the accompanimental figures gradually develop into individual melodic lines, to which the players can lend individual expression.

Wagner himself, Liszt, Baudelaire, all tried to interpret the prelude in words. At the climactic unfurling of the Grail theme in full, Porges astonished Wagner by quoting the lines of the Pater ecstaticus from the last scene of *Faust*:

> Arrows, pierce through me, and
> Lances, subdue me, and
> Clubs, leave no form in me,
> Thunderstorms, storm in me![12]

But at a performance of *Lohengrin* the prelude has a dramatic function in addition to its musical effect. It has been asked how Lohengrin convincingly established his higher nature and mission, in view of the tragic conflict that results from them. It is a pertinent question if based on the text on its own: but the prelude entirely satisfies our instincts on that score in its evocation of the realm of the Grail whence he comes, and which is recalled at every decisive moment in the action. This is one of those instances that prove that no proper assessment can be made of Wagner's skill in characterization and motivation without taking the music into account.

Although he had whole-heartedly adopted Lohengrin's cause from the first, he demonstrated, as in his other works, the genuine dramatist's ability to penetrate the other characters objectively. This power of empathy enabled him to enter so fully into Elsa's femininity that he felt a real, deep distress on her behalf that often moved him to tears. Porges found particularly interesting a comment he made about Ortrud and Telramund which showed the profound sympathy he brought even to them: they epitomized the 'misery of the outcast'.

On the title-page *Lohengrin* is designated a 'romantic opera', and it was customarily represented as such, although Wagner himself was energetically rebutting the term as early as 1851. 'Anyone who does not see anything in *Lohengrin* that goes beyond the "Christian–romantic" category, sees only a fortuitous exteriority, but has failed to grasp its essence.' (*A Communication to my Friends*, RWGS, IV, p. 298) In the final analysis romantics are reactionary beings: with their medieval subjects they are liable to medieval ideals. For himself, Wagner affirms, 'all our wishes and burning desires are in fact carrying us on into the future, and we search among the images of the past for the forms in which to give them an existence discernible to the senses, because the present day cannot furnish the forms they need.' (RWGS, IV, p. 311)

Thomas Mann concluded his memorial address on the occasion of the fiftieth anniversary of Wagner's death with a consideration of his relationship to the past and the future. It was possible, he said, to interpret Wagner's love of myth and the past as reactionary, and yet every grain of understanding of the true character of his artistry, instinct as it was with the drive towards innovation and liberation, categorically forbade taking his language and mode of expression literally instead of seeing them for what they were: an artistic idiom of a peculiarly uncharacteristic kind, conveying at every turn something quite different, something completely revolutionary. 'Every will that is directed towards the future can invoke him in its cause.'[13]

Wagner's origins lay in romanticism, but the disciple of the Greeks, the herald of Beethoven, the poet of mythology was on the point of leaving romanticism behind him.

13

Money Troubles

'Do you know what money troubles are?' Wagner asked Gaillard at the time of his retreat to Gross-Graupa in May 1846 to write *Lohengrin*. 'Lucky man, if you don't!' Newman remarks that we have been told in great detail about 'the women in Wagner's life', but the story of 'the talers in Wagner's life' is much more important. So a chapter devoted to the subject, in addition to passing references, hardly needs an apology.

In spite of his full-time appointment at the Dresden opera this perennial problem was once more on the point of developing from a crisis to a catastrophe. He had been 'penniless Johnny' when he returned to Dresden in 1842, but no sooner had he scored a success with *Rienzi* and been appointed hofkapellmeister than his old creditors, going back even to his schooldays, presented themselves again, so that he exclaimed that he fully expected a bill for services rendered from his wet-nurse.

As a consequence he never enjoyed his monthly salary of 125 talers to the full, while on the other hand he was never remotely near paying off all his debts. On a generous impulse Schröder-Devrient lent him 1000 talers at 5 per cent – a loan that was to prove fateful. Half of it was immediately despatched to Paris, to Kietz who was as poor as a church mouse, to his patient tailor Monsieur Loizeau, to the shoemaker, and to the pawnbroker with whom he had left his watch and silver cutlery. The other half had to go to pacify his Magdeburg creditors, who were threatening to sue. After meeting the most pressing demands in this way he was still left with commitments of a not immediately 'hostile' character, the sum total of which he was not precisely sure of himself. Chief among them was the new, large debt with which he had paid off some of the old ones.

This method of dealing with his debts is typical of Wagner's financial management. It could be described as an improvident gamble, staking everything on a single card. But from his point of view it all looked quite different. At no time did he ever experience a moment's doubt that he would triumph in the end, and even in a situation as desperate as he found himself in in London in 1855 – exiled from his homeland, hounded by the press, without any prospect of ever seeing his new works performed – he amused Berlioz with his assurance that in fifty years' time he would be supreme in the world of music: a prophecy that proved literally true.

Wagner was convinced that he possessed incomparably greater assets with which to balance out his ludicrous liabilities, only that he had not yet had the chance to realize them. The error in this calculation was simply that he was the only person who saw things that way, except perhaps for a loyal friend here and there who shared his faith. 'The one thing on which it all depends for me is: *winning time*, which is *winning life*,' he wrote to Ferdinand Heine in 1849. Those who loved him, who regarded the survival of his art as a matter of prime importance, would have to help him. 'They must not look on me as someone who needs help on his own account, but as an artist and a movement in art which they want to preserve for the future and not allow to founder. They shall own the works that I am eager to create, until such a time as they are able to present them to the *people*, as a property preserved for them.' (19 November; RWBC, pp. 352ff.)

Once *Rienzi* and the *Holländer* had been performed, his first priority was to find a publisher, so that he could supply scores as well as the performing rights which he confidently expected would very soon be in demand. The success *Der Fliegende Holländer* had enjoyed in three theatres, he wrote to Raymund Härtel on 11 July 1843, meant that he could no longer postpone the steps necessary to publication. 'If I do myself the honour to offer you herewith the publication . . . I am confident of making you a not unadvantageous proposition.' At first Breitkopf & Härtel expressed delight, especially as he had not mentioned the matter of an honorarium, and asked him for more details. But when he asked for a fee, and one of the order of 2000 talers, they found themselves regretfully obliged to decline his proposal.

Their letter revealed, Wagner replied, that they regarded his opera as worth the substantial costs of publication, but not worth a fee for him. 'Great as is my amazement, because I cannot grasp how anyone can risk a considerable capital outlay on something of which one is not sure whether it is worth the purchase price, yet at the same time it confirms the sorrowful opinion I have hitherto held that an original *German* opera, however fortunate the auspices under which it made its appearance, does not seem as safe a business proposition to a *German* publisher as a *French* opera, even though . . . it saw the light under the most inauspicious signs.' As Newman says, he was simply telling them, politely enough, what he thought of this attempt 'to rook a poor German composer'. (NLRW, I, p. 410)

Relations between the parties remained amicable, however, Breitkopf & Härtel undertook the publication of *Das Liebesmahl der Apostel*, and early in January 1844 Wagner even made them two further proposals with regard to the *Holländer*, suggesting that his fee should be made entirely dependent on its success. When, after renewed hesitation, they replied that they could not see their way to pay any royalties until sales had reached one hundred copies of the vocal score, Wagner realized that it was useless to pursue the matter any further.

We have no way of knowing whether it was his own idea or put to him by someone else; at all events Wagner now made one of the most fateful decisions of his whole life: to publish his scores himself. At first everything went smoothly. Schröder-Devrient approved his estimates and was ready to lend him the necessary capital at an appropriate rate of interest, and the court music publisher C. F. Meser was willing to publish on a 10 per cent commission. But after the contract had been signed, and substantial orders had already been placed with suppliers, an engraver and a printer, Devrient announced out of the blue that she had entrusted the management of her finances to her latest lover and husband-to-be. Wagner could not withdraw from his commitments and so had to try to raise the capital elsewhere.

Three of his friends in Dresden had the confidence in him to advance the money: the oboist Hiebendahl, the actor Hans Kriete and Anton Pusinelli. Pusinelli, a medical practitioner and amateur singer, had first approached Wagner to express his admiration of *Rienzi* when the Liedertafel male-voice choir serenaded their conductor on his thirtieth birthday. 'I have few friends,' Wagner wrote to him in August 1843, 'because I lack entirely the talent for going out to seek them. I am able to win very few by my own deserts, I have to rely on my good star to grant me them. But there is a certain look by which one at once recognizes another person – we only need to exchange names and we have gained a friend. And this brings happiness – so how could anyone doubt your faith? Let us both hold to it and be friends for life!'

His wish was granted, in spite of the occasional strains placed on the friendship by Wagner's financial demands. Pusinelli attended the Bayreuth Festival in 1876 and was able to offer his congratulations and share in the triumph for which he too had made sacrifices. He died two years later. On his deathbed he whispered 'My Richard, O my Richard, how you have had to fight, how misunderstood you have been! Only future centuries will know how to appreciate you! And you have been my friend.' 'He had a great heart, an unshakably great heart, which enabled him to understand everything,' Wagner mourned when he had the news of his death. 'It is hard to think of anyone who stood by me with the same heartfelt, unwavering loyalty.'

In 1844, when Pusinelli became the principal creditor in the young conductor's publishing venture, it was certainly a gesture of great confidence in his future. A contract was concluded on 25 June 1844 between Wagner on the one hand and Pusinelli, Hiebendahl and Kriete on the other, whereby the latter were to receive the proceeds from the publishing rights as collateral and interest. The success of the undertaking rested on two factors: the growth in demand and Meser's business efficiency. It emerged that Wagner had been mistaken about both.

He had twenty-five copies each of *Rienzi* and the *Holländer* printed by lithography. He wrote *Tannhäuser* straight out on to a paper suitable for reproducing by the same method and had a hundred copies of it printed. Every one of the copies of the full score that he sent out to theatres was sent back, Munich not even having troubled to open the package. 'I am learning by experience that here in Germany the more stir my works have created and the more they have made my name, the slower they are to spread,' he complained in a letter to Kietz in December 1844; 'why that should be, God alone knows!' In the final resort it was because his successes in Dresden remained of local importance, and only success in Berlin would have counted for anything more. And those in Dresden who

envied or disagreed with him, unable to shake his popularity with
the Dresden public, saw to it that in Berlin, as had been the case with
the *Holländer*, he was received by a press that was already predis-
posed against him.

The other important factor in Wagner's calculations, the court
music publisher, soon proved completely useless. Even when
demand for the music did pick up, from 1850 onwards, Meser was
incapable of exploiting the opportunities. 'Of all the music publishers in the world he is the least fit for such a business,' Wagner
raged in 1851, 'and if you distil the quintessence of the most shit-
scared, unreliable and cowardly philistine, what you get is Meser.'
(RWBC, p. 777)

By the end of 1845 at the latest, Wagner must have abandoned the
hopes he had placed in the publishing venture. 'I couldn't go on any
longer, taking steps I found most repugnant to ward off the
impending catastrophe in my financial status.' A ridiculous accident
struck him as an omen. Meser had arranged to meet him in a
wine-parlour to discuss the idea of doing business at the next Easter
trade fair. Wanting to encourage him, Wagner ordered a bottle of
the best Sauternes so that they could drink to success at the fair.
Suddenly they both shrieked and tried to spew out the tarragon
vinegar which had been served them by mistake. 'Good Lord!'
Meser gasped, 'that couldn't have been worse timed.' 'You're
right,' Wagner agreed, 'I think it bodes that a lot of things will turn
sour on us.' His sense of humour showed him in a flash that he
would have to save himself by some other means than dabbling in
trade fairs.

He had already had recourse to his usual method of raising
money by incurring new debts, with only partial success. He tried
in vain to borrow 2000 talers for two years from Ferdinand Hiller.
His luck was better with Pusinelli: 'God willing, this is the last time
that I shall bother you with a request like this.' He also borrowed
500 talers on this occasion from Heinrich Brockhaus, the brother of
his two brothers-in-law – this was the debt for which Heinrich took
his library as collateral in 1849. It is not known whether Heinrich
Schletter, a Leipzig patron of the arts who was a friend of his sister
Luise, lent him the 1000 or 1200 talers he asked for or not. He even
took it into his head to borrow the same sum from Meyerbeer, who
noted in his diary on 26 November 1846: 'wrote to Richard Wagner
(turned down his request for a loan of 1200 talers).'[1] He was, in

short, like a drowning man clutching at every straw to keep his head above water.

His economic circumstances could not be kept a secret any longer, and the rumours that spread in the city were fanned to the utmost by his opponents. 'You exhort me to do something about the gossip in the city, which is taking such an unprecedented and assiduous interest in me at the present time': the only answer he had for these fictions and exaggerations was contempt. Pusinelli published this letter in the *Dresdener Anzeiger*, giving it as his belief that to do so was in the best interests of his greatly maligned friend.

What finally caused the catastrophe to break over him came from a quarter where he had least looked for it. The arrival in Dresden of Wagner's niece Johanna, the stepdaughter of his brother Albert, unleashed first the jealousy and then the hatred of Schröder-Devrient, who sensed that she had passed her peak. She announced in public that Wagner had helped to oust her from her position, called in the 1000 talers she had lent him, together with the accumulated interest, and started legal proceedings.

Wagner had no alternative but to render Lüttichau an account of his debts. It says much for the intendant's esteem for him, in spite of everything, that on 16 August 1846 he was awarded an advance from the court orchestra pension fund of 5000 talers at 5 per cent to be repaid in instalments of at least 500 talers per annum from 1851. Since it was a condition of the loan that Wagner had to take out life insurance at an annual premium of 3 per cent of the borrowed capital, Lüttichau could hardly be accused of rash irresponsibility in the light of reasonable expectations, for no one could have foreseen Wagner's flight and exile. The payment of what amounted in effect to interest at 8 per cent – without taking the later amortization into account – took up almost two months' salary in a year, so Wagner succumbed to the temptation of not declaring some of his commitments, which he considered less urgent, and this in turn was a source of new embarrassments.

But his efforts to get the better of his desperate situation were not confined to making new debts. In spite of the experience he had had with the *Holländer* in Berlin, in spite of the failure of his attempt to dedicate the score of *Tannhäuser* to the King of Prussia – which had elicited the suggestion that he should set numbers from it for military band and get them performed at a colour-trooping – his hopes nonetheless rose again when the king commanded a performance of *Rienzi* in 1847. He travelled to Berlin in September to direct the rehearsals and conduct the first three performances. His letters to Minna show that he was doing his best to interpret all the signs favourably and that he even dreamt of a post in Berlin: '*Here* is more the place for my works, there's no denying it! – Well, – let us leave these fantasics!'

It is no wonder that the rumour became current that he was trying for an appointment as conductor and even that he had good prospects of getting one, garnished with special powers. Of course it spread at once to Dresden. 'You foolish friend, do you still allow yourself to be misled by gossip?' he reassured Ferdinand Hiller. 'As long as I am unable to exist without kapellmeistering, I much prefer to do it in Dresden, for a thousand reasons, all of which I will swear to on oath. You know how much I would like an adequate pension, enough to allow me to read all the books I already own and those I have yet to add to my collection.' (6 October 1847)

Secretly his wishes were more ambitious: apart from scoring a success with *Rienzi* he hoped for an audience with the king, word of whose interest in his operas had reached him. He wanted to obtain leave to read the text of *Lohengrin* aloud to him, in the hope of getting a first performance for it in Berlin. But all these hopes were dashed. *Rienzi*, handicapped by the shortcomings of the singer in the title role, nevertheless pleased the audiences, but the critics were the more ruthless for that very reason in demolishing it. Furthermore, a hunting party prevented the king from attending the first performance. Wagner set himself a date up to which he would leave the door open for the sudden summons to Potsdam that might seal his fate, but when the date was past he was forced to admit the failure of all his hopes of Berlin.

Just how deeply these hopes and disappointments had stirred him, more profoundly perhaps than he admitted to himself, is shown by the fact that in later years he had the same dream over and over again: Friedrich Wilhelm IV showed him boundless love and heaped consideration and favours upon him, so that when he stood before Ludwig II for the first time it was as though his dream was at last coming true. (DMCW, I, p. 554)

Since Count von Redern, who would have been the intermediary in arranging an audience, was a friend of Meyerbeer, it used to be surmised that the latter in some way influenced Wagner's lack of success. But his letters and diaries for the period in question offer no evidence whatever to support the suspicion. 'Today I am dining with Meyerbeer,' Wagner wrote to Minna on 3 October. 'He is leaving Berlin soon – so much the better' – presumably because he feared that a success with *Rienzi* might arouse Meyerbeer's jealousy. On the same day Meyerbeer wrote in his diary: 'Took Kapellmeister Richard Wagner to dine at mother's.' 23 October: 'In the evening to the dress rehearsal of Richard Wagner's opera *Rienzi.*' 26 October: 'First performance of the opera *Rienzi* by Wagner under the composer's direction. Wagner took two curtain calls.' The reason for his not writing anything about the work itself is that he had already heard it in Dresden. He had noted on 20 September 1844: 'In the evening I went to *Rienzi*, grand opera in five acts by Richard Wagner. Although dulled by a senseless over-abundance in the orchestration, there really are some truly beautiful, excellent things in it.' For the rest Meyerbeer proves to mention Wagner far less often than was generally expected. He was interested in the Wagner phenomenon, but he had as little inner sympathy for his work as Mendelssohn and Schumann, witness an entry in his diary for 23 October 1862: 'Because of the mental fatigue that listening to Wagner's *Lohengrin* caused me, I had never listened properly to the third act, never even stayed until the end. In order to accomplish it I went to the third act alone today.'

The last straw was when Küstner, the intendant, revealed to Wagner that he could not claim any fee for the two months he had spent rehearsing the work, since the management had only expressed a 'wish', but had not issued an 'invitation'. The only money he received was royalties for the three performances he had conducted 'as an advance'.

It was in a bad mood, Wagner wrote in his autobiography, that he finally took his leave from Berlin and his Berlin hopes. Seldom had he suffered so much from the eternal grey skies and the cold, damp weather. Moreover everything his friend Hermann Franck had told him about political and social circumstances in Prussia contributed to discouraging him completely. 'As I travelled with my wife along the homeward road through the bleak landscape of the Mark, I felt that the deep despair I was experiencing was a mood that I could be plunged into only once in a lifetime.'

Lüttichau was amazed when his second conductor came to him, straight from his guest appearance in Berlin, with the request for more money and for an increase in salary and parity with the principal conductor, Reissiger.[2] Even so he promised to pass on the request with his own recommendation that it should be granted. Wagner was astonished and ashamed when the intendant sent for him one day and showed him his letter of recommendation together with the king's consent. Wagner's version of it in *Mein Leben* could be taken for an overstatement, if it were not surpassed by the original, published by Glasenapp (II, pp. 262f).

'I beg most humbly to offer in the following my unqualified approval of Kapellmeister Wagner's deferential petition.' After the preamble, Lüttichau began by expressing the view that Wagner's stay in Paris had unfortunately given him so light-hearted a view of life that experiences as serious as the difficulties he was now undergoing were probably the only means of curing him. He had not known how to appreciate properly his good fortune in obtaining his post as kapellmeister with a salary of 1500 talers. Inflated praise of his talent had strengthened him in his extravagant ideas, so that he had envisaged making as much money with his operas as Meyerbeer had earned in Paris. The illusory notion of channelling the profit from his compositions to himself instead of leaving it to his publisher had led him to undertake their publication at his own risk and expense. After the disappointment of the hopes he had entertained of the Berlin production of *Rienzi*, he found himself in such straits that he was emboldened to approach the king directly with a petition for an increase in salary of 500 talers.

The intendant's letter concluded,

> As to the question of whether his retention here would
> be of sufficient value to justify granting him so
> exceptional an increment, I must indeed confess that it
> does not really appear proportionate to his overall
> achievement so far; nevertheless it is beyond dispute that
> in particular cases, where it matters, as for instance in
> the production of the opera *Iphigenia in Aulis* last year,
> or in the current series of subscription concerts, he does
> exert all his powers and displays a zeal that can only
> redound to his credit and would make his loss a matter
> for regret.

Wagner handed the sheet of paper back to his advocate without a word. Sensing the hostile reaction, Lüttichau hastened to emphasize that his request had in fact been granted. In fact the consent

depended, at the intendant's suggestion, on two conditions: that the
sum in question was to be regarded not as an increase in salary,
which would have put Wagner on the same footing as the principal
conductor, but as an *ex gratia* payment; and that if he got into new
financial difficulties he would be instantly dismissed.

Still Wagner was to know no respite from his troubles. Perturbed
by a speech he made to the Dresden Vaterlandsverein on 15 June
1848, some of the creditors of his publishing concern terminated his
credit. His first move, as five years previously, was to approach
Breitkopf & Härtel. He had been ill-advised enough to publish three
of his operas on his own account, he wrote on 17 June; even now he
would not regret it, if the money had been his own. But now some
of the principal had been called in and he sought a speedy settlement
of the matter in order to recover the peace to devote himself to
artistic creation. 'I therefore offer you the opportunity to purchase
this business: namely, the three operas *Rienzi, Der Fliegende Holländer* and *Tannhäuser* . . . Since my previous dealings with you give
me reason to suppose that, had I asked for no fee, you would have
been willing to undertake the publication of my operas on your
own account, I am reasonably confident that you will not have any
substantial objections to such an arrangement.'

But Breitkopf & Härtel were no longer disposed to agree even
to those terms. They feared that the uncertainty of the times
threatened the theatre. They declined the offer and at the same time
asked Wagner not even to inform them further about his new opera
Lohengrin, which he had already mentioned to them. (20 June 1848)

Without losing any time he next turned to Liszt, on 23 June: 'For a
number of contributory reasons the matter is becoming very peril-
ous for me: and privately I wonder what will become of me. The
sum involved is 5000 talers: after deducting what has already been
gained from the investment, and forgoing any fee for myself, this is
the money spent on publishing my operas. Can you raise the
money? Wouldn't it interest you to be my publisher? . . . I should
become a human being again, a human being for whom existence
had become possible . . . Dear Liszt, with that money you buy me
out of slavery!' And a week later: 'I am fighting for my life here, and
do not know how it will end.' But Liszt, who had given up his
career in the concert hall, could not help him.

By the end of July the situation had grown unendurable and only
Pusinelli remained as the last hope. Wagner proposed that he should

buy the publishing concern, but he replied to Wagner's lawyer: 'I cannot permit my friendship for Wagner, my respect for his talent or my admiration of his art to lead me to take any further rash steps. I have shown my readiness to make sacrifices, great sacrifices, but my conscience forbids me to do any more and I am fully resolved not to consider his proposal of a sale in any circumstances whatever. I may lose much, very much indeed, by acting in this way, but I must console myself with the conviction that I was fired with enthusiasm for an ideal, and that I have paid a heavy price for that enthusiasm.' (1 August)

To Wagner himself he wrote begging him not to make any personal approach about the transaction: he feared that he might then weaken after all. Wagner replied that this request aroused many bitter thoughts: while it showed no change in Pusinelli's feelings for him personally, it confirmed his views on the devastating effect money could have on the human soul. The full significance of the comment can be seen only if one remembers that by that time he was fully absorbed in the thoughts he was eventually to formulate in his essay on the Nibelung myths. A coolness was created between the two friends, which thawed only slowly.

Wagner's flight from Dresden did not entirely put an end to the publishing venture. The after-effects caught up with him nearly thirty years later, when the publisher Fürstner, one of Meser's business assignees, laid claim to the performing rights of *Tannhäuser*, but on 2 January 1877 Wagner at last emerged victorious from the case.

It is interesting to read the interpretation that Newman, with his no-nonsense grasp of affairs, places on the whole episode. Time was to prove that, in begging his friends one by one to pay his debts in return for the rights to his scores, Wagner was making them a perfectly sound proposition.

> In 1848, anyone could have become the out-and-out proprietor of *Rienzi*, the *Flying Dutchman*, and *Tannhäuser* for about £750 in all – an investment that would have one day brought him in some hundreds per cent. The commonsense of the thing seemed so self-evident to Wagner that he frankly could not understand why it was not equally and immediately self-evident to others. (NLRW, I, pp. 419f.)

Part III: The Revolutionary (1848–1852)

14

Revolutionary Ideas

It is as well to remind ourselves at this stage, immediately prior to the great turning point in Wagner's life and work, that the various threads we have traced in his Dresden years were all unwinding simultaneously. At the same time that he was writing *Tannhäuser* and *Lohengrin* he was delving into Greek and German antiquities, conducting operas and concerts, devising theatrical reforms, publishing his own music and fighting for his financial life, but he was also already bringing an artistic ideal into being that led him far beyond the confines of his own century.

The first products of his classical and German studies were the scenarios of two historical plays on Alexander the Great and Frederick Barbarossa. The former is known only from what Wagner told Cosima about it: 'I had written a sketch for a play, "Alexander"; the first act was the murder of Cleitus, the second the decision to withdraw from Asia, the third his death. Nowadays they usually go for the burning of Persepolis, Thais with a torch, something lyric. I also sketched a three-act "Achilles" and a "Barbarossa".' (1 April 1878; BBL 1937, p. 5)

Wagner read the life of Alexander in Droysen's *Geschichte Alexanders des Großen und des Hellenismus*, and from that one can imagine quite vividly his three scenes in the royal tent at Marakanda, the encampment on the bank of the Hyphasis and the palace in Babylon. It was the incommensurable, as Jacob Burckhardt calls it, that attracted him to the figure of Alexander throughout his life.

His 'Barbarossa' survives as a brief sketch entitled *Friedrich I.*, written on 31 October 1846 – that is, during the composition of *Lohengrin* – with some additions made in 1848. (RWGS, XI, pp. 270ff.) In it, the concept of kingship is invested with the most

127

powerful and immense significance possible; the emperor's dignified yielding to the impossibility of putting his great ideals into
practice would have gained sympathy for the hero and, at the same
time, demonstrated the proper recognition of the 'self-activating
multiformity of the things of this world'. Wagner was thinking, as
with 'Alexander', of a play without music, to be written in 'popular
rhyming form', in the style of the twelfth-century *Alexanderlied* by
Pfaffe Lamprecht. The scenario is only a few pages long, but it must
have been preceded by a long process of cogitation, just as it
stimulated further thought and writing that eventually crystallized
in the text of the *Ring*.

But before that final step could be taken one more powerful
stimulus was needed: the experience of revolution.

'What is the use of all our preaching at the public?' he wrote on 23
November 1847, after the collapse of his Berlin hopes, to the writer
Ernst Kossak, who had told him about *Rienzi*'s fortunes. 'I am so
sorry that you are giving yourself all this trouble over it and, in the
last analysis, doing it for my sake! What we have here is a dam that
we must force our way through, and the means to that end is:
Revolution!'

There for the first time he uttered the fateful word that was to
direct his thinking from then on. It is significant that it was not the
February revolution in Paris that first gave him the idea; indeed it
was not inspired by politics at all. The heights and depths the
thought opened to him are suggested in a letter he wrote on 4
January 1848 to his old friend Johann Kittl, by then the director of
the Prague Conservatory, who had helped him in his publishing
difficulties and whom he had thanked by giving him the text of *Die
Hohe Braut*, which Reissiger had rejected. Kittl had suggested some
changes, and Wagner replied that the excitement and lightning
speed of the ending were quite intentional and the frightful catastrophe was not to be softened in any way. 'The one dreadful,
exalting element is the inexorable advance of a great world destiny,
personified here by the French revolutionary army, marching in
terrible glory over the ruins of the old order.' The great reconciling
factor lay in the fact that 'we see literally before our own eyes the
entrance of a new world order, whose birth-pangs were the suffer-
ings in the events of the drama up till then'.[1]

All he meant here, of course, was an operatic revolution – he did
not believe that there would be a real revolution, even in France: he

had seen the construction of the circle of *forts détachés* around Paris while he was living there. When August Röckel interrupted a rehearsal of *Martha* with the triumphant announcement of the flight of Louis Philippe and the proclamation of the republic, he was extremely surprised, even though he expressed his doubts as to the significance of these events with a slight smile.

As long as he was preoccupied with the composition of *Lohengrin* (finished 28 April 1848), he was shielded by the aura of the Grail kingdom and could not be touched inwardly by events in Paris, Vienna or Berlin. He welcomed Friedrich August's appointment of a liberal government in Saxony in March, but feared that changes to the constitution in the democratic interest could mean cuts in the Civil List and thus, as the first economy, in the subsidy of the court theatre. To forestall this possibility he worked out a plan for the 'organization of a German national theatre for the kingdom of Saxony', which, taught by his experience with his plan for reforming the orchestra, he sent direct to the ministry rather than to the intendant.

The gist of this very detailed document, filling forty pages in print, was that the theatre should be taken out of the competence of the court bureaucracy and placed directly under the control of the elected representatives of the people. 'The king . . . could not but enhance the standing of this institution, if he appointed the authorities through whom he imparts his wishes to it from the members of the Ministry of State and not any longer from the officials of the court.' (11 May)

The manuscript ended up in the royal archives in Dresden, and later study revealed that, when Wagner published the text in his collected writings in 1871, he left out a passage about the competence of the intendant, to the effect that the position might be filled by one of the two principal conductors; but since a divided rule was always less efficient the reorganization should be entrusted to only one of them, together with the responsible minister, while the other might be put in charge of church music.

One of the people to whom the document was referred, obviously Reissiger, wrote in the margin against this 'That's the poodle's heart!' – in other words, here the author betrayed his true purpose. In another marginal note replying to the 'honoured reader' who had written the first comment, Wagner explained that no material benefit, at any event, would come to himself if he were to be given such a position; on the other hand, since the choice would have to fall on the most industrious and energetic, he had indeed meant it for himself, as the previous annotator had correctly guessed. He assumed that no one who read his document would believe that he had gone to so much trouble for purely egotistical reasons. 'So I am deeply grieved that the honoured reader regards the whole of this plan merely as a poodle, and its heart my own self-seeking.' (RWBC, pp. 297ff.)

After the referees had come out against the document the ministry put it aside, and the revolution that broke out shortly afterwards made it out of date in any case. In 1850, in exile, Wagner toyed with the idea of publishing it with a preface, solely in order to demonstrate that the infamous revolutionary had busied himself with plans for practical reforms until the last moment. (To Uhlig, 18 September 1850)

If his ideas on theatrical reform already had political implications, it was not long before he moved on to overtly political acts. In May he hailed the Austrian revolutionaries' recognition of the 'true nature of freedom' in a poem which appeared, with his name, in the *Allgemeine Österreichische Zeitung*.

> Ihr habt der Freiheit Art erkannt,
> nicht halb wird sie gewonnen . . . (RWGS, XII, pp. 358ff.)

He joined the revolutionary Vaterlandsverein, which was particularly absorbed at the time in discussion of the question: monarchy or republic? Recoiling from the narrow either–or, Wagner put forward a compromise view in a speech which was published in the *Dresdener Anzeiger* under the title 'What relation do republican aims bear to the monarchy?' and which he delivered on 15 June before thousands of people at a meeting of the Verein in a public park.

After proposing the abolition of the Upper Chamber and the formation of a People's Army, he put forward his economic ideals which, by emancipating mankind from the devilish concept of money, would put into practice the unadulterated teachings of Christ.

> Or do you scent the theories of communism in this?
> Are you foolish or malevolent enough to equate the
> necessary release of the human race from the clumsiest
> and most demoralizing form of enslavement to base

matter with the realization of communism, the silliest
and most meaningless of theories? . . . Recognize the
rights bestowed on mankind by God, or you might well
see the day when nature, forcibly denied, will gird itself
for a bitter battle, and the wild shriek of victory might
really be the communism you fear, and even though the
impossibility of its principles enduring is the inherent
assurance that its rule would be of the shortest,
nevertheless that short rule would have been sufficient to
eradicate all the achievements of two thousand years of
civilization. Do you think this is a threat? No, it is a
warning!

He appealed to the king to place himself at the head of the new
movement, for his mystical conception of kingship among the
Germanic tribes was combined with a quite personal respect for
Friedrich August II.

That is the man of Providence! . . . This prince, the
noblest, the worthiest of kings, let him say it: 'I
proclaim Saxony a free state.' And let the first law of
this free state, giving him the most perfect assurance of
his possession, be; 'The supreme executive power resides
in the royal house of Wettin and continues in it from
generation to generation according to the law of
primogeniture.' (RWGS, XII, pp. 220ff.)

Wagner spoke with all his considerable powers of persuasion,
and the applause was tumultuous. But his hearers had understood
nothing more than that the hofkapellmeister had made a speech
attacking the court toadies. The town talked of nothing else for
days. Newspapers published anonymous articles and verses deni-
grating and lampooning Wagner, to which he replied with an
'Open Declaration' in the *Anzeiger*: 'The rogues and scoundrels are
hereby informed that I make no answer to their anonymous
attacks.' He tried to explain himself in a long letter to Lüttichau: he
had attempted to present a poetic image of kingship, as he saw it, to
a predominantly prosaic crowd. That it might not have pleased the
demagogues gave him no concern; but it was a different matter if he
had reason to fear that he had been completely misunderstood by
the other side as well. (18 June)

He asked, and was readily given, leave of absence, and went to Vienna to find out whether conditions there would be more favourable to his plans for theatrical reform. He found the city in the grip of nationalist and revolutionary fervour: the National Guard wearing black, red and gold sashes, students in Old German tunics, sporting plumed hats and bayonets, the women with tricolour ribbons in their hats, and a German flag waving on nearly every house. Vienna had five theatres, which dragged themselves laboriously along. With the sense of the practicable that never deserted Wagner when he was on his own ground, he worked out a plan for a federative constitution for them, which he read to a number of leading figures in the musical and theatrical world. But politics took first place for the time being, and when the entry of Prince Windischgrätz's troops in October put power back in the hands of the reactionaries, it was an end of any plans for theatrical reform as well.

By the time Wagner got back to Dresden the unwelcome attention aroused by his speech to the Vaterlandsverein had so far abated that he was able to resume his conducting duties. The celebration of the orchestra's third centenary on 24 September, when Wagner proposed the toast, had the effect of a feast of reconciliation. (RWGS, II, pp. 229ff.)

Foremost among those who had introduced Wagner to politics was August Röckel, whose father occupies a place in musical history as the Florestan in the 1806 revival of *Fidelio* in Vienna. Röckel had been an enthusiastic socialist ever since witnessing the July revolution in Paris at the age of fifteen. He was appointed assistant conductor in Dresden in 1843, and when he got to know *Rienzi* and the *Holländer* he voluntarily withdrew an opera of his own which he had submitted for performance. He was the young musician whose sympathy went to such lengths, as Wagner wrote in *A Communication to my Friends*, that he surrendered his natural preference for his own works. It was not long before he came to view his badly paid post as forced labour and devoted himself to reading books on economics, which he discussed on walks with Wagner. In 1848 he at once took the side of the radical Socialists and announced that he had at last found his true vocation, as an 'agitator'. All at once, to the general amazement of his acquaintances, he stood revealed as the 'voice crying in the wilderness'. After losing his job for addressing an appeal to the army, he published weekly newssheets, the *Volksblätter*: three articles published anonymously in them were obviously by Wagner – 'Germany and her princes' (15 October 1848), 'Man and society as it is' (10 February 1849) and 'The Revolution' (8 April 1849). (RWGS, XII, pp. 414ff., 240ff., 245ff.) The increasingly strident tone betrays the general heightening of political excitement in the face of the threat of reaction.

The apocalyptic language of the last article is thought to be a sign of the influence of the Russian revolutionary Mikhail Bakunin. Wagner had met him through Röckel and had been fascinated by the 'colossus', the flowing mane that gave his Slav features a leonine air, the combination of ruthlessly challenging energy with refined delicacy of feeling. Without halting the flow of his terrible doctrines, Bakunin once held up his hand for a full hour to shield a bright light which he saw was dazzling Wagner. Neither succeeded in making a convert of the other: to Bakunin, Wagner's hopes for a future human society shaped by artists were the purest castles in the air, while Wagner could not help but see that Bakunin's insistence on the need to destroy all cultural institutions rested on premises of vertiginous implications. When Wagner conducted the Choral Symphony for the third and last time on Palm Sunday 1849 Bakunin secretly attended the performance. 'All, all will perish,' he exclaimed, 'not only music, the other arts too, even your Cornelius' – he had seen the *Nibelungenlied* print over Wagner's desk – 'only one thing will not perish but last for ever: the Ninth Symphony.'

In view of the profound differences between their outlooks, it is ludicrous to call Wagner a Bakuninist and to see a portrait of Bakunin in his Siegfried, as Bernard Shaw did. But it only needs one intelligent mind to propose an amusing paradox for ten less intelligent ones to spring up and adopt it in all seriousness. Bakunin for his part had nothing but contempt mingled with pity for Wagner's politics. According to the minutes of the hearing at Königstein on 19 September 1849 he said: 'Wagner I at once recognized as a dreamer, and although I discussed politics with him I never undertook any joint action with him.' (LWVR, p. 214)

Newman regretted that no catalogue of Wagner's Dresden library existed, which would have shown whether he had read Marx and Engels; now that the library has come to light and been catalogued we can see that it contained no political texts whatever. It is another piece of evidence that, in spite of his activities in the field, politics as such hardly impinged at all on his inner life.

It was during this period that he told Gustav Adolf Kietz, on one of their walks, that he was contemplating a work drawn from German mythology. His only fear was that he was already too old to be able to master the immense subject: he should have undertaken it earlier in his life.

When he had taken up his Barbarossa sketch again to make some additions to it, it occurred to him that the subject had a 'generic similarity' – one that only the eye of faith will perceive – to the Nibelung myths. The train of thought set off by this led to an extraordinary essay written in the late summer of 1848, 'The Wibelungs: World History from Saga', in which he attempted to show that the history of the Hohenstaufen dynasty derived from the Nibelung sagas, by associating 'Waiblingen' (the name of the Hohenstaufen stronghold Italianized as 'Ghibelline') with 'Wibelung' and thence 'Nibelung'. It was all fantasy, of course, but interesting insofar as it shows how the historical subject was being transformed in his mind into the mythological one.

The Nibelung myth had developed for him into a form which 'contained much and yet [was] compressed down to its principal elements', and the time was ripe for him to work out a dramatic text from it. What he said to Kietz gives some notion of his struggle with the immensity of the subject which, as he guessed, would be his fate. The first prose outline of all, *The Nibelung Myth as the Scenario for a Drama*, finished on 4 October 1848, already contains in narrative form the whole of the eventual plot of the *Ring* apart from a few, admittedly significant, factors. The fragmentary nature of the literary tradition vanishes from sight and the sketch reads like a new-minted original text from the authors of the Edda and the Volsunga saga. It owed its homogeneity to the Greeks: the close interrelation of the divine and the heroic myths, in particular, was quite unknown to the early Germans and was inconceivable without the example of the *Iliad*.

Even in this first version, Wagner's text broke spontaneously into dialogue at the point where Brünnhilde recognizes the ring on Siegfried's hand, and Wagner realized that the final stages of the fable would serve as the material for a 'drama executed in music'. In view of the contemporary state of the lyric theatre he was slow to muster any great enthusiasm for the prospect: only when he had nothing left to lose did he find the courage for the task.

Precisely there, in the creative courage born of despair, lay the deeper significance of the revolution for the conception of the *Ring*.

Even if Wagner himself had not stressed the matter, it would be clear enough that social factors also played a part, but such factors have no bearing on the value or non-value of a work of art. If the artist does not succeed in sublimating those factors, whatever they may be, into the substance of pure art then there remains a sediment that draws the work down to the level of its time and allows it to perish with its time. To translate the *Ring* back, nowadays, into a piece 'about' those factors and to pride oneself on doing so amounts to a failure to recognize the timeless substance behind the temporal, and indeed renders it unrecognizable.

The last straw for Wagner came when the production of *Lohengrin*, for which the sets had already been commissioned, was abruptly postponed by Lüttichau without a word of explanation. 'Silently abandoning my last hope of reconciling myself to the theatre by means of a fine production of my *Lohengrin*, from that moment, absolutely and fundamentally, I turned my back on the theatre and on every attempt to come to terms with it. . . Now I set to work to carry out the plan that I had long nurtured in seclusion, of *Siegfrieds Tod*.' (ML, pp. 445f.)

He completed the first full prose sketch, in dialogue form, on 20 October 1848. (SERD, pp. 38ff.) When he read it to Eduard Devrient, the dramaturg of the Dresden theatre, the latter pointed out that in order to enter into the quarrel between Siegfried and Brünnhilde it was essential for the listener to have known them in their earlier, unclouded relationship. Wagner at once sketched the introductory scene in which they take leave of each other and, while he was at it, the Norns' scene, an addition of much greater consequence, referring the 'great heroic opera' to its mythological background for the first time.[2]

Rewriting the text in verse took him from 11 to 28 November. For the first time, he used not iambics but the 'free rhythmic verse' that he developed out of the requirements of musical declamation. Early in December Gustav Kietz had a note from Wagner inviting him to a reading of the new text, 'if you have nothing better to do'.

> I arrived punctually [Kietz wrote in his memoirs], and found Professor Semper, Fischer the chorus master, Heine the costume-designer and his son already there. The last arrivals were the musicians Hans von Bülow and Karl Ritter, who made their entrance in full evening

dress, tails and white tie, balancing top hats on their
arms. Laughing, Wagner met them with the words, 'Ah,
gentlemen, you do me too much honour.' . . . Now he
began to read the text in a clear voice and with the
enthralling expressiveness which lay uniquely at his
command . . . His listeners were spellbound, the general
excitement grew from act to act! The reading was
followed by a discussion about the musical realization of
it with old Fischer, who kept on shaking his head.
Excited by his demurrings, Wagner explained the
important part the orchestra would play in the dramatic
expression, and how the 'word' projected from the stage
would have to carry more weight than hitherto.

It was, Kietz concluded, an unforgettable evening for everyone
present – and, we may add, a red-letter day in the history of the
writing of the *Ring*, not least because it shows how clearly Wagner
already envisaged the new kind of musical realization.

But the immediate effect of writing the text was to bring home to
him even more painfully his isolation as a creative artist. He had
been immersing himself in the Gospels, and the copy of the New
Testament that he owned at that time bears more underlinings than
any other book in the whole of his Dresden library. His reading
made him very aware of the man Jesus as opposed to the symbolic
Christ, and drove him to sketch a drama 'for the ideal theatre of the
future', presenting the self-sacrifice of Jesus as the revolt of a spirit
that loved, and needed love, against a loveless world. The sketch of
Jesus von Nazareth runs to more than fifty pages in print. (RWGS,
XII, pp. 273ff.) The first act, outside the house of Levi the publican,
expounds the contrast between Judas and Barabbas, who are planning an insurrection, and Jesus, who develops his teaching of love
(the tribute money and the woman taken in adultery). The second
act takes place on the Sea of Gennesaret and ends with the sermon
on the lake. The third depicts the entry into Jerusalem, the fourth
the last supper and the agony in the garden. In the fifth, the trial
takes place outside Pilate's palace, and the two Marys and John,
returning from Calvary, recount the end and look forward hope-
fully to the founding of the communion of followers. Arthur
Drews believed that it was probably no exaggeration to describe
Wagner's version of the life of Christ as one of the most successful.

It is significant of the relationship between Wagner and Bakunin that the latter was no more interested in the *Jesus von Nazareth* project than he was in the Nibelung plans: he begged Wagner to spare him, but in any case to present Jesus as a weak character. He recommended musical variations on a single text: the tenor singing 'Behead him!', the soprano 'Hang him!' and the bass 'Fire, fire!'

Wagner passed the spring of 1849 in a state of numb expectation. The political situation seemed to be heading straight for a catastrophe, and it gave him a certain satisfaction to picture his personal fate as bound in with the general position. Indignation with the reactionary party reached a peak when the king, contrary to the constitution, dissolved both chambers of the Landtag on 30 April, and sent a government commissioner to order the deputies home. In the face of deputations from every sector of his kingdom appealing to him to reverse his decision, the king, normally the most malleable of men, preserved a firmness of purpose worthy of a better cause. He understood very well that his refusal was bound to lead to civil war, but he relied on his troops and the military aid promised by Prussia. The government's moral position was as poor as could be in the eyes of the country: the dissolution of the Landtag was seen as a breach of the constitution and the threatened Prussian aid as an invasion, and the expression 'revolution from above' was heard.

The dissolution of the Landtag deprived Röckel of his immunity as a member of it, and he fled to Prague. Wagner wrote to him on 2 May: 'It is very unsettled here . . . People are preparing themselves for a decisive confrontation, if not with the king, then at any rate with the Prussian army; the only fear is that a revolution may break out too early.' That sentence turned out to be fateful for Wagner, when the letter was later found on Röckel. Item 5 in the Saxon Ministry of Justice document of 1862, collating all the charges against him, reads: 'The letter written on that account by Wagner to Röckel compromises the former to the utmost.' (LWVR, p. 18) In this the court was over-estimating Wagner's political status, for if a date had really been set for the revolution, the last person to whom the secret would have been confided was the musician shrugged off by Bakunin as a 'dreamer'.

The chapter about the revolution is one of the most exciting in *Mein Leben*. It is very possible that he represented his own part in it as less active than it really was. The reader must not forget that when he began to dictate the autobiography his exile, after lasting thirteen years, had been lifted only two years previously, on 28 March 1862. Apart from that, there is the consideration that he had perhaps already admitted almost too much for a reader like King Ludwig, at whose behest he was writing the book.

There are some undisputed facts. He had handbills printed saying 'Are you with us against foreign troops?', which he distributed in person during a cease-fire to the Saxon soldiers stationed on the square outside the palace and on the Elbe bridge. It was a miracle, according to an eyewitness, that he was not arrested or even shot while he was doing it. He spent the night of 6–7 May on the tower of the Kreuzkirche and watched the approach of bands of insurgents from the Erz mountains in the early morning. He did not go to the barricades and join in the hand-to-hand fighting; nor was it he, contrary to what was claimed, who set fire to the Old Opera House. A curious incident made that particular event unforgettable for him. As he went past the Annenkirche on his way home on the morning of 7 May, he heard a shout: 'Herr Kapellmeister!' and when he turned round he saw a fine figure of a man on the barricade who called to him 'Joy's beautiful divine spark has *kindled*!' ('Der Freude schöner Götterfunken hat *gezündet*!'). When Wagner told this 'peculiar story' in 1873 he also made the movement of the arm with which the man had visibly underlined the word 'gezündet'. 'It was very strange', he added in a voice that betrayed emotion.

Some things remain obscure, for instance whether Wagner – as alleged by the brassfounder Oehme, one of the 'most severely incriminated persons' – really did order a substantial number of hand grenades for Prague from him. The protocols give a general impression that the revolutionaries who were arrested – not excepting Wagner's friend Röckel – did not scruple to lay as much as they could at the door of one who had managed to escape.

But our concern here is less with the legal side of the affair than with the psychological. While the elemental force of an event of such a nature seems to draw Wagner wholly in its wake, his better conscious judgement remains untouched by it, like an uninvolved spectator. When the tocsin suddenly started to ring as he was crossing the Postplatz he experienced a phenomenon which, he realized, was exactly the same as Goethe had experienced during the cannonade of Valmy: 'The whole of the square before me seemed to be lit with a dark yellow, almost brownish light' (Goethe: 'as if the world had a certain brownish tint'). There were others on the tower of the Kreuzkirche with him. While they were trying to keep out of the line of fire of the Prussian snipers on the tower of the Frauenkirche, he started a philosophical discussion with a schoolteacher called Berthold, which led them to the remotest areas of religion. A Professor Thum, who was also on the tower that night, recalled that he had a long and lively conversation with Wagner about the classical and Christian views of the world. 'In this way,' Wagner wrote, 'in the immediate proximity of the terrible clamour of the bell and under the constant hail of Prussian bullets against the tower wall, I spent one of the most remarkable nights of my life.' Slowly making his long way home past the numerous abatis during the short cease-fire on the morning of 7 May, he worked out in his head the plot of a play about Achilles. Thetis would appear to her son as he was mourning for Patroclus and offer him immortality if he would forgo vengeance for his friend. But Achilles would disdainfully reject divine immortality at the cost of the loss of human striving. Then the goddess would bow before him, recognizing that he was greater than the gods. 'Man is god perfected. The eternal gods are only the elements which create man. Creation finds its ultimate conclusion in man. Achilles is higher and more perfect than the elemental Thetis.' (RWGS, XII, p. 283)

Wagner kept the project in mind for years. In 1865, after completing the prose sketch of *Parsifal*, he wrote to King Ludwig that he still hoped his *Achilleus* would see the light of day eventually. (16 September 1865) In the meantime one of its important features had been transferred to the figure of Brünnhilde in the third act of *Siegfried*, renouncing divinity and accepting her humanity.

Wagner avoided arrest after the failure of the revolution solely because of one of those remarkable chances that always played a large part at the turning points of his life: travelling on from Freiberg he lost contact with the members of the provisional government with whom he had fled from Dresden and with whom he would otherwise have been arrested in Chemnitz. 'My soul was transfixed as if by lightning, remembering the extraordinary way that once before, when I was a student, I had been saved from certain defeat in the duel I was to have fought with the experienced bully-boy.' Fate had some other strokes of luck in store for him: the fact that his brother-in-law Heinrich Wolfram lived in Chemnitz and was able to hide him and drive him secretly to Altenburg; that

Liszt was able to give him advice and practical assistance in Weimar; that a Professor Widmann in Jena was ready to give him his passport, so that he could cross the Saxon border under a false name. If any one of the links in this chain had been missing, his flight would have failed.

The account in *Mein Leben* is supplemented by what Wagner wrote at the time in letters to Minna and his brother-in-law from Weimar and Eisenach. (RWBC, pp. 303ff.) What these principally reveal is his concern for his wife: he had been so happy to have a letter from her on his arrival in Weimar: 'the evidence of your pure, warm love which you assure me of this time without torturing me with reproaches'. He went on that he would not leave Germany without having seen her again.

'The ways of human fate are incomprehensible! The dreadful catastrophe I have just experienced and the day I spent yesterday in Weimar have made a different person of me and have shown me a new path.' In his extreme dissatisfaction with his position and almost with his art, he had been at odds with the world and ceased to be an artist. While he had spent the journey to Weimar thinking about finding a quiet place in the country, Liszt had turned his thoughts to the whole wide world, to London and Paris. 'That gave me fresh heart, and at a stroke I am once again all artist, *love* my art again and *hope*, too, that it will be the means whereby I will make my poor, sorely tried wife happy again.'

He was in a state of 'dreamy detachment' which made it hard for him to judge how far he had compromised himself. To comfort Minna he wrote: 'To be sure, if the reactionaries wanted revenge on everyone who took any kind of part in the rising – they would have to prosecute half Saxony!' With all the insouciance of Goethe's Egmont he went off to Eisenach, intending to explore the Thuringian countryside on foot and visit the Wartburg. By chance the Grand Duchess Maria Pavlovna was on his train and she invited him to call on her in Eisenach that evening. He presented himself at the castle in his travelling clothes, and she received him among all her noble guests with uncommon kindness, talked to him for a long time and made him promise to visit her later in Weimar.

On his return he used his first free hour to write a long letter to Eduard Devrient, giving him a full account of his part in the rising and clearly intended for the eyes of Lüttichau. 'I shall hold out the olive branch, so as not to make the breach with Dresden irreconcilable,' he told Minna.[3]

While he was lulling himself in such illusions, the warrant for his arrest had already been drawn up. He heard from Minna on 19 May that its issue was imminent. At Liszt's urging he went into hiding in the nearby ducal domain of Magdala under the name of 'Professor Werder from Berlin', and there Minna paid him a birthday visit on 22 May. Their initial conciliatory mood quickly dispersed under the pressure of events and she could see in him only an 'ill-advised and thoughtless man', who had plunged them both into the most dreadful situation. When they took leave of each other in Jena on 24 May the breach, which was never again to be completely mended, had already taken place within them.

On 27 May Wagner travelled by express coach via Rudolstadt, Saalfeld, Coburg, Lichtenfels and Nuremberg to Lindau on Lake Constance. Stepping on to the steamer for Rorschach the next day, on a beautiful spring morning, with the Swiss mountains shimmering on the other shore of the lake, he was quite unaware that he had escaped a sentence of death.

But he had incurred one lifelong enemy. Among the Prussian troops who fought in Dresden in May 1849 was a lieutenant in the Grenadiers called Botho von Hülsen, who was appointed general intendant of the Berlin court opera two years later. The reluctance with which he allowed Wagner to be performed in the theatre is already well known, the motive less so. When Wagner wanted to call on him in 1863, after his amnesty, Hülsen wrote to Hans von Bülow on 14 February: 'I cannot deny my personal feelings, and after our encounter in Dresden in May 1849 it is repugnant to me to enter into any kind of personal relationship with the aforesaid.'[4] And when it was expected, after Wagner's death, that the Berlin opera would commemorate a great German composer in some fitting way, Hülsen refused the Wagner Society permission to hold such a ceremony in the house, on the grounds that the theatre could not be made available for private functions.

15

Wieland der Schmied

On the night of 29 May 1849 the doorbell began to ring loudly in the house of the musician Alexander Müller in the Rennweg in Zürich. Müller put his head out of the window. 'Who's that at this hour?' 'Hurry up and open the door,' came a voice from below, 'it's me, Richard Wagner!' Müller's daughter said later that she would never forget Wagner's arrival at their house. 'He stormed up the stairs, threw his arms round my father and cried: "Alexander, you must let me stay with you, I'm safe here!" '

He and Müller had become friends in Würzburg in 1833, and it was another of the strokes of luck that helped him on his flight that Müller now lived in Zürich and could take him in, introduce him to two cantonal officials, Jakob Sulzer and Franz Hagenbuch, and help him to get a Swiss passport for his journey on to Paris. 'To my complete astonishment I have found that I am famous here,' Wagner wrote to Theodor Uhlig, his friend in the Dresden orchestra, 'thanks to the vocal scores of all my operas, whole acts of which have been frequently performed at concerts and by choral societies.' (9 August)

He arrived with no luggage but a lightweight brown coat and what he could carry in a single bag slung over his shoulder. At the moment when he caught his first glimpse of the Lake of Zürich framed by the Glarner Alps as he approached Zürich from Oberstrass, he made a subconscious decision that he wanted to stay there. All at once he felt a surge of new strength to create the most important work of his life but, to please Liszt and Minna, he tried to persuade himself that he had to do it in Paris. Planning to leave Switzerland again after only two days, he felt like closing his eyes to the land he was travelling through, like Tannhäuser: 'Verschloßnen

Aug's, ihr Wunder nicht zu schauen'. (29 May, RWBC, pp. 319ff.)

Renewing his acquaintance with Paris was worse than he had anticipated. 'What is going on inside me is indescribable,' he complained to Minna. 'Memories, the present and the future, are all pressing in on me . . . Alas, my Swiss courage has already nearly gone.' While he still held fast to the necessity of Paris for his future, he confessed to Liszt that he would not be able to create works with which to storm the French capital if he stayed there. 'I cannot work in Paris and without hearth and home – by which I mean peace of mind: I must find a new spot where I can feel at home and resolve to stay at home. I think that Zürich is that spot.' (18 June) Meanwhile he passed the time by reading Proudhon's *De la propriété*, which afforded him in those circumstances, as he said, strangely lavish consolations.

He returned to Zürich early in July, with the idea for an essay on art and revolution as his sole gain. He submitted it to one of the larger French periodicals, which returned it with the remark that it would be of no interest to their readers. He promptly sent it to the Leipzig publisher Otto Wigand, who paid him 5 louisdor, in view of the stir it was likely to cause.

Art and Revolution was the first of the Zürich essays which were, in a sense, the means of sublimating his revolutionary ideas. In the one-sidedness of their point of view, in their simplification of the problems they discuss, they cannot be described as contributions to an objective philosophy of art. But those same qualities make them all the more valuable as the documents of Wagner's struggle to create a new artistic ideal, which can be seen taking an ever surer form from one essay to the next: *Art and Revolution, The Artwork of the Future, Opera and Drama* and *A Communication to my Friends*.

Even in the first of these essays we can see him 'hewing out' this ideal for himself from the Greek experience: re-creating a day at a festival in the Attic theatre, the references to *Prometheus* – the profoundest of all the tragedies – and to Apollo in *The Eumenides* – evoked by the tragedian under the inspiration of Bacchus – these are the products of his reading of Droysen and Karl Otfried Müller in Dresden. (*Die Kunst und die Revolution*, RWGS, III, pp. 8ff.)

Forced though his exile was, it was freedom to Wagner; he enjoyed the understanding and sympathy of his new friends, especially Jakob Sulzer, and when he read the text of *Siegfrieds Tod* to a small group he declared that he had never had a more attentive male audience. The one cloud in his happiness was Minna's obstinate silence to his imploring letters: 'I must always feel that I have a home – and only you, my dear wife, are my home.' (29 May; RWBC, pp. 319ff.) At last on 18 July she announced her readiness to join him in Zürich. 'I hope you will appreciate, my dear Richard, that in coming to you I am making *no small sacrifice*. What kind of future lies in store for me, what can you offer me?' (RWBC, pp. 337ff.)

She finally arrived at the beginning of September, with the dog, the parrot and Natalie. Her immediate threat that she would go straight back to Dresden if her husband did not behave himself cast a slight chill on the joy of their reunion, so he had to fall back on the affection of Peps and Papo. The odd little family moved into a modest apartment in the Hintere Escherhäuser, where Minna made them quite comfortable, thanks to her domestic talents and the generosity of Sulzer – whose office of 'Staatsschreiber' (secretary in the employ of the cantonal government) she initially understood to be the loftier position of 'Stadtschreiber' (town clerk).

Wagner, who had had to promise her to make an effort to have an operatic success in Paris, devoted himself to theorizing about art the while. Sitting in the Café Littéraire one afternoon, surrounded by card-players and tobacco fumes, he was dreamily surveying the cheap wallpaper covered with scenes from classical mythology, when his thoughts turned from the recent upheavals in the world at large to his own inner life. And suddenly a picture he had seen as a boy flashed upon his mind: Bonaventura Genelli's *Dionysus among the Muses of Apollo*. 'There and then I conceived the ideas of my *Artwork of the Future*.'

It must have been at about the time when he first saw Schröder-Devrient as Fidelio, while he was still a pupil at the Nikolaischule, that he first saw Genelli's watercolour in the house of his brother-in-law Brockhaus. He often stood gazing at it in enchantment, and confessed that it was one of the first things to give him an idea of the Greek spirit of beauty. When he visited Genelli's patron, Count Schack, in Munich thirty years later, he spent a long time looking at the works he owned by this neglected artist, especially at his *Bacchus among the Muses*, another version of the Leipzig painting. He told the count that he had known the artist in his youth, and his compositions had exercised an important influence on his own work. What attracted him to Genelli was the intimation of a new conception of

Greek culture that went beyond Winckelmann's classical ideal of 'noble simplicity and reposeful grandeur' and that was here epitomized in the encounter of the Dionysian and the Apollonian. It is significant that *The Artwork of the Future* was conceived under this sign. (*Das Kunstwerk der Zukunft*, RWGS, III, pp. 42ff.)

Keeping up a running battle with the cold in their sunless apartment and the worry as to where their next meal was coming from, Wagner finished the essay on 4 November. He later dedicated it to the philosopher Ludwig Feuerbach: 'To none but you, honoured sir, can I dedicate this work, for with it I have given back to you what is your own.' (RWGS, XII, pp. 284f.) Feuerbach's reply gave him great joy: he did not understand how opinion could be divided over the book; he had read it with enthusiasm, even delight, and he had to assure him of his fullest sympathy, his warmest thanks. (Quoted by Wagner to Uhlig, 20 September 1850)

Wagner confessed that it had always been his ambition to immerse himself in philosophy in much the same way as he had plunged into the depths of music under the mystical influence of the Choral Symphony. After wrestling in vain with Schelling's *System of Transcendental Idealism* in his youth, he had later tried again with Hegel's *Lectures on the Philosophy of History*, which was in his Dresden library: much of it had impressed him deeply and the greater the difficulty he had in understanding some things the harder he had tried to get to the bottom of the 'absolute'. During the retreat from Dresden a German Catholic preacher, a serious young man in an enormous sombrero, had recommended Feuerbach to him as the 'right and only philosopher of modern times'. In Zürich Wagner lost no time in acquiring a copy of his *Thoughts on Death and Immortality*, which was banned in Germany; it had struck him as bold and rewarding to find that true immortality was conferred solely on sublime deeds or inspired works of art.

Feuerbach's influence can already be seen in *Art and the Revolution*, but the claims to have traced it in *Jesus von Nazareth* or even in the articles published in Röckel's *Volksblätter* are refuted in the first place by Wagner's own account of his reading of Feuerbach and above all by the total absence of any of his works from the Dresden library.

It is because it was conceived as a vision that *The Artwork of the Future* is so difficult a text to understand: it is as a vision that it must be read. 'I have no desire to make any alterations,' Wagner wrote when he sent the manuscript to Uhlig; 'once something like this has been written it has to be allowed to stand as it is: the strengths and weaknesses are quite accurately related to each other for the most part.' In the event it was fundamentally misunderstood and only gave rise to two indestructible new catch-phrases. Professor Bischoff, the editor of the Cologne *Niederrheinische Musikzeitung*, achieved immortality of a kind by coining the howler 'music of the future', but Wagner's friends on Brendel's *Neue Zeitschrift für Musik* hung a worse millstone round his neck with their theorizing about the 'total artwork'. Anyone who goes to the original sixteen volumes of Wagner's *Schriften und Dichtungen*, in search of further information about this apparently central concept, will encounter an initial difficulty: the term is not to be found in the 132-page index. Wagner does in fact use it once, in *The Artwork of the Future*, at a point where he is contemplating the supplementation of the 'three purely human arts' – music, poetry and the dance – with what, in an unpublished note, he called the 'ancillary aids of drama': architecture, sculpture and painting. The Utopian character of a work of art that would absorb all the separate arts into itself in such a way is further emphasized by the proviso that it would be the creation not of a single genius but of the 'genius of community', of a free association of artists, led by the performer, who is both the writer and the composer. That is the context in which Wagner used the expression 'total artwork', or to be more precise 'total artwork of the future'. It is obvious that he meant two complementary things by it: a totality of the arts and a totality of artists.

But disciples are usually the same: with unerring skill they single out the exceptional and extravagant among their teacher's dicta. Not content with rallying to the 'artwork of the future', they plucked 'total artwork' out of its context in the book, so that Wagner was to write to Liszt in complete despair that they weren't even capable of understanding his writings when they read them. (16 August 1853) 'There is no other reason why the fruit of all my efforts should be this wretched "special art" and "total art". Honestly: it makes me sick to talk to people without intelligence about things they do not and never will understand, because they simply have no trace of artistic and true human essence in them. If I were ever to write another polemic it would be far more likely to be against these "enlightened" wretches. . . But first and foremost, no mention of that wretched "total art" in the title!!!' It is as though he foresaw that the 'wretched' total artwork would still be a topic of discussion a hundred years later.

Wagner concludes his vision of the 'artwork of the future' with a vigorous coda in which he interprets the legend of Wayland Smith as a parable of the artist driven to forge wings for himself out of his own distress. When he finally had to give way to Liszt's and Minna's urgings to produce an operatic project for Paris, that was the subject he wrote up in a prose sketch, with dialogue, for a three-act drama, with the idea that the librettist Gustave Vaez should put it into French verse.

Then what seemed to be a last-minute chance of escaping the Parisian doom presented itself. Frau Julie Ritter, the widow of a merchant from Narva, now resident in Dresden and the mother of the young Karl Ritter, had heard of his straits and sent him 500 talers, as the first instance of the help she was to give him in the future. Furthermore, a young friend of hers, Jessie Taylor, who had visited Wagner with Karl Ritter the previous year in order to express her admiration of his work, and who was now married to a Bordeaux wine merchant, Eugène Laussot, wrote in terms of heart-felt sympathy. But when he put it to Minna that they would be able to manage on what they could get in Zürich after all, she completely lost her temper: if he did not make a serious effort to succeed in Paris then she would have to wash her hands of him; she was not going to sit and watch him go to the dogs in Zürich as a penniless writer and conductor of hole-and-corner concerts.

Wagner returned to Paris on 1 February 1850 and found, as he had expected, that the city where Meyerbeer was just celebrating the triumph of *Le Prophète* was no place for him. 'I am ill and my illness is called Paris,' he wrote to Sulzer. 'The struggle between my inner unwillingness and the urging of some of my friends and my good wife in particular has perhaps been sowing the seeds of my present illness for a long time . . . How can people fail to understand that no activity satisfies us and makes us happy, no activity is useful, in fact, except one that is in sympathy with our whole true nature!' (22 February 1850, FWSZ, I, p. 355)

Then something happened that threatened to bring about another fateful change in his destiny. It remained a secret for many years, until the publication of *Mein Leben* in 1911. The tale Wagner told there was confirmed and amplified by the publication of his correspondence with Frau Ritter in 1920 and of documents from the Burrell Collection in 1950.

In a letter to Liszt dated 6 February 1850 – not included in the official edition of their correspondence – he had mentioned that a third person – obviously Frau Ritter – had told him that a Madame Laussot of Bordeaux had put aside a not inconsiderable sum of money for him, with the intention that it should assure him a modest living. 'You know, my dear Liszt, I have few friends . . . Acknowledge that woman as your sister and one of like mind with you.' We now know, in fact, that the Ritters and the Laussots planned jointly to provide him with an annual income of 3000 francs. (RWBC, pp. 368ff.)

Now, in Paris, at the beginning of March, he received an invitation from the Laussots to visit them in Bordeaux. His meeting with Jessie in Dresden had been very brief, and it was only now that he got to know her well: she was young, beautiful and gifted and, since hearing *Tannhäuser* in Dresden, an ardent admirer of him and his work. She listened enthralled as he read the texts of *Siegfrieds Tod* and *Wieland der Schmied*, preferring the latter, as she found it easier to identify with the part of Wieland's bride Schwanhilde than with the unhappy Gutrune. For her part, she demonstrated her musical talent by playing him Beethoven's Hammerklavier Sonata with great understanding. Her intellectual and artistic calibre is further confirmed by the life she led, after divorcing Laussot, with her second husband the historian Karl Hillebrand, in Florence, where she took up a position at the centre of musical life, founding and directing the Società Cherubini, for which Liszt wrote her twelve anthems. She also wrote scholarly treatises and translated Schopenhauer's *Fourfold Root of Sufficient Reason* into English.

Bordeaux was like a new world for Wagner. The belief in his mission that he encountered there restored his self-confidence. He was now determined not to allow himself to be forced back into the operatic rat-race in Paris. When he confided to Jessie that all he really wanted to do was seek oblivion in Greece and the Orient, far from European civilization, she was surprised and overjoyed, and told him she was ready to share his lot.

Returning to Paris his first task was to inform Minna of his decision to leave her. He may have thought that, having made the same threat herself, she would agree to it with not too heavy a heart. But since she had just received a letter from Jessie, telling her of

Wagner's visit to Bordeaux and expressing the wish that he might now live and work entirely according to the promptings of his heart and advance towards his great goal unhindered by any exterior considerations, her female instinct recognized a rival to whom she could not afford to concede a single inch of ground. 'O false, treacherous creature!' she scribbled at the foot of the letter. (RWBC, pp. 376f.) She rallied their friends in Zürich to write an imploring letter to her husband, and herself set out for Paris, where she missed him, as he had gone to Geneva to avoid her.

He had already planned his flight, via Marseilles and Malta to Greece, and from there to the Near East. Jessie declared her determination to accompany him without hesitation. But on the point of departure he had a letter from her confessing that she had let her mother into the secret, that her husband had forthwith threatened to shoot Wagner, and that she herself had made up her mind not to follow him. Thunderstruck, Wagner wrote to tell Laussot that he was coming to Bordeaux to see him. But the house was empty: the outraged husband had preferred to take his household to the country and leave it to the police to send his rival packing.

Wagner retreated to Villeneuve on Lake Geneva, where he met Karl Ritter, whose mother also came hurrying when she received a despairing letter from him. They spent his thirty-seventh birthday together. The most bitter disappointment was yet to come, when Karl had a letter from Jessie letting it be known that in future she would throw any letters in Wagner's hand into the fire unread. It is easy enough to guess what induced her to make the break. The Burrell Collection contains a letter from her mother accompanying 'important papers' returned to Minna. Obviously some of Wagner's letters to Minna were used to turn Jessie against him. (RWBC, pp. 412f.)

One of the few people who knew of the episode, Hans von Bülow, a friend of Jessie's in her youth and again in age, later wrote to Karl Klindworth that this very attractive, intelligent and musical woman had some years earlier experienced an uncommon passion for Wagner, 'a passion that was, moreover, mutual and was brought to a sudden rift solely by the crossgrained counterpoint of unfavourable circumstances'. If she should visit Klindworth in London in the immediate future, Bülow went on, he could give her immense pleasure by playing her some of the music from the *Ring*:

'she deserves, as few others do, to be initiated in it'. (10 October 1858, NBB, p. 2)

In Villeneuve Frau Ritter's maternal solicitude restored Wagner's spirits. The way she stood by him even then and did not withdraw her hand from him was the best reassurance he could have had. Karl was despatched to Zürich to intercede with Minna, and gave so favourable a report of her reaction that Wagner himself wrote her a long letter recapitulating everything that had happened. (RWBC, pp. 403ff.) At the bottom of it she wrote: 'Not this letter, which contains many accusations that are untrue as well as hurtful, only my all too great love, which lets me forgive and forget what happened, do I thank for our reunion.'

'I arrived in Zürich with Karl Ritter four days ago', he wrote on 7 July to Ernst Benedikt Kietz, whom he had told of his plan for flight in Paris, 'without my horsetail and turban' – the oriental insignia of manhood. (RWBC, pp. 413f.)

On the face of it, the Jessie Laussot episode was an ordinary love affair, but at bottom it was yet another of the often violent attempts that Wagner the artist made to free himself. As the revolution had torn him from his position as kapellmeister, so the Bordeaux adventure released him from the phantom of making an operatic career in Paris. That subject was no longer mentioned.

In May, while he was still in Villeneuve, he had written a preface for *Siegfrieds Tod*, which he was thinking of publishing, believing that he would have to abandon the idea of ever setting it to music. 'So receive this work of literature that I offer you as what an honourable artist, after mature deliberation, can now offer only to his friends.' (RWGS, XVI, pp. 84f.) But in Zürich he wrote a composition sketch of the first two scenes, and with that we move into a new phase in the history of the creation of the *Ring*.

16

From Heroic Opera to Mythic Drama

Minna had set up house in a modest apartment in Enge, the first suburb of Zürich along the left-hand shore of the lake. There was nowhere else in the whole wide world he wanted to live but here, Wagner wrote to Uhlig after his return. 'I go down in my house coat and bathe in the lake. There's a boat, which we row ourselves. And an excellent race of people, sympathy, kindness, the most touching readiness to be of service at every turn . . . Let me . . . say nothing of the very recent past and tell you briefly only this much, that I have got a new wife.'

   Things were looking much better outside the home, too. 'Perform my *Lohengrin*!' he had appealed to Liszt from Paris. Now the first performance was due to take place in Weimar on 28 August, on Goethe's birthday and the occasion of the unveiling of a memorial to Herder. The theatre management had spared no expense and Liszt had spared himself no pains. He even touched on the possibility of performing *Siegfrieds Tod* and hoped to be able to procure Wagner an advance payment so that he could work without worries. 'I need the actors to play heroes such as our theatre has never yet seen,' Wagner replied; 'where are they to be found?' But in the first flush of enthusiasm he was ready to put such doubts on one side: 'I believe you are going about things in the best way to get them growing out of the ground for me.' (20 July 1850)

   In this optimistic frame of mind, on 12 August he drafted a composition sketch for the Norns' scene and the opening of the Leavetaking scene between Siegfried and Brünnhilde.[1] The very first bars reveal an astonishing coincidence. The Norns' scene of *Siegfrieds Tod* differs somewhat in the text, but the music begins – as in *Götterdämmerung*, composed twenty years later – in E♭ minor (and in 6/4 time): a proof of how involuntarily and compellingly in Wagner the key proceeds from the situation. In both versions the rondo-like refrain of the question-and-answer framework returns, after temporary modulations, to the mysterious atmosphere of E♭ minor in the end. There are motivic reminiscences, too: the words the Norns repeat like a formula, 'In osten wob ich . . . ', anticipate the theme of the Ride of the Valkyries, though without the final modulation into the major; according to Jacob Grimm the Norns and the Valkyries were related. The setting of the Leavetaking scene is particularly interesting, since the words are the same as in *Götterdämmerung*: a piece of luck which will allow us to make a stylistic comparison in due course.

The composition sketch breaks off at Siegfried's words 'Brünnhildes zu gedenken!' and although Wagner assured Liszt on 16 August that the music for his 'Siegfried' (as he then called it) was haunting him in his very bones, he did not resume it. There were three reasons for this. His courage failed at the thought of finding, within a year, a singer capable of giving life to his Brünnhilde; there seemed to be too much bald narrative of events that had preceded curtain-rise; but the principal reason was the third, though as yet he was only dimly aware of it: the composition sketch is written in an astringent saga style, completely *sui generis*, but does not reveal the extensive background of the myth. His writing and thinking during the next six months were devoted to the problem of how to open up those perspectives.

Meanwhile he plunged once more into polemics, which he had believed himself to have done with. There was an association from his past that had long been irking him. As we have seen he had tried to accommodate his liking for Meyerbeer the man with his distaste for the composer. Then, in 1847, on the occasion of the Berlin *Rienzi*, he lost confidence in the man as well, suspecting some intrigue, although, as we now know, there is not the slightest shred of evidence for it even in Meyerbeer's diaries. When Meyerbeer tried to avoid him on a chance encounter in Paris in 1850, Wagner interpreted it as the sign of a bad conscience, though it is much more probable that Meyerbeer feared that a meeting with a man wanted for insurrection and high treason would compromise him, in his position as General Musical Director to the King of Prussia.

At all events, Wagner now believed that he was no longer under an obligation. His dislike of Meyerbeer's work had recently been revived by a performance of *Le Prophète* in Paris, and when he came upon the term 'Hebraic taste in art' in a review in the *Neue Zeitschrift für Musik* it became the watchword of his *Jewry in Music*.

He frankly admitted to Liszt in a letter of 18 April 1851 that the article was aimed solely at Meyerbeer: his relationship to Meyerbeer was odd and quite unique; he reminded him of what might almost be called the most vicious period of his life. 'It was the period of old-pal networks and backstairs arrangements, when we are made fools of by patrons to whom inwardly we are most decidedly not devoted. It is a relationship of the utmost dishonour: neither is sincere in his dealings with the other.' Meyerbeer's favours made it impossible for Wagner to make him the least reproach, so that he was actually glad not to be so much in his debt as, for instance, Berlioz. 'But it was time to free myself completely from the dishonest relationship to him: outwardly I did not have the least cause to do so . . . But inward reasons eventually forced me to abandon every regard for normal circumspection where he was concerned: I cannot exist as an artist in my own sight or that of my friends . . . without roundly declaring that in Meyerbeer I find in every respect my opposite . . . This is an act necessary for the complete birth of my mature being.'

Anticipating Liszt's disapproval, he added: 'These are secular matters, on which we can from time to time disagree, without ever being divided on sacred matters. – Whatever you don't care for here, just shut your eyes to!'

Wagner had never objected to Jewish origins among his friends and acquaintances before this time: he has often been accused of ingratitude, and yet he wrote in *Mein Leben* of Samuel Lehrs, for instance, by then long dead, with affection and gratitude. That he now singled out Meyerbeer's race for attack was the outcome of his efforts to give his criticism a completely personal edge. In the last resort that edge was directed against himself, against 'the most vicious period of his life'.

He returned to the subject of Meyerbeer in *Opera and Drama*, when he criticized contemporary grand opera. After sending the manuscript to Uhlig he began to have second thoughts: 'It would be dreadful if it proved possible to take the book as just an attack on Meyerbeer. I wish I could take back some of the things in that vein: when I am reading it, the mockery never sounds venomous – but perhaps when others read it it often sounds passionately embittered

to them, which is not how I would wish to appear even to my
enemies.' (10 March 1851)

The criticism in *Opera and Drama*, which refrained from any
attack on his ancestry, wounded Meyerbeer more deeply than the
earlier pamphlet. He felt so debilitated by an illness, he wrote in his
diary on 24 November 1851, that he could not carry out his intention of getting on with the composition of his new opera.
'Moreover I am greatly demoralized by hearing from Burguy [his
mother's secretary] that Richard Wagner has attacked me violently
in his book on the future of opera.' He goes on to refer to his turning
up again a manuscript essay by Wagner 'on the standpoint of
Meyerbeer's music', in which Wagner praised him extravagantly
and which he had sent him for publication ten years ago; this can
only be the essay mentioned in Chapter 7, on *Les Huguenots*, to
which Richard Sternfeld gave a date of 1837, since its wording
corresponds to a letter Wagner wrote to Meyerbeer in that year.
(*Über Meyerbeers Huguenotten*, RWGS, XII, pp. 22, 422; RWGB, I, p.
101)[2]

In the meantime *Lohengrin* had been performed for the first time,
on 28 August 1850 in Weimar. Wagner and Minna celebrated in
advance by making an excursion up the Rigi, and took it as a good
omen when they saw the rare phenomenon of the Rigi spectre,
when Richard, who had advanced to the very edge of the precipice,
was reflected giant-size in the sky in the evening sunlight. They
spent the evening of the performance itself in the inn Zum
Schwanen in Lucerne. Stirred by a multitude of emotions, Wagner
kept his watch in his hand to time the start and the probable ending,
but he always felt a little strained, ill at ease and irritable, he later
confessed, when he tried to share what should have been agreeable
and exciting occasions with Minna.

The whole opera was a single, indivisible miracle, Liszt reported,
and like the pious priest who had gone through the *Imitation of
Christ* underlining the text word by word, he could underline
Lohengrin note by note, though if he did he would go first to the
duet in the third act, which to him was the acme of beauty and truth
in art. (2 September)

'As far as I can now . . . judge the overall character of the Weimar
production of my *Lohengrin*,' Wagner replied, 'the first most certain
and incontestable thing that emerges from all the accounts is your
incomparable exertion and dedication for the sake of my work,

your touching love and the manifestation of your genius for doing the impossible as well as it possibly can be done.' (8 September) When he dedicated the score to Liszt two years later he wrote: 'You it was who awoke the dumb notation of this score to the bright life of sound: but for your rare love to me my work would still lie silent – perhaps forgotten by myself – in a box with my domestic effects: no ear would have been reached by what moved my heart and delighted my imagination when I wrote it, nearly five years ago now, performance always vivid in my mind.' (May 1852)

Though the theatre at Weimar was not one of the great houses of Germany, this première marked a new epoch in Wagner's career. The world was accustomed to look on the first performances of his works as local, Dresden occasions and waited to read about them in the spiteful columns of the local critics, Carl Banck and Julius Schladebach. But *Lohengrin* had been presented to a new forum, an audience of strangers, and its success could neither be denied nor concealed. The mere fact of the presence at the première of leading figures from the musical world both in Germany and abroad proved the standing of the exiled composer. For the first time, too, voices were heard expressing good will, even enthusiasm: Franz Müller, a senior civil servant in Weimar, who wrote for the *Konversationsblatt* of Frankfurt, Adolf Stahr in the Berlin *Nationalzeitung*, J. C. Lobe in the Leipzig *Signale*, Uhlig in the *Neue Zeitschrift für Musik*, and Gérard de Nerval in *La Presse* of Paris. If Nerval showed more good will than actual understanding, he nevertheless deserves to be hailed as the precursor of the French *wagnéristes*. Wagner was now a phenomenon so widely discussed that even adverse criticism could no longer put him down but, as Newman points out, only added to his publicity. Moreover the Weimar production broke a taboo, the idea that only theatres with performers of the calibre of Tichatschek and Schröder-Devrient at their disposal could dare to stage Wagner's works. From now on there began a steadily increasing demand for them at the smaller houses – or at those where the musical director had no operatic aspirations of his own – the most sought after, to begin with, being *Tannhäuser*. If Wagner had earned any royalties from the performances he would soon have been in the position to support himself without being a burden on his friends.

The Weimar *Lohengrin* had no less profound consequences for his new work. According to Karl Ritter, his emissary at the first performance, the musical execution was good, but the dramatic side was all wrong. This had a decisive effect on the fate of *Siegfrieds Tod*. The first person to whom he mentioned it was his old Parisian friend Ernst Benedikt Kietz. He was still thinking of setting his 'Siegfried', he wrote on 14 September, but he was not prepared to let it be performed in just any theatre that happened to make an offer for it. On the contrary, he was laying the most audacious of plans, the realization of which could not cost less than 10,000 talers. With that sum he would build a wooden theatre right there where he was and employ the most suitable singers. He would invite all those who were interested in his works and give – gratis, of course – three consecutive performances in one week, after which the theatre would be pulled down and that would be the end of the whole affair. Something on those lines was all that appealed to him now. now. 'If Karl Ritter's uncle dies I shall get the money!' (RWBC, p. 415)

A week later he wrote to Uhlig that whether he would let Weimar give the first performance of 'Siegfried' was a question he would probably be able to answer only with an unconditional No. Although the intendant had assured him that *Lohengrin* was and would remain a success at the box office, nevertheless he probably didn't need to emphasize that he hoped 'Siegfried's' launching on the world would be different from what the good people there were capable of giving it. Then he again unfolded the plan he had revealed to Kietz which, he admitted, looked a real chimera on the face of it. 'Now do I seem downright mad to you? It may be so, but I assure you that achieving it is the hope of my life!' (20 September)

For the time being these were dreams of the future which he confided to no one else. 'I have had a great deal to think about again,' he told Liszt, 'alas, to think about *again*! But now once and for all I've come to a point where I cannot go back: I *must* think things through to their conclusion, before I can become an instinctive, completely confident artist again.' (2 October) And even more urgently after quite a long silence: 'I regard the eventual adoption of my artistic plans, to which I am now applying myself, as one of the most important factors in my life . . . I had to make a clean sweep of a whole life, bring all that was dawning in me to full consciousness, master by its own agency the reflection that inexorably rose upon me.' (25 November)

He was referring to an article he was writing on the 'nature of opera', which grew during the course of the winter to a whole book, *Opera and Drama*. 'It is a very remarkable work,' he told Cosima in 1879, 'and I was very excited when I wrote it, for it is without a predecessor in the history of art, and I was really aiming at a target no one could see.' (BBL 1937, p. 106)

The excitement that pursued him on his lonely way vented itself in some strange, exalted ideas. With true fanaticism he prescribed a 'water cure' for himself and his friends, on the grounds that 'radical water' is the only release any of us have from an unnatural physical state. At the same time he proposed a 'fire cure' for mankind in the form of a new revolution which was to start with the firing of Paris as a beacon. 'You'll see how much better we shall be after this fire cure!' he exclaimed to the horrified Uhlig.[3] The following year he survived two months of a hydropathic cure in Albisbrunn, though he was in a terrible nervous state and lost a great deal of weight, which goes to show the fundamental soundness of his constitution in spite of all his complaints and suffering.

Opera and Drama was nothing less than the theoretical expression of an 'artistic–productive process' – the outward manifestation of his great drama on the Nibelung's ring, which was developing deep within him while he was writing the book. The third part of it, 'Poetry and Music in the Drama of the Future', as he told Uhlig, penetrates to the fundamentals. It is illuminating that artistic practice had already preceded the theory. 'I had to wait until now to realize that I would not have discovered the most important factors in the shaping of the drama of the future, if I had not already stumbled upon them completely unawares as an artist in my "Siegfried".' The great significance of the 1850 composition sketch lies in its illustration of how the preliminary practice was not confined to the text alone, but also affected the musical setting as well.

'Here is my testament,' he told Uhlig when he sent him the manuscript. 'I wrote the last pages . . . in a mood that I could not describe lucidly to anyone.' He had withdrawn so far from the present that it had grown completely still about him and he had sometimes seemed to himself to be dead.

Shortly before completing the book, he had suffered the loss of his familiar spirit and domestic genius: the little parrot, which had always had a cheerful whistle to greet him with, had died. 'Oh – if I could tell you all that has died for me with that little creature!!! I don't care in the least if people laugh at me: what I feel, I feel . . . It happened three days ago – and still nothing can soothe me: – and it's just the same with my wife: – the bird was something unforced between us and for us.' (To Uhlig, mid–February; to Liszt, 18 February 1851)

It had not been long before it emerged that they had little left in common; and the pets, the dog and the bird, had had to take the place of the children and interests that might have linked them. For all Minna's excellent qualities she unfortunately did not have the least understanding of his essential being, he complained to Liszt: 'I am inwardly a stranger to her.' (9 March)

At the same time that he was working on the book, he had not been able to rid himself all winter of an idea for a comic opera based on the Grimms' fairy tale about 'the boy who left home to learn fear', which threatened to distract his attention from Siegfried altogether. 'Imagine the shock I had', he wrote to Uhlig on 10 May, 'when I suddenly recognized that that boy is none other than – young Siegfried, who wins the treasure and wakes Brünnhilde.' *Der Junge Siegfried* would have the immense advantage of presenting the myth to the audience playfully, as a fairy tale does to a child, and it would moreover prepare the performers for the daunting task of *Siegfrieds Tod*.

He had just drafted the first prose sketch before he wrote that letter, and the confidence of the scenario reveals how much the plan had already matured in his head. He wrote the full-scale prose draft between 24 May and 1 June and completed the verse text in the following three weeks, 3–24 June. *Der Junge Siegfried* had entered the world, entire and well rhymed, that very morning, he wrote hastily on 24 June to Uhlig, who was on the point of leaving Dresden to come and visit him in Switzerland.

Liszt, too, was made privy to the new plan, partly because it occurred to Wagner that perhaps it would after all be possible to entrust the two 'Siegfrieds' to the Weimar theatre. But he hesitated to send him the text: 'What I have written is – I'm afraid – not good enough for my purpose, but if I can read it aloud to you – giving some idea of how I think it ought to be – then that would completely reassure me as to the impression I want my text to make on you.' (29 June)

But although he had thought that this text would absolve him once and for all from ever writing prose again, he had, once more, crowed too soon. Breitkopf & Härtel were going to publish an edition of the texts of *Der Fliegende Holländer, Tannhäuser* and *Lohengrin*, and for this he wrote a long autobiographical preface, the *Communication to my Friends. (Eine Mitteilung an meine Freunde*, RWGS, IV, pp. 230ff.) As he put it in a letter to Liszt, the *Communication* is an admission of how far he too had wandered trying to find the right artistic path, and he was not one of those elect of God into whose mouths the one true, solid food of art drops as manna from heaven. Only the *completed Tannhäuser*, the *completed Lohengrin* made him conscious of the direction in which an unconscious instinct had steered him. What he wanted to explain to his friends was the turn he was now making away from romantic opera to mythic drama. (22 May)

As chance would have it, the printing was held up because Breitkopf & Härtel took the preface for a delayed revolutionary tract: as businessmen, they indicated, they held aloof from political involvement of any kind; but as Wagner lived outside the frontiers of the German Federation, they would be held accountable. By the time the offending passages had been altered and the book had gone to press the situation had fundamentally changed.

Wagner had embarked on his drastic hydropathic cure at Albisbrunn on 15 September: the idea of being in perfect health when he went back to his 'Siegfried' appealed to him as both pleasing and seemly. After only a fortnight he reported to Uhlig that Albisbrunn was doing him the world of good: whereas to begin with he had still been plagued by theory, it was now gradually dispersing from his brain like a grey mist. Two weeks later still, on 12 October, came the first announcement of the tetralogy: 'More big ideas for "Siegfried": three dramas with a three-act prologue – if all the theatres in Germany collapse, I will put up a new one on the Rhine, issue my summons and perform the whole work in the course of one week.' In November he made the first drafts of the prose sketches of *Das Rheingold* and *Die Walküre* and returned to Zürich on 23 November, where he had in the meantime moved to rooms on Zeltweg.

It was clear to him that his plan entailed a break not only with Weimar but with the contemporary theatre as a whole. 'With this conception of mine I *totally* abandon all connection with the theatre and audiences of today: I break decisively and forever with the formulas of the present time,' he told Uhlig. And then followed an admission that was omitted from the edition of their correspondence and first published in *Bayreuther Blätter* in 1892: 'I cannot think of a *performance* until *after the revolution*, only the revolution can give me the artists and the audiences . . . Then I will summon what I need out of the ruins: I will find *then* what I must have.' (12 November; RWBC, p. 783)

He had hoped that *A Communication to my Friends* would appear before his new plans became known, so that Liszt would have been assured of his original good intentions, at least, in respect of Weimar. As a result of the delay he was obliged to alter the conclusion so as to announce the project of three dramas and a prologue, of which it was as yet still quite uncertain when and how they would eventually reach the public. At the same time, on 20 November, he wrote Liszt a letter, running to ten pages in print, rendering him a full account of the development of his idea from the first draft of 1848 to the tetralogy: the expansion was not the product of wilful calculation of extraneous factors, he explained but had forced itself upon him as the necessary consequence of the nature and content of the material.

'You just get on with it,' Liszt replied, 'and don't concern yourself with anything but your work, for which we might as well now give you the same commission as the cathedral chapter in Seville gave their architect: "Build us a temple such that future generations will surely say that the chapter was mad to undertake something so extraordinary." And yet the cathedral stands!' (1 December)

It was another of the eleventh-hour strokes of luck in Wagner's life that a sudden legacy enabled Frau Ritter to ensure him an annuity of 800 talers. That it should have come precisely at that moment could not but seem almost providential. 'Thanks to this security I am . . . as one newborn,' he wrote to the friend who had become like a mother to him; 'my head is full of the most provocative and exhilarating artistic plans.' (9 December)

All the time his plan was growing, he was alive to the natural beauties of Switzerland. In a letter to Otto Wesendonk in 1859 he wrote with nostalgia of 'glorious Switzerland', where he had conceived his works 'with the sublime, gold-crowned mountains before my eyes'. Before going to Albisbrunn, inspired by the quincentennial celebrations in Zürich, he had spent a week with Uhlig following the paths traced in Schiller's *Wilhelm Tell*, which led them from Brunnen on the east shore of the Lake of Lucerne through 'the fearful mountains of the Surennes' to the Maderaner valley, where the 'sublime Alpine world' of the Tödi came into view. He made no further progress with his work during the winter, but he wrote the full prose draft of *Das Rheingold* in March 1852, and both the prose sketch and the verse text of *Die Walküre* in May and June, while staying in the Pension Rinderknecht on the slopes of the Zürichberg, 'in the open air, with unimpeded views of the lake and the distant Alps'. It was here that he first thought of the episode of the May night bursting its way into Hunding's hut, which is absent from the earlier sketches: in the full prose sketch, 'Siegmund points to the beauty of the spring night, no one has gone out: Spring has opened the door and entered; the fresh, intoxicating scents of the forest reach us; the nightingale tells her sad tale . . . '

On 1 July he told Uhlig that he had finished *Die Walküre* the day before after a month's work, 'I am rather worn out once again: I am simply putting too much passion into my work!' So the next thing he did was set off on another tour, mostly on foot, from Interlaken via the Gries glacier to Domodossola, climbing en route the Faulhorn and the Siedelhorn, which gave him amazing views of Mont Blanc and Monte Rosa.

After that, he found the courage in the autumn to write the verse text of *Das Rheingold* and make a final revision of *Der Junge Siegfried* and *Siegfrieds Tod*. 'My only major concern now is the Nibelung poem,' he confessed in the middle of his work, 'that is the only thing, it uplifts me, high and powerfully, whenever I turn to it. I am averse to the thought of posterity, and yet this vanity of vanities creeps up on me now and then, when my poem issues out of my soul into the world. It is and it contains everything I can do and everything I have.' (To Uhlig, 14 October)

The fundamental structure of the fable of the *Ring* was already present in the 1848 essay, *The Nibelung Myth as the Scenario for a Drama*, but it acquired certain new characters and new situations during the next four years. The *Scenario* lacked Loge, Freia and Erda: the last is unknown to German mythology and was Wagner's own invention, a Greco-German mother–prophetess, uniting Aeschylus's Gaea (*The Eumenides*, V, 2) and the Eddic Völva (from whom Jacob Grimm deduced an Old High German Wala).

Two important elements were not incorporated until quite a late stage. Alberich's curse on love took from the ring its purely magical power and made it an ethical symbol of universal significance: as the material shaped itself in Wagner's hands, the renunciation – or the denial – of love became the governing dramatic motive up to the moment of Siegfried's death. And the World-Ash, slowly withering away from the wound incurred when Wotan tore off a branch to make his spear, now provided the mythic background to the revised version of the Norns' scene, Waltraute's narration and the finale.

But the most significant departure from the 1848 sketch is the turn the work takes into tragedy. Originally *Siegfrieds Tod* ended with Brünnhilde proclaiming the restoration of Wotan's reign:

> Nur einer herrsche:
> Allvater! Herrlicher du!

('Let one alone rule: Allfather, Lord, you!');

while *Götterdämmerung* ends with his freely chosen eclipse:

> Ruhe! Ruhe, du Gott!

Two interpretations have been put on this, one philosophical, the other political, and both mistaken. The former, attributing the change to the influence of Schopenhauer, is easily answered: the Annals record Wagner's first reading of *The World as Will and Idea* in September 1854, eighteen months after the private first edition of the text of the *Ring* in February 1853.

According to the other interpretation, Wagner the revolutionary, disillusioned by Louis Napoleon's *coup d'état* of 2 December 1851, inwardly admitted defeat, gave up the struggle against the nineteenth century and gave the *Ring* a pessimistic, nihilistic construction. The reasoning is attractive, but it is false for all that. Apart from the version of *Siegfrieds Tod* published in the complete edition of Wagner's writings, there is a later manuscript copy that can be dated early in 1849, owned by the Sulzer family of Zürich. In that, Brünnhilde's final words are crossed out and replaced initially by a few lines in which she speaks to the guilt of the gods and promises them 'blessed expiation'. But this change still did not satisfy Wagner: following a sudden inspiration, he scribbled a third version sideways up the margin:

> erbleichet in Wonne vor des Menschen Tat,
> vor dem Helden, den ihr gezeugt!
> Aus eurer bangen Furcht
> verkünd ich euch selige Todeserlösung!

('Grow pale in bliss before the deed of the man, before the hero you begot! Out of your dread I proclaim to you blessed absolution in death!')

This is no less than the complete reversal of Wotan's destiny into a tragic one. The note in the margin can moreover be dated fairly precisely: since it is in the old German script it must have been written before Wagner changed to using Latin script, which he did in 1850. Nothing tangible came of it for some time, but when Wagner started to draft the first sketches for *Der Junge Siegfried* in May 1851, the following immediately meets the eye:

> Wodan and the Wala: the gods' end. Wodan's decision: the Wala sinks away.

The tragic theme crystallizes here, in the scene between the Wanderer and Erda in the third act, the 'heart of the great cosmic tragedy', and from here it reaches out to inform every section of the tetralogy. The sketches for *Rheingold* and *Walküre* followed in November, with the greatest space allotted to the tragic catastrophe in the second act of the latter, and by the time the news of the coup in Paris on 2 December 1851 broke on the world, the tragic turn to the *Ring*, which had started to take shape two years before, had already been accomplished.

But while the political event was too late to exercise any influence on his text, it inflamed rather than dampened his thoughts. Together with the poet Georg Herwegh, he wrote to Uhlig on 18 December, he had decided on something which could prove to be a turning point in history. He was going to devote his literary activity to nothing else from that time forth, his goal being a positive, practical purpose of immeasurable consequence and moreover one that no reactionary power in the world would be able to hinder. (RWBC, p. 784) Whatever these cryptic hints may have meant, the last thing they suggest is inward defeat.

He expressed himself in even more radical terms to Ernst Benedikt Kietz: 'The whole of my political creed is nothing other than the bloodiest hatred of our whole civilization, contempt for everything that springs from it, and longing for nature. . . Everything in our country is riddled with servility: there is nobody in all France who knows that we are nonetheless human beings, except perhaps Proudhon – and even he is none too clear about it! – In all Europe I prefer the dogs to these doglike people. And yet I do not despair of a *future*; but only the most fearful and destructive of revolutions can

make our civilized beasts "human" again.' And then he voices for
the first time an idea that stirred him again a quarter of a century
later: 'I am thinking about America a great deal now! Not that I
would find right there, but because it would be easier to implant
there.' (30 December; RWBC, p. 257)

But violent outbursts like this do not disguise the fact that his
belief in revolution was by now only a habit of thought essential to
his creative work. As the hope of a revolution in 1848 had given him
the desperate courage necessary to embark on the Nibelung plan, so
now he had to sustain the illusion so as not to lose his courage in the
face of the dissatisfactions of his present circumstances. Once he had
established the dimensions of his plan, laid down the width, height
and depth of it, the idea of revolution lost its creative importance
and nothing more was heard of it all the time that he was at work on
the music.

It was neither philosophy nor politics that dictated the tragic turn
taken by Wotan's fate in the *Ring*: his tragedy revealed itself to
Wagner in exactly the degree that the mythological figure took on
the attributes of individuality, of *humanity*.

The many stages in the composition of the text, from the first
notes and sketches to the first and then the final drafts of the poem,
amounting to more than 750 pages in all, can be traced more
completely in the case of the *Ring* than any other of the major
works. It emerges all the more surely that research into the sources,
or historico-biographical interpretations, will not plumb the mystery of its genesis. The final form of the work was not the product of
wilful calculation, Wagner had told Liszt: it forced itself on him as
the necessary consequence of the material. As Thomas Mann
remarks, we have to relive the 'ecstatic amazement' Wagner himself
experienced in the course of writing the text, if we are to realize how
little the artist originally knew about his work. 'The ambition is not
the artist's, it is the work's: the work's own will to be far greater
than the artist believed he might hope, or dare, imposes itself upon
him.'

'The work imposes its will upon the artist' – and how relent-
lessly! His whole day was a strict regimen, he told Frau Ritter, in
order to gain two beneficial hours in the morning to work in. 'As
the result of a gestation like this I have now brought the complete
poem of my *Ring* into the world: this birth gives me great joy; like
an enfeebled mother I have diverted my best fluids to it and with

luck no one will notice how it came about.' (29 December 1852)

As usual he was impatient to unveil the new work to his friends. On 18 December he set off with Georg Herwegh to read it to their friends François and Eliza Wille in Mariafeld on two consecutive days. He spent a fee that he had had for *Tannhäuser* on printing fifty copies of it for private circulation. He derived especial pleasure from the thought of sending it to his friend Uhlig already in print, but it was too late: Uhlig died on 3 January 1853. In the middle of February Wagner arranged a reading of the tetralogy on four evenings in the Hotel Baur au Lac, and was astonished to find the room was fuller on each successive evening.

Part IV: *Der Ring des Nibelungen* (I) (1853–1857)

17

The Vision of La Spezia

'I am greatly occupied with the musical setting now', Wagner wrote to Frau Ritter on 29 December 1852, a fortnight after he had finished his text. But the preoccupation had started much earlier. Even before the composition sketch of August 1850 he wrote down some preliminary sketches for *Siegfrieds Tod* on a folio sheet which has survived:[1] fragments of the Norns' scene and the Leavetaking scene, and the Valkyries' chorus from the first act ('Nach süden wir ziehen, siege zu zeugen . . . '), sung to a melody that later became the orchestral form of the Valkyries' motive. This theme, so very characteristic of the style inaugurated in the *Ring*, is thus the earliest surviving leitmotiv of the entire work. (The theme turns up again in an *Albumblatt* of 23 July 1851 and in an inscription in an autograph album dated 12 November 1852.)

It is less easy to know precisely what other musical developments came out of these years of preparation, apart from notes of individual motives and remarks Wagner made during the period about singing the free, rhythmic Nibelung line. Certainly the most important thing was that, although against his will, Wagner engaged once again in the performance of music. On his recommendation Karl Ritter had been appointed conductor at the Zürich municipal theatre for the 1850–1 season. However, when it became all too apparent at Ritter's first rehearsals that he was almost completely unequipped for the post, Wagner recognized that he had an obligation to the management to take his place. The fact that Hans von Bülow also wanted to come to Zürich to study conducting with him was, in his eyes, yet another burden.

Bülow, though consumed by a passion for music, was being forced by his parents to study law. 'Pray allow . . . a man who, now in his maturity, has become accustomed to think and to act not by halves but always whole-heartedly – so far as it lies in his power – to tell you his opinion on this matter,' Wagner implored Frau von Bülow. He had observed, he wrote, that her son's love of music was founded on great, indeed exceptional, ability. 'Give your consent, freely, gladly and soon, to your son's not living an instant longer under a yoke that is incompatible with his well-founded and tested inclination.' His plea was in vain. Bülow asked him once more for advice, to which Wagner replied: '*You alone* must know the strength of your love for art and your dislike for the law; I have no doubts about your ability.' (5 October 1850) That message was conveyed to him by Karl Ritter at his father's house, Schloss Ötlishausen in the Thurgau. After walking through foul weather for two days the two young men arrived on Wagner's doorstep in Zürich on 7 October. 'I had to act,' Bülow wrote to his mother, 'act wholly, leave no bridge behind for return, for possible repentance. There is no going back on this decision now. I am going to be a musician.'

By contrast with Ritter, he at once demonstrated an innate ability to govern an orchestra. But he had the misfortune to earn the displeasure of the all-powerful prima donna, and had to resign after only two months. The post was filled by Franz Abt, while Wagner, carefully avoiding any permanent appointment, continued to conduct certain works until the end of the season.

The choice he made from the limited Zürich repertory, with the *Ring* stirring inside him, is illuminating. He began with *Der Frei-schütz* and finished with *Fidelio*. *Norma* was a voice from the past, recalling his enthusiasm for Bellini when he was twenty-four. As he said in a letter to Liszt, he regarded the works of the older French school as the most suitable for developing a dramatic performance style, because they embodied a natural dramatic intention in the most easily assimilable form. How was a company that could not put on competent and effective performances of works by Cheru-bini, Méhul or Boieldieu to cope in the fullness of time with the enormous demands of his operas? (22 May 1851) In fact he only had the opportunity to conduct *La Dame Blanche* during that season, and the deficiencies of the Zürich theatre are illustrated by the fact that, in the absence of a harp, the music for that instrument which accompanies the appearance of the White Lady had to be played by Bülow on the piano; he did it 'with a wonderfully beautiful effect'.

Of the two works by Mozart that he conducted, *Die Zauberflöte* and *Don Giovanni*, the latter has a certain significance in that he did not limit himself to preparing the musical performance, but undertook also a cautious editing of the text and the recitatives. He told Uhlig that he had put in some careful shading in the orchestral part, made a new translation of the dialogue and run some of the scenes together, to reduce the need for changing the set. As an instance of this he cited the combination of the scene in the cemetery with Donna Anna's aria. 'After Don Juan and Leporello have gone off over the wall, the orchestra softly holds the F major chord: the two mourners [Donna Anna and Ottavio] enter (accompanied by servants with torches) to lay a wreath on the Commendatore's tomb; a short dialogue takes place (to music), leading directly into the aria, which gains a very beautiful, elegiac colouring from being sung in the graveyard.' (26 February 1852)

Wagner and his two apprentices spent several days and nights correcting the deficient orchestral parts, and making up for the lack of some instruments by rewriting the parts for others – low trumpets in place of trombones, for instance. Bülow wrote of how angry it made him to recall that Wagner had been accused in Dresden of deliberately conducting Mozart's operas badly because he detested them out of sheer conceit: the warm sense of piety that Wagner expressed in his selfless action would never be displayed by any of those pseudo-admirers.

Unfortunately the edition has been lost. It was probably destroyed when the theatre caught fire on the night of New Year's day 1890. Throughout his life Wagner opposed the fashionable idea of making a serious opera of *Don Giovanni*. Of course the work was divine, incomparable, but that was precisely due to the fact that its perspectives opened out from a popular basis: to take those wider perspectives as the starting point was to destroy them, to make nonsense of the frivolous and light-hearted elements, to render the work as a whole stiff and dull. In short, it was *opera giocosa*. (BBL 1937, p. 53)

The stimulus he received from this renewed contact with the theatre is shown in the pamphlet he wrote in April 1851, *A Theatre in Zürich*, which approached the question of theatrical reform, which he had already tackled in Dresden and Vienna, from a completely different angle. Instead of entrusting the fortunes of the institution to the arbitrament of chance, he suggested the evolution of an 'original theatre' out of a root-stock of local, indigenous forces. 'Let us take a look . . . at Zürich! Are there no artistically creative forces to be found here? Unrecognized they may be, but they surely exist.' (*Ein Theater in Zürich*, RWGS, V, pp. 20ff.)

The Zürich writer Gottfried Keller, then in Berlin, at once sent for a copy of Wagner's pamphlet and read it rejoicing, as he told Wilhelm Baumgartner, a Zürich musician who knew them both. In his opinion, it would unfortunately have little effect in the immediate future, but it strengthened his hope of finding somewhere where he could work in the air of his own home.

Wagner also conducted concerts in Zürich, and this activity had a direct bearing on his principal concern, the composition of the *Ring*. The Music Society in Zürich, in competition with the theatre, maintained its own orchestra, consisting of twenty-four professional players assisted by some dozen amateurs. After Wagner had accepted their invitation to conduct Beethoven's A major Symphony 'with an augmented orchestra' in January 1850, the society were bold enough to engage him as a guest conductor for future concerts. During the winter seasons of 1850–1 and 1851–2, in addition to the overtures to *Euryanthe, La Vestale* (to mark the death of Spontini), *Coriolan* and *Tannhäuser*, Wagner conducted the *Egmont* music and Beethoven's Third, Fifth, Sixth, Seventh and Eighth Symphonies, some of them on two occasions.

Even the rehearsals, with musicians who in some cases had travelled long distances to play, were in a sense solemn occasions. And since Wagner was able to concentrate on one overture and one symphony at a time, he had the leisure to refine his interpretation and performing style as never before. He rehearsed the oboist in his part like a singer, with such success that the little adagio passage in the first movement of the C minor Symphony was played more movingly than he ever heard it again. He put a gifted horn-player in charge of the brass section, under whose leadership they played the loud sustained chords in the last movement with an intensity that reminded him of the Paris Conservatoire orchestra.

When rehearsing the *Coriolan* Overture, the first thing he did was give the players a programmatic exposition as a foundation, in terms of a dramatic scenario which he explained to them step by step as they went through the work. (RWGS, V, pp. 173ff.) The

result was striking: he made ordinary dance-band musicians capable of achievements that they themselves had never dreamed of.
And later, when he was rehearsing the *Tannhäuser* overture with
them, they asked him on their own initiative for a similar exposition, as it would help them to 'play better'.

'A miracle!' Bülow exclaimed after the 'Eroica', 'beyond belief!'
What particularly pleased Wagner, however, was the effect his
performance had even on such as his friend Jacob Sulzer, who had
had no interest in music until then.

The effect that performing Beethoven had on Wagner himself
was to stimulate him to reflect on the other composer's procedures
of melodic formation and development: how he burst the narrow
mould, broke up the melody into its separate motivic elements,
mixed these elements together in all kinds of different associations,
in order to link them all together again during the course of the
piece in a new organic whole – that is, his presentation, not of a
completed melody, but of the act of its creation. (*Opera and Drama*,
RWGS, III, p. 315)

The only person with whom Wagner could discuss matters like
this was another musician given to thinking about music, like
Uhlig. He read his articles in the *Neue Zeitschrift für Musik* and wrote
to tell him what immense pleasure they gave him and, more important, how much they frequently taught him as well. 'I am very
grateful to you. You are a master in your field, there is nothing
more that I can say.' When the two of them went on their walking
tour of the four Forest Cantons in July 1851, Uhlig had the misfortune to fall into a mountain stream. Making the best of it, he spread
his clothes out in the sun and walked up and down stark naked
waiting for them to dry, while continuing his conversation with
Wagner about the weightier problems of Beethovenian thematic
processes, until at last Wagner shook his aplomb by declaring that
he had just caught sight of a respected Hofrat from Dresden and his
family coming along the path towards them.

The outcome of these exchanges was an essay by Uhlig on the
'choice of motives and the manner of their deployment in larger
instrumental compositions'. After his death Wagner offered it,
together with other essays by his friend, to Breitkopf & Härtel for
publication: he believed it to be no exaggeration, he wrote, to
regard it as the most significant work of its kind. (5 April 1856)
'But, however,' went their reply, declining, 'collected essays in the

field of music are very hazardous projects for the publisher.' When Uhlig's writings were eventually published, nearly sixty years later, the manuscript of his most important work had vanished without trace.[2]

Motivic development was the musical problem that exercised Wagner most with the *Ring*. In the case of the *Holländer* he had been unaware of what he was doing when he set the motivic germs in Senta's Ballad, whence they had grown to spread a complete network over the entire drama; but since then he had become aware of the process, and it must have been a wonderful moment for him when he recognized that the principle of motivic development, with its wealth of emotional associations and its capacity for recalling the past and foreshadowing the future, was ideally suited to the task of creating the omnipresent mythic background to his drama.

It can be said that it was the poet who refined the process of musical motivic development for the sake of his drama. But it could be asserted with equal truth that it was the musician who made his text go back to the very beginning of things for the sake of these new musical possibilities. It is probable that Wagner's musical instinct, always the stronger force, had the last word here, as elsewhere. At all events the first and perhaps the most difficult step on the road to understanding the Wagnerian work of art is the realization that the text and the music are only two different facets of one and the same thing.

It is significant that this stage in the development of his compositional technique took place under the aegis of Beethoven: 'I would not have been able to compose as I have, had it not been for Beethoven.' (GLRW, VI, p. 408)

Wagner's appearances on the podium in Zürich were the occasion of his at once stepping, as he was fated to do wherever he went, into the centre of controversy, This time, however, there was a comical exchange of roles: while the conservative *Eidgenössische Zeitung* espoused the cause of the revolutionary musician, the *Neue Züricher Zeitung*, then a radical, liberal paper, took the side of his opponents, on account of the various choral societies and their director, Franz Abt, who were among its readers. On the occasion of a performance of the *Holländer* overture in 1852, the *Tagblatt* published a poem by 'an Aargauer', accusing the opera of immorality, to which Wagner replied with an antistrophe:

Daran erken ich schnell, mit leichtem Rat,
du Ärmster seist ein – ganzer Literat . . .

('Therein I see at once, as well I can,
poor wretch, thou art – a literary man.')

His conducting had a more serious consequence, however, in that it drew him to the attention of the police of the German Federation. A young violinist from Lemberg (Lwow) called Haimberger, whom Wagner had known at the time of the Dresden rising and who had also fled to Switzerland, appeared at one of his concerts. An enquiry went from Prague to Dresden as to whether the Wagner who was one of the ringleaders of the Swiss Revolutionary Party in Zürich, associated with the Galician fugitive Haimberger, and had Austrian connections, was identical with the 'known Richard Wagner'. The Dresden police enquired of the Zürich police about the 'said individual', and received the following reply: 'The refugee Richard Wagner from Dresden composes and occasionally obliges by conducting the orchestra in concerts and in the theatre here; he holds no specific appointment. The Jewish embezzler Lehmann Samuel, *vulgo* Braunschweig, was handed over to the district magistrates in Hall on 1 February. The notorious confidence trickster and counterfeiter Mitalis Georg, alleged Prince of Smyrna' – and so on. (LWVR, p. 28) Wagner knew nothing of the illustrious company in which he had been included. But we can see the effect that the Saxon police's interest in him was to have on his future.

To begin with Wagner refused even to think of appealing for pardon. As late as 13 April 1852 he asked Liszt to deny as firmly as possible the rumour that he had made any such application. By accepted standards he could count himself satisfied with his lot: a refugee without means, he had found friends here who helped him, and was the centre of a circle who admired him as an artist.

Of all his Swiss friends, it was Sulzer whom he singled out in his autobiography for the highest praise: if he was asked if he had ever encountered in his life what could be called true moral character, then, after very careful thought, he had to name Jakob Sulzer. Another intimate in Zürich was Wilhelm Baumgartner, 'Boom' to his friends, whose settings of poems by Gottfried Keller Wagner actually reviewed in the *Eidgenössische Zeitung*: 'May . . . true song, no more separable from the poem than from the melody, blossom from the common creative power of these two.' (RWGS, XII, pp.

286ff.) The attempt to introduce him to the senior members of the university was less successful: 'Recently I was invited to take tea with some of the German professors here – horror seized me and drove me, pining, back into the arms of my Swiss friends.'

After her initial reluctance, Minna, too, had settled down in Zürich. 'My wife is radiantly happy,' Wagner wrote to Frau Ritter in April 1852, 'she has lovely clothes and a lot of lady friends; she has never, anywhere we have been, enjoyed a winter so much as this last.'

But all of a sudden, in the following autumn, he began to complain: 'The desert in which I now find myself is becoming intolerable,' he wrote to Liszt on 3 October 1852. Then, even more passionately, 'I shall very shortly be ruined here and everything – everything will come *too late*!!' He weighed up all the possibilities open to him: should he appeal for pardon to the King of Saxony, or rather to his scoundrels of ministers? Who would ever expect that of him? But there were princes – and here he was hinting at Liszt's employer, the Grand Duke of Weimar – who loved his works and could bring about his return without his needing to humiliate himself. 'You, my only friend, the dearest that I have, you who are prince and world – everything in one to me, have pity on me!' (9 November)

What had happened? Wagner suffered from depression throughout the whole of this winter of 1852–3. 'I wanted to work,' he told Uhlig, 'but felt so bad that I had to spend the whole morning on the couch, half sleeping, half waking.' He had no doubts as to the inner cause of his malaise. 'Something has got to happen, to wrest me out of this eternal existing only in my thoughts. This occupying myself with art *à distance* is killing me!' 'I am suffering from "mind",' he wrote to Kietz, 'and the mind is an incurable disease.' (7 September; RWBC, p. 263)

Early in 1853, immediately following his readings of the text of the *Ring*, he felt so ill that he feared he was on the verge of following poor Uhlig. Again, it was the constriction on his material circumstances that sapped his strength for living and creating. 'Give my new poem the greatest attention,' he exclaimed to Liszt, 'it includes the beginning and the end of the world!' The prospect of setting it all to music stimulated him greatly: 'in its form' it was completely finished in his mind, and he had never been so certain about a composition as now. All he needed was some pleasure in his life to induce the cheerful temper where motives would pour out freely and gladly. 'I *must* hear *Lohengrin* once: until I have, I neither want, nor am able, to make music again!!' He outlined a new scheme: the Grand Duke should arrange a safe conduct to Weimar for him for four weeks, and then he would punctiliously return to Switzerland. (11 February 1853) 'I am afraid that I can hold out only very timorous hopes,' Liszt replied.

So Wagner had to help himself. On 22 February 1853 he wrote to the committee of the Zürich Music Society, proposing to give a special concert *hors saison* in the civic theatre in May, with a programme of excerpts from his operas, which he would repeat twice. 'I would . . . look for my sole reward in the artistic execution, in the joy of success itself, and I expressly decline any part of any kind of pecuniary profit.'

It was in fact the first Wagner Festival. An orchestra of seventy was assembled from far and wide – only Munich refused its players leave. Zürich provided a choir of 110 singers, of both sexes. The programme consisted of items from *Rienzi*, *Holländer*, *Tannhäuser* and, most important of all, from *Lohengrin*: for the first time Wagner heard the sound of the eight-part string writing in the prelude, the woodwind chords enriched by the 'third group'. The third of the concerts took place on his fortieth birthday. At the end a singer stepped forward and read a poem in his honour. As the whole house applauded Wagner was presented with a silver cup and a laurel wreath. 'It made an uncommonly moving impression on me,' he told Liszt; 'I had to take a good grip on myself not to break down.' Artistically it was an immense success: there was a demand for more repeat performances, but Wagner wanted to preserve the special character of the occasion. 'There is *one* beautiful woman . . . at whose feet I laid the entire festival,' he confessed to Liszt. It was Mathilde Wesendonk.

Not only did these concerts permit him to hear how his *Lohengrin* orchestra sounded; they also revived his hopes of performing the *Ring* in Zürich and he actually selected a beautiful meadow at Hottingen as a site for his timber festival theatre. 'My music festival was wonderful,' he wrote to his old friend Ferdinand Heine in Dresden on 10 June, 'and has given me great hopes of accomplishing unheard-of things here in the future. Certainly I shall perform . . . the "Nibelungs" here too.'

It even seemed now as though his pardon was likely to come

through. There was to be a wedding in the Saxon royal family, and Wagner's friends counted on his being included in the amnesty usual on such occasions. They took it as a good omen that the theatre in Dresden, obviously acting on instructions from above, had recently revived *Tannhäuser*.

Then a mere week before the wedding ceremony, there appeared in the Dresden police bulletin, under the rubric 'politically dangerous individuals', the old warrant, adorned with the old portrait by Kietz printed on its side, such was the official haste: Wagner, who was believed to be intending to leave Zürich for Munich, was to be detained if he should cross the border, and handed over to the jurisdiction of the Dresden magistrates. The whole procedure smacks of a desire on the part of the reactionary court bureaucracy to forestall the chance of a royal pardon. Not only did it put paid to any hopes of a safe conduct to Weimar; it also diverted Wagner on to a course that took him further and further away from Germany.

But in the mood that he was now in Wagner was not to be discouraged by the news. In May, at a banquet given by the patrician music-lover Konrad Ott-Imhof, he had outlined the plan for a larger orchestra to be available both to the theatre and to concert-promoters. On one of his mountain rambles he now spent a rainy day drawing up a nine-point programme – first published in the Burrell Collection – which neglected none of the organizational and financial aspects involved. (RWBC, pp. 459ff.) It was, after Riga and Dresden, his third plan for orchestral reform and, like the Dresden plan, it was not put into practice.

At last on 2 July his passionate wish to see Liszt again was granted. They came close to smothering each other in their embraces, Liszt reported to Princess Wittgenstein. 'At times Wagner has something of the cry of a young eagle in his voice.' Their friendship was of a rare kind, not one to be measured by the usual standards. Wagner often said that a large piece of him remained alien and incomprehensible to Liszt. But in spite of all reservations and some estrangements there was one thing that bound them together for life: the secret affinity between the souls of two men of genius.

Wagner had just moved from no. 11 Zeltweg to a larger apartment in no. 13, marked today with a plaque. 'You will find I've got things very nicely,' he had written to Liszt, 'the demon of luxury has got into me' – as was usually the case when he was turning from writing words to writing music. 'When one can't get what is exactly right, one does the best one can!' Liszt was amazed by the 'petite élégance', though he found it 'fort modérée'. (The furnishing of the new flat contributed in no small measure to Wagner's pecuniary difficulties over the next few years.)

'A veritable tempest of news and views raged between us,' Wagner told Otto Wesendonk. He read to Liszt from the *Ring*, and Liszt played some of his own compositions.[3] They went up the Rütli with Herwegh, and drank brotherhood in the three springs on the mountain. Liszt recalled years later how he and Wagner had chanted the Eddic lay of Helgi the slayer of Hunding: 'In days of old, when eagles sang and sacred waters flowed from the mountains . . .' 'Eagles – that's what we are,' he wrote to his daughter Cosima in 1877, 'and the sacred waters are flowing.'

They also discussed the possibility of performing the *Ring* in Zürich, and Wagner was amazed by Liszt's enthusiasm for the plan: he was ready to ask for contributions from every source under the sun and was confident of being able to raise enough money. When François Wille asked Liszt whether he did not have the influence in Weimar to arrange for Wagner to return to Germany, Liszt replied that he knew of no theatre suitable for Wagner: the theatre, the singers, the orchestra – in short, everything, would have to be exactly as he wanted them to be. 'That could cost a million,' Wille said, to which Liszt, speaking French as usual when he was excited, exclaimed: 'Il l'aura! Le million se trouvera!'

There was more ceremony to come, to conclude the exhilarating events of that spring, when the choral societies of Zürich united to bring Wagner a torchlight serenade on 13 July. Zeltweg was packed and there was loud applause when a spokesman voiced the wish that the man who had been driven from his homeland would continue to live, to the country's honour, in free, beautiful Switzerland.

There seemed to be no obstacle now to his making a start on the composition. But still Wagner shrank back from this 'gigantic task'. 'He had before him a task', Newman writes, 'such as had faced no other composer in the whole history of music, the task not merely of "setting the text to music" but of giving organic musical unity to the enormous dramatic mass.' His themes had not only to be musical in themselves but also to sustain the most varied, subtle musical and psychological relationships to one another. In addition they had to possess an inexhaustible capacity for variation and furthermore lend themselves to contrapuntal treatment. 'At every point in the score he would have to look both before and after, seeing the whole in each part, and each part as contributing to the whole.' (NLRW, II, p. 389)

The importance for him of the study of motivic formation and development in Beethoven is understandable, even if the technical difficulties of the process in a four-part drama went far beyond what they are in a symphonic movement.

At the same time he was assailed again by the dangerous longing to break with the past that had recurred repeatedly since the revolution, to rid himself of all compromises and seek out new, virgin territory for his life. He had to close the door behind him on a whole section of his life, in order to begin a new one, he wrote to Otto Wesendonk. For that he needed new impressions: Italy, perhaps Paris too, in order to find creative peace. And Wesendonk was generous enough to finance his journey to Italy, in the form of a loan for which royalties for *Tannhäuser* expected from Berlin stood as security.

But first Wagner wanted to recover his health completely. He persuaded Herwegh to go to St Moritz with him to take a cure. Forced to spend time in Chur he read *Der West–Östliche Diwan*. The only accommodation they could find in St Moritz was primitive, and Wagner complained about 'food fit only for dogs'. Once again he discovered that he was not a fit subject for this kind of 'cure': the mineral waters and baths agitated him more than they soothed. To aid recovery he read *Die Wahlverwandschaften*, swallowing down every word, disagreed with Herwegh about the character of Charlotte, and in the end would gladly have been rid of his companion in order to have peace and quiet.

But he received two indelible impressions from the mountains. When he saw the Julier on the way from Chur to St Moritz, he was able to imagine Wotan and Fricka on its heights: 'there, where all is silent, one pictures the beings who reign there, no longer touched by growth and becoming'. On an excursion to the Roseg glacier he received once more, more strongly than the first time, 'the sublime impression of the holiness of the empty waste'. Both impressions became music: the 'open space on a mountain summit' depicted at the beginning of the second scene of *Das Rheingold*, and the 'blessed emptiness on blissful height' where Siegfried finds the sleeping

Brünnhilde. But it was not only the artist in Wagner who was susceptible to the majesty of the mountains; the man, too, felt the challenge to prove himself through danger. Wagner once told Heinrich von Stein that he had climbed the Alps in his younger days with the feeling that he must be able to overcome even them.

At last he set out for Italy on 24 August. In Turin he enjoyed a performance of *Il Barbiere di Siviglia*. In Genoa he encountered for the first time a genuine Italian city, beside which London and Paris seemed to him to be mere agglomerations of houses. On the very first evening he had his courier Signor Raffaele take him on a tour of the streets around the old mansions of the nobility and enjoyed a night fit for the gods beneath flowering oleander trees as high as houses in the garden of one of the Palazzi Brignole-Sale, where a café had installed itself on the ground floor. But the noise from the harbour, right outside his hotel, drove him along the coast to La Spezia. And there, suddenly, there came the moment that released everything that had been building up in his musical imagination for five years – 'unasked-for, unsought', as Egmont says, and 'unimpeded flows the circle of inner harmonies'.

Wagner recounted in his autobiography how, after a night spent in sleepless fever, he forced himself to go for a walk and in the afternoon, exhausted, lay down on a hard couch in his inn in the hope of sleeping at last. But sleep did not come: 'Instead I sank into a kind of somnambulist state, in which I suddenly got the feeling that I was sinking into a strong current of water. Its rushing soon developed into a musical sound as the chord of E♭ major, surging incessantly in broken chords; these presented themselves as melodic figurations of increasing motion, but the pure chord of E♭ major never altered, seeming by its persistence to give the element into which I was sinking an infinite significance. With the sensation that the waves were now flowing high above me I woke with a violent start from my half-sleep. I recognized immediately that the orchestral prelude to *Das Rheingold* had come to me, as I had borne it in me but had been unable to find exactly; and quickly, too, I understood the essence of my own nature: it was not from without but only from within that the current of life was to flow to me.'

'Whether it be a demon or a good genius that often takes control of us in decisive hours,' he wrote to Arrigo Boito in 1871, 'enough:

the impetus for the music of *Das Rheingold* came to me as I lay sleepless in an inn in La Spezia; and without delay I returned to my dismal home to set about writing the immense work, whose fate, more than anything else, binds me to Germany.'

18

The Myth Becomes Music

On the same day that Wagner experienced his 'vision' in La Spezia, 5 September 1853, he wrote to Minna, complaining of his loneliness and the state of his health: 'I have only one thought in my head: how to get back home to you quickly.' This was published for the first time with the Burrell Collection, but the editor is wrong in assuming that Wagner deliberately concealed from Minna the true reason for his wish to go home, because she would not have understood it: he overlooks the fact that the letter was written in the morning, while the vision did not occur until the afternoon. As Wagner travelled back towards Genoa by stagecoach, his pleasure in the Italian scenery revived, and in the midst of the musical sensation that now filled him, it was the colours that made a particularly strong, even impressionistic, appeal to him: the blue of the sea, the red of the cliffs, the green of the pine trees, the white of a herd of cattle. But the mere thought of postponing his departure was enough to cloud his spirits again.

Since he had arranged to meet Liszt in Basel at the beginning of October he had to possess his soul in patience for a while, in any case. Princess Wittgenstein also put in an appearance, with her fifteen-year-old daughter Marie, whose youthful grace earned her the title of 'the Child' from Wagner. 'I have come to venerate the Child,' he confessed to Bülow, 'now, as I compose, I live under her blessing.' (25 November) It is not too fanciful to see a reflection of this feeling in Freia's delightful D major melody. His letters to Princess Marie during the next few years contain a number of revealing comments on his work, but this did not prevent her from joining the camp of his enemies in Vienna, after her marriage to Prince Konstantin Hohenlohe. He told Cosima that he regretted every confidential and enthusiastic remark he had ever made to such a deceitful being.

From Basel the party set out together for Paris, where two events occurred of great significance for Wagner. Liszt took him to visit his children, who were being brought up there under the strict tutelage of Madame Patersi. Wagner read them the third act of *Siegfrieds Tod* and was particularly struck by the exceptional shyness of the sixteen-year-old Cosima.

The other event was a performance of Beethoven's E♭ major and C♯ minor Quartets, by the Maurin–Chevillard quartet, whom Wagner used to cite as exemplifying the blend of thoroughness, imagination and intelligence typical of the best French musicians. Even as a boy he had been drawn to the late quartets, and at sixteen a copy of the E♭ major had been his most treasured possession. But just as it had been a performance by the Paris Conservatoire orchestra that had first enabled him to recognize the full stature of the Choral Symphony, so it was only now that the C♯ minor Quartet was fully revealed to him. 'If I remembered nothing else of that visit to Paris, it would rank as unforgettable for that alone.' This is a significant admission, above all because the 'differentiated texture' of these quartets became the model for the polyphonic writing of the works of his second creative period: in them, as in the quartets, linearity is wrested out of the predominantly homo-phonic textures.

At last, on 1 November, he was back in his study on the Zeltweg and wrote down the chord of E♭ major that had sounded for him in La Spezia, with the famous sustained pedal point on the low E♭. But any expectation that the visionary nature of its inspiration would have led to a free fantasy is disproved by the first version, with its regular sequence of four, precisely compartmented, sixteen-bar variations, with a note already anticipating the 'poco dim.' in the last bar of the fourth of them. 'Friend, I stand amazed!' he wrote to Liszt after finishing the first scene. 'A new world is revealed to me. The great scene in *Das Rheingold* is finished: I see an abundance before me greater than I ever dared to hope. Now I believe my capabilities are limitless: the making of music floods through every fibre of my being.'

As always he began with a continuous composition sketch, writ-ten in pencil and later inked in for the most part, usually combining the vocal and instrumental parts on two staves, occasionally three.

He used a kind of shorthand, decipherable for us only by reference to the score, which made it possible to write out the whole of *Das Rheingold*, words and music, on thirty-nine half-sheets of manuscript paper, with fourteen staves on each side.

The first remarkable thing is the shortness of the time in which he wrote it, and the second is how complete the sketch is. It is dated at the end '14 January 1854', followed by the cryptic question: 'And nothing more?? Nothing more??' That means that, not counting a period when he was laid up with a feverish cold, Wagner took only nine weeks to set down on paper this composition which not only was completely new in style but also laid the thematic and compositional foundations of the whole tetralogy. This could only have been possible if he had it all fixed and ready in his mind when he started, which in turn presupposes that its essential elements must already have been present in his mind when he was writing the text. And so the claim he had made to Liszt at the beginning of 1853, that the form of the music was already finished in his mind, was no exaggeration.

But this means, furthermore, that the verse itself must owe its form to the music that already existed within the composer, in a way such as had never been known before. The well-meaning literary critics of Wagner's texts concede readily enough that they ought to be judged only in association with the music, but they then invariably proceed to judge them from a purely literary point of view. It is only in perusing the documents of his creative processes, pre-eminently the composition sketches, that we can appreciate how close, how mutually dependent, how organic the relationships are between the words and the music.

From the very first words – 'Weia! Waga!', the undying target of so many pawky jokes at Wagner's expense – it is quite obvious that the melody is the primary consideration, and the words, developed from the Middle High German 'heilawâc' ('holy wave'), which Wagner had found in Jacob Grimm and elaborated after the model of the 'Eiapopeia' refrain of German nursery rhymes, are secondary. But coming after the impersonal natural phenomenon of the orchestral prelude, how effectively words and music combine to create the first impression of conscious life and sensation!

This close alliance of words and music is not confined to the emotional content, it extends to the linguistic expression as well. From a few examples in the second scene of *Das Rheingold*, August

Halm illustrated how Wagner even composed the syntax: an antecedent clause ends with the triad not in its root position, but in the second inversion that indicates the statement is incomplete; a parenthesis is declaimed as such in the musical line; an unsingable pluperfect tense, for which an imperfect verb does service in the text, is yet discernibly present through the medium of the accompanimental motive. These are isolated fingerposts for a future assessment of Wagner's texts.[1]

No less astonishing than the speed with which the composition sketch was written down is its correspondence to the completed score: everything is already there. It is as if it was written at one sitting, taken down in great haste from uninterrupted dictation. There can be no question of its having been composed at the piano. Wagner never created anything at the keyboard, though he found that improvising stimulated his 'creative memory' to recall ideas that had occurred to him 'God knows how or when'. Moreover, playing things at the piano after he had thought of them prevented him from writing down something that was permissible according to the rules but did not sound right.

The concision of the composition sketches allowed him to take a general, bird's-eye view of lengthy passages and large-scale forms: it kept him from getting bogged down in too much detail. Since the frequent changes of key signature sometimes obscure the overall, *real* key of a period, he often used to write that key down in letters and words for his own reference as he worked: 'F major', 'A major', 'B minor'. Against Alberich's 'Holder Sang singt zu mir her' he wrote expressively 'B♭ tonalities'. This bears out Alfred Lorenz's analyses of Wagnerian form, which mark off the periods according to their underlying, though not always obvious, tonalities. It also demonstrates that Wagner was always conscious of what he was about in his construction of musical forms.

Some occasional alterations were made later to the vocal line without affecting its essence, but all the themes are already in their final form in the composition sketch. The harmonization is also already fully realized, not only within the themes but in their development as well. When Donner vanishes into the gathering stormcloud, for instance, already in the sketch the tonality, too, darkens threateningly at the impending catastrophe, sinking into low B♭ harmonies, like the development section of the first movement of Beethoven's 'Appassionata' (cf. Ernst Kurth).

There are already notes indicating the characteristic instrumentation: even such specks of colour as the pianissimo strokes on triangle and cymbal after Fricka's 'Gewänne mein Gatte sich wohl das Gold?' are already marked – evidence that Wagner's instrumentation was not a gloss that he worked out separately later. Only the statement of the Valhalla theme at the beginning of the second scene differs in being assigned to trombones, although it is already distinguished by the metallic demisemiquaver triplets on the trumpets – the idea of devising his own tubas specially for this work (a development of the horn from the romantic into the mythological) had not yet occurred to him.

Emendations and later alterations are few and far between, and are confined to relatively unimportant matters, with two exceptions. The first concerns the Rhinemaidens' final song: the original two bars setting 'Um dich, du klares, wir nun klagen' are replaced already in the sketch by the version found in the score, with the characterful sharpening effect of the chord of the dominant seventh. The result is what Ernst Kurth calls 'one of the most marvellous refractions of colour': as he says, shading like this is too subtle to be expressed in words.

Yet there is nothing in the least rarefied about this subtlety. Furtwängler once noted: 'Some composer, any composer in the world, should just try to cap Richard Wagner in the Rhinemaidens' final song in *Das Rheingold*, if nothing else! This power to speak from the very depths of popular feeling, and yet in a completely direct and original voice, was something only he possessed.'[2]

The other change affected the introduction to the first scene – the last place, in view of its inspiration, where one would expect to find any alterations. It is an astonishing discovery which gives completely new insights into the origination of one of the most important musical symbols in the *Ring*. In the sketch the introduction is admittedly in E♭ major and in 6/8 time, it comprises variations that roll on, steadily crescendoing, over the pedal point of the low E♭. The melodic line of the very first horn motive is already indicated, developing out of the E♭ major triad. But the profound difference between the version in the sketch and the eventual version in the score is the total absence from the former of the two variants of that motive which now set their stamp indelibly on the introduction. In its place there are figurations for the strings, running up and down as in the transition to the second scene.

It is as Wagner had heard it, but it is as yet nothing more than pure nature-painting. How it was to be informed with a symbolic content worthy of the cosmic drama it begins was still hidden from Wagner. The solution to that problem – indeed, the problem itself – occurred to him only at a later stage in the work, at a moment that had nothing to do with the Rhine or its waters: at the apparition of Erda in the fourth scene. We do not know how the idea came to him, but we do know how he felt his powers increasing, in the conviction that his work would succeed and that he himself would win through in the end. To others he appeared taciturn and introspective: but what visions he beheld within! 'Believe me,' he wrote to Liszt, 'nothing has ever been composed like this before; it seems to me my music . . . is a morass of horrors and sublimities!'

It was one of the great moments in the process of composition when the idea came to him of projecting the two themes associated with Erda back to the prelude and blending them into the music of his vision. The two images, the flowing water and the goddess rising up out of the earth, are now merged in a single image of inconceivable simplicity and symbolic potency, and each of the two passages, the prelude and Erda's appearance, gains a deeper significance thereby. It is true that when we first hear the prelude we do not know the themes' associations, but we sense that the music is more than a depiction of natural phenomena. What is truly remarkable is that the symbolism was not premeditated: the writer of the text knew nothing about it: it was born to the composer out of the spirit of the music.

Finally, has enough credit yet been paid to Wagner's accommodation here of the demands of poetry and the idea with those of music and form? In the terms of the latter, Erda's apparition is no longer an isolated episode: unbidden, one hears it as a varied reprise of the prelude, and one's sense of musical form approves it.

He had achieved, after all, what he had despaired of when he started the composition sketch of *Siegfrieds Tod*, when it was no more than an idea: beyond the foreground action played out on the stage there lay the broad background of the myth, revealed by the orchestra. Completing the composition of *Das Rheingold*, so difficult and so important a work, had restored a great confidence to him, he wrote to August Röckel on 25 January 1854. He was now again able to recognize how much of the intention of his text was disclosed only with the music: as a result he could no longer bear to look at the words without the music. 'In due course,' he went on, 'I expect to be able to let you see the music too. For the moment I will say just this much, that it has turned out to be a firmly entwined unity: there is scarcely a bar in the orchestral writing that does not develop out of preceding motives.' He was now fully alive to the technique of motivic development that he had first used unconsciously in *Der Fliegende Holländer* and had then studied in Beethoven, but significantly the creative process itself still remained a mystery to him: 'it is something that will not be spoken of.'

This is still not the end of the story of the *Rheingold* prelude. The newness of its conception obliged Wagner to abandon what was usually the second stage in composition, the writing of an orchestral sketch on three staves. 'I am now writing *Das Rheingold* straight out in full score, with the instrumentation: I couldn't think of any way of writing out the prelude . . . comprehensibly as [an orchestral] sketch.' (To Liszt, 7 February 1854)

This first draft of the full score of *Das Rheingold* had an eventful history, typical of many of Wagner's manuscripts. From the estate of Karl Klindworth, who had made the vocal score, it made its way to New York, where it was sold at auction in 1927 for $15,400. In 1928 it became the property of Mr John H. Scheide of Titusville, Pennsylvania, and it is now in the Scheide Library at Princetown University (as Dr Daniel Bodmer of Zürich tells me). But this copy was not complete: it lacked the first two fascicles, which had been given by Liszt to the pianist Louis Köhler of Königsberg, who returned them to Cosima on 17 September 1878.[3] These eight pages of thirty staves each, now in the Wagner archives in Bayreuth, contain the opening of the prelude, up to six bars after the entry of the trumpets. At the head the first page is dated 'Zürich, 1 Febr. 54', that is, a fortnight after the completion of the composition sketch.

And from this manuscript, the very first draft of the score, we see that the synthesis of the La Spezia vision and the apparition of Erda had already taken place: the draft corresponds to the final version. Only the first horn theme is still as follows:

while it was, of course, eventually to take the following form:

It is an apparently insignificant alteration. But its effect is twofold: the larger interval, a fifth, coming right at the start, gives the motive a stronger lift, and the mediant (G) to which it now rises imbues the final note, too, with a latent tension. It demonstrates the simplicity that was as much part of Wagner's genius as his complexity: at one stroke an ordinary sequence of notes has become a living tonal shape.

Up to the last few bars, the dynamic swelling in the prelude is due entirely to the successive entrances of new groups of instruments, and not to any crescendo marking: as Wagner stressed at the 1876 rehearsals, it should make the impression throughout of a natural phenomenon unfolding of its own volition. It is therefore interesting to observe that the first draft of the score is marked with small expressive crescendos and decrescendos, subsequently crossed out in pencil, however, never to appear in any later version.

In the letter Wagner wrote on 15 January to tell Liszt of the completion of the sketch, he was already complaining: 'Ah, how the want of gold encompasses me, too!' By the summer his situation was menacing. 'I am sending you . . . a shipment of "Rhine gold",' he wrote to Bülow, who was originally to have made the vocal score; 'how I wish it was minted.'

Apart from the 3000 francs he received yearly from Frau Ritter, he had no regular income. The Dresden publishing company could not even meet the pressing demands of its creditors. The fourteen concerts of the Zürich Music Society that he took part in between 1850 and 1854 earned him 1400 francs altogether. There were also occasional fees for articles and pamphlets. Breitkopf & Härtel took on *Lohengrin* in 1851, after all, but since his payment for that consisted of the cancellation of an old debt of 200 talers for a concert grand, he could not help but feel that their decision to publish the score was an act of charity, of which he could almost be ashamed.

Then suddenly in 1852 applications to perform *Tannhäuser* began to flood in: requests from twenty-two theatres within a period of eighteen months, and they made single payments of between 10 and

25 louisdor – Hamburg, exceptionally, paid 50. This brought him in 7500 francs. Since there were still a number of theatres where he had hopes that *Tannhäuser* would be staged – apart from Berlin and Vienna, where he met with particular difficulties – and since *Lohengrin* had as yet been performed in only four houses, he believed he could afford to furnish his new lodgings in 1853 with the 'petite élégance' Liszt admired; Liszt was also pleased to find that his larder and his cellar were well stocked to provide for the friends who were always welcome at the Wagners' supper table.

But Wagner's expectations were severely disappointed, when the hoped-for applications to do *Tannhäuser* failed to arrive by the autumn of 1853. 'If opera money doesn't come from Germany soon, and in massive amounts, then I shall be in truly the most disagreeable position I have yet to know.' (To E. B. Kietz; RWBC, p. 269)

The German theatres had good reason for their caution: the recent re-issue of the warrant for Wagner's arrest inhibited them from having anything to do with a man who would be thrown into gaol if he set foot on German soil.

In his predicament Wagner hit on the idea of selling to Breitkopf & Härtel the performing rights for *Lohengrin* as well. On the basis of his earnings from *Tannhäuser* he decided to ask them for 15,000 francs. 'If you think, my dear Franz,' he wrote to Liszt on 16 November 1853, 'that what I'm offering for sale is not rubbish . . . then you will probably agree that my price is not, after all, unreasonable, and – here it comes!!! – *recommend it to Härtel's.*' Liszt passed on this proposition in person, when he went to Leipzig for the première there of *Lohengrin* on 7 January 1854, but he met with a point-blank refusal. It was hardly surprising, for Dr Härtel was a close friend of Otto Jahn, the future biographer of Mozart, who had recently published in the *Grenzboten* an article on *Tannhäuser* which was, as Newman observes, 'of a quite monumental stupidity, even for a "classicist" of that epoch'. (NLRW, II, p. 399)

In the event, the production of *Lohengrin* in Wagner's birthplace, under the direction of Julius Rietz, who was simply not up to its demands, gave so false an impression of the work that the agent Michaelson, who was supposed to negotiate the purchase of the performance rights for the Berlin firm of Bote & Bock, decided that it was not a commercial proposition.

Some bills of exchange were due for payment in April. 'God

knows what I am to pay them with! If I could only manage to hang on till the autumn, then I shall be getting something from the theatres again,' he told Liszt. 'Well, that's how it is, when one acquires a taste for luxury, but is in reality condemned to sackcloth and ashes.' But no theatres applied to perform anything during the summer or autumn of 1854. It was no secret to his friends in Zürich that his situation was now desperate. 'Whether and how to render any assistance can only be decided when all the circumstances are known,' Wesendonk wrote to Sulzer on 26 July. 'This much is clear: no money must be given to him directly . . . From the very first I thought of giving funds to Madame Wagner, but it seemed too humiliating.'

Wagner finally opened his heart to Sulzer in a long letter on 14 September: he had nothing with which to meet the reproaches, silent or open, which he had brought upon himself on account of his domestic expenditure, except by pleading that certain processes were going on inside himself which no one could understand, unless they could imagine themselves in his position and with his nature, and faced with a task of that kind and that scale. 'So I say nothing of that, and willingly admit that anyone who accuses me of folly is right. And I am also completely ready to atone for my folly.' He had earlier expressed himself more explicitly to Liszt: his senses were uncommonly delicate, sensitive, strongly responsive to any stimulus, and needed to feel pampered in some way or other if he was to succeed in the 'desperately difficult task of bringing a non-existent world into being'. (15 January 1854)

He asked Sulzer to be his intermediary with Wesendonk in launching a rescue action. His debts amounted to 10,000 francs, and he estimated that *Tannhäuser* and *Lohengrin* would still bring in a minimum of 21,000 francs. If Wesendonk would let him have the means to settle the debts and also allow him 500 francs a quarter for the next three years, then all his income from theatres should go to Sulzer and be administered by him. (FWSZ, I, pp. 309ff.)

Wesendonk agreed to this proposal, but he authorized Sulzer to say on his behalf that he was not prepared to listen to any further requests of the same nature. Sulzer acquitted himself in the delicate task of managing Wagner's income for him with tact and efficiency, and was rewarded by the affectionate title of 'my dear guardian'.

During the summer, while the financial crisis was at its height, Wagner put the final draft of the score of *Das Rheingold* on one side, in the hope that starting a new work would rescue him from the despair that threatened to crush him: he began the composition sketch of *Die Walküre* on 28 June. 'You know, now it really *is* getting started!' he exclaimed to Liszt. 'Extraordinary, these contrasts between the first love scene in *Die Walküre* and the scene in *Das Rheingold*!' He was now leaving the world of elemental beings for the human world, and the 'plastic nature motives' of the first part of his tetralogy were now re-forming as the 'vehicles for the promptings of the passions' roused by the action and experienced by the characters. Or, as he was to express it later to Brahms, when he sent him a copy of the score of *Das Rheingold* in 1875, ironically alluding to Hanslick: his music had been accused of being 'painted scenery' and the same would certainly be said of this work. All the same, he thought Brahms would be interested to see the variety of thematic material he had been able to construct in the later scores of the *Ring* from the 'scenery' set up in the first part.

Das Rheingold ends and *Die Walküre* begins with a thunderstorm. But what a contrast! The first is seen through the eyes of the gods, the second is part of the experience of human distress: 'Gewitterbrunst brach meinen Leib', Siegmund says. But as well as the skilful, stretto-like treatment of the string figures, stormily overrunning each other, the prelude to the first act of *Die Walküre* also features the call with which Donner summoned the thunder, now played on the tubas and trombones, and so this orchestral passage, like the *Rheingold* prelude, is more than a mere depiction of nature: we sense the god's authority. 'Play it with more awareness!' Wagner exhorted his brass-players in 1876.

Divine authority has a very special role to play in the first act itself. In the earliest prose sketch Wotan actually puts in an appearance; he does not reveal his identity and is received warily by Hunding, while Sieglinde and Siegmund dimly sense who he might be. He drives the sword into the trunk of the tree and spends the night behind a partition at the back of the stage, the unseen witness of his children's love. The intention was to rid the theme of love between siblings, an essential and basic element of the Volsunga saga in Wilhelm Grimm's view, of any taint of moral aberration and present it as Wotan's will. But Wagner soon abandoned the idea and trusted in the power of his music's associative magic', as Thomas Mann called it, to express Wotan's presence *in spirit*.

In the margin of the sketch, against Sieglinde's 'Gast, wer du bist, wüßt' ich gern', there is the note 'Answer, when I get back from Sitten, 13–14 July'. Wagner had agreed to conduct Beethoven's A major Symphony and the *Tannhäuser* overture at the Confederation Music Festival at Sitten, on condition that he first approved the arrangements for himself. He found them so unsatisfactory that he left without conducting a note, fuming at the 'village fair'. Sheer vexation prevented him from resuming his work at once, as the next entry in the manuscript shows: '3 August!!' It is followed by a further note, 'W. d. n. w., G.!!!', decipherable as 'Wenn du nicht wärst, Geliebte' ('Were it not for you, beloved'), which relates to the adjacent stage direction and Siegmund's words: 'Siegmund looks up, gazes into her eyes and begins: "Friedmund darf ich nicht heißen".' There are sixteen similar notes in the first act of *Die Walküre*, all of them undoubtedly to be interpreted in the light of his growing love for Mathilde Wesendonk.

He confided in only a few: Liszt, Bülow, Julie Ritter. To her sympathetic, motherly ear he confessed that he was living a life completely divorced from reality; in the mornings he sat down in his 'luxury' and *worked*; in the afternoons, solitary walks in the mist; on some evenings he called on the Wesendonks, where he could still find the one thing that roused his spirits: 'the graceful woman remains loyal and devoted to me, even though much else in this association is necessarily a torment to me'. (20 January 1854)

Having resumed the composition sketch of the first act on 3 August with Siegmund's narration, Wagner finished it on 1 September, thus composing the major part of the act in thirty days. The music had been present in his mind for a long time, as we know by chance. He had made a note of the characteristic rocking rhythm of the Spring Song in the margin of the manuscript when he wrote the verse text in 1852. While he was writing it he used to go for morning walks with the writer Hermann Rollett, to whom he read each new part of the text as he finished it. When Rollett said he hoped he would write a 'really full-blown melody' to this 'in every sense poetic passage', Wagner tore a page out of his notebook, drew a five-line stave in pencil, wrote out the text and its melody and then sang it, more or less as he intended it to be. This first version of the melody, later published in facsimile, cries out for the rocking to go on longer, to arch across a wider span; that in turn demanded an expansion of the text, such as Wagner wrote out one day in his pocketbook. But he still had to make further alterations to the words and the melody and even to the metre – replacing the 3/4 time with its triplets by 9/8 – before the song reached the score in the form we know today.[4]

At the rehearsals in 1876 Wagner explained that he did not want it performed like a kind of concert number, but so as to make the effect of an episode which momentarily halts the dramatic progress without interrupting it. Porges, in his record of these rehearsals, defines the overriding characteristic of the style of *Die Walküre* as the way in which essentially reflective sensations are expressed in a completely spontaneous fashion.[5] Some of the questions and answers ought to sound exactly as if they were spoken; the temptation to draw out emotionally charged, extended melodic phrases was to be resisted, until at the end the primitive force of elemental passion sweeps all before it in a whirlwind.

This unleashing of passion is mirrored in the manuscript of the composition sketch; to begin with the handwriting is a model of calligraphic beauty, but it becomes increasingly hurried, and by the end of the act the pen can hardly keep up with the pace of the invention.

'I have finished the first act of *Die Walküre*,' Wagner wrote to Bülow a day or two after doing so; 'when I shall get on to the second, God knows – I am in a very bad mood now!' In fact he started it within three days of ending the first, on 4 September. In an undated letter to Liszt he poured out all his rage at the world: 'It is bad, *bad, fundamentally bad*, and only the heart of a friend, only the tears of a woman can redeem it from its curse.' Then he went on: 'I have started the second act of *Die Walküre*: Wotan and Fricka: as you can see, I'm bound to succeed with it.'

In the middle of this crisis in his economic, intellectual and emotional affairs, Wagner began the composition of the second scene, in which Wotan's despairing renunciation of the will to power marks the turning point of the entire drama:

> Auf geb ich mein Werk;
> nur eines will ich noch:
> das Ende.

And then, after a long pause, in which he seems to be communing with himself in the very depths of his spirit, once more, accompanied by the disturbing pianissimo of the chord of C minor:

das Ende!

Then one day Georg Herwegh entered his lonely study with a copy of Schopenhauer's *The World as Will and Idea*.

19

The London Inferno

The history of Schopenhauer's major work aroused Wagner's fellow-feeling: it was completely ignored by an entire generation of academic philosophers, until attention was focused on it in 1853 by a brilliant article in an English journal, published soon afterwards in translation in Germany.[1] The 'great clarity and manly precision' of the language at once captured Wagner's interest. The importance Schopenhauer attached to music in his aesthetics surprised him, but when, as one passionately aroused by the business of being alive, he turned to the philosopher's handling of the ultimate questions of ethics, he was appalled to read of denial of the will as the only means of release from the trammels of the world. It was Herwegh who pointed out to him that recognition of the worthlessness of the world of appearances was the only *tragic* world view: intuitively, it must dwell in the heart of every great creative artist, and of every great human being.

Then Wagner looked again at the text of the *Ring* and suddenly realized that the idea that perturbed him when he read Schopenhauer's theory had long been familiar to him in his own poetry. Had not a poetic impulse inspired him to refashion his drama so that tragic resignation became a principal theme? 'So at last I myself understood my Wotan and, shaken, I began to study Schopenhauer's book more closely.' The fundamental idea was dreadfully serious, he told Liszt, and no one could begin to understand it unless it was already alive in him. (16 December 1854)

The World as Will and Idea affected him as the Choral Symphony once had, as the 'Fundamental of his own life'; more than the thoughts expressed, Schopenhauer's metaphysics and Wagner's music share something that is outside the province of reason. It was more than a book, it was a friend who entered his loneliness like a gift from heaven. Wagner wanted everyone to share in his experience. He undertook personally the initiation of Karl Ritter and Robert von Hornstein, and hoped that they would be his emissaries on a pilgrimage to Frankfurt. He exhorted Hans von Bülow to get a copy as quickly as possible: he would be amazed when he made the acquaintance of Schopenhauer's intellect. (Late 1854) He even sent a copy to his comrade of the revolution, August Röckel, now languishing in Waldheim prison, expressing the hope that he would find in it the consolation more necessary to the strongest spirit than to all others. (5 February 1855)

Only with Liszt, who was so close to him in friendship and in art, and often so distant in things of the mind and spirit, did he abstain from any attempt at proselytization. But he had to affirm his belief in their essential unanimity in a matter that had become so important to him. 'It is queer that I have often . . . recognized your thoughts as my own,' he wrote, 'even if you express them differently because you are religious, yet I know you mean exactly the same thing.' (16 December 1854)

On fine Sundays he and Herwegh walked out to visit the Willes, who owned the patriarchal country house of Mariafeld overlooking the Lake of Zürich. François Wille, who had represented Schleswig–Holstein in the Bundestag for a time, had returned to the land of his fathers to get away from the forces of reaction in Germany. He too was made a convert, and the conversation often turned to questions of Schopenhauerian philosophy. His wife Eliza, who sewed while the men talked, was amazed by the speed with which Wagner had absorbed the philosopher's ideas. He later compared their effect on him with the benefit he had had from his rigorous study of counterpoint with Weinlig: he meant that what he had assimilated from Schopenhauer consisted not in preformed conclusions but in a mode of thought. Even here his intellectual freedom was important to him; once, fearing that Princess Wittgenstein would 'scent Schopenhauer again' in what he said, he complained that people would not credit him with any independence in crucial matters: 'It only remains for someone to prove that Reissiger wrote my operas.' (FWSZ, II, pp. 376f.)

The small community's greatest wish was to receive the Sage of Frankfurt in their midst. 'A whole coterie of fine minds . . . ', Schopenhauer growled, 'invited me in all seriousness to travel to

Zürich in December, to satisfy their curiosity! Replied in a polite and friendly tone but briefly that I could not embark in a controversy in writing and that I no longer travel anywhere. This brought me a book from Richard Wagner, printed only for his friends, not for the trade, on superb, thick paper and in a decent binding: it is called *Der Ring des Nibelungen*, a series of four operas which he intends to compose one day – the artwork of the future itself, I suppose: seems very fantastic: have only read the prologue: I'll read the rest before making up my mind. No letter with it, just an inscription: "in respect and gratitude". ' (To Julius Frauenstädt, 30 December 1854) Wagner had thought that if Schopenhauer could not tell what manner of person he was from the poem, then no letter, however long, would make any difference.

As is well known, Schopenhauer wrote disapproving notes all over the margins of the book, complaining especially of the, in his view, 'hair-raising morality' of some passages.[2] Nevertheless, comments he made in conversation with Wagner's friends show that his overall impression of the work was more favourable than would appear from the notes. 'Thank your friend Wagner on my behalf for sending me his "Nibelungs",' he said to Dr Wille, 'but he ought to forget about the music, he has more genius as a poet! I, Schopenhauer, remain true to Rossini and Mozart!' To Robert von Hornstein he said, 'the man's a poet, not a musician', and Karl Ritter reported that while Schopenhauer thought highly of Wagner as a poet, he could not agree on the 'joint stockholding' of words and music. He praised the *Ring* as a work of poetry: the language was in every way worthy of the subject, which he meant as high praise.[3]

But Wagner was never quite able to get over the fact that Schopenhauer never wrote him a line in acknowledgement of the book. 'I cannot think of any other poem which depicts the will – and what a will! one that has created a world for its own pleasure – broken without the intervention of grace, solely through the strength of its possessor's own proud nature, as Wotan's is . . . I am convinced that Schopenhauer must have been annoyed that I created this before I knew his philosophy: I, a political refugee, whose theories were shown to be untenable in the light of his own philosophy by his disciple Kossak, on the grounds that I have 'no melody'! But it doesn't look well. It's exactly how Goethe treated Kleist, whom he ought to have hailed as joyfully as Schumann did

Brahms. But that', he added cheerfully without a shred of bitterness, '– that seems to happen only among donkeys!' (GLRW, VI, pp. 62f.)

It did not prevent him from trying to do something for Schopenhauer, who wrote to his apostle Julius Frauenstädt on 28 March 1856: 'Jam de re nova magnaque: arrigite aures! Four days ago Ritter came to see me from Zürich . . . He disclosed to me that they are thinking of founding a chair of my, and exclusively my, philosophy at Zürich University, and they think the best occupant for it would be you.' Going on to say that the scheme was being promoted by a Regierungsrat Sulzer, he evidently had no idea that Sulzer was acting solely in response to Wagner's urging. What Schopenhauer thought of this plan – which came to nothing in the end – can be judged from the glowing colours in which he painted the prospect to Frauenstädt: life in that 'Swiss Athens' would be very different from what it was in 'horrible, pinched Berlin . . . I should be greatly honoured by it.'

Besides occupying himself with Schopenhauer – he read *The World as Will and Idea* from cover to cover four times in the course of a year – Wagner continued to work on the composition sketch of *Die Walküre*. By now, as he admitted, he was having to hold a new creative idea forcibly at bay. 'Conceived *Tristan*', he wrote in the Annals. The entry is undated but clearly relates to October 1854. He gave Liszt a fuller explanation in the letter of 16 December: since he had never enjoyed the true happiness of love in his life, he wanted at least to set up a monument to that most beautiful of all dreams, in which his yearning should for once be completely satisfied. He was less extravagant in *Mein Leben*: the earnest frame of mind engendered in him by Schopenhauer had induced the urgent need to give ecstatic expression to its fundamentals. Finally, in conversation with Cosima in 1878, he commented on people's ignorance of how remote the creative processes are from all experience, all reality. 'I felt the need to let myself rage in music, just as if I had to write a symphony.'[4] These are three very different admissions over a period of twenty-five years, and the full truth emerges only from placing all three together. Even if the third was tempered by consideration for Cosima, we can see today that it delves deepest into his creativity: the composer, conscious of the mastery he now possessed, had to express himself without restraint, 'let himself rage'. Mathilde Wesendonk and Arthur Schopenhauer were the two particular experiences that his genius needed and that destiny generously granted him.

In November he wrote to Princess Wittgenstein that he had been able to continue working away on *Die Walküre* but it was going much more slowly than he had expected. What he finally sketched was always the best he could do, but the mood to work visited him less and less often in his dreary life. And then, he found the subject of *Die Walküre* too painful by far: there was really not one of the world's sorrows that it did not express, and in the most painful way. Playing artistic games with that pain was taking its revenge on him: several times it had already made him so ill that he had had to stop altogether. 'I am now on the second act, in the scene where Brünnhilde appears to Siegmund to foretell his death: something like that can hardly be called composing any more!'

The beginning of the Annunciation of Death scene is one of the few passages in the composition sketch which Wagner had to cross out twice before eventually getting it right the third time. The trouble was caused by the second motive, which is subsequently taken up by the voice at the words 'Wer bist du, sag', and which, so far as it is possible to decipher the first deleted version, originally lacked the rising interrogative cadence at the end. The sketch of this scene offers a particularly large number of instances of Wagner's use of letters and words to keep the overall key of longer musical periods in mind when he was working. The indivisibility of expression and form in his work is well illustrated by the fact that precisely this most moving of scenes was, as shown by the formal analysis of Alfred Lorenz, one that required the highest degree of artistic contrivance.[5]

It was while he was working on the second act that Wagner wrote a letter to Bülow discussing the latter's compositions very thoroughly and tactfully — a rebuttal of the charge that he had no time for his friends' works. He knew from his own experience, he wrote, that there were some things that could not be expressed musically in any other way than by the use of harmonies that were bound to affront the ear of the musical philistine. When he recognized this in his own work he always made an effort to disguise the difficult nature of the harmony as much as possible. The art consisted in 'communicating precisely the strangest, least familiar sensations to the listener in such a way that he is not distracted by the material substance of what he hears but surrenders to my blandishments unresisting, so to speak, and willingly accepts even the most unaccustomed of sounds'. (26 October 1854)[6]

He was writing there of something he had just been putting into practice, setting Wotan's despairing outbreaks in the great second scene of Act II. The notes he made in the margins of the composition sketch show he was already thinking out the instrumental blends that would distract attention from the difficult harmonies. The readiness with which his imagination was able to give him what he wanted is well illustrated by the note against the line 'Ich berührte Alberichs Ring': the cor anglais, three clarinets, horns, bassoons and tubas listed in the sketch all appear in the scoring of the following passage.

The composition sketch of the second act was finished on 18 November 1854, having taken two and a half months. Below the date Wagner wrote 'that was a bad time!!!'

He began the third act directly, on 20 November, and, relieved now of his financial worries, finished it in the incredibly short time of five weeks, on 27 December. It was written down in great haste, some of it no more than the bare indication of his intentions: the elaborate ensemble for the eight Valkyries at 'Unsern Schutz flehte sie an' appears here in the form of a single unison line, and at the close of the act he wrote out only the sustaining melody of the wind, without the Magic Fire figuration.[7]

But the sketch of this act has one most unusual feature, of which the prelude to *Das Rheingold* is probably the only other example: it lacks an important musical motive. Sieglinde's thanks to Brünnhilde, 'O hehrstes Wunder! Herrlichste Maid!', is set merely to a declamatory phrase, not to the melody of Redemption through Love. It has been asked why Wagner should have destined this motive, which occurs only at this one place, for its transfiguring role in the finale of *Götterdämmerung*, but it would appear from the sketch that Wagner originally conceived the motive for that role, and only subsequently decided to anticipate it in *Die Walküre*, so as to allow a ray of that transfiguration to fall upon Sieglinde in her grief.

As he now came to start scoring, Wagner was glad of the opportunity to work with an orchestra again. He replied to another invitation from the Zürich Music Society with a letter, dated 23 November, that, as Max Fehr says, is a masterpiece in both substance and form. While reminding them of the lack of results from

his efforts of the last five years, he affirmed his readiness to conduct
for them again, if the society and the theatre would come to an
'arrangement' over their two separate orchestras. This was accomplished, and he undertook a performance of the 'Eroica' on 9 January
1855. For the next concert, as he told the orchestral manager,
Salomon Pestalozzi, he had something special in mind which would
require extra players. 'I recognize, to my sorrow, that this will cause
you a great deal of trouble and that I am driving the Music Society
into certain bankruptcy.' (FWSZ, I, p. 411)

The 'something special' was the first performance of the *Faust*
Overture he had originally composed in Paris and had just re-
written in a single week. 'I cannot be vexed with this composition,'
he had told Liszt back in 1852, 'even though it has things in it that
would not flow from my pen now.' Now he wrote a completely
new score, expanding the middle section with cadential phrases,
toning down the brass throughout, and adding a 'dying fall' coda.
He felt that revision of that nature showed more clearly than
anything else what sort of person the composer had become and
what crudenesses he had sloughed off. According to Mathilde
Wesendonk he originally intended to dedicate the overture to her,
but had suddenly decided that it was 'impossible for me to burden
you with the dreadful motto [from *Faust*]:

> The God who dwells within my bosom
> Can make my inmost soul react;
> The God who sways my every power
> Is powerless with external fact.
> And so existence weighs upon my breast,
> I long for death, and life – life I detest.'

So he contented himself with presenting her with the score and
inscribing it on the last page: 'R. W. Zürich 17. Jan. 55, to his dear
friend, in remembrance.'

When he performed the work on 23 January he discovered that it
was difficult to put across. He soon regretted having published the
score: it had been more than rash, it had been foolish and irresponsible to place a composition like that in the hands of the time-beaters
without any assurance of an even tolerable degree of understanding.
(To H. Gottwald, 30 December 1855; FWSZ, II, pp. 353f.)

As well as his own works, the four concerts he conducted in
January and February 1855 included the overtures to *Die Zauber-*

flöte, Iphigenia in Aulis and *Der Freischütz*, and Beethoven's Septet and Fifth and Seventh Symphonies. He also took a great deal of trouble rehearsing some members of the orchestra in Beethoven's C♯ minor Quartet, observing the while that simply teaching dynamic nuances by rote could never achieve the kind of results that were only to be obtained through the individual cultivation of a higher artistic taste.

When Wagner mentioned his loneliness during these months it was no more than the literal truth, for Minna had left Zürich at the beginning of September, ostensibly to visit relatives in Germany, but in reality on a special mission. As long ago as the summer of 1852, an enquiry about the terms for performing *Tannhäuser* had come from Botho von Hülsen, the intendant of the court opera in Berlin, transmitted through Wagner's brother Albert, whose daughter Johanna was now one of the stars of the Berlin company. In order to avoid repeating the experience he had had with *Rienzi* and the *Holländer*, of the performances being cancelled after he had done a lot of work for nothing, Wagner's terms included a payment of 1000 talers in advance, as well as the supervision of rehearsals by his 'other self', Liszt. The negotiations had come to grief on the latter condition, and when they were resumed in May 1854 between Hülsen and Liszt personally, there was again no agreement, in the face of Liszt's insistence on a completely free hand. In his financial predicament, Wagner was embarrassed by his friend's lack of diplomatic compliance, but could not bring himself to let him down. The easiest way for Liszt to retreat honourably would be if Wagner himself could assume control of the rehearsals.

So when Minna arrived in Dresden in October she presented a personal petition to the king: 'May Your Majesty accord grace and pardon to my husband, Richard Wagner, who was led astray, and grant him leave to attend the performances of his works in person.' The answer from the Ministry of Justice did not reach her until she was back in Zürich: the petition was refused. (LWVR, pp. 48ff.)

Before that, Hülsen had condescended to see Minna in Berlin on 9 October, when he gave her a number of empty assurances, so that she was encouraged to write to him from Zürich on 4 November, probably at Wagner's dictation, asking him to lend support to her petition. Quite apart from Hülsen's total lack of any desire to intercede for the amnesty of someone found guilty of high treason, it was not long before the refusal arrived from Dresden, so shelving the whole rescue operation.

Unless Wagner was prepared to renounce the royalties from Berlin, he had no remaining recourse but to capitulate. He could not afford to defer the Berlin *Tannhäuser* business any longer, he told Liszt in mid-March 1855; his financial situation was too grave. A friend in Zürich (i.e. Wesendonk) had rescued him from catastrophe the previous year, paying his debts in return for supervisory rights over all his future income. The person in question was a businessman, and a sincere friend, but, being a businessman, was unable to grasp why they did not give way, since it had become clear that there was no hope of Liszt being employed. 'Let us allow the matter to take what now seems to be the only course it can take. I regret bitterly that you have expended so much trouble in fulfilling my condition, and have had to endure so much tiresomeness.'

To Hülsen he wrote on 23 March: 'I hereby authorize you to perform this work, without attaching any further conditions.' His only request was for an advance payment of 100 friedrichsdor. *Tannhäuser* was at last performed in Berlin on 7 January 1856. By the fiftieth anniversary of Wagner's death, 13 February 1933, it had been given 711 times.[8]

Meanwhile Zürich had stolen a march on Berlin, and *Tannhäuser* was performed there in February 1855. He complained to Bülow that he had been squeezed dry. 'To please Frau Wesendonk I even consented to conduct one performance in their divine theatre. What stupid things one does!' The modest scale of the production can be judged from the scene-painter's bills, quoted by Fehr: 'Background to Venus Grotto with transparency, fr.55.–; repainting the horizon, fr.15.–; image of the Virgin, fr.8.–; two tiger skins, fr.3.–.' In addition, the soubrette cast as Elisabeth sang her role in white kid gloves with a fan dangling from her wrist. But modest as the singers' abilities were, Wagner wrote to Frau Ritter, they showed such willingness that he was moved to play a larger part in the production than he had originally intended, 'and to my sincere astonishment my – admittedly appalling! – exertions resulted in a success far beyond what I had expected. I did not conduct [the first two performances] myself. . . and so, as a listener for the first time, I had a truly thrilling impression of my work.' After conducting the third performance himself he addressed a few guarded words to his audience: if they now had only a feeble conception of his work, he was ready to do everything he could, if Zürich would also do its part.

He left Zürich on 26 February 1855 to travel to London by way of Paris. A Mr Anderson had turned up at the beginning of January, introducing himself as treasurer of the Old Philharmonic Society and offering him a fee of £200 for eight concerts. 'The prospect filled me with gloom,' Wagner wrote to Liszt, 'going to London to conduct philharmonic concerts is not my line of country.' But he had seen very clearly that if he did not accept the proffered hand it was tantamount to turning his back once and for all on the idea of making an impression in the artistic world as it was. (19 January)

It was soon plain that his forebodings had been justified. He had already learned before leaving Zürich that the London press was howling for the blood of the Old Philharmonic management committee over his engagement. As soon as he arrived he was advised to call on the most powerful critics, such as Chorley and Davison: they were of course rogues and fools, but they had influence, and it would be a pity if he allowed his talent to be wasted in London to no purpose. 'I don't know what *you* think of it,' he told Otto Wesendonk, 'but I have felt all along that there is nothing here for me with my talents, and I can really do without the praises of scoundrels.' (21 March)

He had to conduct those interminable programmes beloved of mid-nineteenth-century England in which one item followed another without rhyme or reason and was applauded with an equal lack of discrimination. He could not even console himself with the thought of his fee, for life in London was more expensive for a foreigner than he had anticipated. One cause for satisfaction was that the orchestra took a liking to him very quickly, although he brought them almost to despair at rehearsals with his 'Once more, please!' (in English). It was hard to wean them from the uniformly fast tempos and lack of dynamic variation instilled in them by Mendelssohn and persuade them to play in his own more richly shaded style. The 'faults' with which Henry Smart of *The Sunday Times* charged him give an approximate idea of his conducting: he took quick tempos faster than usual and slow tempos slower; he prefaced important entries or returns of themes with exaggerated ritardandos; he reduced the speed of Allegro movements by a third on the entry of cantabile phrases. This corresponds, broadly speaking, to his recommendations in his later essay *On Conducting*, which have been followed by all the great conductors since, especially in Beethoven.

He caused sufficient stir to bring Queen Victoria and Prince Albert to the seventh concert of the series, on 11 June. They asked for an encore of the *Tannhäuser* overture and received him, outlaw from Germany though he was, in their box during the interval. The queen's diary indicates that it was no empty act of courtesy: 'His own overture to *Tannhäuser* is a wonderful composition, quite overpowering, so grand, & in parts wild, striking and descriptive. We spoke to him afterwards.'[9]

But no amount of success could prevent him from comparing his lot in London to that of 'one of the damned in Hell'. He tried to spend the mornings scoring the second act of *Die Walküre* but felt so disorientated that he often sat staring at his pencilled sketches as if they were written in utterly foreign characters. Nevertheless, he managed to write the first draft of the score of the first and second scenes while he was there, including Wotan's great narration, of which Richard Strauss wrote in his edition of Berlioz's treatise on instrumentation: 'For all its simplicity, this passage is to me the rarest miracle of a genius more richly endowed than any other with the gift of transforming every nuance of feeling, every tremor of passion, into orchestral timbres, with an exactness that invincibly captivates and convinces every listener.'

In the afternoons Wagner threw himself despairingly into reading Dante, whose *Inferno*, he said, gained an unforgettable realism from the atmosphere of London. When Liszt told him he was going to write a *Dante* Symphony, he was aroused to write the long letter of 7 June which amounts to a complete treatise on the subject. He had followed Dante with sympathy through Hell and Purgatory, only to learn in Paradise that God had created the hell of existence to his own greater glory. He pointed out the contrast offered by Brahmanism and Buddhism: a sublime doctrine, the only satisfying one. For with Schopenhauer, another culture had dawned upon his spiritual horizon beside ancient Germany and Greece: India. He had brought Adolf Holtzmann's *Indische Sagen* to London with him: reading the legends had been his only pleasure there. They were all beautiful, but Savitri was divine. 'How hangdog our culture looks beside these pure revelations of noble humanity in the ancient East!' (To Mathilde Wesendonk, 30 April)

The external events of the four months in London were few: he struck up an acquaintance with the orchestra's leader Sainton, a Frenchman from Toulouse, and his friend Lüders, who were responsible for Wagner's engagement without knowing him: they had supposed that there must be some virtue in an artist who was so violently attacked. He met a young pupil of Liszt's, Karl Klindworth, who was supporting himself in London by giving lessons and in whom Wagner found only one fault, namely that he did not possess the voice for Siegfried. He met Malwida von Meysenbug, who had left Germany on account of her political ideals and was then living in London, and was later to become an intimate of the Wahnfried circle. He met Meyerbeer in the house of an English music-lover, who was astonished that two great composers should greet each other so coldly. He spent a few stirring evenings with Berlioz, who was in London to conduct the 'New' Philharmonic orchestra: they would have become even closer in their shared antipathy for the contemporary musical scene, had not Madame Berlioz, jealous of Wagner's fame, come between them. 'I have one genuine gain from London,' Wagner wrote to their mutual friend Liszt on 5 July, 'a sincere and intimate friendship with Berlioz, to which we are both party.' Berlioz, too, wrote to Liszt, 'Wagner a quelque chose de singulièrement attractif pour moi, et si nous avons des aspérités tous les deux, au moins nos aspérités s'emboîtent.' (Liszt to Wagner, 10 July)

The London tragedy does not lack its satyr play. Ferdinand Praeger, a German who lived in London teaching music, was recommended to Wagner by August Röckel's brother, and proved helpful in numerous mundane matters – 'an uncommonly good-natured fellow, only too touchy about his educational qualifications', as he was described in *Mein Leben*. Wagner corresponded with Praeger in later years, and the latter occasionally visited him in Zürich, Paris, Munich, Tribschen and Bayreuth.

To general astonishment, in 1892, a year after Praeger's death, a book by him entitled *Wagner as I Knew Him* appeared in both German and English editions, containing 'sensational revelations' about Wagner. To his personal 'reminiscences' were appended thirty-four letters to him from Wagner, but the discrepancies between the English and the German versions of these were so glaring as to arouse the suspicion of forgery. The following year Houston Stewart Chamberlain discovered twenty of the original letters in the possession of Lord Dysart, which he copied out in full. The result surpassed all expectations: not a single sentence corresponded to Praeger's text! When Chamberlain published the originals in 1894, together with a critique demolishing Praeger's book, Breitkopf & Härtel withdrew it, admitting that professional integrity required them to do so.

But what had become of the fourteen letters still missing? Chamberlain drew up a table demonstrating that these on the one hand were the most sensational, and on the other had no dates in Praeger's text, unlike those he had found, and contrary to Wagner's habit. It is not unreasonable to conclude that they were out-and-out fabrications or else distorted beyond recognition, so that Praeger had not dared to give dates, which would have led to their flat contradiction by other reliable sources.

And someone who forges letters will certainly not shrink from forging unsubstantiated conversations: the sheer impossibility of some of the dates and facts in Praeger's 'recollections' proves it. With anyone else that would have been an end of the matter, but not with Wagner. Praeger's inventions continued to be touted as facts for long after. It is only as an example of a very large sub-species of 'Wagnerian literature' that the case merits as detailed an exposition as it has received here.[10]

It is not even possible to attribute the line taken by Praeger in his book to senile decay, as has been suggested. Karl Klindworth warned Wagner in 1859 that Praeger was abusing his confidence. Wagner's reply, in a letter of 18 May, shows how easily he could be deceived by those who purported to be his friends: Klindworth had no cause for alarm on his behalf, it was impossible for Praeger to abuse any 'confidence': 'he really is not on such terms with me'.

Unproductive as his stay in London was so far as his creative work was concerned, it nevertheless represented another step in his growing awareness of alienation from contemporary artistic activities. This is most clearly expressed in a long letter to Sulzer of 10–12 May 1855: that he had once again allowed himself to be tempted to have truck with the world with which he had really long ago severed his ties was due to the contradiction within himself that would probably endure his life long. The realization that he could only sully himself by contacts with the public world of art had already led him to wish that he could slough off his artistic nature altogether. What would then be left for him? Probably Schopenhauerian sainthood!

> But there is no need for me to rack my brains over that
> one, because as long as a spark of life remains within
> me, it is unlikely that my artistic illusions will release
> me: they are really the decoys the life-urge uses to
> ensnare my judgement to do it service again and again. I
> really cannot imagine anything clearly and plainly that
> does not at once get mixed up with visions of that kind,
> and in the end it is my own judgement that time and
> again makes me the artistic dreamer that I am.

It was a nice state of affairs, he concluded. He probably hurt a lot of people in this way, but he caused none such hellish torments as himself, and he could assign the blame almost entirely to his artistic nature. 'Therefore anyone who gains some pleasure from the products of it really has nothing to complain about if I cause him any distress, for I certainly suffer more from it than he.' Resignedly he added, 'I hardly believe that you will be able to understand me entirely.'[11]

Although he was sometimes on the point of throwing away the baton he finally stuck it out for all eight concerts. 'I shall be bringing 1000 francs back from London with me,' he wrote to his 'guardian' on 15 May; 'it is simply *not possible* to save any more than that, and I can only assure you that this is the *hardest* money I have ever earned in my life, compared to which the piecework I once did for a Parisian music publisher, humiliating as it was, now seems child's play. I may say that I have had to pay for every one of these 1000 francs with a sense of bitterness such as I hope never to have to experience again.'

20

The *Ring* Crisis

'London' had prolonged itself throughout the rest of the year, Wagner wrote to Julie Ritter, looking back over 1855. 'On my return, my old dog received me and lived just one more week to show me he had been waiting for me; then he died . . . it was yet another heavy blow for me.' He will have remembered Homer's lines about the dog Argus, who 'had no sooner set eyes on Odysseus after those nineteen years than he succumbed to the black hand of death'.

In the middle of July he and Minna went to Seelisberg, a resort high above the Lake of Lucerne with views across to the mountains of Schwyz and Uri. 'A few days ago I arrived up here in Paradise,' he wrote to Praeger. But his stay was spoiled by the weather and the other people, and he went back to Zürich on 15 August to take up the scoring of *Die Walküre* again, from the third scene of the second act. He was so unsettled that all memory of the ideas he had in London seemed to have abandoned him.

Then during the winter he began to suffer attacks of an inflammation that was diagnosed as erysipelas, though it is more likely to have been an allergy of some kind. Hardly had he started to settle to his work again, he complained to Julie Ritter, than a 'face-rose' [to give a literal translation of the German name for erysipelas] had flowered on the briars of his existence. Like a conscientious gardener he had been tending it carefully for almost three months, 'and I still have not been able to get my big child, the Valkyrie, to go to sleep yet'. (29 December)

In such periods of illness, which made it impossible for him to compose, his mind was always particularly active in adopting and elaborating new ideas. The Indian studies sparked off by his reading

211

of Schopenhauer had led him to Eugène Burnouf's *Introduction à l'histoire du Bouddhisme indien*, where he read the legend of Prakriti, the Jandala girl, and Ananda, the Buddha's 'beloved disciple'.

Once on his wanderings Ananda came to a well where a girl was drawing water. When he asked her for a drink she replied that she was of the Jandala caste and not permitted to approach a holy man. Ananda answered: 'My sister, I did not seek to know your caste, I asked you for a drink of water.' And as she handed him the cup she was suddenly overcome by passionate love. She hurried to her mother and bewailed her distress. Her mother told her to adorn herself and put on her finest clothes. Then she wove a powerful love-spell that would bring the youth to the spot. When Ananda felt the pangs of love he prayed to the Buddha, and the Enlightened One heard him and destroyed the spell. But the girl did not abandon her desire. She went outside the city gate, sat down beneath a tree and waited for the Buddha. When he came past, begging for alms, she threw herself at his feet and confessed her love. Then the Enlightened One asked whether she was willing to wear the same robe as Ananda and to follow him wherever he went, and whether her parents consented. The girl, thinking only of her love, answered 'Yes'. But then she realized the deeper significance of the question and she joined the Buddha's followers.

When the Brahmans heard that the Buddha had taken a Jandala girl as a disciple they murmured together and went out to the garden where he taught. And the Enlightened One, knowing their thoughts, told them the story of the girl in her previous incarnation: then she had been the daughter of a Brahman king, and her father had rejected the proposals of a Jandala king who had wanted her as a bride for his son.

For the time being Wagner stored this legend in his heart. But it never left him, and he only finally abandoned the idea of composing it in 1882.

At least the state of his health guarded him against the temptation to throw himself into another adventure like the London one. America was working on him now, he told Klindworth, trying to persuade him to go to New York for six months, but they had small hope of success. 'I am too stupid even to earn money.' (4 October) When the Zürich Music Society invited him to conduct another series of subscription concerts, he refused on health grounds. He told Mathilde Wesendonk that his London experiences had made him determined to withdraw from public music-making. 'I need all my inner repose now, in order to complete my great work, which could easily . . . become a grotesque chimera, ruined by this everlasting, injurious contact with the second-rate and the unsatisfactory.'

Even so, he very nearly succumbed to the temptation of conducting Mozart's *Requiem* in celebration of the centenary of his birth in 1856. The arrangements came to grief, however, over the matter of finding a hall for the performance that satisfied Wagner: the German-language press seized this as a welcome excuse to accuse him of hostility to Mozart. He lost patience and wrote an 'explanation' for the *Eidgenössische Zeitung*: since his refusal had been exploited by a number of 'journalistic idiots' in the style that had become standard practice for use against him, he thought he might as well explain himself. He would be ready to sacrifice his health if the music-lovers would make corresponding sacrifices and provide him with a proper concert hall.[1]

As Wagner saw his hopes for Zürich as the location of his future artistic activities receding, he increasingly withdrew from the public eye. He had formed a small circle of tried and trusted friends, to whose number Gottfried Semper and Gottfried Keller were added in 1855.

Semper had gone through the Dresden uprising with Wagner, who commended him to Sulzer in 1850, writing from Paris: 'It would give me extraordinary happiness if so excellent a man and artist were to join you all – and me – there.' (FWSZ, I, pp. 355f.) He had then met him again in London, where Semper was struggling to gain a foothold. Thanks to the combined efforts of Wagner and Sulzer, in the autmn of 1855 he was appointed to the staff of the newly established federal Polytechnic in Zürich, where he became a stimulating member of the circle of friends, always ready for a lively argument. While Wagner followed with interest the writing of Semper's book on style, his chief theoretical work, and had a copy of it in his library in Wahnfried, Semper thought that the dramatist in Wagner took his work too seriously: what he particularly liked about *Don Giovanni* was that the tragic types were encountered in it only as in a masquerade, in masks and dominoes.

Gottfried Keller had returned to Zürich from Berlin in December 1855, and as early as 13 January 1856 he was writing to Lina Duncker, his publisher's wife, about dainty suppers at the house of an elegant member of the cantonal executive council – Sulzer – where Richard Wagner, Semper and some native Zürichers used to meet. Wagner himself sometimes offered a decent midday meal and didn't stint the wine. On 21 February Keller wrote to the literary historian Hermann Hettner: he often saw Richard Wagner these days: come what may, he was a very gifted and likable person. 'And he is certainly a poet too, for the text of his Nibelung trilogy is a treasure house of original national poetry.' In a letter of 16 April he repeated, emphatically, 'I am seeing a great deal of Richard Wagner, who is a genius and a good man as well. If you find the opportunity . . . do read his Nibelung trilogy. You will find it is informed by an impressive poetry, quintessentially German, but clarified by the spirit of classical tragedy.' His intuition of the Germanic and Greek elements behind the inspiration of the *Ring* is amazing. And on 21 April he wrote to Ludmilla Assing (another of his female friends) that Wagner was a genius and the most entertaining of men, extremely cultivated and a really profound thinker. 'His new libretto, the Nibelung trilogy, read simply as a poem on its own account, is full of passion and felicities, and has made a far deeper impression on me than any other book of poetry.'[2]

In view of these letters there is something curiously brazen about the assertion of Marcel Herwegh, Georg's son, in his memoirs (*Au banquet des dieux*, 1932), that after Wagner's public reading of the *Ring* in February 1853 his father had walked home with Keller, who had disparaged the work – the more so as Keller was not even in Zürich at the time! Evidently some people would give a great deal to be able to call Keller as witness for the prosecution. In 1951, in a review of the newly published Burrell Collection, Thomas Mann launched a furioso attack on Wagner, taking Keller's description of him as 'hairdresser and charlatan' as his text: of course a realist like Keller could have had no time for the Wagnerian hotch-potch of worldly renunciation and worldly lust, the arch-romantic exploitation of the unwholesome contrast of sensuality and chastity, and so on. Mann does not give the source of his quotation, but, coming from a man of his integrity, one takes it for granted that it must have been said in a context where Keller was discussing fundamental principles of art and life. It is therefore all the more surprising to track it down in a letter to Ferdinand Freiligrath of 30 April 1857 where Keller for once really lets off steam. After slandering a string of 'notabilities' he writes: 'Then there's Richard Wagner, a very

gifted man, but something of a hairdresser and a charlatan as well.
He has a bric-à-brac table, with a silver hairbrush in a crystal dish
etc. etc. on it . . . But that's enough tittle-tattle.' And then in a
postscript he tries to take back what he has said: 'Once again I've
written a lot of feeble jokes, which I already regret.'[3]

For his part, Wagner had lost no time in asking Sulzer for a copy
of Keller's novel *Der grüne Heinrich*, but he had the greatest pleasure
from *Die Leute von Seldwyla*, Keller's collection of tales about the
inhabitants of a mythical but archetypal small Swiss town. To the
end of his days *Die drei gerechten Kammacher* and *Spiegel das Kätzchen*
were, together with Hoffmann's *Der goldene Topf*, the stories that he
most loved to read aloud. The 'town warlock of Hottingen', as he
dubbed Keller, was much gratified by Wagner's special appreciation of these two tales, of whose formal excellence he himself had a
high opinion. 'I have just passed one of the pleasantest hours of my
life,' Wagner declared after reading the much later *Züricher Novellen*
in 1879, and praised Switzerland for being a country where a writer
like Keller was still possible. 'If only I could hear something comparable in music from a contemporary.' Then he recalled his
memories of Keller from his years in Zürich: when he said something truly fine and witty, it came blurting out in a rush, as if
somebody had tipped over a sack of potatoes. When he and Cosima
read *Das Sinngedicht* together, when they were in Sicily in 1882, he
made up his mind to see his old friend once more after so long an
interval. The reunion did not take place. On 19 February 1883
Keller wrote to Cosima, asking if she would permit an old neighbour and friend to express his deep sympathy, sorrow and distress
at Wagner's death. Daniela replied on her mother's behalf, saying
how much Wagner had continued to admire and enjoy Keller's
works – 'your charming, touching characters, the sublimity of your
observation and thought' – in the last years of his life.

Of all his other friendships in Zürich, Wagner was affected most
deeply by his relationship with the Wesendonks, embarrassed as it
was during that winter of 1855–6 by his growing love for Mathilde
and his dependence on Otto. His not daring to be godfather to their
son Guido gives some insight into the conflict of his feelings. In the
Annals he noted for September 1855: 'Bad, capricious moods,
particularly against the Wesendonk family. Refused to be godfather, because unlucky.'

Forever interrupted by attacks of erysipelas, work on the third act of *Die Walküre* proceeded only slowly, which obliged him to put off once again the visit from Liszt that he was longing for. 'I am pining for him,' he told Princess Wittgenstein in November. Moreover, a year after the first mention of the idea, a new project was again urging itself upon him. 'More defined conception of *Tristan*,' he noted in the Annals for December 1855, 'third act the source of the mood of the whole (interweaving Parzival searching for the Grail).' A few lines about this earliest conception were preserved in a notebook dating from 1854–5.

> *3rd Act.* Tristan on his sickbed in the castle garth.
> Battlements to one side.
>
> Waking from slumber he calls to his squire, if he can see anything, thinking him to be on the battlements. He is not. He comes at last in response to the calls. Reproaches. Apology. There has been a pilgrim to make welcome. Then and now. Tristan's impatience. The squire still sees nothing. Tristan reflects. Doubt. Song from below, receding. What is it? Squire tells him about the pilgrim. – Parzival. Deep impression. Love as torment.
>
> My mother died when she bore me;
> now I live, I die of having been born.
> Why? – 'Parzival's Refrain' – repeated by the shepherd.
> = The whole world nothing but unsatisfied yearning!
> How shall it ever be satisfied? –
>
> Parzival's Refrain. (BBL 1915, p. 145)

The words and melody of 'Parzival's Refrain', with the rising sixths of the Grail theme coming at the end, have also survived, in a note Wagner wrote to Mathilde Wesendonk:

> Wo find' ich dich, du heil'ger Gral
> dich sucht voll Sehnsucht mein Herze.
> ('Where shall I find thee, thou holy grail,
> full of longing my heart seeks thee.')
>
> You dear, errant child! Look, that's what I was on the point of writing down, when I found your beautiful, noble verses![4]

At last, in March 1856, he was in the position to tell his friends that he had finished *Die Walküre*, after suffering agonies. 'It is more beautiful than anything I have ever written – but it has exhausted me dreadfully.' (To Pusinelli, 28 April)

Throughout the whole period he was dogged by his everlasting money troubles. A large debt to Karl Ritter had been left unpaid in the reorganization of his affairs in 1854, and repaying it now in instalments perceptibly diminished his income. In November he had approached Wesendonk, through Sulzer, with a plea for his subvention to be increased from two to three thousand francs a year, but Wesendonk mantled himself in silence. When the Wesendonks then paid him a formal call to congratulate him on the completion of his score, he spoke in such bitter terms, as he admits in his autobiography, about this manner of expressing interest in his works, that the visitors abruptly left in confusion: it cost him a good many laborious explanations to repair his offence.

On 26 April he invited his friends to hear a run-through of the first act with piano accompaniment, in which he sang both Siegmund and Hunding. While the impression this performance made on him was still fresh, Wesendonk wrote to tell Wagner how much he had enjoyed the evening and that he wished heartily that Wagner might be able to bring the work he had begun so magnificently to an equally magnificent conclusion, untroubled by mundane worries. 'I will take charge of that and authorize our friend Sulzer to pay you 250 francs a month forthwith, on the understanding that you regularly transmit all the income from your operas to Sulzer, as hitherto.' (FWSZ, II, p. 38)

As his hopes of Zürich faded Wagner was again directing his thoughts towards Germany. After the failure of Minna's attempt to win him an amnesty, he appealed to Liszt to seek an audience with King Johann of Saxony on his behalf, with Grand Duke Carl Alexander of Weimar acting as intermediary: in requesting pardon for him, Liszt was to put all the emphasis on the fact of his being an artist. 'Could you perhaps take the opportunity to give the king a copy of my *Ring* text?'

Liszt, recognizing the uselessness of such a step, advised Wagner to present instead a plea for permission for nothing more than to hear his works in Weimar, on the grounds that to do so was essential for his future works. For his part, in the meantime, he persuaded the duke to write personally to King Johann in the hope of influencing him to receive Wagner's request favourably.

The king's reply, on 25 April, was that many benefits had been bestowed on Wagner in the past, his thanks for which had been to take part in the May uprising: 'had he not absconded, he would probably have been sentenced to death for high treason. It is as clear as day that even the greatest talent cannot weigh in the scale against such ingrate and shameful conduct.' Nor did he refrain from administering a reprimand to his 'dearest cousin': in propriety he had to leave it to his conscience as to whether, in the circumstances, he wished to allow a man like Wagner to appear at his court.

Evidently Carl Alexander was so wounded by this letter that he did not even tell Liszt about it. It is otherwise improbable that Wagner would have composed his lengthy plea for pardon on 16 May, admitting and attempting to justify his error. Since he had once more become capable of conceiving a great, purely artistic work, in which he had regained his moral poise, an inner conversion had led him to a deeper insight into the essence of things, thanks to which he had now come to recognize that his previous opinion in one particular matter, the 'relationship of the ideal to the reality of all human, earthly affairs', had been erroneous. (LWVR, pp. 62ff.)

'Here is the letter to the King of Saxony,' he wrote to Liszt, 'it has cost me much, very much – even so, I am afraid that it may not serve its purpose, and let that be the end of the matter. For even this letter is a profanation; just to mention my "inner conversion" to the King of Saxony and his ministers amounts to sacrilege. But I thought I might go so far in this extremity.' His fears proved justified: the reply that came from the Ministry of Justice at the beginning of August held out no hope of his petition being granted. He sent it on to Liszt: 'Read the splendid answer to my letter to the king.'

After finishing *Die Walküre*, Wagner composed no more of the *Ring* for six months, but his imagination was busy. On the same day that he wrote his letter to the King of Saxony, 16 May 1856, he wrote down in his notebook the prose sketch for a drama to be called *Die Sieger* ('The Victors'), based on the legend of Ananda and Prakriti. (RWGS, XI, p. 325) It was not alone the beauty and the profundity of the subject that appealed to him, but also its peculiar suitability to the compositional procedures that he had now developed: as the life of every being in earlier incarnations is apparent to the eye of the Buddha, so the listener should be able to share in the previous lives of the two principal characters through the musical reminiscences heard throughout the action. This is an example of how, in Wagner's work, the poetic and dramatic ideas on the one hand and the musical techniques on the other mutually condition and support each other.

It was in the same period that he devised a new ending for *Siegfrieds Tod*, with a large-scale choral finale. On 22 June he wrote to Franz Müller in Weimar that he was going to make changes of some substance to the last two dramas, including their titles, which would probably become plain *Siegfried* and *Götterdämmerung*. The principal change would be in the finale of the latter, for which he was going to write a completely new text: 'the interpretation of the character of Brünnhilde, now that she has become all-knowing, will be different, broader and more decisive. The men and women, too – for the first time in the whole work – will take a larger part and express a wider interest at the very end.'

He was referring not to the two versions of the concluding words which are to be found in the complete edition of the writings (the first beginning 'Nicht Gut, nicht Gold, noch göttliche Pracht...' and the second 'Führ' ich nun nicht mehr nach Walhalls Feste...'), but to a third version he had sketched, which was first published by Otto Strobel in 1933. The second and third versions both introduce the idea of rebirth, which has been regarded as an uncalled-for fusion of the Germanic and the Indian ; but Ettmüller's commentary on the Vaulu-Spá (Völuspa), which Wagner is now known to have had in his library in Dresden, lists some examples of the belief in rebirth of the 'old Northmen', so Wagner must have believed that he was not proposing anything contrary to the spirit of Germanic myth.[5]

If, in the end, he used none of the three, it was because 'the meaning they had to convey is already expressed with utmost clarity in the musical rendering of the drama'.

Before beginning the composition of *Siegfried* Wagner wanted to overcome his susceptibility to erysipelas. On 5 June he set out on one of the 'unhappiest and most wretched' journeys he had ever made, by train, mail coach and steamer, to seek a cure in a change of air. He had been recommended to consult a Dr Vaillant, who ran a hydropathic institution in the small village of Mornex, in the vicinity of Geneva, at the foot of the Petit Salève, where the regime was more like the milder observances of Priessnitz than the killing measures of Albisbrunn.

When Wagner had described his symptoms, Vaillant smiled: 'Monsieur, vous n'êtes que nerveux.' He promised to cure him so effectively within two months that he would never suffer from erysipelas again, and it was in fact another twenty-four years before he did. The only unwelcome aspect of the cure was that he had to abstain from all serious work, so he devoted his time to reading the novels of Sir Walter Scott and designing a house for himself, doing his best to draw plans as accurate as an architect's.

This ambition was born of negotiations he was conducting at the time with Breitkopf & Härtel, with a view to their publishing the *Ring*. There was no longer any reference to the resignation of two years previously, when he had declared that he wanted to perform it for Liszt and himself alone.

He saw very plainly, he wrote to the Härtels,

> that only the future in a quite literal sense (and not in the sense of the label that a number of empty-headed scribblers have stuck on me) will be able to establish the genuine, unquestionable success of my dramatic works; and if I was previously without hope in that respect, you must admit that after the extraordinary, quite unprecedented fate that has befallen my most recent works, I now have good reason for hope . . . It is impossible that I shall ever again conceive, let alone write, anything resembling my 'Nibelungs': rich and abundant, it is the most important work of my life, and in the text alone I believe that I have already given the nation a work that I am proud to think can be commended to it for the future as well.

He suggested that, as there were no precedents for so extraordinary a publication, his fee should be calculated according to what he would need to live on while he finished the work: 'That sum, for all four parts, is . . . 2000 louisdor, or 10,000 talers in gold.' He would make over the two parts already completed to them at once and unconditionally, on payment of half that sum; the remainder to be paid in instalments of 500 louisdor each on delivery of the scores of *Siegfried* and *Siegfrieds Tod*. Whatever their decision, he felt compelled to tell them that if they could come to no agreement he would find it impossible to finish the great work. In that case he would start something else, which he would be able to finish in a year. (20 June)

The Härtel brothers' counter-proposal revealed, to his delight, that they were by no means unwilling to bargain. He therefore invited them to join him and Liszt when they met, as they were planning to do, in Zürich. 'You will have no better opportunity, *before* hearing a performance, of getting a really clear idea of what is in hand.' But they unexpectedly revoked their proposal: 'Circumstances leave us no choice: we beg to withdraw.' Once again, Newman remarks, 'a fortune was to be lost to people whose business instincts were a guide to nothing but the immediate future'.

Wagner suspected, not without reason, the influence of Otto Jahn; instead of getting to know the work at the fountainhead, as he had suggested, they had preferred to trust the advice and opinion of a third party. 'My negotiations with the Härtels have come to nothing again,' he wrote to Princess Wittgenstein, 'and the little house I have so long been yearning for, as a quiet place to work, is still only a castle in the air, probably next door to Valhalla.' (4 September)

The collapse of his hopes in Weimar and Leipzig was followed by the failure of his attempt, through the good offices of Mathilde Wesendonk, to rent a cottage in Seefeld; but then Otto Wesendonk came up with the suggestion of providing something for the Wagners in the property overlooking the Lake of Zürich where he was having a house built for himself. 'Entre nous, do you really want to take the place, as far as you are able, of princes and publishers?' Wagner wrote in reply. 'I scarcely thank you for this wonderful offer, for I am sure that the sensation of being able to make one like it must be a joy that is more rewarding in itself than any expression of thanks could hope to be.' (1 September)

The prospect gave him the courage, in spite of five pianos and a flute in his immediate neighbourhood on Zeltweg, to begin the composition sketch of *Siegfried* in the middle of September. He reverted to his earlier practice of making an orchestral sketch while he was still working on the composition sketch, having often experienced difficulty in deciphering his hectic scrawl when he came to score *Rheingold* and *Walküre*. He started with Mime's 'Zwangvolle Plage! Müh' ohne Zweck!' and did not write the short prelude until he was on the verso of the second sheet of paper. 'It was utterly new ground,' he wrote to Frau Ritter, 'and after the dreadful tragedy of *Die Walküre* I entered upon it with a sensation of freshness such as I have never felt before.' But he came close to despair when a tinsmith across the road added his percussion to the other musicians in the street. In an access of comic rage he threw himself at the piano to sing Siegfried's G minor Allegro: 'Da hast du die Stücken, schändlicher Stümper . . .'

Work was interrupted on 13 October by the arrival of Liszt, followed a few days later by Princess Wittgenstein and her daughter Princess Marie. Liszt played his *Faust* and *Dante* Symphonies from the score, making Wagner exclaim that it was a miracle to hear him. Liszt's forty-fifth birthday on 22 October was the high point of his visit. A brilliant company gathered in the Hotel Baur au Lac to hear Wagner and a young Zürich soprano, with Liszt at the piano, perform the first act and the Annunciation of Death scene from *Die Walküre*. At the end Liszt held out both hands to his friend in admiration. A well-wisher wrote in the *Neue Zürcher Zeitung* that Wagner's efforts towards reform were realized in this composition, which was one of music's most magnificent creations; his ideas 'mark an epoch and will move the whole world'.

'I . . . have now luxuriated – without getting intoxicated – in Liszt's company for three weeks,' Wagner told Karl Klindworth on 1 November, 'and hope to keep him here for some time yet.' His desire to unbosom himself to Liszt on artistic matters was accompanied by a need to pour out his heart on more confidential concerns. Liszt had just had a letter from Jessie Laussot, telling him that she was on the point of creating an independent existence for herself by founding an educational institution. This prompted Wagner to tell him the whole story of his unhappy adventure in Bordeaux. Liszt was so moved that he walked home with him all the way from the Hotel Baur au Lac to Zeltweg, and kissed him as they parted. 'Were it possible', Wagner wrote to their mutual confidante, Julie Ritter, 'that Jessie has gathered the strength to withdraw from an unworthy dependence . . . no one would owe her the heartiest interest more than I; indeed, I could call myself shamed by her . . . I ought to draw some comfort from being able to offer Jessie my hand in friendship, now that passion need no longer cloud our relationship.' Clearly the pain of that experience still lodged in his heart.

But Wagner's pleasure in Liszt's company was clouded by the

hubbub Princess Wittgenstein created around her: it was, he said, as though Zürich had become some kind of metropolis overnight; dinner parties, supper parties followed hard upon one another; suddenly one found oneself surrounded by a throng of interesting people, of whose existence in Zürich one had previously had no inkling. His only choice was to put a good face on it or take refuge in illness. 'By all that you and I hold holy,' he excused himself to Liszt, 'believe me and my assurance that I am ill and need complete rest and care today, in the hope of being able to enjoy you again tomorrow.' (2 November) He particularly detested the princess's 'appalling mania for professors', now keeping each one individually to herself, now serving them en masse to her friends. Gottfried Keller remarked that the 'Ferschtin' (as her title of 'Fürstin' was pronounced in Zürich) had made a friend of every person of prominence, and was a clever woman, for all the learned fire-eaters and Brutuses sang her praises – he alone had remained in the outer darkness and was quite out of countenance. (To Lina Duncker, 8 March 1857) He had almost despaired of Wagner, who, encouraged in his follies by the presence of Liszt, had again become cracked in the head and very selfish.

Wagner, too, was taken aside for a tête-à-tête one day, as she wanted to know all about the 'plot' of the downfall of the gods in the *Ring*. She grasped the significance of the finest and most abstruse elements, he recalled, but in somewhat too arithmetical, mathematical a spirit, so that by the time he had finished he had the feeling that he had been explaining the intrigues of some French play to her.

Liszt was often unwell and irritable during the six weeks and did not always have the self-control to sustain his usual air of serenity. Wagner observed this on several occasions with alarm: he was put on his guard by it, and things never reached a pitch of intensity between them, 'only it gave me the obscure feeling, which has never since left me, that it might come to such a pitch, and it would then be frightful'. (ML, p. 629)

One outburst he witnessed was directed against Karl Ritter, who was mortally offended and was not to be pacified even by a personal visit by Liszt. For the first and only time Wagner was reproached by Frau Ritter, because he had allowed her son to suffer offence in his house. As a consequence he felt he could not continue to accept her money: 'Permit me to tell you candidly that I could accept such a sacrifice only so long as I was sure that the source from which it flowed was a completely unclouded sympathy, a sympathy strong enough to extend forbearance even to my weaknesses and errors.' (24 December) To Sulzer he wrote that it gave him no pleasure to have to remind him that he was now without means of subsistence. The recognition that his financial affairs would never regulate themselves was gradually eating down so deep into him that he was afraid of becoming totally apathetic. (FWSZ, II, p. 373)

But in spite of all its drawbacks, Liszt's visit gave him a lift that is reflected in his letters to Princess Marie. After Liszt had gone he had swallowed Goethe and Schiller's correspondence hungrily. It was the case with him that he seldom read what was actually in front of him, but what he put between the lines. 'And now I was reading into it everything that I could promote, initiate and disseminate with Liszt if we were closer to each other! I even read our rare friendship into it, printed in letters of gold.' (January 1857)

He had resumed the composition of *Siegfried* on 1 December with Mime's 'Einst lag wimmernd ein Weib'. But he was already telling Princess Marie on 19 December that he had imperceptibly found himself in *Tristan*: 'for the present music without words'. A sheet of musical sketches of the same date has survived, with the heading 'Love scene. *Tristan und Isolde*', which includes not only the proto-type of the theme 'Lausch, Geliebter!' from the second act, and some variants on it, but also the famous rising chromatic motive of yearning which was destined to revolutionize the history of music – and this before a single line of the text or even of the prose sketch had been written! 'For some things I will sooner write the music than the words.'[6]

Nor was that all that was occupying his thoughts: three weeks later he told the princess of a new idea for *Die Sieger*, inspired by Count Schack's *Stimmen des Ganges*: the girl, now called Savitri after his favourite character in Holtzmann's *Indische Sagen*, who, while waiting for Ananda in the second act, 'rolls in the flowers in ecstasy, luxuriantly drinking in the sun, the trees, birds, waters – everything – the whole natural creation, is told by the Shakya, after she has taken the fatal vow, to look about her and then asked "How does it all seem to you?" – "No longer beautiful", she replies gravely and sadly, for now she sees the other side of the world.' Characteristi-cally, in view of the counterpoint of his creative activity, Wagner went on: 'In the second act of *Tristan* – but you shall not learn anything about that yet. All that is only music at present.' (January 1857)

Finally, he felt compelled to take arms on behalf of Liszt, who was under fire as a composer, in an open 'Letter to M[arie] W[ittgenstein] on Franz Liszt's Symphonic Poems', published in the *Neue Zeitschrift für Musik*. (*Brief an M. W. Über Franz Liszts symphonische Dichtungen*, RWGS, V, pp. 182ff.) It in fact mirrors something of Wagner's feelings on the subject: by keeping to general aesthetic reflections, he avoided having to touch on details that were unsympathetic to him. Privately he did not conceal from his friends his reservations about some of the more theatrical effects, such as the pompous conclusion of the Dante symphony: 'No, no! Not that! Away with it! No majestic Lord God!' 'You are quite right,' Liszt wrote back, 'I said the same; the princess persuaded me to write it like that: but now it shall be done as you think it should be.' Wagner was all the more distressed, then, that not only was the finale retained after all, but the original ending of the *Faust* Symphony, which died away gently, was replaced by a grandiose chorus with tenor solo. Nevertheless the open letter is an unequivocal affirmation of his high opinion of Liszt the composer. Thanking him, the latter wrote: 'You said it as no one else would have known how.' (19 April 1857)

In the meantime Wagner had finished the composition sketch of the first act of *Siegfried* on 20 January and the orchestral sketch on 5 February. He finished the first draft of the score on 31 March during a visit from Mathilde Wesendonk. This first act had succeeded beyond all his expectations, he told Julie Ritter, and he was now convinced that *Siegfried* would be his most popular work. He had not only trodden completely new ground in it, but developed a completely new compositional technique as well. Whereas there are still alternating passages of arioso and recitative in *Rheingold* and *Walküre*, which had confused Liszt at first in the third act of the latter, here Wagner succeeded for the first time in sustaining the uninterrupted flow of melody: one is hardly aware that the structure rests on a sequence of songlike periods.

He had just got to Siegfried's 'Des Vaters Stahl fügt sich wohl mir', and was actually thinking about the motive that was to define the beginning of the forging, when Wesendonk's letter arrived confirming the purchase of the cottage next to his villa on the

Gabler hill. 'You dear, good people!' he exclaimed. 'What shall I say to you? Everything around me is suddenly different, as if by magic!' (To Otto Wesendonk, January 1857) 'Wagner's letter truly warmed our hearts and was the best possible reward, if an action which in itself gives the greatest happiness even needed one,' Mathilde wrote to Minna. 'I hope this house will be a true haven ['Asyl'] of peace and friendship, a sanctuary in a world of envy and hatred.' (11 January) The house, henceforth called 'Asyl', was ready for them to move into on 28 April. Minna occupied the ground floor, Wagner the first. From his writing-desk he had a wonderful view of the lake and the Alps. A chaise-longue, on which he used to rest, stood in the middle of the room. He stood at a lectern to compose, often taking a turn up and down the room, sometimes going into the next room to try out a chord or a phrase on the grand piano there.

It seemed a good omen when the first letter to arrive in his new home was from Frau Ritter, offering to renew her support. With what melancholy he had thought of her all that time must remain his secret, he wrote in reply, for she was really the closest to him of all her family: her age and her frank, open character enabled her to maintain her boundless indulgence in the face of the fierce idiosyn-cracies of his own nature, 'which is something people like me need if we are in our turn to remain patient and persevering in our contact with a world that is always hostile at bottom, alien and injurious towards us'. (6 May)

On the first warm, sunny morning of spring he had taken a walk out to the new house while it was still in the builders' hands. Green buds were opening in the little garden, the birds were singing and bells were ringing in the distance. He recalled that it was Good Friday and then remembered the significance of the same reminder for the hero in Wolfram's *Parzival*. All the intransigence of exis-tence subsided, and an inner voice cried out: 'God is in us – the world is vanquished! Who created it? Idle question! Who van-quished it? God in our hearts!' It acted as a pointer to the fundamen-tal idea of the poem. 'Starting with the Good Friday idea, I rapidly conceived a complete three-act drama, which I at once sketched in outline.'

'Good Friday, fantasy on the terrace. Conceived "Parcival" ', he wrote in the Annals. (10 April 1857)

But before turning to one of the new projects – *Tristan, Die*

Sieger, Parsifal[7] – that were clamouring for his attention, he made one last attempt to create a material basis on which he could then have proceeded to complete the *Ring*. With Liszt acting as mediator, he again resumed negotiations with Breitkopf & Härtel in March. The most important thing, he wrote to them, was to set right their misconceptions about the nature of the work. He was expecting some leading singers and a pianist of the first rank – Klindworth – during the summer. If they could come and see him at the same time, then he would gladly let them know the precise date. 'In issuing this invitation I assure you at the same time that no pressure of any kind from me will be exerted on you to make a decision.' (19 May)

Their noncommittal reply to this was an end of the matter, as far as Wagner was concerned. 'I shall have no more trouble with the Härtels now,' he told Liszt, 'as I have now decided at last to abandon the stubborn enterprise of finishing my "Nibelungs".' He had conducted his young Siegfried as far as the solitude of the forest and bidden him farewell with heartfelt tears. And he added that if he was to take the work up again after all, then it would have to be made possible for him to *give* it to the world, in the fullest sense of the word. (28 June)

But inspired by the walks he used to take in the nearby Sihltal, where he listened attentively to the songs of the forest birds, he did complete the composition and orchestral sketches of the second act of *Siegfried* before laying the work aside. What he took home with him of their songs he imitated by his art, and the music reproduces distinctly the songs of the yellowhammer (oboe), oriole (flute), nightingale (clarinet), tree-pipit (flute) and blackbird (flute and clarinet).

Sitting on the veranda on the evening of 22 May, his forty-fourth birthday, he was surprised by the song of the Rhinemaidens, which he had rehearsed with some singers in the previous year, and which now reached him across the gardens as if from some little distance. Coming now in the composition sketch to the point where Siegfried emerges from the cave with the ring and the Tarnhelm – 'Was ihr mir nützt, weiß ich nicht' – he added the melody of the Rhinemaidens' lament in the accompaniment, writing it very lightly in pencil. Scoring the passage twelve years later, he wrote to King Ludwig in similar terms, telling him that the melody was now heard on six horns, as if coming from a distant dream-world of nature: 'As we take in the full significance of it, our emotion is overwhelming!'(23 February 1869)

With the music of the Woodbird leading Siegfried off, he laid his most important work on one side as a 'chimera' – at the time it seemed that it might be for ever.

Part V: *Tristan* and *Die Meistersinger* (1857–1868)

21

In Asyl

The Härtels' refusal to come to Zürich would not in itself have influenced Wagner to abandon the 'stubborn enterprise' of the *Ring*, but it was just one more in a series of reasons. He felt the necessity of appearing before the public with another new work, after an interval of seven years: his friends feared, so he wrote later, that he might have strayed into the realms of 'the unstageable and the unsingable'; the leading critics treated him as no longer in the land of the living; and in his own eyes, as he laid one unperformed score aside after another, he resembled a sleepwalker with no real idea of what he was doing. (RWGS, VI, pp. 266f.) Perhaps, too, he sensed that he was not yet ready to tackle the composition of *Götterdämmerung*. We, at any rate, with the advantage of hindsight, can see that he would not have been able to write it without first having mastered the harmonies of *Tristan* and the counterpoint of *Die Meistersinger*.

There was a psychological factor, too. Having severed one link with the outside world after another during the last few years, his need to immerse himself in an inner world had grown ever more imperative. Hence his yearning for the friendship of Liszt, his longing for the understanding and love of a woman who would open her soul before him like a blank sheet of paper; hence, too, his receptivity to Schopenhauer and Buddhism, and his attraction to the subject of *Tristan*.

His acquaintances, in different ways, must have sensed his isolation in those years. Wagner was indescribably lonely there, Eliza Wille wrote to Princess Wittgenstein, but would he not be so everywhere? And Eduard Devrient, the first guest the Wagners received in Asyl, wrote to his wife, 'He is a totally disquieting character.'

With great self-control, he was on the point of leaving Siegfried alone in the forest for a year, in order to give himself some relief in writing a *Tristan und Isolde*, as he reported to Frau Ritter. He shrank from admitting to this good friend, whose generosity had inspired him with the courage to start the tetralogy, that he saw no prospect of ever finishing it: she died in 1869 and never saw its completion. 'The text [of *Tristan*] is still dormant within me,' he went on: 'I shall shortly start to rouse it.' (4 July 1857)

The way for his new enterprise seemed to smooth itself of its own volition. In March Wagner had received a letter from a Dr Ernesto Ferreira-França, who introduced himself as the Brazilian consul in Dresden: the emperor, Dom Pedro II, an admirer of his music, wished to invite him to Rio de Janeiro, so that he could perform his operas there in Italian. Strangely enough, Wagner observed, the idea had attracted him: he thought he would have no difficulty in writing a libretto full of passion which would turn out excellently in Italian. He wrote to Liszt that he was thinking of getting *Tristan und Isolde* translated into Italian, dedicating it to the Emperor of Brazil, and offering it to the theatre in Rio for its first performance. His correspondence with Ferreira went on for several months, but in the end nothing came of it: in *Mein Leben* he wrote that he never heard from the Emperor of Brazil again. But ten years after he had dictated that section of his autobiography, a foreigner arrived in Bayreuth, on the day of the very first performance of *Rheingold*, who entered his name in the hotel register as 'Pedro'; profession, 'emperor'. Late that same evening he called at Wahnfried, and talked enthusiastically about his impressions of the performance.

The proposal Devrient made during his visit to Asyl held out more concrete hopes. As intendant at the Grand Duke of Baden's theatre in Karlsruhe, he offered to interest the duke, whose liking for Wagner's music was well known, in holding the première there. Wagner also had plans for a performance, with the Karlsruhe orchestra, in Strassburg, the home town of Gottfried, the author of the German medieval epic poem of *Tristan*, 'and so I believe that, with God and in my own way, I shall once again produce something in which I shall achieve renewal and self-awareness'. At all events, *Tristan* was going to be a thoroughly practicable work which would soon bring him in good financial returns. (To Liszt, 28 June)

On 22 August the Wesendonks moved into their new house,

built in the style of a patrician Renaissance villa. Mathilde had christened it 'Wahlheim' ('chosen home'), quite possibly at Wagner's suggestion, in allusion to the idyllic hamlet of that name where Werther decides to live. Wagner had begun the prose sketch of *Tristan und Isolde* two days before. The sense of seclusion, the beauty of his surroundings, the neighbourly association with Mathilde combined to speed the work, so that he had completed the verse text by 18 September. As he recounts in *Mein Leben*, he made the best use of his reading in Dresden, and the catalogue of his Dresden library reveals just how extensive that must have been. It includes Gottfried's poem, not only in the modern German translation by Hermann Kurtz, but also in the Middle High German editions of H. F. Massmann and F. H. von der Hagen, the latter also including the surviving texts of the Middle English, medieval French, Welsh and Spanish poems on the same subject. His possession of Ziemann's 750-page dictionary of Middle High German with grammatical introduction shows that he really made the effort to read Gottfried's text.

Even then Hermann Kurtz's comment that the legend has the stuff of a tragic drama in it must have stirred his imagination to trace the outline of its original form – perhaps we might say its ideal form. As was so often the case with him, the material lay dormant for years in a half-conscious creative sphere of his brain, then suddenly came to the fore and was written down, prose sketch and verse text, in twenty-nine days. Bülow, who was visiting Asyl at the time with Cosima on their honeymoon, had the feeling that Wagner was in a state bordering on 'transfiguration'.

Although he always aimed at stripping his legendary subjects of specific historical conventions, he recognized that the knightly ethos of the Middle Ages had to be retained as the necessary setting for Tristan's conflict of love and honour. It was in consequence of this that the language of the text is more deliberately archaic than usual. The language has been much abused, but it is strongly influenced by Middle High German, not only in the choice and inflection of the vocabulary, but even more in the sentence structure.

To give just one example in each category: in Kurwenal's 'Nun bist du daheim . . . auf eig'ner Weid' und Wonne', the word 'Wonne' (which means 'bliss', 'great joy' in modern German) is imbued with the double meaning of MHG 'wünne': not only 'what is longed for' but also 'pasture' (a synonym of 'Weide', so a non-singing translation of the line could be 'Now you are at home . . . among your own meadows and longed-for pastures'); in Isolde's 'den hell ich haßte', 'hell' ('bright', 'light' in modern German) is used in the original sense of 'resonant', extended to mean 'violent', and showing that it is cognate with 'hallen' (which still means 'to ring' or 'resound'); a form like 'sehren', lacking the usual prefix ('versehren'), is much closer to the medieval 'sêren'; case inflections are used to make their point on their own, without prepositions, as in the use of the genitive in Brangäne's cry 'Des unsel'gen Tranks!' ('[Because of] the accursed drink'). Then the sentences often use constructions that are medieval in inspiration: in 'Das Schwert – das ließ ich fallen' ('the sword – I let it drop') the caesura after the noun and the subsequent pronoun duplicating the noun reproduce a characteristic of Gottfried's own style ('liep und leit, diu sind alleins'); the placing of adjectival and adverbial phrases in front of, and outside, the main body of the sentence: 'Siech und matt, in meiner Macht, warum ich dich da nicht schlug', where the first two phrases refer to 'dich'; the placing of a whole relative clause, or even a series of them, in front of the main clause, before the noun to which they relate has been spoken: 'Die im Busen mir die Glut entfacht, die mir das Herze brennen macht, die mir als Tag der Seele lacht, Frau Minne will, es werde Nacht' ('[She] who . . . Dame Minne wills that it be night').[1]

There is nothing amateur about this archaicization, nor is it so abstruse that only scholars can appreciate it. It might nevertheless be open to a charge of artificiality, were it not also determined by the spirit of the music. The concise forms of words, the avoidance of auxiliaries and expletives, the more flexible construction, the defiance of linguistic logic make the sentences akin to the melody, which also knows only the logic of emotion. Yet even so sympathetic a critic as Erich von Schrenck can criticize the 'favourite advance positioning of the relative clause', which wearies by its artificiality.[2] He fails to see that the practice, as in the last of the examples in the preceding paragraph, results in a peculiarly intimate fitting of the words to the climbing melodic line, as it mounts to a climax of monumental grandeur. The sequence of short relative clauses anticipated the musical sequence: or rather, since it is quite clear that the music formed the words rather than vice versa, the sequence of clauses was determined by the needs of musical sequence.

Finally, towards the end of the great duet in the second act, there are passages where the words read on their own seem empty, because their emotional content is provided by the music alone: it would have been a contradiction of Wagner's concept of the living work of art to create a poetic illusion on the page which would then be annulled by the writing for the two voices and obliterated by the flow of the orchestra. The words here are nothing more than the raw material for the vocal parts.

On the other hand, all the passages where the words arc intrinsically important possess the highest degree of poetic strength and beauty: Isolde's 'Mir erkoren – mir verloren', Marke's 'Mir – dies? Dies – Tristan – mir?', Tristan's 'Muß ich dich so verstehn, du alte, ernste Weise', can stand comparison for expressive pregnancy with any of the greatest works in dramatic literature.

But the poetry, as in *Tannhäuser*, is not confined to the expression and content of the words. Wagner presents a symbol at the beginning of each act – the young sailor's song, Isolde holding the torch, the doleful tune of the shepherd – which is then transposed on to a psychological and metaphysical plane. Interpreting a simple theme in a series of poetic variations like this is also an act of creation out of the spirit of music. As a matter of interest, the poetic motive of the torch is absent from the prose sketch: Brangäne stands on the steps leading to the gate and Isolde calls to her to open the gate to Tristan. The extinguishing of the torch, which is far more striking both as a visual image and as an imaginative association, appears for the first time in the verse text itself. 'Even the ancients', Wagner told Eliza Wille as he was playing to her from the second act, 'placed a lowered torch in the hand of Eros as the genius of death.'

The *Hymns to the Night* of Novalis are frequently referred to as the model for the love scene, and there are indeed reminiscences.[3] But Novalis's works were not in Wagner's library either in Dresden or in Bayreuth, nor is there any other evidence that he ever took any interest in the poet. If, instead of being content with comparing a few lines in isolation, one reads both poems in conjunction, then it is the differences that make the far stronger impression. The *Ring* is as remote from the verses the romantic poets wrote about elves and goblins as *Tristan* is from their poetry of love and death, and the affinities of the subject matter make the contrast with the spirit in which it was conceived all the more striking. The major difference between *Tristan* and the *Hymnen an die Nacht* is the complete absence of Christianity from the former. There is only one divinity in *Tristan*: Frau Minne, 'des Weltenwerdens Walterin'. The imaginative world is closer to that of India, as is the idea of the 'Weltatem' ('world breath'), and – say what you will – Schopenhauer: even though the longing for the night, 'wo Liebeswonne uns lacht', has nothing to do with the denial of the will to live, yet Thomas Mann is right in this instance when he demonstrates that such denial is only a secondary intellectual element of Schopenhauer's philosophy: his system is a metaphysic of the will, fundamentally erotic in character, and to the extent that it is so, *Tristan* is filled, saturated with it.[4]

'On 18 September', Wagner wrote in the Venetian Diary intended for Mathilde, 'I finished the text and took the last act to you. You went with me to the chair beside the sofa, embraced me and said "Now I wish for nothing more."'

A few days later an encounter of truly portentous significance took place in Asyl. When Wagner read the text aloud to a small gathering, the audience included Minna Wagner, Mathilde Wesendonk and Cosima von Bülow. Minna, as she told a friend, saw nothing in Tristan and Isolde but a 'much too odious and slippery couple'.[5] Cosima was then nineteen. Wagner found her shy and reticent, and complained to Hans that she was too reserved. But her reserve already concealed an instinctive animosity towards Frau Wesendonk. When the last act provoked a particularly emotional response from Mathilde, Wagner comforted her by saying that such an outcome was really the best, in an affair of such seriousness – and was supported by Cosima.

Who was Mathilde? Her importance as Wagner's muse was beyond all question sublime. But it is the privilege – or the fate – of the poet to see his muse through the eyes of love. Who was Mathilde Wesendonk in sober reality, and of what order were her mind and spirit? Ernest Newman, who can certainly not be accused of favouring Cosima unduly, was very sceptical about Mathilde. Was she able to follow Wagner's thoughts? Did she ever love him as much as he loved her? Her avowals of love, apart from her poems, have come to us only through Wagner's pen; she destroyed her own letters, except for a few from later in her life, and she made her own selection and edition of his letters for posthumous publication, some of them reaching the editor Wolfgang Golther only in copies in her handwriting.

Perhaps we shall do her the greatest justice by referring to a

comment Wagner made in a letter to her after he had been reading
Goethe's *Tasso* a year after leaving Asyl: 'The only important
confrontation for those who seek the essence of things is that
between the Princess and Tasso . . . If we look . . . beyond the play,
we are left with only the Princess and Tasso: how will their differences be reconciled?' It is obvious that this remark had a personal
relevance: when Wagner's passionate nature had made it hard for
him to obey the stern command of voluntary renunciation,
Mathilde had admonished him as the Princess admonishes Tasso:
'There are many things that we should grasp eagerly: but there are
others that can only become ours through restraint and self-denial.
Such, they say, is virtue; such is love, her kinswoman. Consider it
well!' (II, 1) 'Will Tasso be taught by her?' Wagner asks.[6]

On 1 October 1857, twelve days after finishing the text, he began
the composition sketch of the first act, which he finished by 31
December. The dates shed light on the 'force' with which the
conception 'erupted' from him, in Ernst Kurth's words: there are
few instances in the history of music of the evolution of harmony
being similarly pressed forward in one enormous jolt by the genius
of a single individual. An epoch was closed, and the assembled
ranks of his contemporaries were able to witness it like a natural
phenomenon.[7]

Not that there was anything new about the famous *Tristan* chord,
the first chord of the prelude: it is to be found in the Andante of
Bach's A minor Violin Concerto, and in the Andante of Mozart's
Eb major Quartet. The chromaticism is even less of a novelty. What
was new was the elevation of these two features into the form-
giving principle of a whole work on a large scale. The chord
provides an inner dynamic which sweeps the music on from tension
to relaxation to renewed tension. 'You know the Buddhist theory
of the origin of the world,' Wagner wrote to Mathilde: 'a breath
clouds the clarity of heaven' (and here he writes the four chromatically rising notes which he had written down as early as 1856 as the
germ of this music):

'This swells, grows denser until finally the whole world stands
before me in impenetrable vastness.' (3 March 1860) His words act

as a description of the impulse which led on to the creation of the musical world of *Tristan*.

For all its dynamism, the music is informed by a stream of thought that is, as Richard Pohl wrote of the prelude as early as 1859, 'of eminent logic and consistency'. Eighty years later Paul Hindemith analysed the logic and the consistency:

> The prelude to *Tristan* is one of the finest examples of the elaboration of a two-voice [i.e. two-part] framework. The observer of the intervals formed by the outside lines of the harmony will be astonished to see how intervals of varying tension are juxtaposed. The procedure is illustrated beginning with the very first chord . . . the tensional development of the framework is calculated from beginning to end.[8]

The epoch-making significance of the music of *Tristan* was so little a conscious intention on Wagner's part that to begin with he did not even notice it. The effect it had on him, when it did suddenly strike him, is recounted in a letter to Mathilde Wesendonk, written in January 1860: nothing that had happened to him in Paris (where he was at the time) was of any significance beside a realization, a discovery he had made during the first rehearsal with the orchestra for his concert series, because it would determine the whole of the rest of his life. 'I played the prelude to *Tristan* for the first time; and – saw, as though scales had fallen from my eyes, the immeasurable distance that I had travelled from the world during the last eight years. This little prelude was so incomprehensibly *new* to the players that I had to lead them directly from note to note, as though hunting for jewels in a mine.'

One cannot avoid the impression that in writing *Tristan* Wagner was the unconscious agent of a higher power, and all the personal and intellectual experiences that contributed to it were merely release mechanisms. This is in direct opposition to the popular belief, shared by Frau Mathilde, as Newman ironically remarks, that she was the work's onlie begetter. (NLRW, II, p. 524)

The direct artistic outcome of their relationship was the group of *Wesendonk Lieder*, composed between 30 November 1857 and 1 May 1858. He had spent a little time dabbling in trifles, he told Liszt, and had set some nice little verses that had been sent him, 'which is something I have never done before!' (1 January 1858) The order of composition of these 'five poems for a woman's voice' is somewhat different from that in which they were published: *Der Engel*, *Träume*, *Schmerzen*, *Stehe still*, *Im Treibhaus*. As one can see from the dates, Wagner must have set the poems virtually 'by return of post'. Only in the case of *Schmerzen* did he revise the setting, changing the coda twice in the following two days. Sending Mathilde the second version, he wrote on the manuscript: 'After a good, refreshing night, my first thought on waking was this improvement to the coda: we shall see if Señora Calderón [an allusion to what they had been reading together] likes it if I play it today in the depths [at Wahlheim].' Below the third version he wrote: 'Another ending, it must be getting more and more beautiful.' He explicitly identified two of the songs as studies for *Tristan*: *Träume* for the second act, and *Im Treibhaus* for the third, while the Destiny motive heard in *Stehe still* is a quotation from the first act, which had already been composed by then.

The first song, *Der Engel*, contains a delicate tribute to Mathilde: the melody of the words 'da der Engel niederschwebt' is taken from the first violin melody after Loge's words in *Rheingold*: 'In Wasser, Erd' und Luft, lassen will nichts von Lieb' und Weib.'

It was a difficult, artificial situation, the stability of which could be maintained only by scrupulous consideration of all the people concerned and was under threat at every instant. While Wesendonk was away from home on business, following a crisis in the American money market, Wagner serenaded Mathilde on her birthday, 23 December, with an arrangement of *Träume* for solo violin and small orchestra, performed in the hall of the villa. On 31 December he presented her with a dedicatory poem:

> Hochbeglückt.
> schmerzentrückt,
> frei und rein,
> ewig Dein –
> was sie sich klagten
> und versagten,
> Tristan und Isolde,
> in keuscher Töne Golde,
> ihr Weinen und ihr Küssen
> leg' ich zu Deinen Füßen
> daß sie den Engel loben,
> der mich so hoch erhoben!

('Enraptured, freed from pain, free and pure, ever thine – what Tristan and Isolde lamented and forwent in the gold of chaste music, their weeping and kissing I lay at thy feet, that they may praise the angel who raised me so high!')

Whether the serenade or the poem was the cause of it, there must at all events have been an exceptionally violent quarrel between the Wesendonks when Otto returned in the new year. A passage in a letter Wagner sent Liszt refers to it: 'For a moment it seemed to me that I would have to steel myself, quickly and decisively, to offer my protection.' (18–20 [?] January 1858) In his first wave of despair he turned once again to his friend in Weimar. 'This time you must come without delay. I am at the end of a conflict involving every-thing sacred to man: I must decide, and the choice facing me is so cruel that when I decide I must have at my side the *one* friend Heaven has granted me . . . Since I hope to find the path on which I shall cause the least harm, I am thinking for the present of going to Paris where – plausibly – my interests take me – at least in the eyes of the world at large and of my good wife in particular.' (Early January) Astonished, Liszt asked: 'Is your wife staying in Zürich? Are you thinking of perhaps going back there later? Where is Mme W.?' On 14 January Wagner left for Paris, and from there he wrote to Liszt that things had all turned out quite peaceably after all: '*For* me – only tenderness, resignation, pining, concern solely for me; *against* me – honourable suffering amidst great magnanimity and irreproachable considerateness towards the delicate, passive ele-ment in the conflict.' A passage in the Venetian Diary shows that he corresponded with Mathilde during this period: 'Do you remember, how we wrote to each other when I was in Paris, and our joint sorrow burst forth from us both at the same time, after we had fervently told each other of our plans?' (31 October 1858) Unfortunately those illuminating letters have not been published.

Wagner did in fact have a genuine business reason for his journey. Dr Hermann Härtel had visited him in Zürich in the previous autumn and reminded him of the necessity of establishing his copyrights in Paris. In pursuit of this end he now made contact with the lawyer Emile Ollivier, later a member of the French govern-ment, and the husband of Liszt's daughter Blandine. Wagner gave him powers of attorney to represent his rights in France. It must have been a picturesque scene when Wagner expounded the plot of

Tannhäuser to the 'most famous advocates in the world', strolling up and down at Ollivier's side in the Salle des Pas Perdus in the Palais de Justice.

The most tangible profit of his visit to Paris came from a visit he paid in Passy to the widow of the piano manufacturer Erard; he improvised from his operas in her music room, and she promised to give him one of her famous grand pianos – the 'swan', as he called it, which had a soft tone that for him became inseparable from the love scene of the second act.

During his visit Härtel had also pronounced an interest in buying the rights to the less demanding new opera. The great warmth of the subject, the music's fortunate propensity for melodic flow, the two effective principal parts which would soon be numbered among the most grateful in the soprano and tenor repertories – so Wagner wrote to the publishers on 4 January – all this made him confident that he had played his hand well. The contract was drawn up after his return from Zürich at the beginning of February, though not without all manner of demurrings on the Härtels' part, and a beating down of Wagner's price of 600 louisdor to 200, with the proviso of another hundred if it should prove an exceptional success. 'It was really funny!' Wagner told Liszt, 'I can do what I like, it will always seem completely or at least half impossible to the philistine.'

On 6 February Wagner resumed work on the score of the first act, which he had barely started before leaving for Paris, and finished it on 3 April, in the incredibly short time of scarcely two months.

It may have been intended as something more than a public gesture of reconciliation when Mathilde gave a soirée on 31 March in somewhat belated celebration of Otto's birthday, at which Wagner conducted an orchestra of thirty in ten separate movements from symphonies by Beethoven in the hall of the villa. After the serenade for 'sa belle Mathilde', a nocturne for Otto was appropriate, Cosima von Bülow commented in a letter to Frau Herwegh.

The whole of Zürich's *beau monde* were present, Eliza Wille reported. Gottfried Keller regretted having been prevented by an accident from attending this elegant concert, which was completely unprecedented for 'a private do in Zürich'.

Wagner's conducting desk, almost completely hidden by flowers, was placed in the vestibule opposite the front door, while the guests were seated in the adjoining rooms. Before the concert began the Wesendonks' seven-year-old daughter presented him with a baton carved with a design by Semper. Frau Wesendonk had received her first decisive impression of Wagner when he conducted Beethoven's Eighth at a subscription concert six years before, and the Allegretto scherzando, which had been one of her favourite pieces ever since, was on the programme on this occasion. It was typical of Wagner's own taste that the concert ended with the 'profoundly consoling' Adagio of the Ninth. Afterwards he went over to the table where Minna was sitting with the wife of the leader of the orchestra, and delightedly showed her the carved baton. The party went on till after midnight and the guests were royally entertained

Even the Wesendonks were deeply moved by the occasion, which was intended primarily as a tribute to them, Wagner recorded in *Mein Leben*. It 'had a melancholy effect on me as a warning that possibly the climax of a relationship between lives had been reached, that the real substance of it had indeed already been overtaken, and the bowstring overdrawn'. Before reproaching him with having concealed the true nature of his relationship with Mathilde in his autobiography, one should remember that he wrote it for King Ludwig and dictated it to Cosima. For those in the know that sentence said all.

Frau Wesendonk had some time previously engaged Francesco de Sanctis, a lecturer at the Polytechnic in Zürich, to give her private lessons in Italian. Since she displayed more interest in excursions and conversation at the tea table than zeal to learn the language of Dante, he asked her to release him, to which she replied that she received him 'en ami, non pas en qualité de professeur'. Her two friends now regarded each other with undisguised dislike, and an attempt to bring them together had failed. On 5 April, a few days after the concert, Wagner had had to do without his evening visit, since De Sanctis remained to tea after the lesson. His chagrin kept him awake all night, and the next day bad weather prevented him from meeting her in the garden.

When he went to see her that evening he was irritable, and they had a difference of opinion. The next morning he sent her the pencil sketch of the *Tristan* prelude as a peace-offering, with a letter. Minna stopped the messenger, took the rolled sheet of manuscript paper, found the letter and opened it. Had she been capable of understanding it, it ought to have allayed all her fears, for, as

Wagner wrote to his sister Klara, its theme was his resignation. She believed, instead, that she now had tangible proof of his infidelity and furiously went to confront him with it. With difficulty he succeeded in so far calming her that she promised to forgo a foolish revenge and to avoid any kind of scene. But behind his back she went to Frau Wesendonk and threatened: 'If I were an ordinary woman I would go to your husband with this letter!' Mathilde, who had no secrets from her husband, had no choice but to tell him of this visit and its cause.

And what was in that fateful letter? Since Minna had appropriated it, it was not to be found among those that were later published. Its history is as strange as the role it played in Wagner's life. Minna left it to her daughter Natalie, who sold it to Mrs Burrell in the 1890s. On her death, shortly afterwards, it was held in trust, together with the many other Wagneriana she had collected. In 1930 two literary adventurers, Hurn and Root, succeeded in gaining access to the Burrell Collection and its secrets. They published what they allegedly found there, together with some of their own inventions and smears, in a disgraceful book to which they gave the title *The Truth about Wagner*. The letter to Mathilde was one of the few documents that they had actually seen, and it was supposed that what they published was the authentic text, especially as Julius Kapp published it in the same form in the next edition of his book *Richard Wagner und die Frauen*. In the meantime the Burrell Collection had been taken to America, having been bought by a patron of music, Mrs Mary Curtis, for the Curtis Institute of Music in Philadelphia which she had founded. When at last, in 1950, the principal items of the collection were published, including the letter which had failed to reach its addressee nearly a century before, it transpired that what Hurn and Root had published twenty years earlier was only its beginning and its ending, and the main substance, and the reason for the letter, was a dissertation on Goethe's *Faust*.

Their disagreement the evening before had been about *Faust*. Wagner had become heated and Mathilde had reproved him for it. Now he had woken with a bad conscience and wanted to make a 'morning confession' to her, excusing his irritability by his 'dreadful hatred for all the De Sanctises of this world'. 'Wretch that I am! I had to say that to you: I had no other choice. But it was very petty of me and I deserved to be suitably punished.'

'What was that stupid quarrel over Goethe about?' he went on. Mathilde had said that Faust was the most significant human type any writer had ever created, while Wagner, with all due respect for Goethe, saw him as an 'over-imaginative scholar' who, sent out to study the world at first hand, instead of learning from Gretchen where salvation and redemption were to be found, woke up one morning and had forgotten the entire incident. 'In the end even the grey-haired sinner is aware of it and makes a visible effort to repair his omission in a final tableau – outside things, after death, where it's no longer inconvenient to him.' To the words of the dying Faust:

> Towards the Beyond the view has been cut off;
> Fool – who directs that way his dazzled eye,
> Contrives himself a double in the sky!
> Let him look round him here, not stray beyond;
> To a sound man this world must needs respond –

Wagner's response was 'Fool, to hope to win the world and peace from out there! Salvation dwells only within, in the inner depths!'

'Be good to me,' he concluded, 'and forgive my childish behaviour of yesterday: you were quite right to call it that! – Today seems mild. I shall go into the garden; as soon as I see you I hope to catch an uninterrupted moment with you! Take my whole soul as a morning greeting!' (RWBC, pp. 489ff.)

Some relaxation of the tension was to be expected after Wagner had taken Minna to the Brestenberg sanatorium on 15 May for three months, to receive treatment for her heart ailment – which had only been aggravated by a 'fearful amount of opium' – and after the Wesendonks, too, had left at the beginning of May to spend a month in Italy. The Erard had arrived on 3 May: this wonderfully soft, sweetly melancholy instrument had fully coaxed him back to music again. The next day he began the composition sketch of the second act, which he finished on 1 July. 'Still in Asyl' he wrote on the first sheet, between hope and fear. The existence he led in his isolation was curiously dreamlike, interrupted by visits from his few friends, and its external events were set down in twenty-nine letters to Minna.

The garden was a picture – but he didn't want to distress her. The gardener was taking care of the lawn, the peas had sprouted, the first asparagus was ready for pulling and if there was plenty she should be sent some. 'I am living so much inside myself now, that I simply do not notice whether anything has happened in the world . . . In addition to that I am now really in the mood for my work and all kinds of the loveliest themes have occurred to me.' As she had broken her ring he had the stone reset: 'Today I am sending you a whole ring for your broken one, and let us hope that it will last better than the old one.'

One morning Liszt's favourite pupil, the sixteen-year-old Karl Tausig turned up. 'He is a terrible boy,' Wagner exclaimed, when he had got to know his young visitor better. 'Musically at any rate he is enormously gifted, and his insane piano-playing makes me tremble.' It was not long before he had found a place in Wagner's affections and had to accompany him on one of his visits to Brestenberg. His 'little Thousand-tara [Tausendsasa]' had taken her to his heart too, Wagner told Minna, and he added, since she had evidently mentioned his Jewish descent, 'his father is a very honourable native of Bohemia, a thorough Christian'. Later, he was to choose Tausig to be the organizer of the society of patrons of the Bayreuth festivals.

At the end of May Minna came home for twenty-four hours to see that everything was in order. Since she mentioned, with a frivolity Wagner found disagreeable, the 'little love affair' she had set to rights, he felt obliged to warn her of the dangers that could jeopardize their remaining at Asyl. It was the first and only time since the devastating letter she had once sent him in Riga that he heard her 'lament in a gentle and dignified manner'. And as on that previous occasion he was ready to believe in a change of heart. 'Your tears and regret during the last night at home moved me more than any other kind of declaration.' Minna's version of this exchange was: 'Richard poured out his venom against me until two o'clock in the morning.' (To Frau Herwegh, JKWF, p. 147) We might despair of ever knowing the truth of the matter, had she not also often told her friends that her husband had again written her a letter full of cruel, mean things, whereupon reference to the letter in question on each occasion shows that, on the contrary, he had expressed himself warmly and affectionately. 'But if she wished posterity to share her opinion of Wagner', Newman observes, 'she ought to have avoided the cardinal blunder of preserving his letters.' (NLRW, III, pp. 175f.)

These were the foreground events of the two months in which

the composition sketch of the second act of *Tristan* was being written. The introduction starts piano in the sketch, with the motive of Impatience in the bass clarinet. The harsh Day motive at the beginning, played fortissimo on horns and woodwind, was not added until he wrote the full score – so presenting the theme of the discussion of Night/Day, that great variation movement, in a form that could not be mistaken.

On the sheet of sketches written on 19 December 1856 (mentioned in the previous chapter), Wagner had set the words of 'O sink hernieder, Nacht der Liebe. . .' to an early form of the 'Lausch, Geliebter' melody.[9] But instead of using that in the composition sketch he began with a melody that proves to be an arpeggiated form of the *Tristan* chord: evidently in the interests of providing a motivic link between the two major elements – the prelude and the love scene.

This scene also contains the only instances of lines set in the composition sketch being subsequently omitted from the score: the eight lines from 'Selbst um der Treu' to 'Geheimnis vertraut' and the fourteen lines from 'Soll der Tod' to 'den Weg uns gewiesen'. While the first omission, of fifteen bars, is of no formal significance, the second, of thirty-six bars, perceptibly shortens the reprise of the period in question, compared to its exposition in the first half of the duet. The gathering velocity of the dramatic action is reflected in the growing speed with which the scene approaches its end musically.[10]

Perhaps the most amazing thing, in view of the intensity of personal experience that seems to be so much in evidence here, is the level of artistic objectivity: one need only think, for instance, of his setting of King Marke's reproach. How much sympathy he had for Marke is demonstrated by his remonstrating with Heinrich Porges over a point in the latter's analysis of *Tristan*: Porges's assumption of a 'quasi-guilt' on Marke's part was uncalled for, in fact wrong: he had failed to notice that the basis of the melodic construction of the coda of the second act was Marke's principal motive, representing his benevolence; 'consequently it contains the motive of self-reproach, which Tristan conspicuously rejects'. (15 March 1867)

The Wesendonks had returned on 1 June, and Otto called on Wagner the next day to invite him to tea. 'I thereupon wrote to him to explain, very delicately, that in future we want to maintain a friendly relationship, but without personal contact.' (To Minna, 3

June) But he was unable to endure more than a month of this
voluntary banishment. 'I shall not visit you often,' he wrote to
Mathilde on 6 July, 'for from now on you shall see me only when I
am sure of showing you a calm, smiling face.'

On 15 July he went to Brestenberg to fetch Minna. During his
absence the gardener, 'a wily Saxon', erected a triumphal porch,
covered with flowers, which, Minna was delighted to see when she
arrived home, was in full view of her neighbour. When the Bülows,
invited by Wagner to stay at Asyl, went to call on the Wesendonks,
they discovered that this welcome had had its effect on Mathilde,
who still nursed a sense of grievance. Wagner wrote in his autobiography of her 'passionate excesses', retailed to him by the
Bülows, and he also wrote to Eliza Wille, telling her that after he
had made his last farewells, Frau Wesendonk had taken it into her
head to torment him again 'with childish and senseless reproaches',
conveyed by one of his friends, because of the terms she supposed
him to be on with his wife. It made him painfully aware that she was
hardly capable of appreciating what he suffered on her account.

He was not going to revoke his decision now: his only regret was
that he had not taken it earlier, at the first catastrophe, in the new
year. If he had weakened again then, he hoped he might be forgiven
by her who had left him uncertain as to her wishes. 'I can see my
continuing to live here in no other light than as a hell from which I
daily long to be released.' (To Eliza Wille, second half of July)
Twenty years later he viewed these events more dispassionately –
perhaps too dispassionately, when he told Cosima about 'Frau
Minna's battle with Frau Mathilde', how they had each tried to rile
the other, 'and I – I had no thought of either'. (DMCW, I, p. 860)

When he told Minna of his decision to leave Asyl he had to admit
that *her* behaviour was not the sole cause of his desperation. In
terms of their personal relationships, Mathilde's refusal ever to have
anything to do with Minna again was the decisive factor. But from a
higher standpoint, it was *Tristan*, it was his work, which, if it was to
be finished, demanded that he find peace and solitude and review his
experiences in a transfigured light.

Putting his decision into practice was fated to suffer delay, as one
party of visitors after another, from far and near, descended on Asyl:
apart from Tausig and the Bülows, no sooner had one famous tenor,
Albert Niemann, and his bride left, than another, Tichatschek,
came, followed by Klindworth, Karl Ritter, a young musician

called Wendelin Weissheimer, and Cosima's mother, the Comtesse d'Agoult, who had come to Zürich 'pour faire ici la connaissance de grands hommes'. 'And so the house was full every day,' *Mein Leben* says, 'and anxious, worried and uneasy friends sat down at our table, their wants catered for by her who was about to give up this household for ever.' The one friend who did not come was the one person Wagner longed for in his emotional turmoil: Franz Liszt.

With only half his mind on his guests, Wagner entertained them with a performance of *Rheingold* and *Walküre*, singing all the parts himself, as Bülow reported, 'with a magnificent unself-consciousness and expending all his forces', while Klindworth provided a thrilling accompaniment at the piano from his difficult vocal scores. The Wesendonks were not present. Mathilde had returned to Wagner a 'precious trifle' which she had kept until then – and about which we know nothing more – 'certainly in order to hurt me very deeply', as he told Eliza Wille. 'You will keep it then, until such time as *she* wants to have it again. Won't you? You will do this for me?' (7[?] August)

By a curious chance we can judge what effect all this had on Cosima. Before her arrival she had written to Frau Herwegh, saying that she was sorry for Minna but could not think it wrong of Richard, driven by his longing for the ideal and for peace at the same time, exhausted by incessant everyday cares of life, if he asked for a little happiness from 'une nature pâle et chétive, aussi incapable de vivre fortement d'une existence simple et droite, que de rompre avec ses engagements antérieurs pour s'abandonner à l'amour et soutenir son amant'. Now she left Zürich for a few days to accompany her mother to Geneva and meet her sister there, and Karl Ritter undertook to escort the ladies. She returned from the journey in a greatly excited state, which alarmed Wagner, to whom she showed it in 'convulsive, violent endearments'. From a passage in a letter from him to Mathilde Wesendonk which was suppressed in the published edition, we learn that in Geneva Cosima and Karl had been close to suicide. She suddenly begged him to kill her and he had declared himself ready to die with her. They both went out on the lake, Cosima intending to drown herself, Karl determined to follow her, and it was because she could not shake his determination that she abandoned her plan. They parted with an agreement to let each other know how they felt in three weeks' time, and in fact Karl did then receive a letter from Cosima, in which she expressed regret for her vehemence and thanked him for his delicacy and consideration. (JKWF, pp. 151ff.)

It was not a tragic mutual passion that led the two to this pass, but the sudden overwhelming recognition of the affinity between their fates. Karl had just separated from his young wife and Cosima had become aware in Zürich of the unhappiness of her own marriage. She was disturbed to the roots of her being by Wagner's personality, his destiny and his art.

Gradually the guests departed. Wagner gave notice of his intention to leave Asyl in a personal call on Wesendonk. He took his leave of Mathilde in the presence of Bülow, and his last words to her were a blessing for her children. The day before he himself was to leave, Hans and Cosima left: he in tears, she stern and silent. Early on the morning of 17 August 1858, after a sleepless night, Wagner left Asyl. Minna was composed, but going to the station in the carriage to see him off, she was overcome by the emotion of the occasion.

'The sky was bright and cloudless, it was a glorious summer's day,' Wagner recalled in *Mein Leben*; 'I do not remember once looking back, or even shedding a single tear at my departure, which almost alarmed me. But as I journeyed in the train I could not conceal from myself a growing sense of well-being; it was obvious that the totally useless torment of the last few months could not have been endured any longer, and a complete separation . . . was what the governing force of my life and my destiny demanded.'

22

Venice and Lucerne

'This is my address,' Wagner wrote to Minna on 1 September 1858: 'Canal Grande, Palazzo Giustiniani, Campiello Squillini no. 3228.' It had not been easy for him to decide where to go after leaving Asyl. In the end Venice seemed to have everything in its favour, except the possibility that there he was not really beyond the reach of the Saxon police. It was not part of the German League, but it was under Austrian rule. Liszt had passed on a warning from the Grand Duke of Weimar, but the Austrian ambassador in Berne believed that with the visa he had given him Wagner had nothing to fear, at least for a while.

'Grandeur, beauty and decay in close proximity.' This first impression, received as he went down the Grand Canal to the Piazzetta, was in harmony with his own grave, melancholy mood. Since his lodgings were important to him as the 'casing of his working mechanism', he decided on the fifteenth-century Gothic palazzo next door to the Palazzo Foscari, where he rented some furnished rooms on the first floor from the Hungarian landlord.

'It has, like all such apartments in a large, old-fashioned palace, large halls and rooms. For my living room I have an imposing chamber overlooking the Grand Canal; in addition a very spacious bedroom with a little closet off it as a wardrobe. Beautiful old ceiling painting, marvellous floor inlaid with splendid mosaic; badly painted walls (no doubt richly tapestried in the past), old-fashioned and at first glance elegant furniture with red velveteen covers, very fragile, miserably upholstered; nothing working properly, doors not shutting completely, everything a bit broken.' (To Minna, 28 September)

To make his living room more habitable he had the grey walls

papered in dark red, and ordered red curtains to hide the shoddy
doors that had been hung in the ancient frames.

Here were peace and solitude in abundance! He was the only
tenant in the whole house. From his balcony he could enjoy the
colourful bustle of life on the canal without any of the street noises
he detested. He looked forward to hearing the Erard in his large
room – twice the size of the Wesendonks' drawing room. The only
drawback was the cold, especially in the winter, when crosswinds
seemed to choose this corner of the canal to intersect.

In a smaller town he would have been unable to avoid social
distractions and would probably not have wanted to. Here he was
surrounded by a world that constantly provided stimulation, but
was alien, remote and moribund – exactly suited to his desire for
solitude. 'Nothing makes the immediate impact of real life; everything makes an objective effect, like a work of art. I will stay here.'
(Venetian Diary, 3 September) Visitors were turned away uncere-
moniously. Apart from Karl Ritter, whom he met in the afternoons
in the San Marco restaurant on the Piazzetta, the only people who
penetrated his fastness were Liszt's pupil Winterberger, a piano
teacher called Tessarin who was a passionate lover of German
music, and the cultured Russian Prince Dolgoruki.

Here he recovered the composure he needed to work and which
had deserted him during the last weeks in Asyl. He could not rid his
thoughts altogether of the two women who had become his fate
even here, but the distance tempered everything, showed much in a
different light.

Minna was still in Zürich, disbanding the household rather nois-
ily and writing heart-rending letters of goodbye as 'the unhappiest
woman under the sun', as she signed herself to Sulzer. Before
leaving for Zwickau and Dresden she wrote one more letter to
Mathilde: her heart bled to tell her that she had succeeded in
separating her husband from her after twenty-two years of marriage. 'May this noble deed bring you consolation and happiness.'
And one to Wagner: he would curse himself in time for having
thrown everything over and wantonly banished his faithful wife.
'That isn't at all what I wanted to write to you about, even that will
come to an end, but it just flows from my pen of its own accord and
only a feeling of vengeance mounts in me, unfortunately there is no
God!' (RWBC, pp. 496ff.)

Wagner's only feeling for her was a boundless pity: he wrote to commiserate with her on her fate, bound once and for all to that of a man who, however much he might wish for contentment, was committed to so extraordinary a development that he had finally had to forgo his wishes in order to fulfil his life's work. 'All I want now is to collect myself inwardly, so as to be able to complete my works.' (To Minna, 1 September) He begged his friends to look after her: 'Be her doctor, her adviser and her helper – if you can,' he wrote to Pusinelli in Dresden, 'her comforter if you cannot.' (1 November) Then he had another letter from her 'and all the old misery starts again'.

Bülow, who had witnessed and played a part in the tragedy in Asyl and knew all the people intimately, formed his own ideas on the matter. He thought that Wagner was 'longing for his wife(!!!)', who kept on bewailing her imminent end and therefore naturally – paltry though the device was – roused his pity anew. 'He wrote in his last letter "no one shall die on my account"! I am afraid – I am afraid – I am afraid! Please heaven I am wrong!' (To Karl Klindworth, 10 October 1858) He could not restrain himself from pleading with Wagner on the same day. 'I have an inexpressible fear that you may profane yourself again out of pity and the goodness of your heart! Don't do it!' (NBB, p. 416)

On the Green Hill in Zürich it had been decided to avoid any contact with Wagner for the time being. 'Do you not even want letters?' he complained in his Venetian Diary. 'I have written to you and have every hope that with *this* letter I shall not be repulsed.' It was returned to him unopened two days later. '*That* shouldn't have happened! Not that!' Only from Eliza Wille did he receive brief bulletins: Mathilde was collected, calm, and determined on complete renunciation – parents, children, duties. 'How strange that sounded to me in my lofty mood of serious cheerfulness!' he commented. 'When I thought of you, parents, children, duties never entered my head: I only knew that you loved me and that everything sublime in the world must be unhappy.'

In fact this disagreement had already come into the open at Asyl. In 1873 he told Cosima that in the dreadful period of Mathilde's jealousy of Minna he had suggested that they should both get divorces and marry each other. She had replied that it would be 'sacrilege'. 'Anyway,' he went on, smiling, 'that incomprehensible word was quite appropriate, because in my heart of hearts and quite unconsciously I was not serious.' (DMCW, I, p. 654)

While the separation only bound Mathilde more closely to her house and family, longing threatened to overwhelm the resignation he had achieved so laboriously. In October Wesendonk informed him that their little son Guido had died. 'Your news distressed me profoundly,' Wagner wrote – an inexplicable apprehension had once prevented him from becoming the child's godfather. 'How gladly I would fly to your side to comfort you both.' The wish was expressed there as something impossible of fulfilment, but his longing soon represented it to him as a possibility. 'Decide on winter visit to Mariafeld,' it says in the Annals. In two unpublished letters he asked Eliza Wille to arrange for him to meet Mathilde again at Mariafeld at Christmas. The reply came from François Wille instead of his wife: Frau Wesendonk had sworn in the most solemn terms that she could not understand how she had given Wagner the least cause to write those two letters: she was horrified at his proposal and begged him not to proceed with it. In his blunt fashion Wille called him 'the most magnificent of all sophists and self-deceivers', who allowed his artistic imagination free rein in everything that flattered his own desires. (6 November) Wagner replied that the motive that had inspired this wish in him so suddenly was too delicate to lend itself to explanation. (13 November; FWSZ, II, p. 402) In his Venetian Diary he wrote: 'The mendicant Buddhist presented himself before the wrong house and hunger became his prayer.' His mood at this time is reflected in a sketch for a song, 'Es ist bestimmt in Gottes Rat' ('It is determined in God's counsels') in A minor. The bass descending stepwise through one and a half octaves, the impassioned cry at 'what we hold most dear' with its augmented triad, give the setting something unrelenting. These were the tones of someone at the convent gate, he commented when he played it to Cosima two decades later, 'and even more, complete renunciation, extinction'. (BBL 1937, p. 109)

He sought refuge from the storms of his passion in *Tristan* – and in writing letters and the diary for Mathilde. His hopes and despair are present in them all, but a world of ideas and observations soon suppressed all personal factors. As always his days were governed by a routine. The morning was reserved for work on his score. At about five he went by gondola to the usual restaurant on the Piazza San Marco, then to the Giardino Pubblico or the Lido where he took his walk. When he got home in the evening a lamp was already burning to greet him in the dark palazzo. At that hour he would open a book, read and think: whatever he read at once stimulated his own ideas. He read history, biography, poetry, philosophy; Count Daru's *Histoire de la république de Venise*, which led him to view the Venetians as 'superb statesmen, quite heartless as human beings'; Wilhelm von Humboldt's letters, which made him laugh at the author's 'nonsense about providence – which certainly provided very well for *him*!'; Schiller, to whom Wagner felt particularly close in the one respect in which he outshone Goethe – the desire for cognition. 'You would think that the man never lived at all, never did anything but peer about him for the light and warmth of the mind.'

'Very solitary,' the Annals say for the November, during a bout of illness, 'dreamy. No work: *Histoire de Venise*. – Schopenhauer. Frequent *Parizival* moods. Shepherd's tune, F minor.'

His renewed preoccupation with his friend Schopenhauer brought him up against what seemed to him to be two gaps in the philosopher's system. Schopenhauer expresses surprise that a pair of lovers should commit suicide, since losing their lives means simultaneously losing their greatest happiness: this moved Wagner to try to demonstrate that sexual love is the saving way to self-knowledge and self-denial of the will. 'You alone give me the material of the concepts through which my views become communicable along philosophical lines,' he started to write to Schopenhauer (RWGS, XII, p. 291), but instead of finishing the letter he asked Breitkopf & Härtel to send the philosopher a copy of the text of *Tristan*. (26 November)

The other problem lay in Schopenhauer's metaphysics of music, in relation to the other arts, especially poetry: this touched on matters that only he, Wagner, could explain properly, 'because there has never been anyone else who has been both poet and musician in the way that I am, and who could therefore have had insights into inner processes such as could be expected from none but myself'. (Venetian Diary, 8 December) These ideas remained with him and formed the subject of his essays on Beethoven in 1870.

The long, slow maturing that was characteristic of his creative processes meant that different works and interests occupied him at different levels simultaneously – like Goethe. While in the middle of composing *Tristan* he could not prevent the mood of *Parsifal* from overtaking him: in particular he was visited by the increasingly vivid and compelling conception of a woman, strange and wonderful, but possessed by cosmic demons: the messenger of the Grail. 'If I ever succeed in writing this text, it is bound to be something very original.' (To Mathilde, 2 March 1859) At the same time, reading Köppen's history of Buddhism encouraged him to expand his scenario for *Die Sieger*. The difficulty was the representation of the Buddha, the man who had shed all passions, in terms suitable for dramatic and, above all, musical realization. The solution he found now was that the Buddha himself, deeply moved by Savitri's fate, should attain to a yet higher level of perception. It was a transfer of emphasis towards the inner action similar to the one he later gave the second scenario for *Die Meistersinger*, away from the foreground action concerning Ananda and Savitri, or Walther and Eva, towards the change that takes place in the heart of the sympathetic observer Buddha, or Sachs. This gave the drama a far greater depth which is revealed in the music.

'My work has become dearer to me than ever,' he wrote to Liszt on 19 October. 'I took it up again recently; it's flowing like a gentle current from my spirit.' Everything in his life in Venice conspired to keep him in the mood for this 'art of resonant silence'. When he rode to the Lido in a gondola of an evening, a sound like the 'soft sustained note of a violin' seemed to waft round him. As he wrote he could hear music outside his window: a brightly lit gondola was gliding past, carrying singers with beautiful voices and players with passable instruments; long after it was out of sight he could still hear the sounds which, while they had no attraction for him as art, were yet native here. One night when he could not sleep he heard the gondoliers' antiphonal singing that had once stirred Goethe so deeply: the melody was older than the verses of Tasso that they sang to it, as old as the canals and palaces of Venice itself. One night, when he was going home along the Grand Canal, a sudden cry broke from the breast of the gondolier standing high above him on the stern, wielding his powerful oar, a mournful sound not unlike the howl of an animal, swelling up from a low, long-drawn-out 'Oh!' to end in the simple, musical cry 'Venezia!' Such were the impressions that surrounded him while he finished the second act and gave him the idea for the melancholy 'alte Weise' of the third act.

His work was the only thing in his life, he told Eliza Wille. But what a work! He was going at it as if he did not want ever to finish it, as though he hoped to force death to surprise him at it. He had never worked so privately: every line had an eternity's significance for him. It was astonishing: when he looked it over as a whole, he was sure he had never written anything possessing such musical unity, such an inexhaustible flow. '*Tristan* will be beautiful! But it is devouring me.' (21 February 1859; FWSZ, II, p. 411)

It was another characteristic of his creative processes that routine in itself could not help him. After an interruption of some length he sat for three days over the passage beginning 'Wen du empfangen, wem du gelacht': he could not pick up the right thread and was at a standstill. 'Then the goblin knocked at my door' – referring to the fairy tales about the goblin's power of inspiration – 'and proved to be the fair muse herself. In an instant the passage was clear. I sat down at the piano and wrote it down as fast as if I had long known it by heart.' (Venetian Diary, 22 November 1858) These are the bars which lead into the melody of the Liebestod.

There were more interruptions and distractions than one might suppose from the pages of the Diary, which is saturated with the mood of *Tristan*. To Bülow, who was preparing the vocal score, he wrote that when he had got to know the second act he would sense how rarely and with what difficulty Wagner was able to wrest from his present way of life the hours when it was possible to write such music. (23 January 1859) There was letter after letter to write, so that he groaned that he really ought to have a secretary: about the Berlin production of *Lohengrin* (23 January 1859), which forced Hülsen to admit at last that he had not expected such an 'outrageous success'; about his efforts to 'exploit' *Rienzi* to earn some money, which brought him from Munich the news that it had once again been withdrawn there 'for religious reasons' – as a result he lost a royalty of 50 louisdor which he had unfortunately already spent in anticipation. In December he was approached again by the agent Dr Hartenfels, who had tried three years previously to persuade him to undertake an American tour. Wagner was once more so deep in financial trouble that this time he gave the proposal serious consideration: five months in New York, a prestigious German opera, he thought he would be well paid. His conditions were that he would conduct only his own operas and that Klindworth must be engaged as his assistant. After three months of negotiations he was finally relieved when the plan came to nothing: it would have been a little too much like London! (To Klindworth, 28 April 1859)

In November 1858 Breitkopf & Härtel, who were in touch with

him over the engraving of *Tristan*, raised the subject of the
'Nibelung' project again of their own accord: they proposed publishing it without making a down payment, but offered him a share
of the net profits. They did not want to let slip the opportunity of
doing business, but still had doubts about the practicability of so
huge a work. Wagner replied that he not only thought his work was
practicable, he knew it, in spite of all appearances. He possessed a
particularly acute sense of the practical, which never deserted him in
any of his ventures, however daring. After a protracted correspondence he broke off the negotiations on 6 February 1859: 'I can
see that the time is not yet ripe.'

He lost no time in turning to Liszt instead. On 23 February,
referring to a conversation he had had with Grand Duke Carl
Alexander in Lucerne in the summer of the previous year, he wrote
to Liszt offering the duke the rights to the score of the *Ring*, for the
same fee that Breitkopf & Härtel were paying him for *Tristan*. Liszt
reported back: 'Our Serenissimus did not find the thick "soup", as
you call it, much to his taste. Neither the palate nor the stomach is
ready for it.' (6 April 1859)

At the same time he was still corresponding with Eduard
Devrient, in the belief that Karlsruhe was going to give the first
performance of *Tristan*. He was relying on the Grand Duke of
Baden to snap his fingers at Saxony and invite him personally to
Karlsruhe, and was unaware that Devrient had long been playing a
double game, as we learn from the letters he wrote to his wife from
Asyl the year before.

So many plans; so many illusions. The only thing to come to
fruition, in fact, was something he had ceased to expect. 'The police
served me with my expulsion order today,' he wrote to Bülow on 3
February. 'Saxony has just kept on at Vienna about it.'

The Saxon government was not alone to blame: he had a powerful enemy in Austria, too, the General Inspector of Police,
Lieutenant-Field-Marshal Johann Freiherr Kempen von Fichten-
stamm. No sooner had he heard of Wagner's arrival in Venice on 29
August 1858 than he sent off a telegram in code to the Venetian
police authorities, on 3 September, making enquiries. After receiving confirmation, he at once approached the Austrian foreign
minister, Karl Graf von Buol-Schauenstein, representing to him
that the presence on Austrian territory of a man notorious as one of
the leaders of the May revolution in Dresden was not only unwel-

come to the police but also likely to offend the government of Saxony. For the time being Buol ordered only that Wagner should be kept under strict police surveillance and that the Saxon government should be informed of this. Kempen had to be satisfied with that, and there was nothing Dresden could do but file the information.

The official documents published by Lippert (LWVR, pp. 94f.) read like a chilling satire on reactionary administrations, while all the more honour is due to Angelo Crespi, the minor police official in Venice who wrote the regular police reports to Kempen and gave Wagner what protection he could in them: Wagner was devoting himself to his work, to the exclusion of all other activities; thanks to his genius he had broken new ground in composition; the doctors had years ago ordered him to live in the south to restore his health. Good Wagnerians, Newman comments, ought to drink Crespi's health after each performance of the second act of *Tristan*.

Wagner's position got worse early in 1859, when the likelihood that Austria would soon be at war with France and the Kingdom of Sardinia engaged so much of Buol's attention that Kempen got a free hand and ordered his expulsion on 1 February. In order to win a little time to finish the second act, on the advice of his friends in the police, Wagner addressed a petition to Archduke Maximilian in Milan, then Governor General of Lombardy and later the ill-fated Emperor of Mexico, who telegraphed his consent without delay.

But as his residence permit was in any case due to expire in the spring, the question of his amnesty again became urgent. He decided to write to 'old Lüttichau', asking him to recommend that he be allowed to return without incurring further penalty: if he were refused yet again then he would have no other choice but, with a heavy heart, to abandon Germany once and for all. 'But it would make me very satisfactory amends that I should not need to denounce my harsh treatment myself: my epitaph would proclaim it, silently but for all the world to hear.' (9 February 1859) Without taking any action himself at all, Lüttichau left it to him to approach the king and so, encouraged by his success with Archduke Maximilian, Wagner wrote to the Saxon minister of justice on 22 February, pleading that his health did not permit him to face the stresses that a trial and the loss of liberty entailed would cause him. The petition was laid before the king; Minna received the refusal on 10 March.

A misunderstanding with Liszt was added to the worries of that winter. 'Thanks to Liszt I had a sad New Year,' Wagner wrote to Bülow on 23 January. It was cleared up in no time, but it left a slight distance between them: he recognized more clearly than ever that he could not let himself go completely with Liszt. 'He doesn't understand my sense of humour at all.' Bülow replied that he had only heard of his awkward passage with Liszt after it was all over. 'Thank God that it's all been settled. You are right to exercise a little diplomacy towards him now and then. He has become distrustful in the highest degree. Hardly a day passes without his being betrayed and traduced.' (5 February)

Wagner finished the orchestral sketch of Act II on 9 March 1859 and the score on 18 March. He wrote to tell Mathilde that he had at last dealt with the big musical problem that had caused everybody so much concern, and knew that he had found a solution such as had never been found before. 'It is the summit of my art so far.' (10 March) Not the least reason for his success, as Alfred Lorenz has shown, was his decision to cast the immensely extended dialogue in symphonic form, in broad outline Allegro – Adagio – Allegro.[1] It was thanks to the complete translation of all the ideas and concepts into musical and visual terms that, as Pfitzner said, a miracle was realized: for all its philosophical profundities and visionary realms of light, even the listener who remains unaware of its poetic depths enjoys it as an opera.

In the meantime the political situation had further deteriorated; troops had been sent to the Riva, and Milan was reported to be in a state of emergency. Since Wagner wanted to spend the summer in Switzerland he made haste and left Venice on 24 March. Coming to Milan and the noise of its streets was like entering a new world, he wrote to Mathilde the following day, and Venice already seemed like a fairy-tale dream. 'One day you will hear a dream that I roused to sound there!' During his short stay he also went to see Leonardo's *Last Supper*. As he looked from the copy, showing the painting as it had originally been, to the original, which was almost completely obliterated, he received for the first time, as he admitted, a clearer idea of the purely artistic significance of a masterpiece of painting. It was probably no coincidence that this revelation first came to him as the composer of *Tristan*. Nietzsche must have had an intimation of this affinity when he said that all the mysteries of Leonardo da Vinci are unravelled in the music of *Tristan*.

While the fruit trees were already in flower in Italy, the St Gotthard was clothed in an abominable cloak of mist, lined with snowflakes. 'A fine business, this snowy passage through wind and weather, on an open sledge.'(To Minna, 30 March) In Lucerne he put up at the Hotel Schweizerhof, managing to get a room in the annexe, which he had to himself until the end of June, with a large balcony and a magnificent view of his 'favourite lake'. At the weekend he visited the Wesendonks in Zürich. 'I feel as though I didn't really see you clearly,' he told Mathilde, 'thick fog lay between us, and even the sound of our voices could hardly penetrate it.' Since Wesendonk thought it was time to resume the appearance of a normal social relationship, to give the lie to gossip, a number of visits were exchanged between Zürich and Lucerne. 'It was, or so we both hope, a salutary demonstration,' Wagner dutifully reported to Minna. 'And I hope that you too will draw from it the conclusions that have given Wesendonk such satisfaction.' (18 April) The immediate consequence was that she at once got in touch with Jacob Sulzer: if his friend Wesendonk knew only a fraction of what she knew, he would abandon this naive idea that it was harmless to receive such a *dangerous* guest in the house. (24 April; FWSZ, II, pp. 164ff.)

After the Erard, delayed by troop movements and snowdrifts, finally arrived, Wagner began the composition sketch of the third act on 9 April. He felt as though he would never invent anything new again: the one period of flowering had produced so many shoots that now all he had to do was help himself from his store. In fact the act prelude is based on the song *Im Treibhaus*, transposed from D minor to F minor, the key of the 'traurige Weise' he had written in Venice, and more oppressive by the change of metre from triple to quadruple. But then the weather took a turn for the worse; he sat gazing out of the windows at the fog and could not get on with his work. In such times of reluctant inactivity he picked up Goethe's *Tasso*, which made him realize that he should not be in any hurry to have the text of *Tristan* published: the difference between a poem intended to be set to music and one intended as a straight play was so great that, if the former was read with the same eyes as the latter, the greater part of its real significance remained hidden. The poet–playwright had to assimilate his subject to real life in innumerable small details, which the poet–composer could simply make good in the 'endless detail of the music'. (To Mathilde, 15 April)

Liszt sent him his *Dante* Symphony at Eastertime. 'As Virgil
guided Dante, you have led me through the mysterious regions of
worlds of music, drenched in life. From my heart of hearts I cry:
"Tu se' lo mio maestro e il mio autore!" and dedicate this work to
you in steadfast, faithful love, your Liszt.'

The dedication reached Wagner at a moment of deep discour-
agement such as only genius knows, when it seems it would be
better to smash the statue and have done with it. In his reply to Liszt
he wrote: 'With this last act I am on the very brink of "to be or not to
be" – the least featherweight pressure from some mundane accident
. . . could kill the child in the act of its birth.' He suggested that they
keep the words of the dedication to themselves: they had made him
blush for shame. 'I simply can't tell you strongly enough how
wretched a musician I am in my own eyes; from the bottom of my
heart I despise myself as a complete bungler.' (8 May)[2]

'Dear Richard, your letter – what a dreadful tempest!' Liszt wrote
back. 'Hamlet's dilemma does not apply to you, because you are
and cannot help but be. Even your crazy injustice towards yourself
. . . is a sign of your greatness.' (14 May)

But Wagner's mood had already changed. He wrote to Mathilde
on 9 May to tell her that only the day before his attempt to work had
been a dismal failure. He had been in an awful state and had poured
it all out in a long letter to Liszt. But after he had been stuck at an
awkward passage for a week her biscuits had reached him today.
'Now I am quite happy: the transition has succeeded beyond expectation, with a quite marvellous blend of two themes. Dear God, the
things biscuits can do, when they're the right ones!'

The transition in question was that from Tristan's passionate
outcry 'Im Sterben mich zu sehnen, vor Sehnsucht nicht zu sterben!' to his recall of his first lonely voyage to Ireland to be healed by
Isolde. What he describes as simply the blend of two themes is the
start of a musical period in which, after the words 'den Segel[3] blähte
der Wind hin zu Irlands Kind', the polyphonic writing for the
woodwind, horns and strings above the pianissimo pedal point on
the timpani expands into the simultaneous blend of four independent themes, but is so fluent and transparent that the accents of each
part can be heard and appreciated individually.

Over and above its intrinsic accomplishment, the passage marks
an epoch in musical history. Richard Strauss commented that the
contrapuntal theory of the old school, according to which the

invention of a new melody had to take into account another melody with which it was expected to fit, had never interested him much. On that principle one could spend the livelong day writing fugues. But the yoking together of themes that were intractably opposed and had to be forced to accommodate each other – that was something else entirely! This modern 'psychological' counterpoint originated, Strauss concluded, in the third act of *Tristan*.[4]

Wagner took his technical inspiration for the passage from Bach and the Beethoven of the late quartets. He had tried to rehearse four Zürich musicians in the C♯ minor Quartet while he was still at Asyl. 'The beggars fiddled and squeaked away again so abominably', he told Minna, 'that Tausig grieved for me.' And an allusion in one of his letters to Mathilde reveals that during this summer while he was working on the third act, he played Bach to her, perhaps from the *Well-Tempered Clavier*, which he held particularly high. 'He has never given even me so much pleasure before, and I have never felt so close to him.' (9 July) Bülow's intuitive understanding of Wagner enabled him to appreciate the unique quality of the style of *Tristan* at once: 'Your *Tristan* bears the same relationship to *Lohengrin* as Beethoven's last quartets to his first. The analogy struck me forcibly. You will have to reckon with the audience of late Beethoven.' (NBB, 24 August)

Wagner, too, was pleased with himself. He had just played through the first half of the third act to himself, he wrote to Mathilde one day, and he had nobody to praise him, just like God on the sixth day of creation – 'and so I said to myself, among other things: Richard, you're a devil of a fellow!' (5 June) This act was like an intermittent fever, he complained while he was working on it. But while someone else might suppose that the passion and suffering in it were as much as his soul could bear, they were putting him into the frame of mind for *Parsifal* again: it was Amfortas who now filled his mind, appearing before him like Tristan in the third act but 'intensified beyond all imagining'. 'And do I really intend to create something like that? and actually set it to music as well? No, thank you very much!' (To Mathilde, 30 May)

Not if he could help it. The nearer he got to the end of *Tristan* the lighter his spirits became. He took up riding – riding! 'My doctor insisted.' He hadn't been on a horse since Riga, but he was managing quite well, with an 'English' seat. But he would have to beware of conceiving a passion for horses: the Wandering Jew had better not have a horse to accompany him on his travels. He had even made up a folksong while he was out riding, to celebrate finishing *Tristan*:

> Im Schweizerhof zu Luzern
> von Heim und Haus weit und fern –
> da starben Tristan und Isolde:
> so traurig er und sie so holde.

('In the Schweizerhof in Lucerne, far from hearth and home, Tristan and Isolde died, he so sad and she so fair.')

It went very well to a folk tune: he had sung it the same evening to Vreneli – Verena Weidmann, his faithful housekeeper, who later looked after him and Cosima in Munich and at Tribschen.

One morning he was woken up by the sound of an alphorn on the Rigi, and the cheerful noise it made inspired the 'lustige Weise' in *Tristan*. While he was pulling it into shape he suddenly thought of a different version of it, far more exultant, almost heroically so, and yet as natural as folk music. He was on the point of crossing out all he had written down when he was struck by yet another thought, namely that the new tune did not belong to Tristan's shepherd but to none other than Siegfried: 'Sie ist mir ewig, ist mir immer Erb und Eigen, Ein und All . . . ' 'And so I found myself all at once deep in *Siegfried*. Am I not right, after all, to have faith in my life, in my – ability to survive?' (To Mathilde, 9 July) Just as the first themes of *Tristan* had intruded as he was writing the second act of *Siegfried*, so now themes for *Siegfried* occurred to him while he worked to finish *Tristan*. As well as this jubilant theme, he made a sketch of a mournful cor anglais tune, heading it 'third act or *Tristan*'. He eventually changed its metre from 3/4 to 4/4 and used it in Act III of *Siegfried* at 'Dort seh ich Grane, mein selig Roß'.

His longing to complete the *Ring* revived, in spite of the Härtels and the Grand Duke of Weimar. When Otto Wesendonk offered him help Wagner at first refused. 'I cannot honourably accept a loan, for I know my position and constitution, which will probably never alter.' (24 August) But a few days later he followed this with: 'Can we perhaps make a *deal*?' He outlined the same proposals as he had made to Carl Alexander: Wesendonk should pay 6000 francs for each part completed, Wagner would sign over to him all the receipts from publication and would keep for himself only the income from public performance. He added that the offer would prove a bargain, even if it took time, which was if anything too modest a claim: it would have been the most profitable investment Wesendonk ever made – if it had not been for an event five years later which no one could have foreseen at the time. The contract was agreed, though it is hardly necessary to say that Wesendonk looked on it not as a commercial venture but merely as a means of saving Wagner's face.

Apart from the occasional society of his friends in Zürich, he felt very lonely. 'Do send me Tausig!' he begged Liszt. But Tausig could not come, and Liszt himself was rushed off his feet with the preparations for the Leipzig musicians' congress that was to lead to the foundation of the Allgemeiner Deutscher Musikverein. 'Don't laugh too much at me for always concerning myself with things like this: they are not without influence on your royalties, and from that point of view I beseech your tolerance.' (14 May) Instead of Tausig he sent the twenty-four-year-old composer Felix Draeseke, who arrived in Lucerne at the end of July and to begin with upset Wagner gravely with his account of the congress in Leipzig, at which his name had not been mentioned once, so as not to incur royal displeasure. Wagner addressed his anger to Bülow: instead of timidly avoiding mention of his name the honourable assembly should have submitted a petition on his behalf to the government of Saxony. 'Truly, I was stupid enough to expect just that . . . And ought I to blame Brendel and his cronies for it? Of course not – but you and Liszt – you I blame.' (2 September) 'You are right,' Bülow replied; ' "We" behaved badly. It is not my fault particularly.' He went on to tell Wagner that he had been so disgusted by Brendel's 'tactless, lickspittle toast' to King Johann, 'the jolly state-coachman, patron of the arts and sciences' – Bülow's allusion here to a well-known satirical poem makes this a far more savage comment on the king than it appears to be – that he had thrown his full glass of wine under the table, to the consternation of the assembled company.[5]

Draeseke stayed for four weeks and bequeathed us one of the few accounts of Wagner at work written by someone who possessed not only the musical training but the grounding in general culture needed to do the subject justice.

Wagner worked throughout the day, while Draeseke read the sections of the score that were finished. In the late afternoon they emerged from their separate rooms to talk and go for walks. One

day, 6 August, Wagner received him with: 'Wait just a moment and
Tristan will be finished.' 'I don't want to miss that!' Draeseke
exclaimed and he was allowed to watch as Wagner wrote the last
bars, with the opening motive dying away in the final, transfiguring
chord. Looking at the score he asked why the cor anglais did not
play in the last chord.[6] Wagner replied brusquely: 'Why should that
old scoundrel still be grunting away?' The instrument that plays the
'traurige Weise' is silent in what Richard Strauss called 'the most
beautifully orchestrated B major chord in the history of music'.

On their walks they held long conversations about art, philosophy, religion and politics. Draeseke soon noticed that Wagner's
thought processes were completely different from Bülow's and
especially from Liszt's: he would call their minds quick, but
Wagner's profound. At the end of his life he still maintained that
Wagner's was the greatest intellect that he had ever known.

Several times there arose the subject of the 'New German
School', whose wilful harmonies incurred the severe condemnation
of the composer of *Tristan*. On one of these occasions he taught
Draeseke a lesson about melody which shed a completely new light
on the subject for the younger man and was of more use to him than
everything he had learnt at the Leipzig Conservatory. 'Quite out of
the blue, I don't know what gave rise to it, he began to sing the first
movement of the "Eroica" one very hot afternoon in August, got
dreadfully carried away, sang on and on, grew very hot, was beside
himself but wouldn't stop until he had finished the first section.
"What's that?" he shouted at me, and I of course replied "the
'Eroica' ". "Well, isn't the plain melody enough? Must you always
have your insane harmonies with it?" To begin with I didn't understand what he meant, but when he calmed down and explained how
the melodic current in Beethoven's symphonies flows onwards
inexhaustibly and the melody alone is all you need to be able to call
the entire symphony clearly to mind, it set me thinking in a way
that had a great influence on my work.'[7]

What Wagner so dramatically demonstrated to Draeseke on that
occasion was the underlying principle of his own creative process:
that the melody ought not to be set moving artificially by harmonic
indulgences, but must flow inexhaustibly by its own power. 'I've
experienced it all at first hand,' he wrote to Liszt, while he was
composing *Rheingold*, 'and now I'm in a phase of development
where I've turned to a completely different method of construc-

tion.' (4 March 1854) He believed that *Tristan* was the closest that he had got to his ideal so far.

He had finished the score of *Tristan* yesterday (actually the day before), he told Princess Marie Wittgenstein. He had saved up this important part of it as a greeting for her. 'Do you remember the trip to Paris? It was a feast of loving friendship fit for the gods, and you presided.' After it he had sat down to compose for the first time in six years. Since then he had finished *Rheingold*, *Walküre*, the greater part of *Siegfried*, and now *Tristan und Isolde*. It was impossible for him to say what the verdict on these works would be. It would certainly be said that they were too unremittingly full of the whole abundance of the subject. A single glance would show that these scores were far richer, more finely woven, more extravagant than all his earlier scores put together. 'Certainly a wonderful blessing must have been laid upon me, to enable me, in these years of worry, want and all kinds of sorrow, to produce what someone who does not know me may well imagine to have flowered from the luxurious womb of a harmonious existence.' (8 August 1859)

23

Tannhäuser in Paris

This time the compulsion to see his new work staged was stronger than ever before. As Germany and Austria were barred to him, perhaps for ever, with Karlsruhe the one uncertain exception and with the alternative of Strassburg hardly to be taken seriously, that left Paris. 'God knows, Paris was not my choice: my readiness to seize it was only that of someone who has no other alternative.' (To Otto Wesendonk, 27 October 1859) Although he at first tried to persuade himself that the sole purpose of his journey was to hear a good orchestra or string quartet, once he was there his true purpose, as strong as fate, swept him ever more irresistibly on to undertakings which brought him to the very brink of disaster.

In 1839 he had believed that he was going to take Paris by storm; in 1849 he went there only at the insistence of Minna and Liszt; this time, in 1859, he obeyed the prompting of his own daemon. 'Something is wanted of me that is more important than consideration of my own personality.' (To Mathilde Wesendonk, 23 September 1859)

Since 1850, however, changes concerning himself had taken place in Paris, of which he was as yet unaware. Little enough had happened on the surface. The *Tannhäuser* overture had been performed twice, in 1850 and 1858, without the press paying it much attention. In October 1850 the *Journal des Débats* had published an article by Liszt about *Lohengrin*: a spirit of flame had sprung to life, whose destiny was to wear a double crown of fire and gold. But public opinion had been more decisively moulded by F. J. Fétis, a formidable scholar of European renown, who wrote a series of seven articles in 1852 in the *Gazette Musicale*, reprinted as a pamphlet, demonstrating that Wagner composed according to a 'system' and that that system was wrong.

But there were also a few finer, more discriminating spirits who felt drawn to him, who studied his scores and honoured him as their liberator. 'The truth is, it was a complete "milieu" that received him,' Maxime Leroy wrote, 'a spiritual milieu that had waited for him and wanted to celebrate his art.'[1]

Bülow had commended him to Auguste de Gaspérini, a retired naval doctor, who now devoted himself entirely to his twin passions of writing and travelling. When Wagner arrived in Paris on 11 September the entire city was on holiday. His letter reached Gaspérini in Marseilles. 'Quick, quick!' the latter wrote to his friend Léon Leroy, 'great news! Leave everything and hurry to no. 4 Avenue Matignon. Ask the concierge if Richard Wagner is at home! He has written me a charming letter. He is in Paris for a time. I beg you to deputize for me with the great man.'

'Thank you very much for Gaspérini,' Wagner wrote to Bülow in October; 'he is agreeable and lively and seems to possess a very obliging nature.' Our greatest debt to Gaspérini is for one of the rare portraits of Wagner as man and artist.

> Wagner was forty-six years old but could have passed for thirty-six. What first struck me was his coldness, his reserve, the severity of his features. But as the conversation got going his expression became more vivacious and I at last recognized him as I had imagined him from his works. Every one of his features was imprinted with the iron will that was the foundation of his character; it was apparent in everything: in the powerfully protuberant forehead, the strongly shaped chin, the thin, tight-pressed lips, the hollow cheeks, which bore the marks of the protracted turmoil of a life full of suffering. Yes, that was the man, the fighter whose history I knew, the thinker who, unsatisfied with the past, pressed ever onwards to the future. In the extraordinary mobility of his features, which his dominant will seemed to struggle against in vain, I saw the born dramatist and the untiring investigator of the human soul, which he explored down into its finest recesses.

   In the alterations of his expression, I thought at times
to discover in its depths Tristan in despair, the disciple
of Buddha and of Schopenhauer. But when conversation
turned to a different subject, one close to his heart,
concerning his future plans and new prospects – he
made courageous efforts in speaking French, though he
had only a poor command of it at that time – I suddenly
beheld a different man: young, enthusiastic, full of life
and confidence and, in spite of all his theories, very far
removed from Buddha and his fruitless contemplation.[2]

Wagner expected to settle in Paris for some time, so he took a
three-year lease on a small house in the Rue Newton, a quiet side
street linking two of the avenues radiating out from the Place de
l'Etoile, where he hoped to resume work on *Siegfried*, undisturbed
by neighbours' pianos. 'Here I am', he wrote to Mathilde, 'settling
in somewhere new again – without faith, without love or hope,
resting on the unfathomable foundation of dreamlike indifference.'
(23 October) Something astonishing happened while he was
arranging for his belongings to be sent from Lucerne. He went to
the Customs bureau to make an enquiry, and when he gave his
name a young official leapt to his feet: 'Je connais bien M. Richard
Wagner, puisque j'ai son médaillon suspendu sur mon piano et je
suis son plus ardent admirateur.' His name was Edmond Roche,
and he was a fervent amateur poet and musician. Wagner invited
him to call on him and later entrusted him with the translation of
Tannhäuser.
   Wagner informed Bülow that he was sending for his unhappy
wife again, since he was the only person who could give her the care
she needed: 'Her dependence on me is life and death to her and that
in turn determines my behaviour towards her.' (7 October) 'So
come here, be cheerful, don't get excited and don't worry,' he wrote
to her. 'You will find that there is still a lot to do here, but there is
nothing waiting for you that will wear you out: we shall be able to
look forward to a bright, cloudless sunset.' (7 November) Their
reunion was under an unlucky star from the first. A short time
before, Wagner had written to Pusinelli: it was a delicate matter that
he could discuss only with a friend and a doctor: in consideration of
the state of her health would he advise her against a resumption of
conjugal relations, a prohibition that she should understand as

being in his interests as well as her own. Pusinelli for his part gave Minna a letter to deliver to Wagner, in which he reiterated the importance of avoiding all excitements that could affect her health adversely. She opened this letter en route and he now refused to accept it from her. There can be no doubt that she made generous use of its contents in future arguments. (RWAP, pp. 106ff.)

The house in the Rue Newton had been in a dilapidated condition and Wagner had had it redecorated at considerable expense. According to Malwida von Meysenbug it looked charming and comfortable; his workroom and the adjacent music room, in particular, were works of art, though tiny. 'Only when I hope to conjure the muse and keep her at my side do I think . . . of furnishing my house with peace and comfort', he wrote apologetically to Wesendonk. 'If I relinquish the muse, then it all ceases to have any importance for me.'

In spite of being in Paris he lived in considerable isolation. His books were his preferred companions. The society of living people cost him more than he could muster, he felt; for the most part it just wore him out. But a book by a noble spirit was the most precious friend anyone could have; all outside excitements fell silent and the voice of a departed, perfected being could speak to one in peace. (To his sister, Cäcilie Avenarius, 31 July 1860)

Wednesday evenings were an exception, when a brilliant company of poets, artists, musicians, writers, politicians and scholars used to assemble in his drawing room: Gaspérini brought his friends, the music critic Léon Leroy and his brother Adolphe, a professor at the Conservatoire, whom Wagner nicknamed 'Monsieur Clarinette'; the poet Jules Champfleury, who had also tried painting and sculpture, and who later became artistic director of the porcelain manufactory at Sèvres: his essay on Wagner said as much that was true and profound in its fourteen pages as a whole library of Wagneriana, in the opinion of Houston Stewart Chamberlain; Frédéric Villot, curator of the art collections in the Louvre, whom Wagner met in a music shop, where he was enquiring about the newly published score of *Tristan*: Wagner esteemed his shrewd judgement, including his opinion of the character of his own nation; the future husband of Judith Gautier, the writer Catulle Mendès, whose admiration for Wagner's music survived the events of 1870; the illustrator Gustave Doré, who wanted to portray Wagner as the conductor of an orchestra of spirits in an Alpine landscape;

there were the musicians Ernest Royer and Charles Gounod, the politicians Jules Ferry and Emile Ollivier, the critics Jules Janin and Emile Perrin; a Monsieur de Chabrol, who wrote for the papers under the name of Lorbac, and proposed the foundation of a 'Théâtre Wagner'; Challemel-Lacour, who translated four of Wagner's operatic texts (*Holländer, Tannhäuser, Lohengrin* and *Tristan*) into French prose, to Wagner's satisfaction; last but not least, the barrister Charles Truinet, who used the nom de plume of Nuitter: he was the second translator of *Tannhäuser*, and his tactful, reliable friendship was to be of lasting value to Wagner.

The host dominated the company so completely, according to Malwida von Meysenbug, that really she saw and heard only him. On one occasion he was talking to a number of people about the rarity of what is called happiness and quoted the Princess in *Tasso*: 'Who then is happy?' She could see in the others' faces that they did not understand him. 'Why does he throw these pearls away on people who can't appreciate them?' she asked herself.

When Klindworth came over from London the social evenings moved upstairs to the music room, and there was always a performance of something from *Lohengrin, Rheingold, Walküre* or *Tristan*; Wagner took all the various singing parts while Klindworth accompanied him. Malwida comments that this might seem very unlikely to create a good impression, 'and yet it did'. Nobody could communicate his intentions as clearly as he did.

Minna felt at a loss and very forlorn in these surroundings. 'I am just the housekeeper here,' she told a friend in Dresden, 'with nothing to do but give orders to three servants and lose my temper with them, but am also allowed into the drawing room to show off my silk dress.' All her hatred for the moment was directed against Blandine Ollivier, Liszt's daughter. 'Blandine is a very commonplace, not to say common, female.' But Madam had noticed that Minna did not want her company, and so she had given up the regular visits she had been in the habit of paying Wagner. (JKWF, p. 186) 'I hardly ever see Blandine now,' he confirmed in a letter to Bülow; 'her husband is always ill and my wife eyes her with implacable suspicion.' (21 May 1860) But it was left to the fecund imagination of Julius Kapp to construct an 'erotic relationship' out of this material and – 'quite comically', as Richard Sternfeld said in his review of Kapp's book[3] – make it the basis of the conception of the new Venusberg music.

Wagner's growing doubts about the Karlsruhe project were confirmed by a letter he received from Devrient on 23 October 1859, saying that in the given circumstances *Tristan* was impossible, indeed that it would be impossible to perform in any circumstances. 'The dramatic idyll in Karlsruhe is completely over and done with,' he wrote to Mathilde. She would accuse him of exaggeration if he tried to tell her how hostile and unscrupulous Devrient's treatment of him had been. He was only interested in an everyday theatrical institution, without any excursions into the exceptional: 'In this sense he was always instinctively opposed to my works.' (23 and 29 October 1859) That he did Devrient no injustice is confirmed by letters, already mentioned, that Devrient sent his wife during his visit to Asyl: while protesting his sincerity to Wagner's face, behind his back his comments on him personally and his works were hostile.[4]

With the abandonment of the Karlsruhe plan, the importance of Paris for Wagner's hopes was greater than ever. He eventually drew up a scheme for conquering the city with three concerts of excerpts from his works, which he thought would earn him the facilities for producing *Tannhäuser*, *Lohengrin* and, as the crowning glory, *Tristan*. So for the time being he put aside his intention of resuming work on *Siegfried* and plunged into an ocean of trouble and vexation.

To avoid having to pay the prohibitively high cost of hiring a hall, on Gaspérini's advice he approached Napoleon III's private secretary for permission to use the auditorium of the Opéra, as an act of imperial favour. Permission was duly granted but came too late: by then Wagner had already arranged to hire the Théâtre Italien for three nights in January and February 1860 at 4000 francs a night. It might have been taken as an ill omen that this was the theatre previously known as the Théâtre de la Renaissance, where *Das Liebesverbot* had *not* been performed twenty years before!

He had a foretaste of what he could expect from the French press from a joke in *Le Figaro* which called him the 'Marat of music', though he could derive some consolation from the designation of Berlioz as its Robespierre.[5] Wagner was provoked to reply in *L'Europe Artiste*: 'I am a foreigner and an exile, and I hoped to be received hospitably by France . . . I have been called the Marat of music. My compositions have no such revolutionary propensities

. . . The French press should wait just a little while; perhaps it will revise its opinion of me.' (RWGS, XVI, p. 28)

All the seats, more than 1500, were taken in the Théâtre Italien on the evening of 25 January 1860. Only the Tower of Babel or a session of the National Convention could give so much as a faint impression of the feverish excitement reigning in the whole auditorium, *Le Ménestrel* reported. Everyone of position and name was present. The court was represented by Marshal Magnan, the Académie by Auber. Meyerbeer, Berlioz, Gounod, Reyer, the Belgian composer Gevaert were all to be seen in the front few rows. The press also appeared en masse, though they had no official invitation. Wagner bowed, with an impassive face, in acknowledgement of the applause that greeted him, then turned to face the orchestra. 'What goes on in the mind of an artist', Champfleury speculated, 'when he turns his back on the audience in the knowledge that in five minutes' time he will hear the judgement of Parisians, that is, of beings who expect first and foremost to be entertained, and whose immediate representatives, the theatre managers, have from the very first protested against all innovations?'

The programme included excerpts from *Tannhäuser* and *Lohengrin*, the *Holländer* overture with the new ending with the Redemption theme, and the prelude to *Tristan* with the concert ending anticipating Isolde's transfiguration. The fact that Wagner conducted without a score created a sensation in those days. Apart from the *Tristan* prelude, which the orchestra too had disliked at the first rehearsal, every item was applauded enthusiastically. Wagner was later to refer to the storm of applause that broke out after sixteen bars of the first cantabile of the march from *Tannhäuser* as a sign of the devout attention with which the audience had followed the development of the melodic idea. (RWGS, X, pp. 73f.)

'A complete success, an immense impression', Gaspérini wrote in the *Courier du Dimanche*. But his was a lone voice. The rest of the press, of all shades, fired off the wildest invective after each of the three concerts: unable to deny the fact of Wagner's success, they did their best to devalue it. But neither applause nor criticism affected Wagner as deeply as his friends thought. 'Evenings like that remain somewhat outside me', he told Mathilde. Only three things made a more distinct impression on him: an article by Berlioz, a pamphlet by Champfleury and a letter from Charles Baudelaire.

He had dedicated the score of *Tristan* to Berlioz on 21 January 1860: 'Au grand et cher auteur de *Roméo et Juliette* l'auteur reconnaissant de *Tristan et Isolde.*' The copy, now in the Bibliothèque Nationale, bears Berlioz's marginal marks against all the musical liberties he took exception to. His applause under the immediate impact of the first concert had been noticed. Reviewing it in the *Journal des Débats* on 9 February, he expressed a not unfavourable opinion of the separate items, except the *Tristan* prelude, of which he admitted that he understood nothing, but at the end of the article he attributed to Wagner theories about an alleged 'music of the future', from which he solemnly dissociated himself: 'I raise my hand and aver: "Non credo".' Wagner's Swiss–French biographer Guy de Pourtalès is honest enough to call the review an 'article perfide'.

Wagner felt the same about it. All the more credit is due, therefore, to the friendly tone of his reply, published in the *Débats* of 22 February, in which he thanked Berlioz for his complimentary remarks and then corrected the distorted picture he had drawn of the 'music of the future' by reference to his ideal of Aeschylean tragedy.[6] Nor was that all: when he read Berlioz's article about *Fidelio* in May he could not restrain himself from writing to him, in his 'horrible French', to thank him for bearing witness to the fact that 'une chaîne ininterrompue d'intime parenté rallie entre eux les grands esprits'. 'God knows what he will make of my gibberish,' he wrote to Liszt, but was astonished to realize from Berlioz's answer that his words must have made a great impression on him: 'Vous êtes . . . plein d'ardeur, prêt à la lutte,' the Frenchman wrote, 'je ne suis prêt moi qu'à dormir et à mourir.'[7]

Champfleury's pamphlet was dated 'the night of 27 January', two days after the first concert. What moved Wagner was the author's understanding, greater than any he had ever encountered, of his suffering as an artist. The signs of exhaustion on Wagner's features, Champfleury wrote, were the result of fifteen years of worry and disappointment, but there was no trace in his works of the martyrdom of this artist, condemned not to hear or see his own creations. Wagner himself had remarked on the same thing in the letter he sent Princess Marie after finishing *Tristan*. He might express bitterness sometimes – in conversation, in letters, in his writings, in his autobiography – but his art lay under the arch of a heaven unclouded by earthly vapours.

Baudelaire had gone to hear the first concert without knowing that he was inwardly already prepared for Wagner's music: 'La musique souvent me prend comme une mer!' And that was how the music had taken him. He wrote to Wagner on 17 February, above all to thank him for the greatest musical experience he had ever known. He said that he would have hesitated to assure him of his admiration, were it not that every day his eye fell on unworthy, ludicrous articles that made every possible effort to denigrate his genius. What he had experienced in the Théâtre Italien had been indescribable, but if Wagner would be so kind as not to smile at him, he would try to put it into words. His next statement is a subtle psychological observation: it had at once seemed to him that he already knew the music – a sensation that others, too, have described on first hearing Wagner's music: completely new and yet completely familiar.

'Ever since the day when I heard your music, I say to myself repeatedly, above all when things look bleak: If only I were at least going to be able to hear some Wagner this evening! . . . Once again, Sir, I thank you; you have shown me the way back to myself.' (TWLF, pp. 198ff.)

Through diffidence he did not give his address, but Wagner managed to track him down and invited him to call on him. 'If you see him before me,' Baudelaire wrote to Champfleury, 'tell him that it will give me great happiness to shake the hand of a man who is reviled by the empty-headed common herd.' (TWLF, pp. 220ff.)

This is the place to mention yet another unexpected amicable encounter. A malicious joke at the expense of Wagner's music, currently going the rounds, was attributed to Rossini, who publicly repudiated it. Wagner thereupon paid him a call and thus made the acquaintance of an honourable, upright man and a cheerful sceptic. Rossini disavowed any ambition to be numbered with the heroes, but on the other hand he could not remain indifferent if he was held so low as to be included among the shabby spirits who derided serious endeavours. When he died in 1868 Wagner recalled their meeting in *A Souvenir of Rossini*, published in the Augsburg *Allgemeine Zeitung*, thereby atoning for the many attacks he had launched on him in his earlier writings. (*Eine Erinnerung an Rossini*, RWGS, VIII, pp. 220ff.)

Of more immediate importance to Wagner than reviews, criticism, applause or fame was the deficit of 11,000 francs remaining after the concerts, and the failure of a financier whom Gaspérini had introduced to him as a future guarantor of his operatic plans for Paris. That was the end of the plan that should have culminated in the performance of *Tristan*, and he counted himself lucky not to end up in gaol, which he accomplished by means of a tangled web of financial transactions of which Newman gives the best account.[8] His only remaining chance was to set all on getting *Tannhäuser* produced at the Opéra, he told Otto Wesendonk. 'Think of me caught up in my efforts, weigh my character and what it is that alone means anything to me: the shifts I shall be put to, the paths I must tread! – and you will know what frame of mind I am in!' (12 February 1860)

The most successful and momentous piece of business he did at this time was with Franz Schott, the proprietor of the Mainz firm of music publishers B. Schott's Söhne, to whom he had offered his transcription of the Choral Symphony thirty years before. Schott wanted to have an opera by the controversial composer on his list, and approached Wagner with this purpose in mind in November 1859 through the agency of his musical adviser Heinrich Esser, the kapellmeister to the imperial court in Vienna. Wagner replied that he had enough material to enter into immediate negotiations with Schott. Esser reported back to Schott, advising him that a certain degree of toughness towards Wagner would not be inappropriate; but apart from that an opera by him would redound to the credit of any publisher; he hoped very much that a satisfactory result would come of his mediation. 'I shall then claim the usual fee of a successful matchmaker.'

Having no new score to dispose of, Wagner quickly made up his mind and offered Schott *Das Rheingold* for 10,000 francs, cash down. To his astonishment Schott sent the money by return. Wagner had intended to repay the 6000 francs that Wesendonk had paid him for *Rheingold* out of the proceeds of his concerts, but the deficit frustrated that plan. In this desperate situation he hit on the extraordinary solution of asking his friend to regard the sum he owed him as an advance payment for the as yet unwritten last part of the tetralogy. Wesendonk agreed to this but, as Newman remarks dryly, as a businessman he must have smiled at this ingenious plan for 'feeding the dog its own tail'.

As usual in such crises Wagner also tried to help himself by his own efforts. He trustingly accepted an invitation to Brussels, to repeat his three Paris concerts in the Théâtre de la Monnaie, on the basis that he would receive half the net profits. Only after making the undertaking did he realize that he had overlooked a clause in the small print making him solely responsible for the musical expenses. After the second concert he decided to forgo the benefits of a third, since the outcome of the management's calculations was that, while he would not actually have to pay anything towards the concerts himself, he would have had to cover his lodging and travelling expenses out of his losses from the Paris concerts. (To Hans Richter, 19 October 1869)

His only gain from the journey to Brussels was making the acquaintance of the elderly diplomat Georg Heinrich Klindworth, a relative of the pianist, and his daughter Agnes Street, a former pupil and friend of Liszt. The meeting needs to be mentioned, because the two were to make one more brief but momentous appearance in Wagner's life, when he was in Munich. The only other consequence of the acquaintance was that Kapp once again leapt to the wrong conclusion, misinterpreting a remark in the catalogue of the Burrell Collection (the contents of the collection itself were of course not available to him) to mean that 'the lovely Agnes . . . seems to have harnessed Wagner also to her love-chariot', with the astonishing result that, as the editor of the Burrell Collection says, 'one more is added to the *Women in Wagner's Life*'.[9] A brief visit to Antwerp, to pay his respects to 'Madame Lohengrin, née Elsa', was disappointing. Wagner had imagined the citadel as being on a hill, but found instead a bleak, bare plain with defences dug into the ground. Thereafter he never saw a performance of *Lohengrin* without smiling to himself at the designer's imagination.

Help came in the end, unsolicited and unexpected, from a woman who had been present at the first performance of *Tannhäuser* in 1845, had made Wagner's acquaintance fleetingly in Paris in 1853, and now learned of his losses on her return from an extended journey: Marie Kalergis, born Countess Nesselrode, later to be Frau von Muchanoff, German on her father's side, Polish on her mother's, Russian by upbringing, Greek through her first husband, an internationally renowned beauty, pupil of Chopin and Liszt, dedicatee of Théophile Gautier's *Symphonie en blanc majeur*. An admirer of all progressive movements, she was also ready to support them out of her considerable means. She sent for Wagner and explained that her regret at having missed his concerts was the greater for her absence having caused her to miss the chance of being able to help him at the right time. She therefore asked him now to accept 10,000 francs from her to go to meet his losses. She was the first person, Wagner wrote to Mathilde, who amazed him quite spontaneously by a truly generous assessment of his position.

To thank her he mounted an impromptu private festival for her, with the first performance of the second act of *Tristan*. He summoned Karl Klindworth from London to play the piano and sang the part of Tristan himself, with Pauline Viardot-Garcia, in whose rooms the event took place, as Isolde. The audience consisted of Berlioz and Madame Kalergis. Her rescue action had been effected so quietly that only those closest to him knew about it. It thus came about that Glasenapp failed to mention it in the first edition of his biography in 1876, which Wagner represented to him as one of its most serious gaps. (GLRW, III, p. 265)

Liszt, too, was delighted at this intervention by his own old patroness: 'Beauty and nobility such as these are, alas, encountered all too rarely!' For the most part he was noticeably reticent during these months. 'Your friendship is indispensable to me; I cling to it with my last ounce of strength,' Wagner had written to him on his birthday, 20 October 1859. 'When am I at last going to see you again?? Have you any idea of the position I am in? Of the miracles of loyalty and love I need, if I am to recover courage and patience over and over again?' And a month later: 'Believe me, my dear Franz, I find it very difficult to give you my news. Our lives do not coincide enough, and we are bound to grow further apart in an important aspect of friendship.' (23 November 1859) He complained to Bülow that Liszt would always remain sublime, deeply sympathetic, greatly admired and loved in his eyes, but – he would no longer be able to expect very much in the way of nurturing their friendship. 'I simply cannot *find* any words to say to him any more: my warmth has been answered with phrases too often. But phrases – are what I do not care to write to him: he is too dear to me for that.' (7 October)

Light is shed on the change in Liszt's attitude by his correspondence with his daughter Blandine. Writing about Wagner in Paris, Blandine said that there was no more dreadful sight than a genius combating the mundane obstructions of life. 'It's the old story, which never fails to move us, of Gulliver entangled in the thousand and one threads of the Lilliputians.' (29 December)

Of course it was regrettable, Liszt replied. But why could a great spirit not muster a little common sense to deal with the practical matters of life? He had himself advised Wagner more than once to settle in Paris, but he had also tried to make him understand that there would be no likelihood of his operas being performed there. 'In my opinion the best thing he could do would be to preserve a quiet, dignified and proud reserve . . . I shall abstain completely from interfering in his affairs, and confine myself to enduring his resentment against me in silence, as long as he is pleased to maintain it.'[10]

Liszt was right in his view that Wagner's activities in Paris were at odds with his true nature. But he failed to understand that there was no other course open to him but to write his works – and to have them performed; that he no longer had the time to wait in aristocratic reserve – until it was too late for him. Wagner knew that he was misunderstood, even though it was more painful for him on the part of his greatest friend. 'A life . . . like mine is bound to deceive the onlooker: he sees me involved in actions and enterprises which he supposes to be mine, whereas they are fundamentally alien to me; how often does anyone realize the reluctance that fills me when I am about these things? It will all be understood only when the sum and the final total are known.' (To Mathilde Wesendonk, 10 August 1860)

At times like these he took refuge in his inner world, as we can see from his correspondence with Mathilde, which underwent a last, late flowering. It is like a great self–communing: 'Mit mir nur rat' ich, red' ich mit dir'. He tells her what he has been reading: after Plutarch's *Lives of Great Men*, he thanks God not to be one of them; Schiller's *Maid of Orleans* inspires him with the desire to fill her glorious, wonderful silence with music. He writes about his 'art of transition' and its masterpiece, the great scene in the second act of *Tristan*. The Wesendonks went to Rome, which gave him occasion to compare Goethe's experience of Italy with his own: unlike Goethe, the great visual observer, he was not satisfied with the perception of the eye alone: there had to be an ineffable inner sense which was wide awake and active, when the external senses were only dreaming. *Parsifal* was occupying his imagination again: 'Have I already told you that the fabulous savage who is the messenger of the Grail is to be one and the same creature as the seductress in the second act?' And again and again he returned to the subject of Schopenhauer, whose morose appearance belied his truly loving nature. 'Clear understanding eases suffering; creases are smoothed and sleep regains its restorative power. And how good it is that the old man knows nothing at all of what he is to me, of what I am through him.'

While he was outwardly engaged in incessant and various activity, his spirit withdrew into a dream life. 'I dream much and often . . . But what poor assistance dreams give! If one is much aware of one's dreams it only indicates the emptiness of our waking existence. I always think of Keller's Green Heinrich, who in the end did nothing but dream.' (To Mathilde Wesendonk, 10 April 1860)

The necessity of limiting his plans to *Tannhäuser* suited the mood of the French public, which now associated his name exclusively with that work. His hopes of the Opéra, as his last chance, seemed threatened by the opposition of the minister of the household, Achille Fould, a friend of Meyerbeer. Then unexpectedly, in the middle of March 1860, Napoleon III commanded the performance of *Tannhäuser*. While his friends rejoiced, Wagner himself remained sceptical: he had no faith in it, and for good reasons, he told Liszt. He would greatly prefer to see *Tristan* performed in Germany and he was thinking seriously of settling his old score with Dresden, if only he could win some decent concessions. (29 March 1860) The course of events proved him right.

The imperial decree was the outcome of the interplay of personal and political factors, in which Bülow had played an enthusiastic part. Hans's diplomatic skill had procured him all manner of Parisian glories, which hovered teasingly before him now like a *fata morgana*. He had hurried to Paris with a letter of introduction from Princess Augusta of Prussia to the Prussian ambassador, Count Pourtalès. In particular, he had been successful in winning the good offices of the attaché at the embassy, Count Hatzfeld, on Wagner's behalf. Hatzfeld, a favourite of the Empress Eugénie, was approached at a masked ball in the Tuileries by a masked woman, in whom he recognized the empress. When they withdrew, at her suggestion, to one of the quieter rooms, he took the opportunity of recommending *Tannhäuser* to her. She promised to see what she could do and asked him to give her details of the matter in writing. This, according to Hatzfeld, was the beginning of a friendlier attitude at the court.[11]

But the decisive factor was the intervention of Princess Pauline Metternich-Sándor, the wife of the Austrian ambassador, who had got to know Wagner through Councillor Klindworth of Brussels. 'She is an imp of a woman,' he wrote to Bülow, 'a distinct oddity, but certainly useful.' Horace de Viel Castel, the chronicler of the Second Empire, describes her in the most repellent terms: this favourite of the empress drank, smoked and swore, was as ugly as sin and a scandal-monger. But we must make allowances for patriotic prejudice: it was generally believed that she had a political mission to improve relations between France and Austria, which made her detested in certain circles in Paris. One day, when Wagner was the subject of conversation at the court, the emperor asked the princess for her opinion. She spoke of *Tannhäuser* with such enthusiasm that he promised her to have it produced in Paris. Thereafter both good manners and policy obliged him, as a man of honour, to keep his word.

The question of the French translation had been a headache from the start. Finally Wagner remembered the customs official Edmond Roche, but as Roche understood no German he had to have a German-speaking collaborator, Rudolf Lindau. 'Travaillez, travaillez comme le diable,' Wagner exhorted his 'chère compagnie de traduction' as early as the beginning of February. And on 12 March: 'The devil's away! The emperor has ordered *Tannhäuser* to be performed . . . If Meyerbeer isn't paying you to lead me up the garden path, let me know if *Tannhäuser* is going to be put on before the end of the world. . . Au nom de l'empéreur, donnez-moi de vos nouvelles!'[12]

With a certain amount of fictional licence, Victorien Sardou describes how Wagner worked with Roche on Sundays, from first thing in the morning till late at night, striding up and down with flashing eyes and wild gestures, hammering something out on the piano, singing, shrieking 'Allez! Allez!' In the evening, when the lamp cast his perambulating shadow on to the wall like something out of Hoffmann, he was still as fresh as when they had started.

The translation was ready at last, but an unrhymed libretto was unheard of at the Opéra, and the manager, Royer, recommended that Truinet, the barrister, should re-do it in verse. Truinet duly produced a satisfactory version, but the matter did not end there. At an advanced stage of the rehearsals Rudolf Lindau brought an action against Wagner, because he wanted his name on the posters as the translator. Thanks to the advocacy of Emile Ollivier, who even offered to sing 'O du mein holder Abendstern' to the court, Wagner won the case easily.

The news from Paris had repercussions in Germany. In view of the facts that *Tannhäuser* was to be performed by order of the emperor, that both the Prussian and the Austrian embassies had intervened on Wagner's behalf and even the Saxon ambassador, Baron Seebach, had taken his part, and finally that Princess Augusta of Prussia put in a good word for him with King Johann in Baden-Baden in June 1860, the king had no choice but to bow to the inevitable. But instead of doing so with fitting dignity he remained true to his nature: he still did not want to see this undesirable person in his own country, and if other German rulers wanted him, then it must be only after consulting Dresden. The draft written by Minister Beust still exists: the clause requiring Wagner himself to apply for permission each time is changed in the king's own handwriting to the effect that the request must come from the *government* in question: he would have nothing to do with Wagner directly. (LWVR, pp. 139ff.)

On 22 July 1860 Baron Seebach notified Wagner of his partial amnesty. On 12 August Wagner set foot on German soil for the first time in eleven years, without, he confessed, feeling any particularly strong emotion. He was received in Baden-Baden on 17 August by the Regent of Prussia, Princess Augusta. He found her the intelligent, clever and vivacious woman that he had imagined her to be, who gladly accepted his thanks for her liking for his works but was skilfully evasive when he raised the subject of the Berlin Opera.

All in all the return to his homeland that he had so long looked forward to was a disappointment. He shuddered when he thought of Germany and of what he meant to undertake there in the future, he told Liszt, writing from Paris again on 13 September: 'Believe me, we have no fatherland! And if I am "German" then I surely carry my Germany within me.'

His French friends tried to counter his lack of faith in the Paris *Tannhäuser* by emphasizing the unprecedented importance of the impression that they expected it to make: how it was received was a matter of life and death for the cultural salvation of Parisian audiences. 'They say to me: "You see *how* things are, and *what* we expect and demand from you! . . . What you are offering is not remotely like anything that has ever been seen here before, for you offer the whole of poetry with your music: you offer the whole . . . formally perfect and with the greatest expressive power." ' (To Mathilde Wesendonk, 10 April 1860) It resounds like a foretelling of the unique '*wagnériste*' movement which grew up after Wagner's death and completely dominated French cultural and intellectual life for twenty years. 'He was the liberator!' exclaimed Maxime Leroy. André Suarès compared him with Prometheus the fire-bringer. Stéphane Mallarmé called him a god: 'Le dieu Richard Wagner irradiant un sacre.'[13]

To promote deeper understanding of his work, Wagner asked Challemel-Lacour to make French prose translations of the *Holländer*, *Tannhäuser*, *Lohengrin* and *Tristan*, which were published with a preface by himself in the form of a *Lettre sur la musique* addressed to Frédéric Villot. This letter, published in his collected writings with the title *Zukunftsmusik* (RWGS, VII, pp. 87ff.), moves away from his earlier theoretical works in placing the emphasis on the musical element – on his innovatory 'infinite melody', which is intended to make an impression on the hearer like that received by a solitary walker in a beautiful forest on a summer evening: however many parts and separate tunes he hears, the swelling notes will yet seem to be just 'the one great forest melody'.

'Meanwhile I must put myself into the right mood to write – a large-scale ballet,' he told Mathilde. 'What do you think of that? Do you find it hard to believe?' He had been asked to provide a ballet for the second act, since the holders of subscriptions to the Opéra, the aristocratic members of the Jockey Club, always arrived at the theatre rather late. 'I explained to them that I could not take any instructions from the Jockey Club and would rather withdraw my work. But I will help them out of their difficulty after all: the opera does not need to start before eight, and so I will rewrite the accursed Venusberg properly once and for all . . . So far I haven't written anything at all: I will try to jot something down here for the first time. Don't be surprised that this should happen in a letter to Elisabeth.'

The scenario he drafted in this letter gives a good idea of Wagner's eagerness to give rein to his poetic imagination again after a long pause. His primary concern was with the dramatic structure of *Tannhäuser*: the court of Venus was the weak part of the work, failing to fill in properly the important background to the tragedy that was to follow. Rectifying it required skills that he had only recently acquired.

It may well be, too, that now that he had expressed in artistic form something of his experience of the Germanic heritage, the desire revived in him to express his experience of ancient Greece, and in particular his conception of Greek culture as the struggle between the Dionysian and Apollonian principles. The Classical Witches' Sabbath (Walpurgisnacht) from the second part of *Faust*, which he admired as an inspired reconstruction of the Greek world, will have been in his mind as a remote model. Goethe introduced a Nordic element with Faust, Mephistopheles and Homunculus, and in this first draft Wagner did the same with the figure of the water sprite, the Strömkarl, who rises out of the whirlpool amid the rejoicing of the Bacchanalian throng and strikes up a dance on his big magic fiddle. 'You can imagine how I'm going to have to exercise my invention to give this dance the proper character.'

Wagner found the Strömkarl in Grimm's *German Mythology*: he plays a tune with eleven variations, of which men may dance to only ten. The eleventh belongs to the Spirit of Night and his horde; if it were to be played, then everything, animate and inanimate, would start to dance. 'I'm very pleased that I thought of using my Strömkarl and his eleventh variation. It also explains why Venus and her court have come to the north: it was only there that they could find the fiddler fit to play for the old gods.' (To Mathilde Wesendonk, 10 April 1860)

In the more detailed second sketch, too, where 'mythological beasts' driven forward from the background are added to the 'mythological rabble', the Strömkarl appears on a rock in the middle of a waterfall, 'an elderly figure of a gentle, jovial appearance, with a misshapen stringed instrument rather like a violin'. Drawing his bow across the strings, he rouses the young men, nymphs, griffins and sphinxes to a wild dance, in which they are joined by a band of centaurs, until a signal from Venus bestirs the slumbering Cupids, who fly up and let loose a hail of arrows on the dancers. Finally the Dionysian riot gives way to Apollonian visions, the Rape of Europa, Leda and the Swan: 'Leda reclining beside a pool: the swan swims towards her, arches his neck, which Leda caresses and draws to her.' This closely parallels the scene on the Lower Peneios in the Classical Walpurgisnacht:

> Now new marvels! Swans are coming,
> From their hidden waters swimming . . .

But one most of all seems vaunting
His audacity and flaunting
Sails through all with eager pace . . .

The Apollonian visions are retained in the final version of the Bacchanal, on which Wagner based his composition. 'Sensuality is transformed into beauty.' But the inspired stroke of the Strömkarl was omitted, and it is an eternal shame that Wagner had to sacrifice it to the limitations of the Paris opera ballet of the time. The company was in any case completely at a loss with what had been written for them. When Wagner pointed out to Petipa that the dancers' little skipping steps were glaringly inappropriate to the music, and explained that he had wanted something 'bold and savage but sublime' in the style of the Bacchanalia depicted on classical reliefs, the ballet master whistled through his fingers: 'Oh, I understand very well!' But if he had said so much as a word of it to his dancers they would at once have found themselves with a cancan and all would be lost.

Yet another trial had been imposed on him to mock his position, Wagner wrote to Otto Wesendonk on 5 June 1860. He had heard from St Petersburg that the director of the Imperial Russian theatre was coming to Paris with the intention of engaging him on advantageous terms. The director duly arrived at the end of May, in the imposing person of a General Saburoff, prepared to conclude a formal contract, but issuing the following ultimatum: either Wagner would go to St Petersburg that summer, spend the winter there, produce *Tannhäuser* and conduct large orchestral concerts, all for a guaranteed sum of 50,000 francs, half to be paid immediately – or nothing at all. The general had been adamant in refusing any of the compromises Wagner suggested to fit in with his Parisian commitment. He couldn't simply sell himself just for the money like that, Wagner confessed to Wesendonk. 'I kept faith with Paris, loaded the apparently unending misery of my Parisian existence. . . on to my shoulders and trudged back to Newton Street.'

Another Parisian catastrophe was already impending. When Wagner had taken the house in the Rue Newton, he had had to pay the whole three years' rent, at 4000 francs a year, in advance. The landlord already knew that the street was due to be relaid at a lower level according to Prefect Haussmann's plans, and that the house would be pulled down. The first the unsuspecting composer knew of it was when the Rue Newton was 'lowered four metres under his very feet'. Litigation to recover the amount paid in rent for the remaining two years of his lease was unsuccessful, and he had to pay the costs of the action as well. When Malwida von Meysenbug visited him in his new lodgings in the dark, noisy Rue d'Aumale, she found him on the second floor of a large tenement house, full of other residents. 'It cut me to the heart to see it. I felt how dreadful it must be for Wagner to live in so uncongenial a house.'

She had heard the sound of music from outside. Wagner was in the act of coaching a young soprano (not a boy) in the shepherd boy's song. 'What a good thing you've come!' he exclaimed. 'You will never hear a better perfomance than this: it is going to be excellent.' This prospect was the only consolation he had. For the first time he had at his command all he needed: everything was going smoothly that would contribute to the success of the production. Whenever, from sheer force of habit, Minister Fould opposed the engagement of anyone Wagner needed to have, he had only to say a word to Princess Metternich and an order from the emperor settled the matter. (To Otto Wesendonk, 5 June)

While Wagner was content to accept the French or Italian singers suggested by Royer for most of the parts, for the title role he insisted on engaging the young tenor Albert Niemann from Hanover. He was admittedly somewhat taken aback when Niemann appeared on his doorstep and asked, without further ceremony, 'Well, do you want me or not?' After an audition, where his giant stature made as great an impression as his powerful voice, he was engaged for nine months from 1 September 1860 at 6000 francs a month, with no other commitments but to rehearse and perform the role of Tannhäuser. The conclusion of this extraordinary contract, Wagner admitted in *Mein Leben*, filled him with a sense of power such as he had never known before. And it was Niemann, of all his singers, who most disappointed him, not only professionally but personally.

In the early stages the rehearsals were encouraging: the artists began to understand him, he wrote, raised no objections to anything and looked forward eagerly to what was to come. In the meantime he was still working on the revision of the text and music of the great scene between Tannhäuser and Venus. He was satisfied with everything to do with Tannhäuser's longing for life and the freshness of nature, everything that breathed the air of the legend.

But he was amazed at his total failure, in the earlier version, to
encompass everything to do with passion, specifically, the feminine
ecstasy of Venus. 'Truly I am appalled at my greasepaint Venus of
those days!' What he had to do was write a free verse sketch, get it
translated and then set the French rhymed version. The German
singing text that we now have is a somewhat contrived translation
back from the French, which differs quite a lot from the text
published in Wagner's complete writings. For instance, the original
German lines:

> Da liegt er vor der Schwelle,
> wo einst ihm Freude floß:
> um Mitleid, nicht um Liebe,
> flcht bettelnd der Genoß!

appear in the score as:

> Auf der Schwelle, sieh' da!
> ausgestreckt liegt er nun,
> dort wo Freude einst ihm geflossen!
> Um Mitleid fleht er bettelnd,
> nicht um Liebe.

One Saturday towards the end of October Wagner sent his
excuses to the chorus master: he was so exhausted, or rather over-
wrought, that he urgently needed a few days of complete rest. His
condition worsened rapidly and Gaspérini diagnosed a typhoid
fever with the possibility of its developing into cerebral meningitis.
The patient became delirious and later had no recollection whatever
of the first week of his illness. But his tough constitution brought
him through the crisis, and by 20 November he was again able to
drag himself the short distance to the Opéra.

They had probably not been expecting him: the rehearsals had
fallen off and then ceased altogether. His opponents had used
his absence to shake the confidence of the artists. Niemann, in
particular, had been susceptible to the insinuations of critics, who
had prophesied the certain failure of the opera. He proved himself a
wretch, both as man and as artist, Bülow wrote, although he had
nothing but profit from the whole venture. (To Alexander Ritter,
10 April 1860)

In this very different atmosphere Wagner had to resume the

rehearsals and at the same time finish the Bacchanal and the scene with Venus. 'Do not entertain the least doubt . . . that I am making superhuman exertions at present', he told Wesendonk in a letter at the end of January 1861. 'Not until yesterday at half past two in the morning – after being up all night – did I finish my new music for *Tannhäuser*.' He had at least the compensation that the new material had turned out to be very significant and at last gave him some interest in the performance.

'One can become omnipotent, just by playing with the world,' he told Mathilde, and that characterizes the essentially new quality of this music. After surmounting the peak of art as experience, as represented by *Tristan*, a new element entered his work: art as play. This is the importance of the new Venusberg music in his artistic evolution. It was born not only from his improved technical mastery but also from the change in his attitude to the world: his desire now to rise above it and look down at it as a 'plaything'.

The 'abundance' of the music gave him lasting pleasure. It was far from easy to write so extensive an Allegro, he remarked in 1881, and he would not attempt it today. (GLRW, VI, p. 446) At the time he wrote it he had had no experience to inspire something like that. 'It is all a *cry*; it's the same in *Tristan* as in the Venusberg, in the latter it dissolves in grace, in the former in death – it is a cry, a lament, throughout. And those accents come from ever so slightly different a source than Berlioz's Sabbath.' (14 July 1880; BBL 1937, p. 159)

The stylistic difference from the Dresden version is obvious. It is revealed in the mere alteration of the Sirens' call from a 4/4 time to the passionate 3/4. The *Tristan* chord is also to be heard in the Paris version, in a different register, fortissimo, as the orgy reaches its climax: Eros here shows his other face – in *Tristan* the spirit of death with lowered torch, here Dionysus surrounded by Bacchantes. But in spite of that kind of harmonic reminiscence the Venusberg music is quite distinct from *Tristan*: nothing like Venus's lament, for instance, 'Wie hätt' ich das erworben, wie träf' mich solch Verschulden', with the painfully sweet, chromatically descending sixths at 'lächelnd unter Tränen', is to be found anywhere else in Wagner, not even in *Tristan* or the second act of *Parsifal*.

Nonetheless, the Dresden version is still often preferred because of the stylistic inconsistency of the Paris version. Even Wagner himself appears to have entertained similar doubts later in life. But when, in Richard Strauss's phrase, 'the opera *Tannhäuser* rose again as drama', in Cosima's Bayreuth production of the Paris version in 1891, it found another champion besides Strauss in Engelbert Humperdinck. He took the line that the important thing was to examine the stylistic discrepancy from the higher viewpoint of dramatic effectiveness as a whole. The simpler musical language in which the full spiritual depth of the Christian medieval world was so convincingly recreated seemed an authentic and appropriate means of expression to oppose to the heightened aural excitements of the pagan Venusberg music.[14]

It was a struggle for Wagner to keep his interest alive in coaching the singers in their parts day in and day out, but at rehearsals in the theatre 'the immediacy of art' exercised its old power over him again. But the two worst disappointments were yet to come. Niemann, who for some time had been given to voicing gloomy prognostications, finally announced that he could not sing the lines 'Zum Heil den Sündigen zu führen, die Gottgesandte nahte mir' in the second-act finale, a passage which is crucial to the character of Tannhäuser. With the first night imminent, Wagner sat down on 21 February 1861 and wrote him a letter about the part, running to eleven pages in print, which has been a bible to every interpreter of the role ever since. 'This is the last request that I shall address to you as author.'

There is a postscript: '11.30. I had got thus far when your letter reached me.' Niemann's brief letter, which is in the Burrell Collection, is an ultimatum: if Wagner did not cut the phrase 'venant en aide au misérable' he would have to look for another Tannhäuser. Wagner goes on: 'I see where you have now got to: you employ towards me a manner of speech which I find myself able to understand only by casting my mind back to the very first period of my painful career.'[15] But with Niemann's gun to his head he had no alternative but to sacrifice the dramatic climax of the second act and the turning point of the whole action.

The other and yet more painful blow came with his renewing his acquaintance with Pierre-Louis Dietsch, the former chorus master and composer of the ill-fated *Vaisseau Fantôme*. He was now the principal conductor at the Opéra and, according to the regulations of the Académie Impériale de Musique, had to conduct the performances of *Tannhäuser*. His inadequacy was obvious to Wagner at the rehearsals. A letter to Royer on 25 February, imploring him to allow Wagner himself to conduct at least the final dress rehearsal and the first three performances, was of no avail. He tried to help matters by sitting at the edge of the stage at rehearsals and conducting with both hands and feet, giving the beat to both singers on one side of him and the conductor on the other. But at the final dress rehearsal it was out of his hands. 'There is nothing more to be done now,' Bülow wrote to Alexander Ritter, 'Wagner is not conducting. Usus tyrannus. One of the shabbiest brutes . . . a dotard with no intelligence, no memory, totally incapable of benefiting from any instruction . . . with no ear – will wield the baton.'

As the prospect of a good rendering disappeared, so Wagner's interest died, so that the three performances had on him the effect 'only of purely physical blows'. There is no need to repeat here the tale of how the outcome of 164 rehearsals was engulfed in one of the biggest scandals in theatrical history. But what cannot be said too often is that it was not the audience as a whole, exercising their critical faculties, who howled *Tannhäuser* from the stage, but a small clique, who had vowed to wreck it in advance. In his report on the production, Wagner wrote that he continued to credit the Parisian public with the very agreeable attributes of a most lively receptivity and a truly magnanimous sense of justice – a verdict that does honour to his own sense of justice. (*Bericht über die Aufführung von Tannhäuser in Paris*, RWGS, VII, p. 144)

It is still astonishing to contemplate the mindless means whereby an entire theatre audience was terrorized for three evenings in a row. At the first performance the clique had agreed to bellow with laughter each time certain words were pronounced, but this failed in its effect as the laughter was drowned by clapping. For the second performance they purchased hunting whistles at a gunsmith's on the way to the theatre, which enabled them to create a far more effective din. The third performance was on a Sunday and outside the subscription series, which, it was hoped, would keep the Jockey Club away. But they were not to be so easily deterred and came in even greater numbers. Malwida recounts that they distributed silver whistles engraved 'pour Tannhaeuser', which they put to their lips each time their leader signalled with his white kid glove, and thereby interrupted the performance for up to a quarter of an hour at a time.

He had blushed for this barbarity enacted before his own eyes, Baudelaire wrote in 'Richard Wagner et le *Tannhaeuser* à Paris'. 'What will Europe think of us, and what will they say of Paris in

Germany? This handful of hooligans brings disgrace upon us all.'

Wagner thanked Baudelaire with the cordiality that this rare instance of tact and courage deserved. 'I can see that the young people, when they do not belong to the Jockey Club, possess a good helping of decent common sense. They understand me. And you, who have devoted so many handsome words to my work, you stand in the front rank of these sincere and likable young people. Et c'est pourquoi je crois que les vieux ont sifflé.'[16]

Jules Janin, the 'king of the Parisian feuilletonists', was another champion, writing one of his most elegant articles in the *Journal des Débats* on 'Princess Metternich's fan', which she broke on the ledge of her box in anger, and advising the gentlemen of the Jockey Club to get themselves a new coat of arms, 'un sifflet sur champ de gueules hurlantes, et pour exergue "Asinus ad Lyram" '.

The unanimity with which the Meyerbeerites in the press fell upon *Tannhäuser* used to be cited as evidence that he was behind the plot. Kapp even asserted that he was present in person.[17] But in fact he was in Berlin and wrote in his diary on 15 March 1861:

> News came today of the first performance of *Tannhäuser* in Paris, which is said to have been a complete fiasco. The audience is reported to have laughed, and at times whistled, many passages (music as well as text) out of court. Princess Metternich and Countess Seebach, whose patronage is held responsible for the production, met with such derision from the audience that they left the theatre after the second act. So extraordinarily unfavourable a reception of a by any standards very remarkable and talented work strikes me as the doing of a cabal and not of genuine public opinion, and in my view will actually benefit the work in subsequent performances.[18]

The rumour, widespread at the time, that Princess Metternich had fled the theatre, was not true: she did not desert in adversity the enterprise to which she had subscribed. When a Marshal of France accosted her with a *bon mot* as she did leave the theatre, 'Madame, you have exacted a cruel revenge today for the defeat at Solferino,' she replied: 'You have laughed Wagner to scorn this time; but in twenty-five years' time Paris will cheer him.'

After the third performance, which Wagner did not attend, Malwida and some other friends called to report events at two o'clock in the morning. They found him alone with Minna, in a cheerful mood. He drank his tea, smoked his pipe and teased Malwida's foster-daughter, Olga von Herzen (the daughter of Alexander): he heard, he said, that she had whistled him off. But when Malwida took her leave she noticed how his hand shook.

A note has survived, asking a friend to take part the following day in a conference 'pur discuter froidement des mesures nécessaires à prendre de ma part'. The outcome was a letter to the minister, Count Walewski, asking leave to withdraw his score as the only means of protecting his work and the artists who had placed their talents at his disposal from demonstrations that had overstepped the limits of criticism and had degenerated into a scandal from which the administration had shown itself incapable of shielding the public. (TWLF, pp. 245f.)

It was generous of the minister to agree to the withdrawal: the production had cost 250,000 francs to mount. The three performances had already brought in a tenth of that; the third alone had raised 10,790 francs, the highest sum since the first Universal Exhibition. The theatre could have reckoned on the opera continuing to be a draw and a box-office success. The only person to profit was Niemann with his 54,000 francs. No payment was due to Wagner for the rehearsals; a fee of 500 francs was due to him for each performance, but it had been settled that the translators should have half the fee for the first twenty performances. Wagner and Truinet agreed to hand over the entire sum from the *droits d'auteur* to poor Roche, all of whose hopes had been dashed by the fiasco. He did not long survive the disaster: he died of consumption before the year was out.[19]

In his friends' eyes Wagner's defeat meant nothing. Quite the contrary! 'Que dieu me donne une pareille chute!' exclaimed Gounod. The performances had acquired a complete 'nimbus', Wagner wrote to Bülow on 4 April. 'Sects are already forming that positively worship me: even among the ordinary people.' The only thing he regretted was what his friends had had to go through. And yet he himself had made a real gain from the whole affair, in that he had found these friends: however poor and inadequate the performance had been, it had nevertheless brought him into close contact with the most estimable and attractive element of the French spirit.

The circle of Wagner's Parisian friends was only a small one, as Houston Stewart Chamberlain remarked, but it included the best names of the day and it gave Wagner what he had not yet received in Germany, except from Liszt and Bülow: respect.

24

Odyssey

'Your Richard Wagner, ὅς μάλα πολλὰ πλάγχθη' ('who roamed the wide world'): the quotation of the opening words of the *Odyssey* with which Wagner signed a letter from Paris to Hans von Bülow (7 January 1862) could serve as motto for the years 1861 to 1864. The letter was about his new work and his need to find somewhere to settle while he got on with it. The tragedy of his wanderings and his conception of the comedy of *Die Meistersinger* make up the tale of this, the most confused and tangled period of his life, in which he was forever on the move, between Paris and St Petersburg, Mainz and Vienna, Zürich and Stuttgart, in which old associations were dissolved and new ones formed, punctuated by incomparable artistic triumphs and an ignominious secret flight, and ending with a reversal of fortune from the darkness of complete despair to a miraculous salvation.

The worst aspect of the *Tannhäuser* débâcle for Wagner was that he not only had earned nothing for his eighteen months' work, but also had accumulated more debts. His friends did their best to help him, but many obligations remained unmet: in a letter of 29 March 1869 he told Ernst Benedikt Kietz that if *Rienzi* were now to catch on in Paris the profits from it, for a *long* time to come, would go to the banker Erlanger, whose loans had kept his head above water at the beginning of the decade. In the end, in 1895, twelve years after Wagner's death, it fell to Adolf von Gross, Cosima's business adviser, to clear things up in person in Paris, in a manner, as Cosima recorded, that was not without its funny side and scored a considerable success for Wahnfried. (DMCW, II, p. 390)

At first it had looked as though something might now come from Germany to make up for the buffeting the composer had suffered in

Paris. On a visit to Karlsruhe in April 1861 he found that the Grand
Duke of Baden was again interested in securing the first performance of *Tristan* for his theatre. It was only a question of engaging
the best soloists. With this end in view Wagner set off for Vienna,
where he received an ovation from the singers and orchestra when
he attended a rehearsal of *Lohengrin* under Heinrich Esser.

It was the first time that he had ever heard the work. The soloists
wore their everyday clothes – Lohengrin in frock coat and top hat,
Telramund with a walking stick, Elsa in an ordinary day-dress – but
the chorus was in costume, the sets were in position and every
aspect of the stage action was punctiliously observed. Wagner sat
on the stage and did not stir throughout. He told Minna that the
rehearsal had surpassed all his expectations, giving him a complete
enjoyment that for the first time made all the pain and trouble he
had endured in his career worthwhile. 'I went on sitting there
without moving. The dear people came up and silently embraced
me.' (13 May)

The critic Eduard Hanslick secured an introduction during one of
the intervals. They had first met in 1845, in Marienbad, when
Hanslick was a law student with hair curling to his shoulders and a
passion for music. He had accosted Wagner as an enthusiastic
admirer and the following year published a long essay on *Tannhäuser*, spread through eleven issues of the *Allgemeine Wiener
Musik-Zeitung* and culminating in the sentence: 'I am convinced that
Richard Wagner is the greatest dramatic talent among living composers.' (MWKS, I, p. 230) After 1850 he went back on that opinion
– he later described it as showing 'all the immaturity of a cocky
young member of the League of David' –and with his essay *On the
Beautiful in Music* (1854) and his reviews in the *Neue Freie Presse* he
became the spokesman of the anti-Wagner faction. It may perhaps
have been embarrassment that made him hesitate to approach
Wagner on this occasion without the friendly mediation of the
Lohengrin, Alois Ander. Wagner greeted him laconically, as if he
had never met him before, and when Ander insisted that they must
know each other already, he simply replied that he remembered
Herr Hanslick very well – and turned his attention back to the stage.
He commented later that his friends in Vienna, as in London,
seemed to have wasted their time in trying to persuade him to
honour the dreaded critics with his regard.

After the emotions he experienced at the rehearsal Wagner was not unduly concerned that the actual performance was delayed. Its reception by the Viennese audience was more enthusiastic than anything he had seen in his life: 'A shout of joy, sounding like a thousand trombones.' (To Minna, 16 May) It weighed on him almost like a burden, he said in a speech afterwards. 'Allow me to carry this burden in humility, allow me to strive towards the goals of my art.' Only Hanslick saw himself obliged to perform the ungrateful task of 'pouring cold water on such a bacchanal'. He hoped that the city of Gluck, Mozart and Beethoven would not purchase a good reputation for Wagner's music at the cost of its own.

Wagner believed he had found the singers he was looking for in Ander and the Elsa, Luise Meyer-Dustmann. 'With these two – we must do *Tristan und Isolde*!' But when he asked the intendant, Count Lanckoronski, to give them leave to sing in Karlsruhe, his request was firmly refused, and instead he was offered the Vienna Hofoper itself for the première. The proposal suddenly threw a very different light on Wagner's plan for Karlsruhe, where he would have had to get everything together himself from scratch, to produce the work properly. 'I think I shall have to seize the opportunity here, where *everything, everything* I need is already to hand.' (To Minna, 13 May)[1]

As he was walking down the steps of the Hofburg, preoccupied with this new turn in his affairs, he was accosted by an imposing, congenial-looking man who offered to drive him to his hotel in his carriage. It was Josef Standhartner, chief medical officer at the General Hospital and physician to Empress Elisabeth, a passionate music–lover who had taken the composer Peter Cornelius under his wing. Together with Karl Tausig and his one-time 'discoverer' Heinrich Laube, who was now the director of the Burgtheater, Wagner won new devoted friends in Standhartner, his stepson Gustav Schönaich, Peter Cornelius, and Heinrich Porges, a young musician from Prague.

He set off back to Paris on 20 May, to wind up his household there, in a mood compounded of resignation and hope. Picking up *Wilhelm Meisters Wanderjahre* in a hotel room en route, he was particularly struck by the aptness to his own situation of the 'almost barbaric song' with which the band of journeymen set off on their travels: 'Can I say, can I know, what chances lie in wait for me as I now depart, as I now roam . . . betake myself far away from here?'

The events and the people he saw during his last weeks in Paris flit across the pages of his autobiography like a shadow-play, in which he himself plays the role of ironic spectator. The only thing to make a deeper impression on him was the loss of his dog: the pets had come to mean a great deal in his and Minna's childless household; their life together had long been an impossible burden and the sudden death of so cheery and lovable a companion seemed to denote the final rift.

After Minna's departure to take a cure in Bad Soden, Wagner moved temporarily into the Prussian embassy in Paris, and here he was overcome by a 'profound sense of well-being in the enjoyment of a complete lack of any possessions and freedom from everything that is usually understood by a stable way of life'. His window overlooked the garden; there was a pool where two black swans swam, and he felt a kind of dreamlike attraction towards them. It was there that he wrote his first music since the revisions for *Tannhäuser*, two small pieces for piano. The first, *Albumblatt* in A♭ major, 'Coming to the Black Swans', dedicated to his hostess Countess Pourtalès, is a reminiscence of Elisabeth's 'Sei mir gegrüßt' from *Tannhäuser*, but drenched in the atmosphere of the prelude to the third act of *Tristan*. The other, *Albumblatt* in C major, dedicated to Princess Metternich and well known in the transcription for violin by Wilhelmj, employs a charming motive that had been in his mind for some time and that seems to anticipate the melodic writing of *Die Meistersinger*.[2]

He spent one of his last evenings in Paris with his friends Gaspérini, Champfleury and Truinet in a café in the Rue Lafitte, and as he walked home in the company of Champfleury very late at night he was delighted by the extraordinary atmosphere of the deserted streets.

On his way to Vienna, to please Liszt, he put in an unexpected appearance at the musicians' congress in Weimar, where he was given an uproarious welcome. There was no question of relaxing and enjoying himself, he told Mathilde Wesendonk; he had had to recount the story of his life to yet another person every half-hour, so that in desperation he had surrendered to his old wild humour. 'I could not permit myself to turn serious, because it is now impossible for me to be so at all without going almost completely to pieces. This is a basic weakness of my temperament, which is increasingly gaining an upper hand nowadays: I fight it as best I can, because I feel as though I should weep uncontrollably if I once gave way to it.' (19 August)

His hectic high spirits continued as he resumed his journey, now in the company of the Olliviers. They had to spend a night in Nuremberg and enjoyed a morning's sightseeing: 'There are a lot of delightful things to be seen here,' he told Mathilde.

On 14 August, as he had informed the theatre management, Wagner arrived in Vienna to begin coaching the musicians in *Tristan*. To begin with he stayed at the Standhartners' house. The family was away on holiday, and he was looked after by the doctor's niece Seraphine Mauro, whom he nicknamed 'the doll' on account of her trim figure and hair curled 'à l'enfant'.

The people at the opera house were astonished that he had been so literal in observing the agreed starting date; they also told him that Ander was indisposed and had to rest his voice for several weeks. Wagner had already realized that the part of Tristan would not lie so well for him as that of Lohengrin, and had commissioned Cornelius to transpose certain individual low notes up by a third, a fifth or an octave. The weeks of Ander's vocal indisposition became months, and as neither Tichatschek nor Niemann was available Wagner was forced to make more and more concessions, including a cut in the third act of as much as 142 bars. Cornelius soon came to the conclusion that Tristan was too low for Ander's voice and too high for his intelligence.

Wagner had no idea that he would not get from Esser the support that the whole undertaking demanded. Esser belonged to the school of conscientious conductors who will not rest until every semi-quaver is correct. But as Cornelius recognized even then, 'The passion which alone brings a work like this to life, which makes its to-be-or-not-to-be a matter of his own life and death – that he lacks.' Nowadays we know more than Cornelius did: while Esser impressed Wagner in their walks together as an 'honest' and an 'upright and serious' man, what he said about Wagner in his letters to Schott was far from complimentary.

The tenor's illness was a misfortune that would be of no further consequence, Wagner wrote to Schott on 30 October, if it were not being used by his opponents as yet another piece of evidence that the opera was unperformable. But the real purpose of this letter was to tell the publisher about a new project that would afford the composer a more agreeable and entertaining occupation, the realization of one of his earlier ideas for a popular comic opera. 'The title is *Die Meistersinger von Nürnberg*, and the principal hero is the jovial poet Hans Sachs.' The subject was extraordinarily rich in pleasant humour, and he believed he could boast of having achieved something completely original in the plot, which was entirely his own invention. He proposed to send the text to Schott as soon as he had finished it. 'I sincerely wish, my dear Sir, that just as I lighten my own heart – in a sad hour – with this sudden inspiration, so the news of it will delight you too.'

The Standhartners had returned to Vienna, and Wagner had moved into a cheerless room in the Kaiserin Elisabeth hotel, where he had time to reflect on his position. 'So this is the outcome, for the time being, of my Viennese expedition which promised so much,' he wrote to Bülow. 'Remarkably, I have nothing to do. I am not expected anywhere, I have not been invited to go anywhere, I am not needed anywhere; I feel as though I'm in a state of the most absolute freedom, you could say the freedom of an outlaw – or a bird: "wie der Fink frei sich davon schwingt".'

It was in this bitter mood that he received a letter at the beginning of November from Otto Wesendonk, inviting him to meet them in Venice. 'God knows what I was thinking of, when I really set off at a venture in that grey November . . . for Venice,' he wrote in his autobiography. But a letter he wrote to Mathilde in the December betrays that one of his motives had been the hope of regaining his 'haven' in Zürich. An hour in her company in Venice had been enough to destroy that illusion, he wrote. He had quickly realized that his proximity robbed her of the freedom she needed. 'I cannot endure it if being near to you means seeing you confined and constricted, overwhelmed, subjected . . . That and that alone was what lay on my soul like lead, in Venice. Not my situation, my other misfortunes; that is, and has always been ever since I knew you, essentially indifferent to me.'

They also discussed his *Meistersinger* plan. Mathilde had kept the scenario he had written in Marienbad in 1845. He seemed so despondent in Venice that, as she later confessed to him, she had hardly dared to hope that he would take it up again. But one day, when he was in the Accademia di Belle Arti, standing in front of Titian's *Assumption of the Virgin* (which had not at that date been restored to its place in the Frari church), he was suddenly overcome by the most sublime sensation which brought all his old strength flooding back to revive him. During the long grey train journey back to Vienna, which lasted a night, a day and yet another night, 'pinned helplessly between Once and Now', the idea of the principal C major section of the prelude presented itself to him with the utmost clarity.

In Vienna Cornelius, who was 'out of his mind' with joy at the prospect, was despatched to borrow Wagenseil's *Nürnberger Chronik* from the Imperial Library. It is barely credible that Wagner then set to and wrote a first prose scenario, which differs considerably from the Marienbad sketch, in only five days and started a second on 18 November. The inner action was now developed for the first time, and its lyrical, contemplative climax, the third-act quintet, is already indicated, though at this stage Wagner anticipated a trio: 'All three sing together gracefully of their gratitude and tenderly of their hope.'

He sent a copy of the scenario to Schott with a letter that Ludwig Strecker, a more recent head of Schott's, has described as a 'magnificent document from Wagner's creative world'. In it he said that he had long been saving this blithe work for when he was older, because he had not expected to summon up the right frame of mind for it among the stresses of his life. But it was precisely the troubles his career was undergoing now that had suddenly recalled this pet project to his mind, because carrying it out was the only thing that would help him over his present difficulties. 'The subject permits me to write lucid, transparent and yet pithy music of the cheerfulest colouring; and yet merely in reading this sketch you will have found that my characteristic note will be struck just as fully and richly here, most persuasively in the blend of fervour and good humour. In sum, precisely at the present time I calculate that I have hit the essential nerve of German life, and in the guise that other countries, too, recognize and love as authentic.'

With his usual optimism he forecast that the opera would be ready for despatch to all the German theatres on 1 October 1862 and ought to have its première in Munich in mid-November. However, that would all depend on Schott's placing complete confidence in him and relieving him of all material worries for the next twelve months. (20 November 1861)

At last he found a haven where he could work. Princess Metternich was in Vienna just then, and he arranged an orchestral rehearsal of *Tristan* in her honour. She offered him the use of a pleasant apartment with access to a quiet garden in the Austrian embassy in Paris. Before he left Vienna a curious interlude took place. Luise Dustmann, foreseeing that he would have no success in the Austrian capital as long as Hanslick was his enemy, invited both of them to a party, at which Hanslick took Wagner aside and confessed with tears in his eyes that it was not malice that lay at the root of his criticism but the 'limitations of personality'. Wagner was so touched that he had no alternative but to comfort Hanslick and assure him of his understanding. Shortly afterwards Hanslick was said to be singing the praises of Wagner's kindness so loudly that the opera management decided the time was ripe to honour their obligation and announce the performance of *Tristan*.

On his way to Paris Wagner made a short stop in Mainz, where he read the *Meistersinger* sketch to Franz Schott and his wife Betty, a woman with a fine appreciation of the arts, and managed to obtain an advance of 10,000 francs after 'uncommonly difficult' bargaining. But in Paris a new disappointment awaited him that affected all his plans: Princess Metternich informed him with the greatest regret that she was unable to keep her promise as the unexpected death of her mother meant she had to take her half-crazy father into her house.

Wagner made do with a modest room in the Hôtel Voltaire on the eponymous Quai, where he settled down to write his text. Gradually his desperation gave way to a cheerful serenity, and he was later to describe these weeks to Malwida as the happiest of his life. He could hardly have failed to be struck with the humour of it, being met, each time he raised his eyes from the paper in order to reflect on the quaint verses and dicta of his Nurembergers, with the view from his third-floor window of the dense traffic on the *quais* and bridges, and the panorama of the Rive Droite from the Tuileries and the Louvre as far as the Hôtel de Ville.

The whim of fate that had tossed him there strengthened his inclination not to take the world seriously any more. Sometimes, he confessed to Mathilde, he had been unable to go on working, either from laughter or from tears. 'Steel your heart against Sachs: you will fall in love with him!' He used little or nothing from the old sketch. 'Ah, you have to have been in Paradise to find out what lies hidden in something like this!'

He lived very quietly, and his only evening entertainment was to visit one of the small theatres where he enjoyed in their original form the farces of which inferior copies were fed, year in, year out, to German audiences. Almost the only person he saw regularly was Truinet, whom he met at midday in the cheap Taverne Anglaise. On his way there one day, passing through the galleries of the Palais Royal, the melody of the 'Wach auf!' chorus suddenly burst upon him. Finding Truinet already at the restaurant, he asked him for pencil and paper so that he could write it down at once, while he softly sang it to him. 'Mais quelle gaieté d'esprit, cher maître!' Truinet exclaimed. Interestingly, none of the three prose scenarios has the least hint of the chorus, which is now the climax of the third act. Such elements in Wagner's work are always spontaneous inspirations, never the outcome of long forethought.[3]

Having finished the text in exactly thirty days, on 25 January 1862, he had to find somewhere quiet, another 'haven', to write the music. 'All the music is already in my head,' he had told Schott on 17 January, 'and God grant only that I fetch up as soon as possible within four suitable walls where . . . I can set my dear Erard sounding again!'

Since the response of the friends and relations of whom he made tentative enquiries was a uniform, undisguised alarm, he even thought of setting up house with Peter Cornelius: '*Friend, you must move in with me, once and for all!*' Since this would be quite impracticable without a woman to keep house for them, he thought of Seraphine Mauro: 'God, how I would like to have the poor doll there! In something like this I am of an indestructibly naïve morality. I could find nothing whatever wrong with it, if the girl came to me and was to me exactly what her nice little nature enables her to be. – But what should we say to society? Oh, heavens! – It makes me smile, but I am still sorry for it!'

But besides his fears for his own artistic identity, Peter was helplessly in love with Seraphine, in whom he saw, not a 'nice little nature' but 'a grim sphinx with the most beautiful bosom in the world and indescribably lovely eyes, but always with that ultimate riddle, threatening to cast me into the abyss if I cannot guess it'.

Finally Wagner decided to take somewhere near Mainz temporarily. 'What pleasure and encouragement it will give me', he told Schott, 'when I start bringing you something every week in the near future, and to a certain extent we complete the work together!' He arrived in Mainz on 4 February and read the text of *Die Meistersinger* aloud to quite a large gathering the following day. The room in the publishing house where this took place, later known as the Wagner-Saal, survived the destruction of old Mainz in the Second World War and is now preserved as a monument.

The young conductor and composer Wendelin Weissheimer was among those present, and his memoirs of Wagner, *Erlebnisse mit Richard Wagner*, contain some graphic scenes, in spite of their self-congratulatory tone. Of the *Meistersinger* reading he recounts that after the audience had all taken their seats Wagner continued to pace up and down restlessly, looking alternatively at the door and at his watch: 'We must wait a little longer, Cornelius is not here yet!' Just then there was a knock and Cornelius came in. Wagner had sent him the fare, and in the middle of winter, defying frost and flood, he had hastened from Vienna to Mainz. 'That's what I call loyalty!' Wagner exclaimed and flung his arms round him. The reading was a virtuoso performance. Wagner's ability to modulate his voice was so great that he soon no longer needed to name the characters. Even when all the mastersingers are talking at once each stood out individually and the audience really had the impression of listening to an ensemble. By the finish they all realized that they had been present at the baptism of an epoch-making work. Wagner's happiness was spoiled only because Cornelius insisted on leaving again the next day. He refused to be dissuaded, in order to preserve the extraordinary character of his expedition.

In the middle of February Wagner at last found a small house in Biebrich, midway between Mainz and Wiesbaden, with a big garden and a view of the Rhine. He had incautiously asked Minna, in a letter of 9 February, whether she would like to join him. Instead of replying she arrived in person on 21 February, as she said, to help him move in. He was moved to tears, and they immediately began to consider settling in Wiesbaden together. But as luck would have it, on the second day of her stay a letter arrived from Mathilde Wesendonk, announcing the belated despatch of a Christmas present, and the parcel itself came the following day. Minna had it opened at the customs office in the belief that it contained music but, as she wrote to Natalie, 'it was from that filthy woman again, an embroidered cushion, tea, Eau de Câlange [sic], pressed violets'. (RWBC, p. 540) Incapable of regarding his relationship with Mathilde in any but a cheapening light, she refused to accept any of his explanations, 'and the whole madhouse is back again, not a brick changed . . . we have been through ten days of hell, and those appalling ten days have at least had the beneficial effect of administering a final warning.' (To Cornelius, 4 March)

Minna went back to Dresden, and as Wagner was not in the mood to settle back to work immediately, he left for Karlsruhe on 8 March to read the text of *Die Meistersinger* to the grand duke and duchess, which he did, by a happy coincidence, sitting under a painting by his old friend Friedrich Pecht, depicting Goethe reading *Faust* to the duke's ancestors.

It was at an evening party given by the Schotts in Mainz that Wagner made the acquaintance of Mathilde Maier. He was at once greatly taken by her intelligent, candid expression. Her blue eyes and curling fair hair reminded him of the young Duke of York in Delacroix's painting. For her part, she admitted: 'When I saw you for the first time the mark left on you by deep suffering made an indelible impression on me. I wanted so much to gather together all the joys of the world in order to blot out your pain, if only for a moment.' He promised to visit her at her home in Mainz, and there he found an idyllic household such as he had hardly come across before. Mathilde, then twenty-eight years old, lived in modest circumstances with her mother, sister and two aunts, and enjoyed a wide circle of friends, including an old friend of Schopenhauer, Gerichtsrat Becker. When Wagner had business in Mainz, usually once a week, he called on her, and she sometimes visited him in Biebrich, accompanied by her sister or a friend.

'Not a love affair, that it was not,' Ulrike von Levetzow said of her relationship with Goethe, and Mathilde Maier could have said the same of her friendship with Wagner. His letters to her breathe the air of *Meistersinger*, and if we did not know that he had already finished the text when they met, we might well take her for the model for Eva. But she was constantly in his thoughts while he was composing the music, and in the turmoil of his existence she gave him peace and reminded him of his true nature and vocation. 'Had I not your dear, resolved, lucid nature, and the lovely person that goes with it, to encourage me, "Teufel möchte Schuster sein!" '

The first rays of spring sunshine revived his zest for work. 'As I sat on my balcony enjoying the magnificent view afforded by a beautiful sunset which shed a transfiguring light on golden Mainz and the majestic Rhine flowing between, suddenly the prelude to *Die Meistersinger* presented itself to me, close and clear, exactly as it had come once before, remote and insubstantial, out of a mood of dejection. I set to and wrote it out exactly as it stands today in the score, with all the principal motives of the whole work clearly delineated in it.'

In the composition sketch, started at the end of March, the majority of the prelude is written out on two staves, increasing to three at the end, where the three themes are welded together contrapuntally. The orchestral sketch, started immediately afterwards, took a week, 13–20 April. The first sketch of the chorale, 'Da zu dir der Heiland kam', survives on a separate sheet, with the chorus parts written in ink and the instrumental interludes very lightly in pencil, and may perhaps antedate the prelude.

While the composition sketch of *Die Meistersinger* has not quite survived complete, there are a large number of separate preliminary sketches still in existence: themes and melodies, some in various different versions, contrapuntal studies of ensembles, and some personal annotations. 'Something for my friend Standhartner's birthday' appears at the bottom of a sketch of Sachs's shoemaking song.

On 22 May Wagner wrote to Mathilde Wesendonk: it was his birthday and somebody had brought him some flowers. 'And there I sat alone. Suddenly I had an idea for the orchestral introduction to the third act.' He went on to describe how he had the bass instruments begin with a profoundly melancholy passage, with the character of complete resignation, and then the horns enter with the bright, joyful melody of 'Wach auf!', like the sound of a gospel. 'I now realize that this will be my most accomplished masterwork and – I shall accomplish it.'

This was one of the sketches that survive, headed 'Introduct. Act III / 22 May 62 morning'. In it the prelude is already in a 'perfect' arch form, that is, a palindromic a–b–c–b–a. It demonstrates that Wagner carved his music from a complete block and did not piece it together from fragments. The chorale melody appears already in its eventual form, whereas the melancholy passage based on the 'Wahn' motive is still very different from what it was to become.[4]

He was not left on his own for the whole of this birthday. Mathilde Maier came later, with a few other friends, and did the honours at the table, skilfully making the most of his deficient stock of china.

Wagner's progress with the first act was not as fast as he had hoped, partly because he was plagued by all kinds of worries and anxiety, and partly because of his attitude to the work: he was only pleased with what he had written down if it was all, to the smallest detail, the result of a happy inspiration. (To Otto Wesendonk, 26 July) Finally he had an accident. His landlord owned a dog and neglected it; when Wagner decided to give it a bath one day it bit him in the right thumb, which prevented him from writing legibly for quite a long time.

He got so behind with the instalments of his manuscript that Schott, who had been very generous to start with, refused to give him another advance. 'You are wrong, my very good Herr Schott!' Wagner wrote to him on 10 October. 'You are very wrong as to the way to treat a person like me. Starvation will compel people to do a great deal, but it will not produce works of a higher kind. Or do you suppose that if my worries will not let me sleep at night, I shall have the serene temper and good ideas that my work needs in the daytime? . . . This letter is the product of a sleepless night, and I thought I was merely following the immutable dictates of justice in not keeping it from you.'

'I had better refrain from comment on the product you have sent me of one of your sleepless nights, my very good Herr Wagner,' Schott replied the next day, 'for although I know what behaviour to adopt towards artists, I prefer not to say to you what I expect from artists . . . I cannot give you the rather large sum you ask for [Wagner had mentioned first 3000 gulden, then 1000]. No mere music publisher could satisfy your needs: it would take an enormously rich banker or a reigning prince with millions at his disposal.'

In their later dealings neither Wagner nor Schott bore the other a grudge over this exchange of letters, but it put an end to the period of happy cooperation and Wagner's life now took a turn which this time led inevitably to disaster. 'If you had supported me that time in Biebrich for another nine or ten months,' he wrote to Schott on 6 November 1867, 'our *Meistersinger* would have been playing in the theatres for the last three years. God knows! It was unfortunate that you made a mistake.'

His correspondence with Minna added to his troubles. While he persisted, with a patience that is hard for us to comprehend, in telling her about his day-to-day existence, she would not stop picking at old wounds until in the end she gave him a real fright with a letter that made him think she must have lost her reason (cf.

his letter to Klara Wolfram, 2 June 1862). He turned to her doctor, Pusinelli, in this predicament: would it not be better for Minna's health if they were to agree to live apart and write to each other as little as possible? He asked him to consult Luise Brockhaus on the matter. (RWAP, 14 June 1862) Wagner did not mention divorce in this letter, but Pusinelli evidently thought that that was what he had in mind and wrote to Minna along those lines. She replied that she would never even consider such a dreadful thing and Wagner had to write to conciliate her. 'In his sympathetic eagerness Pusinelli went further than I meant him to . . . I am sorry such a painful thought occurred to you, which never entered my head. I beg you to calm yourself about it!' (27 June, RWBC)

On the other hand he rejected as foolish and futile the idea that they might resume living together, perhaps in Dresden, which would have been possible by then, since he had been granted a complete amnesty on 18 March. Minna could keep a room ready for him and he would try and see her there, he told his sister Klara; and as long as he had a quiet refuge somewhere else to work in, she could conceal the breach from the world. 'The idea of divorce did not originate with me, although there is much to be said in its favour and although I think I would certainly be forgiven for harbouring the wish to spend my remaining years with a sympathetic being at my side to the greater benefit of my works.' (11 July)

After the rupture with Schott, Wagner had no alternative but to earn his living by giving concerts. The following two years could be regarded as a complete blank in the history of his creative life were it not for the opportunities they gave for audiences, and above all for himself, to hear excerpts from the *Ring, Tristan* and *Meistersinger*.

It was at a concert of his compositions that Weissheimer organized in the Gewandhaus in Leipzig on 1 November 1862 that Wagner conducted the very first performance of the *Meistersinger* prelude, in the city of his birth – in an almost empty hall. 'I have never experienced such a void on a comparable occasion,' he averred. The whole thing seemed to him and Bülow, who was also taking part, like something out of *Don Quixote* and infected them both with an uncomfortable hilarity, until the joyful solemnity of the prelude itself lifted them out of the poverty of the circumstances. It was applauded so vigorously that it had to be repeated,

and at the end the orchestra honoured him with a ceremonial
Tusch.[5]

From Leipzig he went to Dresden, where Minna met him and
took him to her new home. Since his sister Klara was also staying
with her, this, the couple's last meeting, was not spoiled by quar-
rels. 'I am alive and shall return in one day's time!' he wrote to
Mathilde Maier. A new calamity awaited him in Biebrich: his
landlord gave him notice. After a brief farewell from Mathilde he
set off for Vienna on 13 November, to conduct a series of concerts
in the Theater an der Wien. He travelled in the company of the
actress Friederike Meyer, whom he knew from Frankfurt, which
cost him the good will of his Isolde, her sister, Luise Meyer-
Dustmann. He was staying in his old hotel again, he reported,
where they did their best to anticipate his every unspoken wish; he
was basking in his popularity and enjoying the sound of his music
being played on barrel organs.

A week after his arrival in Vienna Standhartner organized a reading of *Meistersinger*, to which Hanslick was also invited. According to
Wagner's account, the critic left at the end in an unmistakable rage,
while Hanslick denied it – though not until years later, after
Wagner's death. His version was that 'after the smoky heat of the
Ring' *Die Meistersinger* had delighted him like a smiling landscape.
(MWKS, I, pp. 323f.) The fact remains that he was from now on
irreconcilably hostile to Wagner, after the short truce. It may be that
he had heard that Beckmesser, the Marker, had been called Veit
Hanslich in the scenario, and he suspected what kind of immortality
might be bestowed on him. Indeed, as Newman says, he was
preserved for posterity in Wagner's work like a fly in amber.

Wagner had done a lot of preparatory work for the concerts while
he was still in Biebrich, extracting the items from their contexts in
his scores, writing concert endings for them, transcribing some for
orchestra alone, as in the case of the Ride of the Valkyries, or, as
with the assembling of the mastersingers in the first act, quickly
orchestrating them for the first time. The instrumental parts
remained to be copied in Vienna, with the assistance of Cornelius,
Tausig, Porges, Weissheimer and – perhaps surprisingly – Brahms.
Brahms had been introduced by Tausig as 'a very good chap' and
was entrusted with copying an excerpt from *Meistersinger*. 'I
suppose I shall be called a Wagnerian,' he remarked to Joachim,
'principally, of course, because any reasonable person is bound to

speak up against the silly tone which musicians here use against him.'

The Wagner tuba did not exist at that date, so Wagner had to supplement the opera orchestra with tuba-players from a military band for the pieces from the *Ring*. 'The trouble this concert is causing is out of all proportion,' he moaned to Mathilde Maier the evening before the first one took place; 'everything I do is just about as difficult as if the world had never known such an event before.' And then he added very seriously: 'I feel as if this may be the last time that I shall ask Fate what change I can expect in my position in the world: it's possible that from now on I shall turn my back on it completely and for ever.'

The first concert was given on 26 December in the presence of the empress and before a full house. With the exception of the *Meistersinger* prelude, every item was a first performance:

> *Meistersinger* prelude
> Assembly of the mastersingers (orchestral arrangement)
> Pogner's address

> Ride of the Valkyries (orchestral arrangement)
> Siegmund's Spring Song
> Wotan's Farewell and Magic Fire music

> Theft of the Rhine gold (second half of Scene 1)
> Donner's conjuration of the storm, *leading into*
> Entry of the gods into Valhalla

'I have never heard anything like the tumult that broke out when Wagner appeared,' Weissheimer recalled. 'Everyone clapped and shouted, the empress leaned out of her box applauding – it went on certainly for five or six minutes, and kept reviving, so that Wagner did not know how to go on acknowledging it and just stood there resignedly, with his arms extended, until the noise died down.' Each piece was applauded more enthusiastically than the one before, and the Ride of the Valkyries drove the excitable Viennese nearly mad.

'Dear child – it's over – but not done with!' he reported the next day. 'There's still an awful lot for me to do! Rebuilding the orchestra: sound not good enough!' He had a sound-board put up, which unfortunately cost 230 gulden. The second and third concerts took place on 1 and 11 January, with slight variations of programme. In the third, Wagner conducted the *Faust* Overture, which Weissheimer thought the most perfect orchestral composition he had ever heard. The applause was beyond belief, but 'Johannes Brahms sat next to me in the box . . . He remained cool and reserved throughout the whole concert. When I rallied him to join in the applause after the thrilling performance of the *Faust* Overture he said "Ah, Herr Weissheimer, you will tear your white kid gloves."'

The reception was the same as almost always: tumultuous applause, bad reviews – notably that of the playwright and non-musician Friedrich Hebbel, who had also tried his hand at dramatizing the Nibelungs – and a deficit. 'Tausig is running round, trying to raise the money to pay off part of my latest concert debts!' (To Bülow, 3 January)

Two significant events took place during the concert series. His various enterprises were proving a nerve-racking gamble, he told Mathilde Maier; a rehearsal with the piano had convinced him that an invalid like Ander, who had ruined his voice, would not possibly be able to sing Tristan. And so he had come to yet another dead end. In this sombre mood he put a question to her which he asked her to consider in a purely hypothetical light, in the first place, like a moral problem.

He needed, he said, a home, not so much a place as a person. He could not marry as long as his wife was alive, and he could not divorce her, because it would kill her. This was the sorry pass that was destroying him. 'I need a female being who, in spite of everything and everyone, will have the resolution to be to me what a wife can be in these miserable circumstances – must be, I say, if I am to thrive. Perhaps I am being blinded by excessive self-esteem when I go so far as to suppose that a woman with the resolution to devote herself to me in such inauspicious circumstances would abandon all human relationships that have no useful place in the life and work of a person like me . . . I want a loving woman at my side, and let her be a daughter at the same time!'

'What will you make of this?' he asked at the end. 'Well, after all, it was only a theoretical problem.' (4 January 1863) He was fairly sure that she would not want to give up her middle-class milieu.

The other event was the writing of a preface to the first edition of the text of the *Ring* to go on sale to the general public. He wrote that he no longer dared to hope that he would live to see it performed, or even that he would find the leisure and the inclination to complete the music. Thus it was really just a dramatic poem, a literary work, that he offered to the reading public. So much in a postscript. The preface itself ended with a pessimistic question. One of the German princes would be in a better position than any other person or group of people to promote the performance of the *Ring*: 'Is such a prince to be found?' (RWGS, VI, pp. 272ff.)

A concert he gave in Prague on 8 February, at which he was presented with a laurel wreath with streamers in the German national colours while the Czechs cheered him with their 'Sláva! sláva!', actually made a net profit of 1100 gulden. Ander surprised him agreeably by his performance at another piano run-through of *Tristan*, so it was in a generally more optimistic frame of mind that he accepted an invitation to go to St Petersburg. Before leaving he commissioned Mathilde to look out for a piece of land on the Rhine where he could build himself a house. 'There, you see, I'm after my quarry: St Peter with his net! And oh, let me catch peace and a home at last!'

'It was downright frightening,' he wrote after the first concert in St Petersburg. 'I've never known it so hot as here in Russia!!! The audience – three or four thousand people – nearly gobbled me up. I've thrown all other concerts into the shade, and my triumph is unheard of.' And he went on to describe what he later called his Jeanne d'Arc vision: 'When I was obliged to repeat the *Lohengrin* prelude my nerves began to sway, and it was as though the whole orchestra – 130 of them – had turned into angels and were greeting me with this strangely ecstatic music on my arrival in Heaven . . . Now may Heaven bless my settling down!' he went on. 'There ought not to be any shortage of money. Do your best! Goodbye – and stay fond of me!' (4 March)

There were another two concerts in St Petersburg, followed by three in Moscow. 'So now I'm in Asia, really in Asia, my girl! . . . It's all gaily coloured, bright, golden, domed – wondrous, wonderful – in my amazement I had to laugh aloud.' The tour finished with two more concerts in St Petersburg.

In spite of his triumph he felt it to be nothing but an interruption of his normal activity. The vision of a little house beside the Rhine was the reward he looked forward to. When Mathilde reported the find of a 'Rose Cottage' near Bingen he immediately sent a telegram telling her to take it whatever the rent; he was so accustomed to seeing every agreeable prospect dissolve again that anything good filled him with anxiety.

What now gave him hope for the future was the interest that the Grand Duchess Helene Pavlovna showed in him. Born Princess Charlotte of Württemberg, and the widow of Grand Duke Michael, she occupied a leading position at the court of St Petersburg, where she brought together all the men of intellectual distinction and also played a part in politics under Alexander II.

Wagner tells in *Mein Leben* of his introduction to her lady-in-waiting and confidante, Editha von Rhaden, after the success of his first concert. He found her a lady of the greatest culture, and she arranged for him to be invited to the Grand Duchess's evening tea circle. This gave him the opportunity to read the *Ring* and *Meistersinger* to the company. Before leaving Russia he told Fräulein von Rhaden of his plans for building a house and of the financial problems they posed. 'Build and hope!' she exclaimed ardently. But a telegram reached him as he crossed the frontier: 'Not too bold!'

This account was supplemented by the publication of eleven important letters from Wagner to Editha von Rhaden, in the periodical *Die Musik* in 1924. 'What marvellous evenings they were!' he wrote from Vienna. 'As you know, the Greeks thought of the realm of Apollo as being in the far, Hyperborean north; there eternal sunshine reigned, there Apollo held his court! Ought I not to think of that Hyperborean court when I remember the quiet liberation from all mundane pressures that I enjoyed on those evenings, in those rooms? . . . And now on to a new life, to the old life, the only one dear to me! "Gib Vergessen, daß ich lebe!" my Tristan cries to the night of love – I cry it to my art.' (9 May)

After paying his own debts and sending Minna the allowance due to her – an obligation he always observed conscientiously, however hard pressed he was – he still had 4000 talers left. In spite of Mathilde's efforts 'Rose Cottage' came to nothing: 'Oh you did everything you could, my dear treasure!' In the meantime his friends in Vienna had been looking for a house in the vicinity with a garden and some trees, and a few days later he wrote to Mathilde again: 'I have some important news; what will you think of it, you dear?' An old Hungarian, Baron Rackowitz, deemed it an honour to place the upper storey of his house at Penzing, half an hour from Vienna, at Wagner's disposal. There was a large garden and some magnificent trees, and the rent was comparatively low, 1200 gulden a year. (10 May)

The next day he wrote to her again. Although he was aware of all the good reasons in favour of settling in Vienna and against a house on the Rhine, he could not rid himself of a sense of regret. He tried to console Mathilde and himself with hopes for the future. 'God knows how far you and your family's bourgeois bigotry will stretch – but suppose the whole family, aunts and all, moved here? – Oh yes! one more Russian campaign and I shall be able to offer you the equally beautiful ground-floor flat of my house. You shall all keep house for me. What about that? What do the aunties say to that?' (11 May)

The expense of decorating and furnishing his flat – which he described to Mathilde in great detail, including a plan he drew himself – gave him an uneasy conscience, though he tried to justify it: 'Good gracious! for how much must not the trivia of an agreeably decorated house be a substitute!'

He felt very lonely on his 'half-hundredth' birthday; only the Standhartners looked in for a moment in the evening. A torchlight procession of choral societies and students' associations made amends on 3 June. As the procession made its way towards him across the Hietzing bridge, the most splendid, glowing full moon suddenly rose above the tall trees in the garden of Schönbrunn. 'And so a dear, old, trusted friend rose to greet me and told me that I was not alone in the midst of all this crowd! (To Mathilde Maier, 5 June)

He was working on *Die Meistersinger* again. He told Editha von Rhaden how curiously attractive he found the work; in it, for the first time, a genial element was developing, an enjoyment of delicate, light-hearted detail such as had never manifested itself in his earlier, passionate dramas. 'I believe that completing this work in peace is the only thing that may heal me and make a new, light-hearted man of me.' (14 September) But his progress was very slow. Having orchestrated the prelude a year earlier, by the middle of June 1863 he had only just finished scoring the first scene of the first act (i.e., up to Eva and Magdalene's exit).

He was constantly being interrupted by conducting engagements: three concerts in Budapest in July, two in Prague and two in Karlsruhe in November, a concert with the private orchestra of the Prince of Hohenzollern-Hechingen at Löwenberg in December,

Breslau on 9 December, Vienna on 27 December. As a conductor he was a 'virtuoso': in that role he could offer the general public the 'personal' accomplishments which were all it knew how to appreciate, while his 'works' really existed for only a few. As a virtuoso he would be at home in St Petersburg, too, he told Editha von Rhaden, only he would not want to take up concert-giving as a career, but rather engage himself for a number of large-scale concerts: he would then build up the Petersburg orchestra into the best in the world. The terms would have to be such as to relieve him of the need to supplement his income in other ways. By his reckoning he would need an annual income of between five and six thousand roubles.

The grand duchess appeared not averse to lending this plan her support. Revolution in Poland, however, barred his way to St Petersburg. An enquiry addressed to Moscow, which he enclosed with a letter to Fräulein von Rhaden for her to forward, was posted in Vienna on 2 February 1864 yet did not reach its destination until 23 March. His friend in Moscow much regretted the delay, as a series of concerts could probably have been arranged had the letter arrived when it should have done. He thought of travelling to Kiev, too, via Odessa, taking Cornelius with him, but again was advised against it because of the political situation.

There remained one last glimmer of hope. At Löwenberg and in Breslau he renewed his acquaintance with Frau Harriet von Bissing, whom he had known in Zürich, a daughter of the wealthy Hamburg shipowner Sloman, and sister of Eliza Wille. She was moved by his exhausted appearance, would not hear of his undertaking another Russian tour and proposed giving him a large sum of money to make up for it. The promise was slow in taking effect, ostensibly because of the objections of her family. In the end Wagner was forced to ask her for an unequivocal declaration: not whether she *could* help him at once, but whether she *wanted* to help him at all. 'You want to know after all if I *want* to? Well then, in God's name: No!' This answer completely bewildered Wagner until Frau Wille gave him the astonishing explanation: in great agitation she told him that her sister had said to herself, 'And if I do rescue Wagner, he still loves the Wesendonk woman!'[6] 'In the end Frau von Bissing's jealousy (I had no idea!) was so powerful', Wagner wrote to Cornelius at the end of March, 'that her behaviour towards me only now – through this discovery – becomes comprehensible.' In 1887, four years after Wagner's death, she called on Mathilde Wesendonk in her home in Berlin, and her agitation on seeing Wagner's bust was such that she began to tremble.[7]

Wagner's fate in Vienna was now sealed. Since he had believed that he only needed to gain time while the help he was sure of getting from Frau von Bissing was delayed, he had been forced to meet the interest due on his debts by issuing bills of exchange. (To Mathilde Maier, 29 March) In the first flush of his hopes he had celebrated Christmas by giving each of his friends Cornelius, Porges, Tausig and Schönaich 'an appropriate little something'. 'That idiot Wagner put up a great big tree and piled a king's ransom in presents under it for me!' Cornelius wrote to his sister. 'Just imagine: a wonderful heavy overcoat – an elegant grey dressing gown – red scarf, blue cigarette case and lighter – beautiful silk handkerchiefs, magnificent gold buttons – *Struwwelpeter* – elegant penwiper embossed in gold, lovely ties – meerschaum cigar-holder with his initials on it – in short, everything an Oriental imagination can dream up – it made me heavy at heart.'

Cornelius's gratitude took the form of a poem wishing Wagner good fortune and immortality, which he recited on New Year's Eve at the Standhartners'.

Wagner must have realized the impossibility of maintaining his establishment in Penzing any longer by the beginning of February at the latest. He asked Mathilde whether she and her family would consider taking a house outside Mainz, 'where I would have a quiet, pretty sitting room and a bedroom; and would you be able to manage if I paid you 100 florins a month for my keep?' But events were moving too fast. 'What I am caught up in is not a catastrophe, it is my approaching end,' he told Editha von Rhaden on 14 March. He implored her to ask the grand duchess to provide a pension of 1000 talers for his wife to be paid in quarterly instalments to 'Frau Minna Wagner, at Walpurgisstrasse 16, in Dresden', the first to be paid on the coming 1 April, and to be discontinued at her death.

Finally Eduard Liszt, an uncle of Franz though younger than his nephew, and an official of the district court in Vienna, advised him to lose no time in leaving for Switzerland to avoid arrest for debt, as one of the larger bills of exchange was about to fall due.[8] On the same day that he wrote to St Petersburg, Wagner also approached Eliza Wille with the request to discuss with Mathilde Wesendonk the possibility of the latter giving him a home for the summer. He

asked only for his keep and would not be any kind of a nuisance. By
the time Eliza Wille's 'total refusal' reached him he had left Vienna.
He had decided on flight. Schönaich and Cornelius went to the
station with him. Peter was gripped by a kind of black humour, a
mood of 'flippant excitement', but in his next letter to his sister he
wrote: 'But Susanne, he is Wagner, after all – by far the most
important poet of our time – and I tell you, in spite of everything he
is a German through and through – in sorrow and joy, in his virtues
and his sins – human, a child, a genius!'

On 23 March Wagner arrived in Munich. In a shop window on
Good Friday he saw a portrait of the new king, the eighteen-year-
old Ludwig II, who had just succeeded to the throne on the sudden
death of Maximilian II. The picture 'gripped me with the special
emotion that beauty and youth arouse in us in what one supposes
must be an uncommonly difficult position'. 'While I was there I
wrote a humorous epitaph for myself.' This is now in the Wagner
Archives.

> Hier liegt Wagner, der nichts geworden,
> nicht einmal Ritter vom lumpigsten Orden;
> nicht einen Hund hinterm Ofen entlockt' er,
> Universitäten nicht mal 'nen Dokter.
>
> ('Here lies Wagner, who never throve,
> tempted no dog from behind the stove,
> earned not the shabbiest star or garter,
> honoured by no Alma Marter.')
> Munich, 25 March 1864

As on his flight fifteen years before, he crossed Lake Constance
and made for Zürich. He sent a few lines announcing his imminent
arrival to François Wille, who was away from home on a trip to the
East. Eliza Wille barely had time to prepare the guest room. 'He
arrived in a pathetic condition, resembling in every respect someone in need of asylum,' she wrote to her husband. In her memoirs
she added: 'He was in a state of mind in which a son seeks out his
mother.'

She had forwarded Wagner's notice of his arrival to Otto Wesendonk. 'I hope . . . that you will be able to give Wagner a refuge,' he
replied on Easter Sunday. 'I can *not* do it; you can fully appreciate
that.' So she took him in. 'That woman is beyond praise,' he wrote

to Cornelius, 'beyond compare, absolutely unique.' And to Mathilde Maier: 'Frau Dr Wille is quite unique; she knows *every-thing* straight away. Also capable, busy and boundlessly kind-hearted. You will like her very much, in spite of her great ugliness.'

She provided him with books: Jean Paul's *Siebenkäs*, the diaries of Frederick the Great, the fourteenth-century monk Johannes Tauler. 'I'm reading the German mystics: today Tauler. The coming of "grace" is particularly enthralling. All the same, everything is more spacious, peaceful and serene on the Ganges than in the cells of these Christian monasteries. One can tell how much bad, grey weather we always have.' (To Mathilde Maier, 5 April) In his diary he noted: Buddha – Luther; India – North Germany . . . On the Ganges mild, pure renunciation; in Germany monastic impossibility . . . Our life here is such a torment that without "wine, women and song" we cannot endure it nor even serve God. Mariafeld, April 1864.' (RWGS, XII, p. 282)

One evening, just after sunset, he was sitting by the window and looking at the floor while Frau Wille talked about the magnificent future that surely lay in front of him. He listened impatiently then jumped up. 'What's the use of your talking about the future, when my manuscripts are gathering dust? Who is going to stage the work that I, only *I*, with the aid of *benevolent* spirits, can give substance to, so that the whole world can know that this is how it is, *this* is how the master envisaged his work?' He was pacing excitedly up and down the room and then suddenly stopped in front of her. 'I am a different kind of organism, my nerves are hypersensitive – I must have beauty, splendour and light! The world owes me what I need! I cannot live the miserable life of a town organist like your master Bach! Is it so shocking, if I think I deserve the little bit of luxury I like? I, who have so much enjoyment to give the world and thousands of people?' He raised his head defiantly and then sat down by the window again.

He slept badly, disturbed by dreams. One night he was King Lear on the heath, in the storm. The Fool sang mocking rhymes at him. With his royal soul Lear hurled his curse in the teeth of the darkness and the storm and felt great and wretched, but not degraded. 'What have you to say of such an experience, where the dreamer feels himself identical with what his dream conjures up?' He dreamed feverishly that Frederick the Great invited him to join Voltaire at his court. 'That's what my secret ambitions do for me!'

'My condition is very disquieting,' he wrote to Cornelius, 'it's balanced on a knife edge: a single push and that will be the end, and there will be nothing more to come from me, nothing, nothing more!' Conjuring fate with daemonic force, he added: '*A light* must shine: *a man* must come, who will help me whole-heartedly, now – while I still have the strength to use his help: or else it will be too late, I feel it!' (8 April)

When Wille returned in the second half of April, Wagner sensed that his presence worried him. He decided to go to Stuttgart and try to resume work on *Die Meistersinger* somewhere in the country. Before leaving Mariafeld he gave Frau Wille a letter for Mathilde Wesendonk, who, however, returned it to her unopened with an accompanying note. 'I am sending that childish little letter back to you,' Wagner wrote to Eliza; 'there is nobody else, dear lady, who can explain to her, as occasion offers, that the most shameful troubles that have befallen me have made me neither wicked nor *bad*, and that therefore the childish exhortation to be *good* is meaningless.'[9]

Wagner left Mariafeld on 29 April. He wrote to Frau Wille from Basel, telling her he would be back and asking her to keep the room and her friendship for him. Her reply, to the Stuttgart address he had given her, caused her some pain: she would not fall in with his plans, one future lay ahead for her, another for him. He replied from Stuttgart on 2 May: 'Your desire not to see me at Mariafeld again is in accordance with my own feelings on the matter. Let the tempestuous, fevered night that not even the loveliest sunshine had the power to lighten from outside be a thing of the past, and let us draw a veil over the changing phantasms that it produced. – My fate, even for the immediate future, is still uncertain.'

NOTES TO VOLUME I

Preface

1 Conversely, Wagner's *Religion und Kunst* was the last thing Carlyle
  read before his death on 5 February 1881. (Cosima to her daughter
  Daniela, 3 April 1881)
2 *L'Opera*, 4, nos. 12/13.
3 Furtwängler, *Ton und Wort*, p. 108.
4 Schopenhauer, *Parerga und Paralipomena*, II, §59.

Chapter 1. The Wagner Family

1 W. Lange, *Richard Wagners Sippe*; Lange, *Richard Wagner und seine
  Vaterstadt*; O. Bournot, *Ludwig Heinrich Christian Geyer, der Stiefvater
  Richard Wagners*; W. K. von Arnswaldt, *Ahnentafel des Komponisten
  Richard Wagner*.
2 H. S. Chamberlain, *Briefe* (Munich, 1928), I, pp. 226ff.
3 Wilhelm Bode, *Der Musenhof der Herzogin Amalie* (Berlin, 1908),
  pp. 13ff.

Chapter 2. Wagner's Mother

1 Both letters were published in the *Bayreuther Festspielführer*, 1933,
  p. 15.

Chapter 4. Beethoven

1 Otto Daube, *'Ich schreibe keine Symphonien mehr'*, pp. 94ff.

Chapter 5. Studiosus Musicae

1 In a letter to Dr Martin Hürlimann, 5 June 1946; published in
  Westernhagen, *Wagner* (1956), pp. 532f.
2 Dannreuther included the full text of what Wagner said in his article
  on Wagner in the first edition of *Grove's dictionary of music and
  musicians* (1879–89). On another occasion Wagner mentioned that
  Weinlig had purposely not recommended Bach as a model because of
  his tendency to break the rules. (Cosima's diary, 20 December 1878;
  BBL 1937, p. 61.)

Chapter 6. The First Three Operas

1 Richard Sternfeld, 'Zur Entstehung des Leitmotivs bei Richard Wagner', *Richard-Wagner-Jahrbuch* 1907, pp. 106ff.

Chapter 7. *Rienzi*

1 An entry in the autobiographical notebook known as the Red Book betrays that Wagner tried to challenge Dietrich on this occasion: 'Became master of myself and a man. Whip, pistols. Failed to find D.' (RWSB, I, p. 83)
2 In *Richard Wagner an Minna Wagner*, II (*Briefe in Originalausgaben*, vol. 2), pp. 90f.
3 The letter is much abbreviated in RWGB, I, p. 101; it is complete in RWSB, I, p. 323.

Chapter 8. *Der Fliegende Holländer*

1 *Bayreuther Festspielführer*, 1939, pp. 61ff.
2 A note in RWSB, I, pp. 414ff., lists a number of points which might be interpreted as evidence that he did not go to prison, but these do not diminish the suspicion occasioned by the disappearance of the first, incriminating piece of paper.
3 G. Leprince, *Présence de Wagner*, pp. 320ff.: '*Le Vaisseau Fantôme* de P. Foucher'.

Chapter 9. *Tannhäuser*

1 Furtwängler, *Ton und Wort*, pp. 163f.

Chapter 10. Hofkapellmeister in Dresden

1 Gustav Adolf Kietz, *Richard Wagner . . . Erinnerungen*, pp. 45ff.

Chapter 11. Germanic Myth and Greek Tragedy

1 J. Grimm, *Deutsche Mythologie*. It must have been a copy of the first edition. The second, which he had in his Dresden library, was published in 1844.
2 Westernhagen, *Richard Wagners Dresdener Bibliothek*. The collection of Wagner's books, stored in a deep bunker, was one of the few things that survived the destrucion of the publishers' quarter of Leipzig on 4 December 1943. After the war the firm of Brockhaus were able to transport it to their new base in Wiesbaden. Their publication of the catalogue in 1966 met a long-standing need among Wagnerian scholars.
3 *Dichtung und Wahrheit*, Book 12. It is interesting to note that when Goethe was writing the scenario for an opera, *Der Löwenstuhl*, in 1814, he thought of casting the narration of the tale of the 'Lions' Seat' in 'Eddic rhythms'.
4 The original title was *Die Nibelungensage* (*Mythus*). (SERD, pp. 26ff.)
5 Spengler, *Der Untergang des Abendlandes*, I: 'Fafnir's hoard' twice, pp.

480 and 482. Spengler heard the *Ring* at Bayreuth in 1931. There is
no sign that he changed his views. Frau Gertrud Strobel, the wife of
the Wahnfried archivist, sat next to him at dinner after one of the
performances, and has told me that 'he didn't speak a single word the
whole time'.

6 Andreas Heusler, *Die altgermanische Dichtung* (new edn, Darmstadt,
1957), p. 39.
7 Kranz, *Stasimon* (Berlin, 1933).

Chapter 12. *Lohengrin*

1 The scenario was published in the *Bayreuther Festspielführer*, 1936,
pp. 141ff.
2 Günther Schulz, *Das Recht in den Bühnendichtungen Richard Wagners*
(Cologne, 1962). Apart from the works mentioned in the text, Wagner
also owned Leopold August Warnkönig's *Flandrische Staats- und
Rechtsgeschichte bis zum Jahr 1305*, in three volumes.
3 The 'Lohengrin house' still stands in the 'Wagnerort Graupa', as it is
now designated (in the district of Pirna), and the museum set up
there is still maintained and, so the curator assures me, is popular
with visitors.
4 Cf. Erich Rappl, 'Vom Werden der *Lohengrin*-Partitur', in Bayreuth
Festival programme, *Lohengrin*, 1954, pp. 21ff.
5 Hanslick, 'Gluck'sche Oper', in *Die moderne Oper*, I.
6 Pfitzner, *Werk und Wiedergabe*, p. 312.
7 Strauss, *Briefwechsel mit Hugo von Hofmannsthal*, p. 628.
8 Ibid., p. 62. Strauss gave the *Meistersinger* quintet as another example.
9 Lorenz, 'Der musikalische Aufbau des *Lohengrin*', in *Bayreuther
Festspielführer*, 1936, pp. 189ff. On Bar-form, see note 11 to Chapter
26, in Vol. II of the present work.
10 The uncut version is to be found in Wagner, *Sämtliche Lieder*, ed. by
Emil Liepe (Breitkopf & Härtel).
11 BBL 1909, 1910.
12 All quotations from Goethe's *Faust* are in the translation by Louis
MacNeice (London, 1951).
13 Mann, *Wagner und unsere Zeit*, pp. 120f.

Chapter 13. Money Troubles

1 Meyerbeer's diaries and correspondence are in the process of
publication, under the editorship of Dr Heinz Becker; to date (early
1978) three volumes have been published, to 1845. I am much obliged
to Dr Becker for placing material from the diaries at my disposal
before publication.
2 Some comparative salaries: Eduard Devrient, dramaturg, 3000 talers;
Reissiger, principal conductor, 2000 talers; Wagner, second
conductor, 1500 talers; Schröder-Devrient, principal singer, 4000
talers, in addition to a pension claim of 1000 talers, wardrobe
allowance of 200 talers, and a payment of 20 talers for each

performance she gave – and frequent leave of absence to make guest
appearances elsewhere. (GLRW, II, p. 261, note.)

Chapter 14. Revolutionary Ideas

1 Kittl's setting, under the title *Die Franzosen vor Nizza* ('The French
before Nice'), was a success when it was produced in Prague – the
one occasion when Wagner appeared in the role of librettist!

2 The first prose sketch of the Norns' scene was published in *Die
Musik*, February 1933, pp. 336ff.; the first verse text is in RWGS, II,
pp. 167ff.

3 The letter of 17 May 1849 to Eduard Devrient is to be found in
RWSB, II, pp. 660–9.

4 Julius Kapp, *Richard Wagner und die Berliner Oper* (Berlin 1933), p. 27.

Chapter 16. From Heroic Opera to Mythic Drama

1 The manuscript found its way into the Bibliothèque Nationale in
Paris as part of the Collection Louis Barthou and was published for
the first time in 1933 in facsimile in *L'Illustration*. When I enquired
about it in 1962, in connection with my 'new Wagner studies', *Vom
Holländer zum Parsifal*, it transpired that this invaluable document had
been sold to a private buyer in 1936 for 11,500 francs. I was therefore
glad of the opportunity to reproduce the sketch from the facsimile in
L'Illustration in the Wagner number of the *Neue Zeitschrift für Musik*,
May 1963, with a transcription, to prevent it from being lost
entirely.

2 Heinz Becker, 'Giacomo Meyerbeer', in the *Year Book of the Leo
Baeck Institute*, IX (London, 1964). It is of no importance if
Meyerbeer gives the essay a different title: he appears unsure of the
title of *Opera and drama*, too.

3 The long section about the 'fire cure' was suppressed in the edition of
Wagner's letters to Uhlig (*Briefe in Originalausgaben*, vol 4: letter 18,
22 October 1850) and was published for the first time in RWBC,
pp. 774f.

Chapter 17. The Vision of La Spezia

1 It was shown at the Wagner Memorial Exhibition in Leipzig in 1913,
when it was part of the Gustav Herrmann manuscript collection. It is
now in the Library of Congress in Washington, D.C. Robert W.
Bailey has demonstrated convincingly that it dates from on or after
27 July 1850. Cf. Westernhagen, *The forging of the 'Ring'*, p. 13.

2 Uhlig, *Musikalische Schriften*, ed. Ludwig Frankenstein, Regensburg,
n.d. [1913].

3 Wagner says in *Mein Leben* that Liszt played to him from his *Faust
Symphony*, but he must have confused this occasion with their
meeting in 1856.

Chapter 18. The Myth becomes Music

1 Halm, *Von Grenzen und Ländern der Musik*, chapter 4, 'Musik und Sprache'.
2 Furtwängler, *Vermächtnis*, p. 31.
3 Otto Strobel, 'Die Originalpartitur von Richard Wagners *Rheingold*', and 'Die Kompositionsskizzen zum *Ring des Nibelungen*', in *Bayreuther Festspielführer*, 1928 and 1930 respectively.
4 Cf. SERD, p. 257. Strobel was mistaken in supposing that this first sketch was in C major: it has to be read in the tenor clef, which makes the key B♭ major. It would otherwise be a unique instance of Wagner conceiving a tune in quite the wrong key.
5 Porges actually used Schiller's terms 'sentimental' and 'naive'.

Chapter 19. The London Inferno

1 John Oxenford, 'Iconoclasm in German philosophy', *Westminster and Foreign Quarterly Review*, LIX, no. 111 (1 April 1853), pp. 388–407.
2 These notes are given in full in W. A. Ellis, *Life of Richard Wagner*, IV, pp. 440–6.
3 Felix Gotthelf, 'Schopenhauer und Richard Wagner', in *Jahrbuch der Schopenhauergesellschaft*, IV (Kiel, 1915), pp. 24–42.
4 28 September; BBL 1937, pp. 55f. ' . . . wie wenn ich eine Symphonie zu schreiben hätte'. The entry in Cosima's diary from which this comes (28 September) actually reads: ' . . . as if I had written a symphony' ('Wie wenn ich eine Symphonie geschrieben hätte'), but she was clearly mistaken.
5 Lorenz, *Das Geheimnis der Form bei Richard Wagner*, I: *Der musikalische Aufbau des Bühnenfestspiels 'Der Ring des Nibelungen'*, pp. 179ff.
6 On the dating of this letter, see Wilhelm Altmann, *Richard Wagners Briefe nach Zeitfolge und Inhalt* (Leipzig, 1905), p. 180.
7 For a more detailed description of the sketch, cf. Westernhagen, *The forging of the 'Ring'*, pp. 101–27.
8 Julius Kapp, *Richard Wagner und die Berliner Oper* (Berlin, 1933).
9 Bert Coules, 'An extract from Queen Victoria's journal', in *Wagner 1976*, p. 212; ill. no. 16.
10 *Richard Wagner and Ferdinand Praeger*, ed. by H. S. Chamberlain (2nd edn, Leipzig, 1908); *Cosima Wagner und H. S. Chamberlain im Briefwechsel*, pp. 354ff.
11 FWSZ, II, pp. 343ff. Wagner praised Sulzer in *Mein Leben*, but that he was nevertheless justified in the reservation he expressed here is confirmed by a recently published letter Sulzer wrote to Mathilde Wesendonk, undated but replying to hers of 17 August 1887 (*Neue Zürcher Zeitung*, 20/21 March 1976; on her letter see FWSZ, II, p. 501). Sulzer's own reservations about Wagner's personality were based on his awareness of something irrational in him that remained a closed book to himself. It was what Goethe called the 'daemonic' and is found in music in the highest degree; because music is on a

plane inaccessible to reasoning or intellectual processes, musicians
have more of the daemonic in them than all other artists. Cf. the
chapter 'Das Dämonische' in Westernhagen, *Wagner* (1956), pp. 427ff.

Chapter 20. The *Ring* Crisis

1 The version in RWGS, XVI, pp. 23f., is abridged; it is to be found in
full in FWSZ, II, p. 28.
2 J. Baechtold and E. Ermatinger, *Gottfried Kellers Leben, Briefe und
Tagebücher* (Stuttgart and Berlin, 1924), II.
3 This somewhat lengthy excursus is made necessary by the fact that
Mann's review, published in the *Neue Schweizer Rundschau* in 1951,
has acquired a form of eternal life through having been reprinted in
book form in *Altes und Neues* (1953), *Gesammelte Werke*, X (1960) and
Wagner und unsere Zeit (1963). It is in any case a classic example of
Wagnerian legends of that kind. Keller's letter is in Baechtold and
Ermatinger, op. cit., II, pp. 439ff.
4 From W. Golther's edition of the *Briefe an Mathilde Wesendonk* (*Briefe
in Originalausgaben*, vol. 5), p. 26. The note is undated. Ashton Ellis
suggests that Mathilde's poem may have been *Im Treibhaus*, which
would give a date of April 1858.
5 Cf. Otto Strobel, 'Zur Entstehungsgeschichte der *Götterdämmerung*';
Westernhagen, *Vom Holländer zum Parsifal*, p. 86; Westernhagen,
Richard Wagners Dresdener Bibliothek, pp. 37f. Newman published an
English translation of the sketch of the third version (NLRW, II, pp.
354ff.).
6 Strobel, ' "Geschenke des Himmels" ', pp. 157ff.
7 There are about as many alternative spellings of the hero's name as
there are medieval versions of the legend. Wagner himself did not
settle for 'Parsifal' until 1877.

Chapter 21. In Asyl

1 For a detailed appraisal see Johann Cerny, 'Die Sprache in Richard
Wagners *Tristan und Isolde*', BBL 1934, pp. 14–30.
2 Schrenck, *Richard Wagner als Dichter*.
3 A. Prüfer, 'Novalis *Hymnen an die Nacht*', in the
Richard-Wagner-Jahrbuch 1906, pp. 290ff.
4 Mann, *Leiden und Größe Richard Wagners*.
5 Friedrich Herzfeld, *Minna Planer*, p. 330.
6 The theme of the play, in a nutshell, is as follows: the art-lovers at
the court of Tasso's patron acknowledge that, in an ideal world of
the spirit, the poet's genius would make him the equal of any
monarch; but in the real world the Princess is immeasurably his
superior and the Prince, her brother, expels Tasso from the court for
daring to love her. (Like Mathilde, the Princess is happy to play the
Muse, but not to accept the full consequences of the artist's love.)
7 Kurth, *Romatische Harmonik und ihre Krise in Wagners 'Tristan'*, pp.
40ff.

8 Hindemith, *The craft of musical composition (Unterweisung im Tonsatz)*, transl. A. Mendel, rev. edn (New York, 1945), I, p. 214.
9 Early in 1857 Wagner sent Mathilde Wesendonk a 'musical letter', with the annotation 'sleepless', consisting of an elaboration of the earlier sketch. (Reproduced in facsimile in *Bayreuther Festspielführer* 1938.)
10 Part of the cut passage is reproduced in facsimile and transcription in Westernhagen, *Vom Holländer zum Parsifal*.

Chapter 22. Venice and Lucerne

1 Lorenz, *Das Geheimnis der Form bei Richard Wagner*, II: *Der musikalische Aufbau von Richard Wagners 'Tristan und Isolde'*, pp. 88–124.
2 Earlier in the same letter he wrote: 'I, poor devil, have . . . absolutely no routine at all, and if it won't come naturally there's nothing I can do about it.' Arnold Schoenberg commented that Wagner, having something new to say, was able to say it: 'That's not routine, but that quasi-animal sureness that a physical organ always shows at the critical juncture. Wagner could not do anything *mechanical!*' (H. H. Stuckenschmidt, *Schönberg*, p. 208).
3 'Segel' is a word of neuter gender in modern German, but the masculine (accusative case) here is one of Wagner's medievalisms. Cf. Wolfram's *Parzival*, I, line 1715 (58⁵).
4 Wille Schuh, '*Tristan und Isolde* im Leben und Wirken Richard Strauss' ', *Bayreuther Festspielbuch 1952*.
5 This reply is dated 24 August in NBB – evidently incorrectly, in the absence of any evidence of a previous letter to Bülow from Wagner or Draeseke.
6 'Bass tuba' in Roeder, which is presumably a mistake.
7 Erich Roeder, *Felix Draeseke*, pp. 102–12.

Chapter 23. *Tannhäuser* in Paris

1 Leroy, *Les premiers amis français de Wagner*, preface.
2 Ibid., pp. 57ff.
3 In the *Richard-Wagner-Jahrbuch* (Berlin, 1913), pp. 339ff., Sternfeld also called Kapp 'hasty' ('schnellfertig') in his review, but, as he later told me, he had meant to write 'irresponsible' ('leichtfertig').
4 The edition planned by the Wagner Archives of Wagner's correspondence with the Grand Duke of Baden and with Devrient about the production of *Tristan* in Karlsruhe in 1859 was abandoned on the outbreak of the Second World War. (RWSB, I, p. 10)
5 Wagner was referring to this when he told Mathilde Wesendonk that a portrait photograph of himself taken in Paris, in a dramatic pose with his eyes turned to the side, made him look like a 'sentimental Marat'. (23 May 1860)
6 *Ein Brief an Hector Berlioz*, RWGS, VII, pp. 82ff.
7 Quoted by Wagner in his letter of 5 June 1860 to Otto Wesendonk.

8 NLRW III, passim. There is also an account of Wagner's relations
with the publisher Flaxland and the banker Erlanger.
9 Three letters from Wagner to Agnes Street are published in RWBC,
pp 696ff., though the editor wrongly describes her as the daughter of
Karl Klindworth.
10 Daniel Ollivier, 'Lettres d'un père [Liszt] à sa fille [Blandine]', in
Revue des Deux Mondes, 15 December 1935 and 1 January 1936.
11 Briefwechsel zwischen Cosima Wagner und Fürst Ernst zu
Hohenlohe–Langenburg, pp. 88f.
12 TWLF, p. 214. Rudolf Lindau was the brother of the journalist Paul
Lindau, who wrote the notorious Nüchterne Briefe aus Bayreuth ('Sober
letters from Bayreuth') in 1876.
13 Cf. Westernhagen, Wagner (1956), pp. 265ff.
14 'Tannhäuser-Nachklänge', in BBL 1892: see Humperdinck, pp. 57ff.,
and Strauss, pp. 126ff.
15 RWBC, pp. 512f., and Wilhelm Altmann and Gottfried Niemann,
Richard Wagner und Albert Niemann (Berlin, 1924), pp. 117ff.)
16 This letter is not to be found in TWLF, but is in Leroy, Les premiers
amis français de Wagner, pp. 177ff. and is abridged in Westernhagen,
Wagner (1956), pp. 267f.
17 Die Musik, 1923, p. 42.
18 Heinz Becker, 'Giacomo Meyerbeer', Year Book of the Leo Baeck
Institute, 1964, pp. 191f.
19 Details in Nuitter (C. Truinet), 'Les 164 répétitions et les 3
représentations du Tannhaeuser à Paris', Bayreuther Festblätter in Wort
und Bild (Munich, 1884).

Chapter 24. Odyssey

1 In any case, Eduard Devrient had again queered Wagner's pitch in
Karlsruhe. Bülow wrote to Wagner on 1 May that he trusted the
grand duke's good faith. 'But I have noticed one curious item: shortly
before your arrival in Karlsruhe [in the previous month], something
appeared in the Didaskalie [the house journal of the opera
management], not merely inspired by Uncle Devrient, I'll swear to it,
but probably written by his own fair hand, explaining yet again that
Tristan und Isolde is impossible to perform. Perfidious scum!' (NBB,
p. 452)
2 Cf. Anthony Lewis, 'A "pretty theme" and the Prize Song', Musical
Times, September 1976, pp. 732f., and CT, I, p. 442: 'he had always
thought it was by someone else . . .'
3 Wagner's Dresden library included Friedrich Furchau's Hans Sachs
(Leipzig, 1820), a two-volume biography based entirely on the
internal evidence of Sachs's works. The second volume contains a
particularly vivid episode where the poet writes Die Wittenbergisch
Nachtigall on a Sunday morning in his workshop.
4 The sketch is reproduced in Westernhagen, Vom Holländer zum
Parsifal, p.136.

5 Vividly described by Berlioz in the sixth of his first set of letters from Germany: 'An appalling hubbub . . . trombones, horns and trumpets blaring out fanfares in a selection of keys, energetically accompanied by the clatter of bows on the wood of the stringed instruments and the din of percussion.' (*Memoirs*, translated by David Cairns (London, 1969).)

6 This episode was omitted from the first published edition of *Mein Leben*; it is in the 1963 edition, p. 848.

7 Mariafeld Archives; FWSZ, II, p. 208.

8 In the *Meistersinger* programme of the 1975 Bayreuth Festival, Manfred Eger published a letter to Eduard Liszt of 25 March 1864, in which Wagner gave an account of his debts. The kind of usury to which he had fallen victim is particularly interesting: taking into consideration the amounts quoted and the shortness of the term, he was being asked to pay interest at rates up to 200 per cent per annum!

9 On his letter and its subsequent fate see Otto Strobel, 'Über einen unbekannten Brief Wagners an Mathilde Wesendonk und seine Geschichte', p. 152. Mathilde later offered the house 'Asyl' to Brahms and also invited him to set her poems – he declined both! See: Erich H. Müller von Asow, *Johannes Brahms und Mathilde Wesendonk, ein Briefwechsel* (Vienna, 1943).